forgotten VILCABAMBA

forgotten VILCABAMBA

Final Stronghold of the INCAS

By Vincent R. Lee

For more information visit the author's website at vince-lee.com

ISBN 978-1-969030-00-0 (Print)

ISBN 978-1-969030-01-7 (Ebook)

Illustrations and Photos by Vincent R. Lee

Cover & Book Design by Sixpac Manco Publishing

Book Production by Sixpac Manco Publishing

"Vincent Lee reveals the secrets and solves the mysteries of Manco Inca's Vilcabamba in a series of splendid expeditions. His detective work and conclusions are totally convincing (and his) drawings constitute a treasure-house of new information."

John Hemming Author of Conquest of the Incas

"Forgotten Vilcabamba is destined to be read and re-read for as long as people are interested in the search for and discovery of lost cities from ancient civilizations. A book that not only captures the excitement of exploration but also tantalizes one with the idea that lost cities are still out there waiting to be found. A great and thrilling read."

Kim MacQuarrie Author of The Last Days of the Incas

"In the category of boots-on-the-ground narratives about the Incas, the true classics can be counted on one hand. Vincent Lee's Forgotten Vilcabamba might just be my favorite. No other book captures so well the history and magic of the once-impenetrable territory that lies just beyond Machu Picchu. With his architect's eye and superhuman curiosity, Lee succeeds in conjuring back to life the stone masterpieces erected by some of history's greatest engineers. In the process he manages to have one hell of an adventure."

Mark Adams Author of Turn Right at Machu Picchu

“No ruin has ever got lost again once Vincent Lee had found it. He combines meticulously thorough exploration with a draughtsman’s eye, resulting both in superb plan maps of the Vilcabamba sites and a text that evokes the endless appeal of this rugged and rich landscape. Forgotten Vilcabamba has the great virtue too that the author always takes the Incas far more seriously than he takes himself; it is one of those rare books that combines both modesty and insight.”

Hugh Thomson Author of White Rock

For

TUPAC AMARU INCA

To whom it is a promise kept

Contents

Acknowledgements

This is the story of an escape that turned into a quest that became an obsession that has solved, I think, a very old puzzle. What began as a simple adventure, soon took on a life of its own and became in time an Odyssey of learning and discovery. Those who think that the frontiers of exploration have all descended into the ocean depths or flown out beyond the rings of Saturn, take heart and read on. Our encounter with the Incas of Peru was not so different from that of Stevens and Catherwood with the Mayas of Mexico, a century and a half ago. High-tech gear and big foundation grants counted not at all. What we did, anyone with a strong back and determined mind could also have done - and can do still. Just as the writings of others led us to the adventures recounted here, I hope this book encourages you to pursue similar dreams of your own , now, while there's time.

Our journey, and like it this book, was inspired by some, aided by others and impeded by a few. All deserve mention here. Absent the writings of Gene Savoy, I might never have ventured to Peru in the first place and once there, the benefits of his advice and field experience were invaluable. But for the subsequent enthusiasm and encouragement of Drs. John Howland Rowe and Patricia J. Lyon, the results of my first expeditions might nevertheless have ended up buried in a file folder and I might never have gone back. Having done so, however, the insights and support of Dr. John Hemming - culminating in his most generous contribution of the Foreword to this book - were critical in making sense of what all we found. To these four, especially, I owe a very great debt of gratitude, for without them, this book would not have been written.

Once the writing began, my agent, Jonathon Lazear, and editors Bob Weil and Leigh Haber were invaluable allies in the long campaign to turn my rough, early drafts into a finished manuscript.

Many others helped out significantly along the way. Prudence Rice rekindled my interest in archaeology and got me started in a belated program of home study. Savoy's Andean Explorers Club co-sponsored our second expedition. Stuart White, Lynn Hirschkind, Bernard Bell, Richard Robinson, Edmundo Guillén and Robert von Kaupp all shared eagerly with me the results of their respective explorations and to von Kaupp in particular must go the credit for dragging me kicking and screaming into the rarefied world of the scholar. Alfred M. Bingham and Adriana von Hagen both permitted me full access to the unpublished records of their respective fathers' work and Adriana managed to find me a rare copy of Christian Bües' original map of the Vilcabamba. Paula Dimmler, Richard Robinson and Manuel Menendez all provided excellent translations of various lengthy Spanish documents, and in so doing saved me many hours of thumbing through my trusty Valesquez dictionary. Renzo Francescutti and Rubén Orellana each gave me updated maps of the Vilcabamba which proved most helpful when it came time to transfer place-names onto the satellite image-based maps included here. Finally, various friends read portions of the manuscript and/or otherwise offered comments and criticisms which have found their ways into the finished work. Notable among these were Bob Weil, John Hemming, Dennis Emory, Jean Pierre Protzen, Stuart White, Bob von Kaupp, Johan Reinhard, Doug Sharon, Jim Little, Ort Steele, Susan Niles, John Hyslop, Nancy Lee, Bernard Bell, Greg Deyermenjian, Margaret Mac Lean and

Judy Eddy. To them and to all the other contributors noted above I offer my deepest thanks.

Special note must be taken of those who actually participated in the field work, a stalwart group without whom there would have been no expeditions and no book. They were crazy enough to go, good enough to do a hard job well and always found something to laugh about. I salute them all : Curtis May and Brooke Tannehill in 1982; Jim Barefoot, Jill Baumler, Paul Burghard, Nancy Lee, Dr. Jim Little, Martha Little and Chris Mattair in 1984; Susan Akers, Bruce Davis, Ben Giles and Nancy Lee in 1986; and Nancy Lee in 1987. No one put more into the trips than they did, unless it was our *campesino* hosts and guides, Juvenal Cobos, José Salas Cobos and Pancho Quispicusi. They cut the trails and packed the horses and paved the way so that we were always welcome among their many friends and neighbors. I'd be proud to share a camp with any of them, anytime, anyplace. Fortunately, theirs is a much happier world just now than it was during much of the period described here and I wish them *buena suerte*, the best of luck. If anyone deserves it, they do. More than anyone, though, my wife Nancy deserves the title "Mrs. Sixpac Manco." She has lived with the Vilcabamba day and night, summer and winter for twelve years and she's been an inspiration all that time. Bless you, Nancy.

Vince Lee, Jackson Hole, Wyoming

Forward

When I studied the conquest of the Incas many years ago, I became increasingly fascinated by the neo-Incas, a small remnant led by Manco Inca, that tried to survive the Spanish conquest of their once-great empire. Manco was a younger brother of Atahualpa, the Inca who was captured, ransomed and executed by Francisco Pizarro in 1532. It was Manco who led his people in a heroic attempt to drive the hated *conquistadores* out of Peru. When his great rebellion finally failed, in 1537, Manco fled north-westwards from Cuzco into the wild, forested "Vilcapampa" (nowadays called Vilcabamba) hills. Despite continuous hostilities with the Spaniards in Cuzco, Manco and his sons continued to rule in Vilcabamba for a further 35 years. Theirs was a tiny fragment of what had been one of the world's greatest empires, but it was at least free from foreign colonial rule.

A contemporary Spanish chronicler wrote that Manco Inca's few followers did their best to embellish this remote enclave at the edge of the Amazonian rain forests. At first, they settled at a mountaintop aerie called Vitcos, founded nearly a century earlier by Manco's great-grandfather, Pachacuti Inca. Then, in the face of mounting pressure from the Europeans, Manco moved his capital deep into the lowland jungles. Like the surrounding province, the Incas called their new city Vilcabamba. In time, it grew into a metropolis in exile, but it was fated for destruction. In 1572, a massive Spanish invasion ended forever the dream of native rule and the Inca's proud capital was abandoned to the forest.

The Spaniards came to call the city Vilcabamba the Old, but no one went there and it passed eventually into the realm of legend. Only in this century did explorers begin to search for its ruins, but none had any real idea where to look. Each new find became briefly identified with Manco's lost city until a better candidate turned up. For many years the famous ruins at Machu Picchu were erroneously thought to be those of Vilcabamba the Old. Almost entirely eclipsed during that time was an obscure site deep in the jungle several days north of Vitcos, at a place called Espíritu Pampa. It was glimpsed in 1911 by Machu Picchu's discoverer Hiram Bingham, and then revisited in 1964 by Gene Savoy. The remains there were so heavily overgrown that explorers were unsure of even the extent of the ruins. The one remarkable feature everyone seemed to agree upon was the presence of charred clay roofing tiles scattered among buildings of otherwise Incan design.

In my research, I pieced together the geography of Vilcabamba from the accounts of the few Spaniards who were allowed into it in the sixteenth century. The documentary evidence all pointed to Manco's capital being in the lowlands beyond Vitcos, a location that fit Espíritu Pampa better than the other candidates, but it was hardly conclusive. Then I came across the chronicle of Martín de Murúa, which contains the missing dispatch of the Spanish commander of the successful 1572 campaign. He told how his men occupied the Inca capital, which was in a broad valley full of tropical produce - a good description of Espíritu Pampa but, again, less than hard evidence. Finally, although it had been torched by the fleeing Indians, he described the Inca's palace as being a fine building "*on different levels and covered in roof tiles*," rather than the Incas' usual thatch. Finding that reference was a thrilling moment for a researcher. It was my personal eureka. This, to me, was absolute proof that Espíritu Pampa is the site of Manco's city of Vilcabamba. It is the only known Inca ruin in the Andes where scorched, Spanish-style roof tiles are found scattered among the remains.

Although I visited a small part of the Vilcabamba region, my research was entirely historical. I ransacked the few surviving narratives for whatever clues I could find. My conclusions still needed to be corroborated on the ground, a formidable task that awaited the arrival of Wyoming explorer, Vincent Lee. He has finally revealed the secrets and solved the mysteries of Manco Inca's Vilcabamba in a series of splendid expeditions. His journeys were arduous but scholarly. He always went in pursuit of Inca remains, but knew the written sources so thoroughly that he was able to positively identify everything he found. His detective work and conclusions are totally convincing.

Best of all, as a professional architect, Lee surveyed all that he found and produced excellent maps and plans of every known archaeological site in the region. The resulting drawings, published here for the first time, constitute a treasure-house of new information about Inca Vilcabamba. Luckily for me, what Lee and his intrepid companions found confirms what I had guessed from the written record. This book, "VILCABAMBA - Final Stronghold of the INCAS", is the story of that physical proof.

John Hemming, London

Prologue

The rain had finally stopped. For the first time in days, the clouds parted and revealed a startling panorama of primeval beauty. The giant ice covered peaks of Peru's remote Cordillera Vilcabamba marched across the southern skyline, gleaming gold in the early morning light. To the north and west, hidden and ominous beneath an immense sea of billowing clouds, the upper Amazon stretched to the horizon and beyond. A rare black collared hawk soared from a nearby crag, intent upon a squawking flight of electric-green parrots wheeling above the treetops far below. Closer by, the northeast sun glistened from steaming rock slabs plummeting vertically from our tiny perch hundreds of feet into the mist shrouded cloud forest. According to some, the final capital of the once-great Inca Empire lay smothered and in ruins somewhere under all that tangled growth.

It was June 21st, 1982, and with two fellow mountaineers, Curtis May and Brooke Tannehill, I gazed from atop an incredible granite crag, shaped in profile like a gigantic human head. For the Incas, it had been a sacred landmark. The local Indians called it Icma Coya, the "Widowed Queen". We had learned of its apparently unclimbed summit from the writings of a mysterious American explorer named Gene Savoy. Twenty years earlier, Savoy had come to the jungle in search of Vilcabamba, the legendary jungle stronghold of the last of the Incas. He was following in the footsteps of another American, Hiram Bingham, the famous discoverer of Machu Picchu. In 1911, Bingham had found what he thought insignificant ruins in an isolated valley about twelve kilometers north of Icma Coya. The place was called Espíritu Pampa, the "Plain of Ghosts", and seemed to him the remains of a small Inca settlement. Nearly three quarters of a century later, Savoy had shown that the site was, in fact, a vast forest metropolis fitting, he claimed, the Spanish *coquistadores'* descriptions of the Incas' final redoubt. Antisuyo, his book about the find, had mentioned Icma Coya only in passing, but that brief glimpse of the strange, untrodden, sacred peak of the Incas had fired my mountain climber's imagination.

The energies of the past days and weeks had been focused myopically on achieving that goal, but now, looking down from our hard-won prize, I realized I'd been equally intrigued by the explorations of both Bingham and Savoy. Much of my childhood had been spent wandering the long-abandoned Hudson River estate of a noted explorer, John Charles Frémont, the controversial "Path-finder of the West". Ever since, as a part-time alpine guide, I had specialized in climbing expeditions to the world's wildest, most untraveled places - places like Icma Coya. Even my work as a practicing architect in Jackson Hole, Wyoming, fit incongruously into the picture. The stone and thatch building technique of the highland Incas was not unlike the log and stone lodge architecture my clients favored in the Rocky Mountains. The land itself provided the materials for both and each, in its way, was shaped by the forces of nature and an abiding respect for the Earth.

A sudden blast of cold, damp air interrupted my thoughts. The weather was worsening and clouds were beginning to boil up from the jungle. Time to go. There'd be no chance to look for Savoy's lost city on this trip, I thought. Putting my old silver ring in a plastic film can, I scribbled a note offering it to the Incas, stuffed it inside and cached the can under a rock while the others got ready for the descent. It was three long days - exactly the time remaining on our government permit - back over a snowy, 13,000 foot pass to the trailhead. Juvenal Cobos, our new-found *campesino* friend there, had said the *policía* might make trouble if we were late. They were increasingly nervous about strangers in the backcountry, wary of the darkening shadows cast by the coming decade of revolutionary terrorism in Peru.

Oblivious to all that, we started down, less fearful of the police than of a long, miserable night out in the clammy, rain-soaked jungle that separated us from camp. Three days later, we collapsed onto the front porch of Cobos's farmhouse near the rustic village of Huancacalle. Cracking us a well-earned beer, Juvenal welcomed us back, but confided he never thought we'd make it. A truck was going down to the railroad the following afternoon, he said, but first he wanted us to join him for a local *fiesta* in some nearby ruins. They were perched atop a high ridge across the river from his farm. The hill was called Rosaspata, the "place of roses," and the ruins were the remains of Vitcos, a famous Inca settlement first reported by Bingham in 1911 - during the same expedition that had led him to both Machu Picchu and Espíritu Pampa.

The celebration turned out to be the Inti Raymi, a winter solstice observance dating from Inca times. All done in costume, it was performed in the scenic courtyard of what the locals called "Manco's Palace." Manco Inca was the rebel leader who had ruled from Vitcos for a time before founding his final capital at Vilcapampa, the sprawling city still hidden somewhere deep in the lowland forests. In contrast to the rebuilt and manicured tourist attractions we'd seen elsewhere, the ruins of Vitcos were tumbled and overgrown. Outside the palace, scattered buildings and tiers of well preserved stone terracing spread all across the crest of Rosaspata and into the isolated valley beyond. How much there was and how it had once fit together, nobody seemed to know. In all the years since Bingham's visit, no one had surveyed the site or bothered to make a map. As I watched the colorful, spinning dancers, chanting age-old prayers against a backdrop of unstudied ruins, unexplored valleys and jagged Andean peaks, I saw that Icma Coya was just a beginning.

Already, I could hardly wait to return to Peru with time enough to really explore Vitcos and find Savoy's city. I'd see for myself whether it was Manco's lost Vilcabamba. What else lay concealed and forgotten in the forest, I wondered? I had no idea at the time, but the answer was to change my life.

KEY TO SYMBOLS

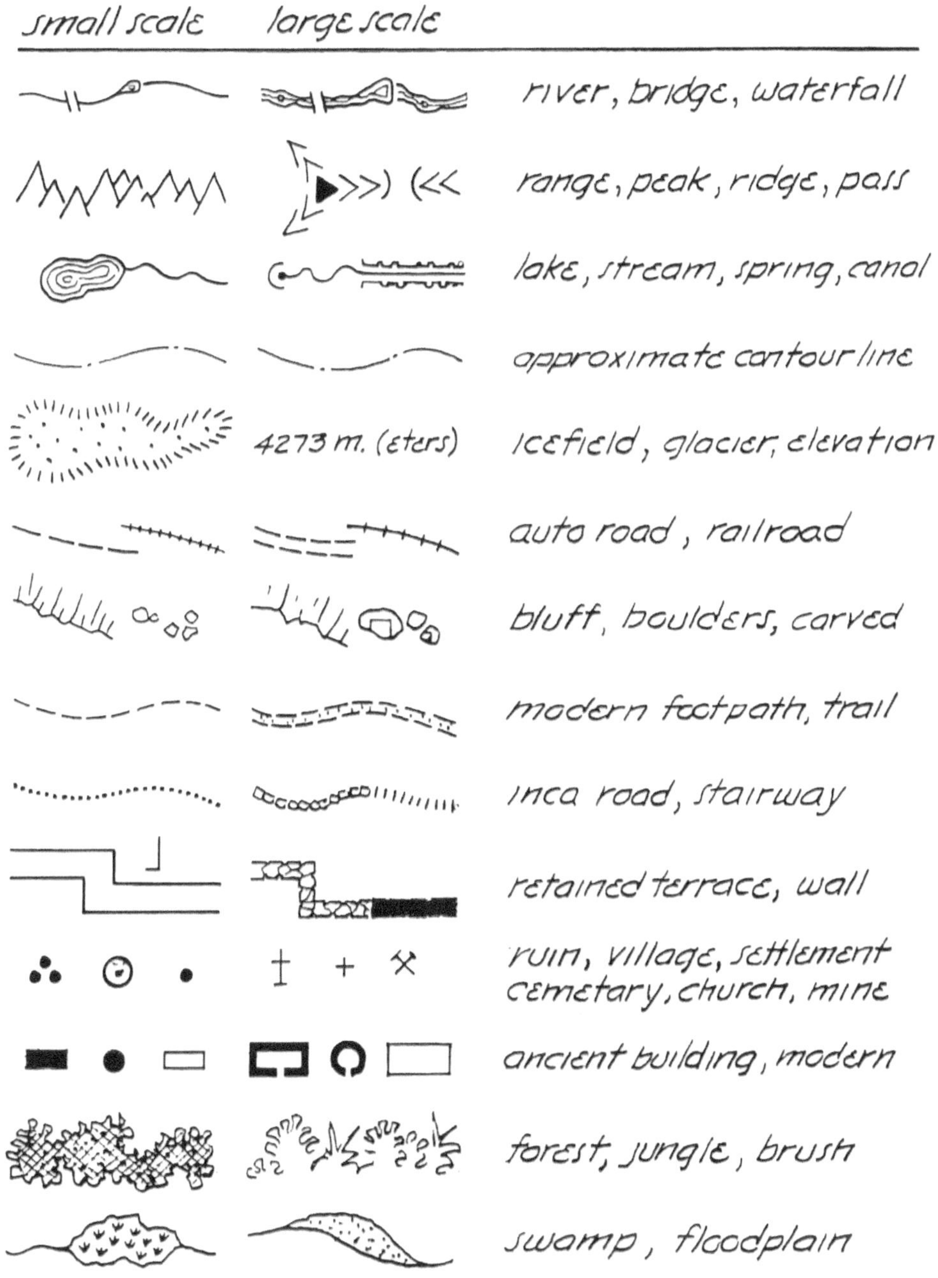

small scale	large scale	
		river, bridge, waterfall
		range, peak, ridge, pass
		lake, stream, spring, canal
		approximate contour line
	4273 m. (eters)	icefield, glacier, elevation
		auto road, railroad
		bluff, boulders, carved
		modern footpath, trail
		inca road, stairway
		retained terrace, wall
		ruin, village, settlement cemetary, church, mine
		ancient building, modern
		forest, jungle, brush
		swamp, floodplain

Part I

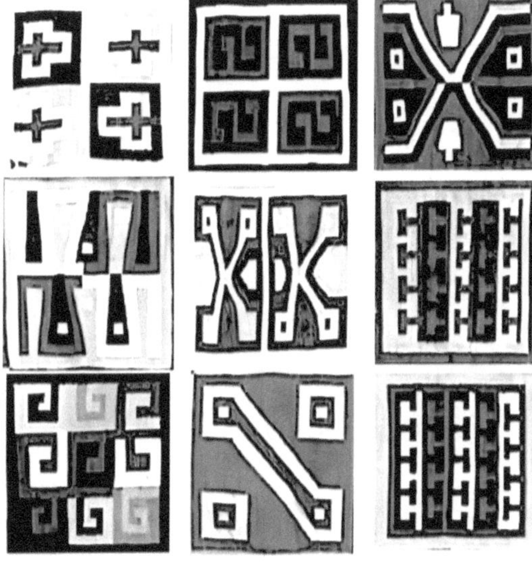

1

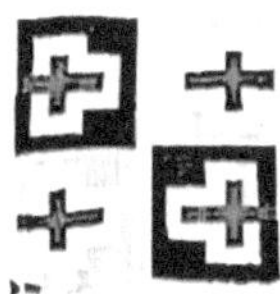

The World Turned Upside Down

Back in the States, I got right to work. All I knew about the Incas was what little I'd read in Bingham and Savoy. Both had focused mainly on the period after the Conquest and neither had given much detail. Now, I wanted to find out everything I could about Manco's illustrious ancestors , especially at the height of their power in the decades before the arrival of the Spaniards. Unlike the Mayas, the Incas left no recorded history and most of what we know of their early years is the stuff of legend. The story begins in the obscurity of an anonymous tribal past, and thereafter follows the exploits of a line of semi-mythical kings. I was amazed to learn that their empire's brief, but spectacular period of fluorescent greatness is credited largely to the inspiration and leadership of a single man. Although revisionists currently dispute the extent of his influence **(1)**, virtually all Andean scholars agree that he was one of history's exceptional figures.

Tradition holds that he was Rameses II, Alexander the Great and Thomas Jefferson, all rolled into one. Divine despot, conqueror, statesman, builder: he was the first New World genius of whom we have any record. He set out to subjugate, unite and civilize the entire Andean world and with his son very nearly did so in less than half a century. He transformed the tribal chaos of his time into a social order so pervasive and powerful that it persists to this day, despite nearly five centuries of alien rule. He left his mark in the fantastic and enigmatic stones of Machu Picchu and a hundred lesser-known marvels of Inca architecture, all connected by one of the best and largest networks of paved roads ever built by pre-industrial man. An early version of the Interstate Highway system, it was built for much the same reasons - rapid movement of arms and material - and was long enough, eventually, to reach nearly around the planet. The man behind all these accomplishments was named Inca Yupanqui, but his people called him Pachacuti, the "Overturner of the Earth."

Pachacuti Încă armed for conquest, ca. 1440; from Guaman Poma de Ayala, 1613

His forefathers had led their small tribe out of obscurity two and a half centuries earlier, sometime around 1200 A.D. After an epic journey northward from a mythical and still uncertain place of origin, they settled into the fertile and well watered valley of the Huatanay River, high in what are now the Peruvian Andes. There, they built a modest capital city - which they called Cuzco, the "navel of the world" - and founded a fledgling, but ambitious dynasty. They believed themselves chosen by Inti, the Sun, to bring order to his children and soon set out to fulfill their destiny. By all accounts, they were a proud, industrious and clever people, humble before no one but their gods and Pacha Mama, Mother Earth. They lived by a simple, three part golden rule: "Thou shall not lie; thou shall not steal; and thou shall not be idle." To the last of these, especially, they were surely true. In time, their influence spread throughout the region and they came to dominate their neighbors as the imperial Incas, the Sons of the Sun.

Pachacuti was the ninth king of the Incas. He came to power after inspiring his people to a great and unexpected victory against the marauding Chancas, a powerful rival tribe whose expansionist ambitions had threatened Cuzco and the Incas' grand designs on the future. To consolidate his newly dominant position, Pachacuti quickly sought to subjugate other neighboring tribes that had loosely allied themselves with the Chancas. Among these were the natives of Vitcos and Vilca"pampa" (nowadays called Vilcabamba), two remote but populous chiefdoms in the jungle-clad peaks several days' march northwest of Cuzco. It was a region soon to become the Province of Vilcabamba, an early conquest of what would eventually grow into a far-flung empire.

According to the 1653 chronicle of Father Bernabé Cobo, a great army was assembled for the invasion of Vilcabamba and set out in about 1440 under Pachacuti's personal command **(2).** At first, the column made good progress down the flat valleys of the Huatanay and Vilcanota Rivers - hospitable, open country which was easily and quickly absorbed into the Inca heartland. Soon, however, the canyon of the Vilcanota narrowed between enormous precipices falling vertically from the ice fields and glaciers crowning a maze of surrounding peaks, some soaring more than 20,000 feet into the cobalt Andean sky. The river Vilcanota, nowadays called the Urubamba in its lower reaches, began to descend into the all-but-impenetrable thickets of the Andean *montaña*, the the *Ceja de Selva* or "Eyebrow of the Jungle." It was the upper fringe of the great Amazonian rain forest then thought to be inhabited by a race of sub-human men who lived like beasts and ate the flesh of their enemies. A lesser leader might have been deterred by such a daunting array of obstacles, but Pachacuti pressed on.

Just where the terrain seemed otherwise impassable, his scouts found a detour through a high breach in the crags north of the river by which the worst of the canyon could be avoided. To this day, a rocky, dirt road through this, the 14,000 foot Pass of Panticalla, provides the only auto route into the region - except when closed by frequent, heavy snows. Descending a steep, but negotiable valley on the far side of the pass, the Incas regained the canyon of the

Urubamba exactly where a deep gash in the mountains across the river invited entry into the fastness of Vilcabamba. But there was a problem. The Urubamba, by then a raging torrent some hundred meters wide, barred the way. The natives of Vitcos and Vilcabamba had destroyed the only bridge for miles in either direction, assuming no one could rebuild it except in conditions of unusually low water. To the dismay of their quarry, Pachacuti's troops quickly erected a long suspension bridge of heavy ropes, high above the rapids. Despite token resistance, the invaders swarmed across followed by trains of llamas laden with food, weapons and supplies for a lengthy campaign. The crossing was called Chuquichaca or, variously, Choquechaca - the bridge of spears or, perhaps, of gold - prophetic names either way, as things turned out. It was not the last time men would fight their way across the river there, eager to possess the mineral riches that lay beneath the peaks beyond.

Once established on the other side and with the natives in full retreat, Pachacuti ascended the steep, narrow valley of the Vilcabamba River westward up into the heart of the province, improving the roads and building other bridges as he went. Little is known about his opponents, except that they were probably tribal Antis or Chunchos, aboriginal forest Indians awed by the sophisticated ways of the Incas. They were so intimidated by the ease with which the highlanders penetrated their homeland, they believed that only the chosen of the Sun could possibly accomplish such feats. Fearing the outcome of a direct confrontation with such a powerful enemy, they conspired to save themselves through trickery.

Into the Inca's camp, they sent emissaries advising that he advance no further. The road, they said, was rough and the country poor and unhealthy. If he would but send word of his demands, he was told, the *caciques* or chiefs of Vitcos and Vilcabamba would gladly comply. To their distress, Pachacuti would have none of it. His response was characteristically unequivocal. "Clear the roads and make ready for the arrival of the Son of the Sun!" they were told, or the Inca would soon drink blood from their skulls and make drums from the skins of their chiefs. Strong words, and the fact that Pachacuti clearly had the power to back them up was not lost on the messengers.

Nervously, they took stock of his host of warriors before scurrying back into the forest to an unexpected and unjust reception among their own people.

We would know nothing of the villages to which they returned, but for an obscure and passing reference in the 1639 treatise of an Augustinian priest named Antonio de la Calancha. The *Padre* describes a place in the forest beyond the head of the Río Vilcabamba called Yanacachi, which:

"*...in ancient times was a great town and capital of that region and home of its shamans and sorcerers - but which had since declined in population.*" **(3)**

Calancha's chronicle goes on to tell where the town was in a confusing reference to several other places, most of which are no longer known, but the most important clue to the whereabouts of Yanacachi was its name, which means "black salt."

Meanwhile, the Inca had presented the *caciques* with a tough choice. It was a technique that Pachacuti and all his successors would use repeatedly and to good advantage for nearly a century thereafter. Much of their enormous domain was eventually annexed without firing a shot, so to speak, as time and again they offered their intended prey a straightforward choice: capitulate and join the empire as welcome citizens or be summarily annihilated by the overwhelming force which invariably hovered in the wings, awaiting only a nod from the Inca to make good on the threat.

The native messengers returned to their leaders with such forceful reports of Pachacuti's prowess that the *caciques* became terrified. In an especially unsporting example of taking bad news out on its bearers , the chiefs promptly cut off their faithful emissaries' heads and sent them back to the Inca with what amounted to a cover story. The chiefs had planned to surrender peacefully all along, they said, but their envoys had betrayed them and paid the price when their rude conduct was discovered. The heads were sent along as tokens of the chiefs' sincerity.

Whether the Inca bought the story or not, it worked. Pachacuti continued unopposed up the Vilcabamba River to its head and crossed the Kolpacasa, or "Salty Pass", just as Brooke, Curtis and I had on our way to Icma Coya. The Inca's army soon came upon a bleak cluster of huts at a place still called Pampaconas. The village occupied the last large clearing before the country plunged into the thick cloud forest beyond. Preferring to remain in the open where his army had the advantage, Pachacuti chose the site for his camp and established court. Here, the frightened natives gradually came out of hiding and welcomed him with all sorts of exotic gifts. Notable among these was an entire mountain they claimed was honeycombed with rich veins of gold and silver. It seemed almost too good to be true, but when the mines were examined, they proved to be even richer than had been promised.

For Pachacuti, it was an incredible bonanza. If his first campaign was any indication, conquest looked like pretty good business. Not only had he subdued several large tribes of potential enemies without a fight, he'd added an entire province to his domain and gotten very rich in the bargain. Cobo says the Inca lingered in Vilcabamba long enough to amass "*many* (llama) *loads*" of gold and silver, with which he triumphantly returned to Cuzco the same way he'd come **(4)**.

The successful expedition and Pachacuti's newfound riches were celebrated by a public *fiesta* that went on for two months thereafter. The Inca Empire was on its way.

Who could have imagined that in less than a century another Inca army would descend from the Pass of Panticalla to the strategic bridge at Chuquichaca, but this time in full retreat from an enemy more terrible even than Pachacuti? The intervening 97 years had seen the virtual fulfillment of Pachacuti's dream of world conquest. Spurred partly by the Incas' sense of mission and partly, too, by their peculiar custom of passing to successors the power of the throne, but none of its wealth, Pachacuti's son and grandson had expanded the supremacy of Cuzco throughout the Andean world. Each, in his turn, had accumulated enormous fortunes. From the Pacific to the Amazon, from what is now southern Colombia to central Chile, untold millions obeyed and paid tribute to the Sons of the Sun.

Theirs was the greatest empire the Western Hemisphere had ever seen - indeed, it was among the largest and most magnificent of the pre-industrial world. To the modern mind, the accomplishment of the Incas is all the more astounding when understood as that of an essentially bronze-age society that survived in isolation well into the Renaissance. Without horses, wheels, iron or a written language, they administered a domain nearly as large and complex as that of the Romans, and administered it well. Even the men who destroyed Tawantinsuyu, "the Four Quarters" as the Incas called their sprawling world, marveled that life there compared favorably with many aspects of European society at the time.

Immutable as it seemed, however, the power structure of the Incas was fatally flawed. Like an immense pyramid balanced on its apex - the person of the king - it was inherently unstable and, in the end, a bizarre coincidence of misfortunes brought it crashing down with cataclysmic finality. By the third decade of the sixteenth century, Pachacuti's grandson, Huayna Capac Inca, was ostensibly the most powerful man in what a strange race of bearded, white skinned voyagers from across Mama Cocha, the "mother lake", were calling the New World. Huayna Capac probably never saw these people, but he received word of their coming at his northern court in what is now Ecuador. His sudden and untimely death in about 1526, amidst the decimation of a terrifying epidemic of previously unknown diseases, confirms that he nevertheless received their calling card - probably smallpox. Working its inexorable way south from newly conquered Mexico, European pestilence had begun paving the way for the destruction of the Inca Empire.

In places, the peasant population was overnight cut in half. The ranks of the bureaucracy and Inca nobility fared no better. No one had immunity, and even the common cold took a deadly toll. Food production and the everyday affairs of state ground to a halt. Just when strong and decisive leadership was most needed from the top, none was forthcoming, since not only the Inca, but his rightful heir was among the victims. A dispute quickly arose between two would-be successors to the throne which soon erupted into civil war. It was a hitherto unthinkable crisis for which the monolithic and now severely weakened empire was totally unprepared. Like all such conflicts, it was an especially nasty affair, with household set against household and much slaughter on both sides. Neither contender for the crown seems to have been up to the remarkably high standards of his forefathers, and for five or so long, destructive years each pretended to rule while the fabric of their kingdom continued to unravel. Subject tribes throughout the Andes quickly sensed the growing vacuum in Cuzco and became increasingly restless. A better time for the arrival of a conqueror from abroad could scarcely have been imagined.

As if on cue, in May of 1532 a Spaniard named Francisco Pizarro, sailing south from Panama, made landfall on the north coast of a place he mistakenly called Peru. Inspired by the already legendary exploits of Cortez in Mexico, he and his motley little band of adventurers had been looking for gold, thus-far without success. In Peru, their fortunes were to change dramatically - and with them, those of the entire world - since they soon encountered wealth beyond even their crazed imagining. The treasure of the Incas had grown many-fold in the nine decades since Pachacuti's highly profitable Vilcabamba campaign and the Europeans suspected they had stumbled upon the richest people on earth.

The epic saga of the tragic Conquest which followed has been told and re-told. Within less than a year after contact with their insatiably greedy visitors, both of the warring Incas were dead and the destruction of their world was well underway. The Spaniards used the relatively benevolent autocracy of the old regime to their advantage by simply replacing it with their own, less benign version. Secular power was thus gained with surprising ease. Control over the "hearts and minds" of their new subjects was another matter, however, since the divinity of the old Inca emperor was something the Europeans couldn't readily duplicate.

They hit on a solution which at first seemed harmless enough, but ended up very nearly their undoing. From among the survivors of the native court in Cuzco, they selected an heir to the still-empty Inca throne. In December of 1533, they set him up as a puppet to pacify the natives while mouthing Pizarro's policies and adding the illusion of legitimacy to his foreign rule. The new emperor's name was Manco Inca and it was a name the Europeans would in time learn to respect.

Young and inexperienced, Manco was at first flattered by the attentions of Pizarro and his fellow *conquistadores*, but what he mistook for their admiration and trust soon revealed itself as condescension and contempt. They paid him none of the deference or courtesy he had always been taught was due an Inca, nor was he given any real authority. Instead, they sought to pacify him with the mere trappings of power while they set about the business of enslaving his own people in his name. It might have worked but for the fact that, like so many of his royal ancestors, Manco Inca turned out to be a proud and able man.

For nearly two years, he endured the insults and injustices of his new masters, pretending loyalty while learning everything he could about their strange, but demonstrably effective ways. He studied their tactics and weapons, learned to ride and shoot and noted the disposition of their forces. He came to recognize the sickness inherent in their insatiable lust for gold and power and educated himself in the subtleties of their corrupt and deceitful diplomacy. His countrymen, meanwhile, complained to him of the daily indignities they suffered and urged him to throw off the Spanish yoke and restore the integrity of the empire. Late in 1535, he finally agreed, but was captured in an abortive attempt to escape into the countryside and begin marshaling his forces. The Spaniards put him in irons and dragged him back to Cuzco like a common criminal. His jailers spat and urinated on him and raped his wives while he was made to look on. For the native population, it was the final straw. Sporadic and isolated uprisings began to plague the Europeans all throughout the old Four Quarters. The only thing preventing a full-scale native rebellion was the lack of a charismatic leader with the stature and know how to make it happen. Early in 1536, a humiliated but far from humbled Manco Inca emerged from prison that man.

Cuzco was by then surrounded by several hundred thousand vengeful "Indians," as their grossly outnumbered masters had come to call them. Manco, now playing by their rules, falsely pledged fidelity to the Spaniards, ventured from the city on an apparently innocent pretext and took command of an enormous army. In May of 1536 he laid siege to Cuzco and torched the heavy, thatched roofs of its desecrated temples, halls and palaces in an effort to drive the Europeans into the open, where his overwhelming numerical superiority could be brought to bear. Instead, they luckily holed up in the one compound that for unknown reasons didn't burn.

Manco Inca takes charge of the native rebellion and sets fire to Cuzco, 1536; from Guaman Poma de Ayala, ca. 1613.

It was a temporary reprieve. The Spaniards' situation was desperate and no reinforcements were likely to help lift the siege from outside the city. Manco's increasingly well orchestrated rebellion had virtually wiped out the pockets of European strength elsewhere in Peru (which included present-day Bolivia and Ecuador at the time). The isolated survivors were completely immobilized. A bold stroke was needed if the entire Conquest was not to be lost and, whatever else one might say of the Spaniards, audacity was their forte. They counter-attacked.

The Inca's headquarters overlooked the embattled Europeans from Sacsawaman, an enormous native citadel crowning the heights north of the city. The original construction had been conceived and begun by Pachacuti sometime in the mid-fifteenth century. For three generations, the work was continued by his son and grandson until being abandoned, unfinished, upon the arrival of the Spaniards. In all those years, it had never been attacked. Some scholars doubt whether it was intended as a fortress at all, but all chroniclers of the period agree that it was a marvel of Inca architecture and construction. One writer even suggested that it belonged among the Wonders of the World. He was referring to the three outer terrace walls which protected the otherwise most vulnerable, northerly aspect of the fort. Together, these are more than fifty feet high and laid in a zig-zag pattern so that every approach can be fired upon from at least two different directions. They are nearly vertical, practically unscalable and virtually indestructible, being formed from huge, perfectly fitted boulders, some weighing over a hundred tons. To this day, Sacsawaman commands the silent awe of all who stand before it and it was this obstacle, swarming with angry defenders, that Pizarro had to breach if his counterattack was to succeed.

Manco's forces set fire to Cuzco, 1536; from Guaman Poma de Ayala, 1613.

The battle raged for several days, with much valor and heavy losses on both sides. Included among the latter was Pizarro's younger brother, Juan, who was killed by a stone flung from the heights. Outnumbered hundreds to one as they were, one might wonder how the Spaniards had any hope at all of prevailing. Three factors tended to even the odds: their horses, their steel armour and swords and the sheer audacity they invariably displayed. An armored swordsman mounted on an armored horse was the equivalent of a heavy tank among light infantry. Used aggressively, it was a weapon against which the Indians had neither an adequate offense nor any real defense and they were cut down and trampled by the hundreds as they tried to swarm the riders and pull them from their mounts.

In the face of appalling losses, the natives were finally driven from the ramparts. The rebellion quickly lost the initiative and the siege of Cuzco was broken. Though the tide of the battle for Peru thus turned inexorably against them, one completely unexpected outcome of the uprising was to work in the Indians' favor for nearly a decade thereafter. Jealousy and competition between Pizarro and one of his fellow *conquistadores*, Diego de Almagro, had been mounting for some time. Almagro, who had been off on a difficult and fruitless expedition into what is now Chile, returned to Peru to find his adversary seriously weakened by his war with the Indians and ripe for overthrow. He even flirted with the idea of an alliance with Manco, but the Inca declined, correctly suspecting that it would only be a matter of time until Almagro turned on him, too.

In the end, Manco was thus forced to withdraw into the hinterland, leaving behind thousands of dead and dying. The Incas were once again outcasts in their own land. Following the route of Pachacuti a century before them, they retreated first to the valley of the Vilcanota river, where they fought a brief, but successful holding action against their Spanish pursuers at the large, fortified town called Ollantaytambo. Realizing, however, that enemy reinforcements would sooner or later render his position there untenable, Manco gathered his forces, their families, herds and possessions and continued on over the pass of Panticalla and down to the bridge at Chuquichaca. Beyond rose the jungle-choked ravines of Vilcabamba - the perfect place, he thought, to make his final stand against the hated Europeans.

In an ironic twist of history, one of the very first provinces conquered by the Incas in their century-long march toward empire had turned out to be their final refuge when their world came apart. Manco briefly entertained alternative sites for what he thought would be his temporary exile. He considered strongholds in the forested maze of Chachapoyas in northern Peru and atop the sheer, thousand-meter cliffs of Oroncota in what is now south-eastern Bolivia. But to reach either he would have to cross a thousand kilometers of country that, though not all yet occupied by the Spaniards, was easily accessible to their all-but-invincible cavalry.

Vilcabamba solved that problem, at least. There were and still are only two or three ways into the province. All were nearly impassable for mounted troops and thus strongly favored the sort of guerrilla defense Manco could best provide. More important, the Inca still entertained the dream of one day throwing the invaders back into the sea and that meant keeping tabs on their activities in nearby Cuzco. Vilcabamba would do well, it seemed, until he was ready to re-take the city and cleanse the Four Quarters of foreign intruders once and for all.

For the moment, though, he needed a safe place in which to settle his people and establish a secure base of operations. His destination was a stone fortress called Vitcos, built nearly a century earlier by Pachacuti on a high, steep-sided hill about thirty kilometers up the Vilcabamba river. It had been expanded and strengthened by every Inca since. The citadel commanded the confluence of several fertile and extensively cultivated glacial valleys high in the Andes, but no more than a day's walk over the surrounding divides from the wild, forested territory of the fierce Chunchos and Antis, loyal allies of the Inca ever since their subjugation by Pachacuti. Best of all, no European had ever set foot in Vilcabamba and it was Manco's intention that none ever would.

2

Trust No One

My crash course on the Incas continued all through the fall of 1982 and into the winter. The deeper I got into their story, the more compelling it was: a sweeping drama-turned-tragedy, set in exotic surroundings with a cast of thousands. Why hadn't Cecil B. De Mille made the movie decades ago? More to the point, how had I gotten through nineteen years of schooling without learning more about it myself? The answer to that was easy. Out of curiosity, I looked up the Incas in an old World History book one of my sons had never quite returned to class. The entire Conquest was covered in two and a half pages. The once-mighty Sons of the Sun had been given three whole paragraphs.

Manco's decision to establish his court-in-exile at Vitcos shifted the scene of action to familiar ground. I was continually reminded of sights we'd seen and places we'd passed through along the way to and from Icma Coya. All of it took on exciting new meaning as I read about who'd done what to whom there, and why. I saw all sorts of interesting projects that cried for attention. And to my relief, what needed to be done didn't seem to be rocket science. It was a combination of the same kind of rigorous field work I'd been doing for years with simple sketch-mapping not unlike what I often did for my architectural clients. For weeks, I couldn't think of anything but Vilcabamba, and I longed to be back there, exploring again.

Fortunately, my most important friend, Nancy Goodman, felt the same. A former Peace Corps volunteer, she'd been stationed in Peru for two years in the early 60s. Curious to see what changes twenty years had wrought, she flew down to Cuzco and spent a few days with me there after my return from Icma Coya. The trip had brought back a flood of fond memories and reminded her how much she missed the Andes. All through the fall and winter, we talked about returning. The obvious time to go was the next dry season, the summer months of 1983, but we'd decided to be married in June. The idea of a honeymoon in the jungle might seem romantic, but we both knew better. The expedition we had in mind would be difficult and demanding. To do the job right, we'd need plenty of time once we got there, and that would mean leaving right after the ceremony. Getting ready for our wedding and a major expedition, all at the same time, didn't seem like a good idea - nor did leaving lots of business at home unfinished until we got back, weeks later. The whole thing struck us both as a formula for early divorce, rather than connubial bliss.

Then, too, there were my architectural clients. Good people all, several of them were as excited about my plans to go exploring in Peru as I was - but with a difference. They wanted their houses before, not after, my great adventure. When we'd started their projects, there'd been no mention of lengthy delays in mid-stream. In the Rockies, summer is by far the best building season and by the time I got back, they'd have lost a whole year. I couldn't ask them to do that. So, enthusiasm aside, we reluctantly agreed to hold off until the summer of 1984. By then, we could spend a full two months in Vilcabamba, meanwhile taking advantage of the intervening year to put our affairs at home in order and get ready for the trip.

The decision made, I sent a note to Juvenal, thanking him for his many kindnesses and telling him of our new plans. I've since learned that remote Andean villages might as well be on Mars, as far as the Peruvian postal service is concerned, and that my letter had next to no chance of getting through. I shouldn't have been surprised, then, when Cobos never responded. The news from Peru all through 1983 wasn't good. The terrorist movement, called the Sendero Luminoso or "Shining Path", was gaining momentum. A group of Maoist fanatics, they were beginning to wreak havoc all over the country, but especially in remote Andean villages like Huancacalle. Juvenal's silence made us all the more fearful for his safety.

Our next priority was finding Gene Savoy and trying to establish communications with him. His book, Antisuyo, had gotten me interested in Peru in the first place, and he seemed the most likely source of help preparing for our new expedition. I'd tried to contact him before the Icma Coya trip, but only succeeded in learning that in the years since his explorations, he'd returned to the states and become a preacher in Reno, Nevada. David Vhay, a fellow Masters candidate from my graduate years at Princeton and native Nevadan, had returned to Reno after school to practice architecture. We'd both been unsuccessful resistance fighters as the mannerist juggernaut of post-modernism swept first through the Princeton faculty and later, the entire architectural profession. Savoy provided a good excuse for us to get back in touch and we found we still felt the kinship of the unjustly defeated. Dave verified that the explorer not only lived in Reno, but was the leader of a local religious group there, the International Community of Christ, headquartered in an impressive downtown temple. Several letters to Savoy in care of the church drew no response, so Nancy and I flew out to Reno hoping to track him down.

A visit to his church office confirmed that we'd come to the right place, but a somewhat other-worldly woman informed us that Reverend Savoy was "in retreat" and thus not available to receive visitors. Disappointed, we decided to drive across town to the residential area where Dave said the explorer lived. There was no missing the house, a large, Frank Lloyd wrong affair plunked in the midst of a hilly cluster of conventional suburban homes. In case one still couldn't figure out where the neighborhood explorer lived, the double masts of a sizable sailing ship towered above the fenced-in back yard, apparently beached there during some past oceanic cataclysm. As we drove by the house, a man in jeans and a snap-front, western shirt was out in the driveway, washing his car. I immediately recognized him as Gene Savoy from his picture in Antisuyo and stopped. Once we'd identified ourselves, he hastily invited us in for a cup of coffee.

He knew of us, he said, from our letters and apologized for his silence. His explorations in Peru had taken place a long time ago and had not had an altogether happy ending. Despite the many inquiries like mine that had been stimulated by Antisuyo, he said, he'd tried to put the entire experience pretty much behind him. He was nevertheless interested to hear of our recent trip and seemed excited by the prospect of our return to the Vilcabamba in 1984. He emphasized that he'd "never again" return to Peru, but wished us well and asked that we keep him informed of our plans. We agreed to stay in touch, thanked him for his hospitality, and left.

Within an hour of our return home to Jackson Hole, the phone rang. It was Savoy. "Had I seen the ruins near Icma Coya?" he asked. When I assured him we'd found no ruins at all, he quickly changed his tune and agreed, having meanwhile satisfied himself that we were who we said we were and had actually been to Icma Coya. Who had he thought we were, I.R.S. agents checking up on his church? I'd never before dealt with anyone quite like Savoy. Suspicion seemed his middle name, as if we were players in some high-stakes game. I had no clue what, exactly, those stakes might be, but the game was at once exciting and a bit unsettling. In the months following that first trick call, we slowly became better acquainted. I kept him abreast of our preparations and sent him copies of whatever my research turned up. Doing business always by phone, he'd call from time to time with bits of advice and encouragement. After years of turning people on by introducing them to the joys of mountaineering, I was especially pleased to see his enthusiasm for the project grow. It seemed we'd rekindled his powerful sense of adventure and, by picking up the exploration of Vilcabamba where he'd left off, we were pursuing some sort of unfinished business there. What business, I wondered, had he left unfinished?

Having finally connected with Savoy, there remained the question of what, exactly, we hoped to accomplish once we got back to Vilcabamba. In addition to spending more time at Vitcos, I wanted to go down to Espíritu Pampa and see Savoy's city. My reading over the winter confirmed what Cobos had said: that more and more expeditions were passing through Huancacalle en route to and from the ruins and that not all of them believed that Manco's Vilcabamba the Old had been found there. Some said the site was too small. Others felt the quality of the architecture was too poor. Many wondered why the ruins of three landmarks reported by the Spaniards, two forts at which they'd fought battles and a populous native village called Marcanay, hadn't yet been found along the only known route into the city. Savoy had come up with a controversial site for Marcanay, but if he was right, then the ancient approach to the capital was not the one used today. By his reckoning, the old road was lost in the now trackless, jungle covered mountains southwest of the city. Not everyone agreed, but even if Espíritu Pampa was Manco's lost capital and the puzzle really had been solved, important pieces were still missing. I wanted to find the old road, wherever it was, and the missing forts, and whatever else might be hidden on the forested flanks of Icma Coya.

The entire problem hinged on confirming the route actually used by the Spanish invaders during their two expeditions into the city. Without a decent map, finding a lost road in the midst of all that cloud forest would be practically impossible. I'd already verified that there were no usable contour maps of the area. The Peruvian government was slowly assembling an excellent series of 1:200,000 sheets using aerial photography to cover the entire country, but Vilcabamba was much too remote to rate such expensive treatment quite yet. North of the thirteenth parallel - the area in question - the sheets were all blank. In desperation, I turned to the most expensive treatment of all: NASA satellite images **(1)**. These can be ordered for any location on earth, but only if the desired latitude and longitude are known - a problem in un-mapped country. Luckily, Gene Savoy's sketch-map in Antisuyo showed Espíritu Pampa a bit less than 13 degrees south and about 73-1/2 degrees west **(2)**, so I ordered an image centering as nearly as possible on those coordinates. The 8 inch square negative that arrived several weeks later showed an enormous jumble of mountains and canyons without a single identifying feature. At first glance, even the scale and direction of north seemed to be missing, and though I eventually saw that both could be deduced from grid marks along the margins of the negative, I was still disappointed. There appeared to be no identifying features at all, and thus no way to tell what you were looking at.

My initial discouragement turned out to be hasty. Careful study of an enlarged print finally showed the distinctive cloverleaf pattern of the Urubamba River at Machu Picchu in the lower right corner of the image. With that as a reference, it was possible to trace the mummy-shaped hilltop of Rosaspata near dead center, and finally, the lightly snow-covered Markacocha mountains, including the jagged peak of Icma Coya, near the upper left corner. About ten kilometers north of the latter, the only large, flat valley for miles in any direction drained out into the low jungle. It had to be Espíritu Pampa. Quite unintentionally, the camera of LANDSAT II had captured the entire Zona de Vilcabamba, as the province is nowadays called, in a single shot from 570 miles out in space. It was a clear violation of the time-honored military adage that important objectives are invariably found at the intersection of four maps, but there it was. The resolution of the negative was so detailed that a postage stamp sized portion yielded crystal clear 11 x 14 inch prints when enlarged. No evidence of man could be seen, but the lay of the land would never again be a mystery. Every terrain feature we'd noted during our Icma Coya trip now stood out in bold relief, and already a few pieces of the puzzle could be seen falling neatly into place.

For openers, any lost road approaching Espíritu Pampa via the site Gene Savoy identified as Marcanay would necessarily have crossed either the main Markacocha divide or a long ridgeline running north from Icma Coya. Remembering that both were open country and easy going in good weather, it struck me that a careful traverse of both ridges would almost certainly intercept an old road there, if one existed. Having found such a road, we could follow it downhill all the way to Espíritu Pampa and explore any intermediate sites encountered along the way.

It would be a serious undertaking, involving six or seven miles of virgin jungle, previously unexplored. It doesn't sound like much, but I knew from painful experience on Icma Coya that six miles is a lot of jungle. At least, I thought, we'd be going downstream, a major advantage over Savoy's uphill attempts to check out the same country back in the 60s. I'd learned that lesson years earlier in the desert canyons of Utah. Drainages there are often blocked from below by overhanging cliffs and waterfalls, but can easily be descended from above by roping down the bad spots. As a sort of icing on the cake, the satellite photo seemed to show several strangely unnatural looking hilltops along the ridges we'd be traveling in search of the road. In my imagination they were all undiscovered Machu Picchus, so our plan of attack became obvious. We would begin by thoroughly searching the Markacocha highlands. Then, with or without a road, we'd descend through the jungle into Savoy's city, check it out and head back over the pass to Huancacalle for a closer look at Vitcos before returning home. That would connect everything I wanted to see along one big loop, like beads on a giant necklace.

Our itinerary decided, it was time to start planning equipment and laying in supplies. If the idea was to find something new, clearly we had to get off the trails and go where nobody else had been. That meant not being tied to a big string of horses, so we'd have to go small and cheap, and travel light. Except for the jungle, I'd been doing that for years and already had most of the food and gear we'd need. Next came putting together the team. As in '82, I wanted it to be a self-sufficient, fast-moving outfit. Nancy and I would be the only ones returning from the 1982 trip, since Brooke and Curtis were supporting themselves in college and couldn't spare two months away from work. Nancy planned to go with me into the mountains, but wasn't too excited about bashing around in the jungle - so I needed some new *compañeros*. I put out the word to see if any of my old climbing buddies wanted to go and was delighted, though not too surprised, that several did. For anyone with an adventurous spirit, it was a hard trip to resist.

The first to sign on was Jim Little, an old friend and neighbor in Jackson Hole. Ever since his days at Dartmouth, he'd been a skier, climber and all-around good hand in the mountains. That he was also a doctor was especially comforting, since we'd be days, or even weeks, away from any medical facilities. His wife Martha decided to join us and follow the same itinerary as Nancy. Jim and Martha had hiked extensively in Nepal several years earlier and were both excited to compare the Andes to what they'd seen in the Himalayas.

Next to join was Paul Burghard, an investment analyst with Merrill Lynch in San Antonio. Paul had been with me on a climb of Mount Moran in the Tetons the previous spring. We'd been caught in a week-long snowstorm, and Paul's performance under pressure in bad conditions had been impressive. I was glad to have him back. Chris Mattair, a college student, also from Texas, decided to come despite the objections of his family. They approved of his climbing with me in the Wind River Range of Wyoming, but felt that the political situation in Peru was potentially more dangerous than any peak. I couldn't help wondering if they weren't right, but both Chris and I shrugged off their concerns as if we knew otherwise.

Unexpectedly, a long-time friend of Nancy's, Jill Baumler, returned from a trip to New Zealand just in time to sign up. She, too, figured to join Nancy and Martha on their return to town after the high country phase of the trip. A bit of a world traveler, she was as excited about seeing Cuzco as she was about exploring the high Andes. For Jill, the trip was to be only the beginning of an adventure of a different sort that would take her eventually to Europe and back. Last to join was Jim Barefoot. Jim and I'd climbed together many times in the Rockies, even though he was a full-time college student in North Carolina. A trek that he, Nancy and I had planned some months earlier in Nepal had fallen through and Peru seemed the perfect place to make up for it.

It was a good group and, once in the mountains, it turned out even better than I expected. Everyone was strong, competent and experienced in the outdoors, but there were no macho men (or women), big names, or fortune hunters. Everyone was along for the fun and adventure of the trip, and each seemed willing to work hard to bring it off successfully. Events were to provide plenty of opportunities for hard work and in time each individual found a niche, becoming the team expert at this or that. The Indians were amazed to see how well we took care of ourselves and how little of their help we needed - their experience with *gringos* being generally quite the opposite, or so they said. Most important of all, as anyone who's ever done a difficult excursion will know, we got along well and laughed a lot.

One final item remained. Curtis, Brooke and I had facetiously named our Icma Coya climb the "Sixpac Manco" expedition. The rebel Inca and his three sons and successors had all been great drinkers of *chicha*, a native beer made from fermented corn. Manco's youngest, Tupac Amaru, was the tragic figure who'd finally lost Vilcapampa to the invading Spaniards in 1572. Over the years, his name had become synonymous with the last of the Incas. Being enthusiastic beer drinkers ourselves, we decided to honor both men and their apparent passion for the occasional brew with a fitting name and a logo showing the Inca carrying a sixpac, with one can raised in final salute. The new team quickly adopted both and, right from the start, called itself Sixpac Manco II.

Shortly before leaving for Miami, expedition rendezvous point for our flight to Lima, Nancy and I flew out to Reno for a second visit with Gene Savoy. He was relaxed and amiable, a different man from the cautious and guarded host of our first visit. It was evident that the months of phone calls and correspondence had drawn him very much back into the Vilcabamba. For old times sake, he showed us the journals from his explorations in the 60s, several large volumes filled with pages of notes, maps and sketches. Then, getting down to business, he handed me a seven page memo laying out his thoughts on our upcoming trip, to this day the only written communication I've ever received directly from the hand of Gene Savoy **(3).** Finally he offered us the co-sponsorship of the Andean Explorer's Club, a group he'd founded in Lima during his exploring years, and, with a certain formality, he even gave us a Club flag to fly over our camps.

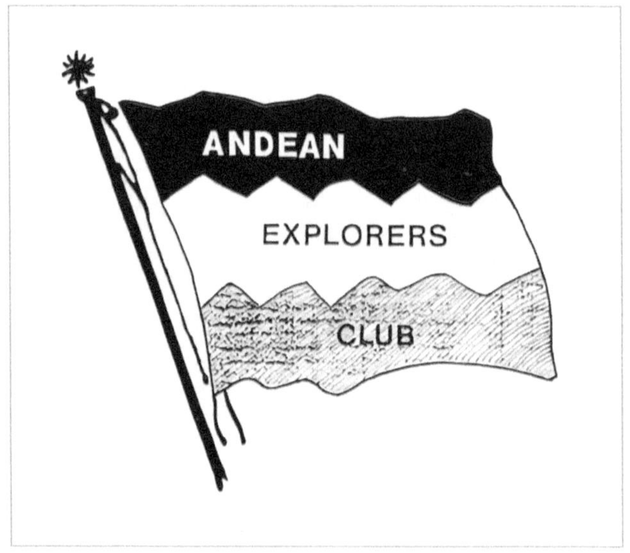

Andean Explorers Club Flag

The whole meeting was a little overwhelming. We began to feel we were entering the larger history of big time exploration in the Vilcabamba, and were carrying on in the footsteps of both Savoy and Bingham. For the first time, I found myself feeling a little nervous. What if we didn't find anything? Almost worse, what if we found something really important? What were we getting into? Gene did little to reassure us.

"Exploring in South America is serious and sometimes nasty business," he said. "But if you're careful and keep a low profile, you'll come out okay. One thing, though: don't trust anyone."

Nancy and I exchanged glances. Come out okay? Trust no one? What on earth was he talking about?

Don't think you can just crash around blind in the jungle and find anything," he continued. "You can't. Listen to the *campesinos*. They know where everything is. Pay attention to their tips and look for old roads. Follow them - they all go somewhere." And, finally, "There's supposed to be a beautiful two-story building made of white limestone somewhere up in the Puncuyoc Mountains. If I were going back, that's where I'd go." It was the best 30 seconds of advice he could possibly have given us.

3

Back To Vitcos

The first of what were to be many changes in our carefully laid plans occurred on June 9th, before we'd even left the States. Everyone except Chris arrived in Miami as scheduled, only to find that all flights to Peru from the U.S. had been cancelled indefinitely due to some flap involving the two governments. We'd bought our tickets weeks in advance, so changing flights was out of the question. "*No problema*," said a fellow from Aero Peru, who finally showed up two hours after departure time. It seemed Air Jamaica was honoring our tickets and would connect us with a Lima flight in Kingston. Sure enough, we soon found ourselves sipping rum collins in the airport there, wondering where Chris had gone wrong. Maybe he'd found out about the flight cancellations in advance, somehow, and assumed the trip was off. He'd be missed, everyone agreed, and we turned our thoughts to Peru. After an overnight bivouac in the cocktail lounge at the airport in Lima, we were off to Cuzco. As the pilot dipped down over Machu Picchu on final approach, the peaks of the Cordillera Vilcanota drew everyone to the port-side windows moments before 20,575 foot Salcantay and the other ice giants of the Cordillera Vilcabamba loomed to starboard. On a fair day, it's as fine a spectacle as can be seen anywhere, and June 10th was crystal clear.

Our headquarters in Cuzco was at the home of Alicia Valle, Nancy's hostess before I'd come out of the jungle in 1982. Never married, Alicia is nevertheless the undisputed matriarch of a charming household of seven Peruvian ladies spanning three generations. In a short time, she became our mother-away-from-home as well. Her guest rooms cluster around the perimeter of a roof terrace with a magnificent view of the city. Enthusiasm was running so high as we gathered there that Alicia asked us to quiet down a bit. It seemed another guest was sleeping in his nearby room. Despite efforts to respect his privacy, we woke him up and out he came. Everyone cheered. It was Chris.

Thus reunited, Sixpac Manco II set out to see the sights and have some fun. The routine was to be much like that of the first trip, beginning with several days of exploring the city and surrounding countryside, meanwhile becoming acclimatized and fit in preparation for a tour of the Inca Trail to Machu Picchu. Having done all that in 1982, I took the time to sort the food and gear, buy last-minute provisions, and negotiate a permit with the Instituto Nacional de Cultura. Not expecting problems with the latter, I saved it for the day before we planned to head downriver. It was very nearly a mistake. The people at the I.N.C. had been so cooperative the first time, I wasn't prepared for the cold reception I received at their offices on Calle San Andreas. The very mention of Vilcabamba seemed to raise eyebrows.

In the two years since our last visit, the Sendero Luminoso had gained strength and become increasingly active. After reading my application, one of the officials warned that Vilcabamba had become a very dangerous place. Another, a woman who knew but seldom spoke English, said there had been many *campesinos* killed there, the most recent incident having been only a month earlier. After some discussion, it was agreed I could go if I were willing to sign a release, absolving the government in advance of responsibility for any trouble we might get into. Without the foggiest idea what I was doing, but having no real alternative, I signed the release and got permission for six weeks in what began to look like a war zone.

As I rose to leave, the man grasped my hand with what seemed a certain finality.

"*Vaya con Dios, señor*," he said, avoiding my eyes. Even with my rusty Spanish, I knew what that meant. The lady followed me out, whispering an added warning in English, just to be sure I got the point. We should be especially careful of the Army and the police, she said. They were arrogant and nervous and would shoot without provocation at anything or anyone suspicious. I thanked her for the advice, but walked away with the uneasy feeling she knew something I didn't.

Later that night, our last in the city, we were all gathered in the Café Roma, drinking round after round of *pisco* sours, the national libation of Peru, and rehashing the days' events. It occurred to me that one of the I.N.C. officials had mentioned another Vilcabamba expedition, led by an Italian archaeologist and due out any day. They'd not been heard from in over a month and there was some concern for their safety. Maybe, I thought, we'd cross their path at some point and find out more about the situation. Our conversation was interrupted by a man at the next table who said he'd just returned from Espíritu Pampa. Along with his older companion, he looked like he'd been to hell and back. They'd overheard our speculations about what we were headed into and offered the benefit of their own experiences. It was a strange story, featuring snakes, spirits, an unreliable guide and a missing doctor. Strangest of all, however, was the fact that in a city of nearly 300,000 people, the only two who had recently been where we were going happened to be sitting at the next table.

They'd seen no terrorists, they said, but echoed the lady's warning about the *policía*. There were armed units patrolling the area, and one had to avoid travel at night and approach villages with great care. I asked about the ruins at Espíritu Pampa, and the older man said the site was the most "powerful" place he'd ever been. We all listened with a combination of skepticism and fascination as he related the bizarre tale of his experiences there. Finally, the other man drew me aside. He was, he said, a hypnotherapist from California and claimed some degree of prescient gift. He said I should follow my instincts and all would be well - ours would be a very successful venture. There was, however, one man of whom I should beware. He didn't know who it was, but said I would know when I met him.

"*Buena suerte*," he added, and with his friend, drifted out into the crowded plaza. First Savoy, then the lady at the I.N.C. and now this fellow all seemed to think we were headed into harm's way. Were we a bunch of naive *gringos* to think we could just hike around in the Andes with impunity, as if we were back home in the Rockies? Ours was a thoughtful group as we strolled quietly homeward down the Avenida Sol that night.

The following morning, June 14th, we were up at 4:30 and off on the local train down the Río Urubamba toward Machu Picchu. The rest of the group got off at kilometer 88, starting point for hiking the famous Inca Trail. Since I'd done that on the way to Icma Coya, my job was to take the mountain of food and gear for the Vilcabamba expedition on down to Aguas Calientes, a raucous little railroad town in the canyon below Machu Picchu where Curtis, Brooke and I had spent a memorable night on our way out in 1982. Burghard, who'd developed a nasty cough in Cuzco, decided to join me in hopes that he'd be feeling better by the time the rest of the group arrived at Machu Picchu. It was a tough break for him, but I was glad to have his help and company. As we threw the last of our duffels onto the platform which doubles as the main street of Aguas Calientes, a *gringo* stepped out of the crowd of Indian faces and identified himself as William Kaiser, ex-patriate American owner of a nearby hostel. For 3000 *soles*, or about 95 cents a night, he said, he'd put us up and feed us breakfast. It was a deal. The price, and for that matter the town, had changed little in two years. Kaiser later turned out to be the "unreliable guide" we'd been told about by the two men in Cuzco, but his side of the story was quite different from theirs and to us, he was most helpful.

Aguas Calientes was then a delightful place. Little more than a shanty town, it clung tentatively to a rocky bench alongside the

Urubamba about three kilometers upstream from the station stop at Machu Picchu. Steep jungle and sheer granite cliffs streaming with flowering bromeliads soar above town in all directions. Two side canyons empty into the river there and relieve what might otherwise be terminal claustrophobia. An old Inca hot spring a short way up one of these gives the place its name. There being no alternative town-site anywhere nearby, a lively village grew up there to house the crews clearing and caring for the ruins at Machu Picchu. Over the years, these locals have been joined by a growing army of tourists, there to take advantage of their handiwork and, more recently, an even larger army of city folk, there to take advantage of the tourists. The result is an increasingly boisterous, multi-national watering hole in an absurdly primitive, isolated setting - a tropical holdover from the Alaskan gold rush. The result isn't much to look at, but I assured Paul we'd have a good time and he wasn't disappointed.

By day, we hiked up to Machu Picchu. Though I'd been there briefly with Curtis and Brooke in 1982, I'd always wanted to have enough time to really explore the place, and this was my chance. We'd get up early and hike down the tracks and up the trail to the ruins, 2000 feet above. Except for us and a few other hikers, the ruins were virtually deserted until the mid-morning tourist express arrived from Cuzco. Then, we'd slip off to some remote corner of the site until the crowds ebbed at about three, in time to catch the last train back to the city. Once again, we could wander about the ruins alone until dark. It was wonderful and got us into pretty fair shape as well. Paul's cough even got better, probably due to the friendlier altitude, more than half a mile lower than Cuzco.

At one point, we were cutting down an old, overgrown path behind the peak of Huayna Picchu, the sharp crag featured in the background of all the best photos of the ruins. It was steep, hot work, and we stopped at one point for a break on the only flat ground we'd encountered, a jungle covered rock ledge. That afternoon, as we backtracked our trail toward home, we stopped there again for lunch. Looking around more carefully, we were amazed to find that the ledge was, in fact, one of several beautifully built stone-faced *andenes*, or terraces, flanking a broad stone stairway leading up into the thick jungle above. For the first time, I understood something Gene Savoy had said about the difficulty of recognizing ruins in the bush. Six years later, Peruvian archaeologists working for the I.N.C. would discover a large complex of fine, previously unknown buildings at the top of those same stairs, not thirty yards from our picnic spot.

On the 17th, we got up early and met the Inca Trail party just as they reached the nearby ruins of Wiñay Wana, my favorite in all of Peru. Meaning "forever young," the name conveys perfectly the exquisite artistry of the architecture and the romantic beauty of its setting. Our friends were dazzled by their four day trek in and above the clouds. Jim and Martha said they hadn't done anything like it since Nepal. Everyone was fascinated by the ruins they'd seen along the way, and Wiñay Wana was no exception. After a quick tour, we joined them as they headed excitedly for the end of the trail and the most famous Inca ruin of all. It was the perfect beginning for the expedition, since all of us were now in high spirits, fit and healthy - Paul's cough having by then nearly disappeared. After a restful day and a half of sightseeing at Machu Picchu, eating banana pancakes, and swimming in the hot springs near Aguas Calientes, Sixpac Manco II was ready for the Vilcabamba.

June 19th found us on the train again, this time en route to the end of the tracks at the sweltering provincial capital at Quillabamba. Beyond, the Urubamba plunges through the gorge of the Pongo de Mainique and on into the Amazon Basin. Though we were now only a day's truck ride from our base camp at Juvenal's place in Huancacalle, no one in Quillabamba wanted even to talk about the Vilcabamba, let alone take us there. The terrorists were bad, we were told, but the Army was worse. We should run the rapids in the Pongo and go home, they said, like all the other *gringos* who came to Quillabamba. Nevertheless, we flashed a few extra *soles* and by noon the next day, we were on our way up the Río Vilcabamba - all eight of us perched atop our gear in the back of a tiny Toyota pickup.

The weather was clear and the countryside even more beautiful than I'd remembered. The only ominous note was the abundance of political slogans painted on rocks, walls and buildings everywhere. Presidential elections were only a year away and a young, Kennedy-style newcomer named Alan García was threatening to overthrow the old order and bring his populist APRA party into power. Such transitions hardly ever occur smoothly in Latin America and there were Army troops in every little village, most of which hadn't even had a police station two years earlier. At Pucyura, we stopped to present our permit to the old policeman who'd waved us through in 1982, only to find an entire company of soldiers out playing soccer in the churchyard. The tension was somewhat eased when the head man, a with-it, good looking young *teniente*, appeared in his running shorts and Grateful Dead teeshirt. Our credentials were fine, he said as our presence was dutifully logged in by one of his troopers, but our planned expedition struck him as "*muy peligroso*," very risky. Still, crazy *gringos* were not his concern and he sent us on our way with a shake of his head. As we drove off, he pointed his finger and hollered after us, "*con cuidado!* " - be careful. Half an hour later, we were unloading our gear in Huancacalle.

Don Juvenal - a title befitting his apparent rank in the community - was glad to see us. He thanked me for my letter, which had somehow made it through, and offered us a good campsite not far from his house. He didn't think we were in any danger from terrorists, he said, but thought it best that we were camped nearby. After setting up our tents and getting organized, we went up to his house for coffee and *choclo*, boiled *maíz* or Indian corn, and met his wife and brother, Flavio, one of Savoy's guides in the 60s. Benjamín, another brother who'd also worked with Savoy, was off working a farm several days to the north. In a ritual universal throughout the Andes, Juvenal hastily covered the low bench at the rear of his porch with horse blankets and animal skins before insisting we all take seats. His wife then served the traditional refreshments while I broke out the equally customary gifts. Savoy had sent along a few things for the Cobos "boys", as he called them, and Nancy and I had brought some presents of our own, for both them and their wives. All these were now passed around to everyone's delight. Surprisingly, a copy of Antisuyo in English, autographed by Savoy, caused the biggest stir. None of the *campesinos* could read it, of course, but they proudly recognized their own names here and there in the text. It was a festive afternoon, and we were welcomed as honored guests by everyone we met.

The Inti Raymi was to be celebrated in four more days and Juvenal again wanted us to be his guests. I much preferred to get going, but such invitations are not politely refused and we decided to delay our departure until the 25th. I figured we could explore the local ruins, get organized for the trail and, if time remained, maybe do some climbing. With our heavy loads, it would be a long, hard haul up into the Markacocha range, our first objective. With that in mind, we turned in that night glad that the next few days would be easy and enjoyable after all- a bit of R and R before the serious work began.

About midnight, Nancy and I were awakened by an hysterical woman and her young son. The woman's husband, it seemed, was desperately ill and needed our help. We woke up Jim Little, who grabbed his medical kit, and the three of us raced up the hill in the dark to the woman's house. Inside, a group of locals was gathered around an old man, writhing in pain on a sweaty bed and barely visible in the candlelight. *Colica*, they called it, but Jim hadn't a clue what was wrong with the poor man. All his family could tell us was that he'd apparently suffered the same acute abdominal cramps in the past, and always recovered. People unused to the over-the-counter medicines we take for granted in the States often respond strongly to isolated dosages. Hoping the old man was no exception, Jim gave him some mild pain pills, and we returned to bed about two AM. As we lay there trying to sleep, all I could think of was the ill-fated Augustinian missionary, Padre Diego Ortiz. It was at precisely that place in 1571 that he'd been asked to treat the seriously ill Titu Cusi Inca, who'd died nevertheless. Ortiz had paid dearly for his failure when the distraught and vengeful Indians had tortured him to a slow and horrible death. What would happen to us, I wondered, if the old man went under after taking Jim's harmless pain pills?

At first light, Nancy and I walked uneasily back up the hill to accompany Jim on his second house call. He was to make many more among the Indians, but none more scary than this one. The young boy ran to greet us at the gate, his wide grin proof that we needn't have worried. The man was not only feeling much better, but the speed of his recovery was seen as a sure sign of Doctor Jim's medical prowess. Despite anything we said, the man's wife insisted on paying him for his services and, having no money, she instead offered us a couple of handfuls of eggs. Gratefully, we got back to camp just as the others were getting up and cooking a skimpy breakfast of dried blueberry pancakes and canned bacon from our packs. With unexpected pleasure, we added in a big fresh omelet.

Tasty as the food was, I was anxious to get to work. The sun was just breaking over the hill of Rosaspata, looming above our camp from the east. I knew its crest and the valley beyond were littered with the sprawling and historic ruins of Manco's Vitcos. Having had almost no chance to do so in '82, I could hardly wait to get up there and check them out. While the others chatted about this and that, enjoying the meal and the morning sun, I sat off to one side gulping my food and trying to recall all that I'd read about the site since my first, quick visit there with Curtis and Brooke, two years earlier.

With their arrival at Vitcos in mid-1537, Manco and his followers were confident they'd finally found a haven, safe at last from the murdering Spaniards and their all-but-invincible cavalry. In this, they were soon disillusioned. Though he'd destroyed the road behind him before descending from the Panticalla Pass and had partially cut the bridge at Chuquichaca before advancing up the canyon of the Vilcapampa toward Vitcos, Manco had nevertheless underestimated the Spaniards' resolve. He left behind no rear guard to block the road or give warning of enemy pursuit. It was the sort of tactical error he would never again make - and fortunately so, since it very nearly cost him his new-found kingdom within days of his arrival at Vitcos.

According to Pedro de Cieza de Leon, one of the principal Spanish historians of sixteenth century Peru, the Inca's successful escape from Cuzco and his victory at Ollantaytambo had given many of his nobles, called *orejones* or "big-ears" due to the large ear ornaments they wore, the courage to follow him into the presumed security of Vilcabamba. Like Manco, they had brought along their entire households, including no small amount of what the Europeans called treasure. Vilcabamba was thus not only a hot-bed of native resistance and pagan souls, but an untapped source of spoils as well. This last, the Spaniards could not long abide.

While Manco had been making good his withdrawal from Ollantaytambo, oblivious to all but the road ahead, his enemies behind had not been idle. No sooner had the Inca abandoned the siege of Cuzco than civil war had erupted among the Spaniards. Returning from Chile at the head of a strong column, the challenger, Diego de Almagro, had won and the severely weakened Pizarros were momentarily out of power. After consolidating his grip on the scattered survivors of the war with Manco, Almagro sent a force under Rodrigo Orgoñez, a trusted supporter and veteran commander, to capture the Inca. The idea was to grab whatever booty could be found and put an end, finally, to the dream of native sovereignty Manco's freedom had come to symbolize. With some difficulty, Orgoñez' troops rebuilt the Panticalla road, repaired the bridge at Chuquichaca and force-marched up the Vilcabamba River toward Vitcos, arriving there close on the heels of their quarry. The Incas, who had chosen the moment to celebrate their apparent good fortune, were taken totally by surprise and, being without either weapons or any organized defense, were nearly wiped out. Great numbers of men, women and children were killed or captured, Vitcos was looted of its wealth and the Indians' vast herds of llamas and alpacas, the native livestock of the Andes, were taken. Although his illegitimate, but closest son, Titu Cusi, was among the captured, Manco himself managed to escape into the forest and - as the Spaniards soon learned to their dismay - lived to fight another day.

Orgoñez returned to Cuzco falsely secure in the belief that the back of the Incas had finally been broken. Neither he nor his superiors yet understood the native mentality. As long as the person of the Inca survived, the empire continued to exist. Manco not only returned to power, but quickly re-established his stronghold at Vitcos. The depleted ranks of its defenders were soon filled by the flood of Indian refugees which began straggling in from all parts of Peru. Within months, Manco's forces were successfully raiding Spanish columns and installations as far away as Lima. Using a vast network of jungle roads unknown to the Europeans, Manco traveled up and down the Andes, attempting to foment rebellion among the many native tribes that had once comprised the Four Quarters. A powerful Spanish force sent to intercept one of these missions at a place called Oncoy was annihilated in November of 1538, just before the onset of the long, Andean rainy season. News of the defeat caused an uproar in Cuzco, and it was decided that another expedition should be sent against Vitcos as soon as the rains subsided.

Mindful of the ease with which Orgoñez had reached that city in 1537 and expecting just such a retaliatory attack, Manco had meanwhile established an alternate refuge deep in the forest beyond the Andean divide. Like the province itself, his new capital city was called Vilcabamba, and to reach it the Spaniards would have to abandon their horses and march single file through miles of jungle, infested with the Inca's allied tribesmen.

Primitive hunters and sometime cannibals, it was their custom to send poisoned arrows and darts from camouflaged positions behind the cover of the nearly opaque screen of trees, roots and vines that pressed claustrophobically from all sides. Seldom, if ever, would such tribesmen confront an enemy openly in the European fashion and if attacked, they simply melted invisibly into the undergrowth. To these tactics, the Incas planned to add one of their own favorite tricks. Having lured an adversary into a confined position on steep, open ground, they would roll huge boulders into his panicked ranks from the safety of the heights above. Such was the surprise Manco hoped to spring on the Europeans when the time came. One particularly narrow and treacherous passage along the road to Vilcabamba especially favored his plan, and it was there that he laid his trap when word arrived of the impending Spanish advance.

In Cuzco, the Pizarros had once more gained the upper hand and managed to capture and execute their rival, Almagro. Thus it was that the invasion of 1539 was led by Francisco Pizarro's half-brother, Gonzalo, a seasoned captain with three hundred of the Spaniards' best men under his command. They marched unopposed up the Vilcabamba river and occupied Vitcos without a fight. It began to look like another rout and they joked that Manco and his rebels would soon be in chains.

From prisoners, they learned that the Inca was waiting for them in a fortified position several days' march beyond Vitcos and they immediately set out to find and destroy his army once and for all. After marching up and over the Salty Pass, they descended to Pampaconas, left their horses and plunged into the jungle on foot. Among those present was Pedro Pizarro, a young cousin of the *Marqués*, as the resurgent Francisco Pizarro called himself. In a detailed account written thirty two years after the fact, Pedro described the near disaster which followed:

"...we were traveling one day by a very narrow road along which we could go only single file, and which was near the place where Manco Inca had his stronghold. Gonzalo Pizarro was in the lead and Pedro del Barco and I came next, followed by all the others. Now it happened that as we neared the fort, we passed through a forest greater and more dense than any we had yet seen and Gonzalo chanced to get a small stone in his shoe. While taking the stone out, he ordered del Barco to take the lead and continue on slowly with the men. They came upon two bridges, newly made in order to cross two small rivers. Not being aware that they'd been made on purpose to lead the Spaniards into a trap, they crossed over and soon came onto an open slope without trees which came down from a very high mountain."

"Not seeing any Indians, because they were all hiding in ambush, about twenty Spaniards proceeded out onto the slope. Suddenly, the Indians hidden above hurled down many boulders, which came rolling with much fury. Three Spaniards were crushed and their body parts cast down into a river, below. The Spaniards who had gone forward into the forest found many archers who began to

wound them with arrows. Had they not found a narrow path by which they threw themselves into the river, all would have been killed." **(1)**

Reeling from this debacle, the invaders fell back to their horses at Pampaconas, re-grouped and sent to Cuzco for reinforcements which eventually carried the campaign. Once again, however, Manco escaped with most of his army and even though the Spaniards penetrated to his hidden stronghold at Vilcabamba, their victory accomplished little. Manco's son, Titu Cusi, the only of the Incas to dictate his memoirs, recalls the second and final fight:

"*My father went to look for the Spaniards about three leagues (about 9 miles) from Vilcapampa, where he had a fortress, in order to defend himself and not let them into the city. It was hard to tell how many there were because of the many trees and thick vegetation. They fought hard for ten days along the banks of a river, back and forth around the fortress. Finally, he saw that he could not win and threw himself into the river. Once safely on the other side, he shouted, 'I am Manco Inca! I am Manco Inca!*'" **(2)**

Inca Vilcabamba would not be seriously challenged for another thirty three years, but Manco was nevertheless destined to die at the hands of his enemies. The civil war between the Pizarros and Almagrists had not ended with Almagro's death after all. His son had continued the fight until his own capture and execution in 1542, but not before having his father's old enemy, Francisco Pizarro, murdered at the Governor's Palace in Lima in mid-1541. In order to escape the wrath of the the dead *Marqués'* brother, Gonzalo, seven of Almagro the Younger's captains fled into Vilcabamba and sought refuge with Manco at Vitcos. Much against the advice of his own captains, the Inca believed that the Almagrists were his only allies against the hated Gonzalo and he received them as such. Ever since the failed Spanish invasion of 1539, the Indians had stepped up their raids in the surrounding countryside and in return for Manco's protection, the seven turn-coats offered valuable intelligence about Pizarro's movements, tactics and weaponry.

Unfortunately for all concerned, as it turned out, the King of Spain sent his own representative to Lima in May of 1544 to be the first official Viceroy of Peru. Gonzalo Pizarro, who'd been trying to regain control since his brother's death, was faced with a new rival and the two were immediately at odds. When news of the ensuing power struggle in Cuzco reached Vilcabamba, Manco's seven visitors quickly saw an opportunity to curry the favor of the new Viceroy and perhaps end their exile in the wilderness. Their plan was simple. They decided to murder their unsuspecting host and claim credit for putting an end to what had come to be called the "Inca problem." Titu Cusi, the young favorite who'd been stolen by Orgoñez during the Spanish raid of 1537, tragically returned home from captivity in Cuzco just in time to witness his father's brutal assassination. According to his account, written in 1570:

"*After these Spaniards had been with my father for several years in Vitcos, they were all playing quoits one day with much good fellowship. Just as my father was raising the quoit to throw, they all rushed upon him with their knives, daggers and swords. He fell to the ground covered with wounds and they left him for dead. Being a little boy and seeing my father treated so badly, I wanted to help him - but they turned furiously on me and nearly killed me with a lance. Terrified, I fled into some bushes and hid.*" **(3)**

Thus died the Caesar of Vilcabamba, though unlike Brutus and his compatriots, Manco's assassins were soon rounded up by the Indians and put horribly to death. Ironically, it was all in vain, since the Viceroy whose attentions they had sought to gain was himself killed by Gonzalo's forces not long thereafter. Nor did Manco's death bring about the collapse of Inca resistance. The throne in Vilcabamba passed naturally to the young heir apparent, Sayri Tupac, who was to rule over the native enclave, unmolested, for another thirteen years. The most visible result of the seven Almagrists' treachery was the grisly sight of their own severed heads, still displayed proudly atop pikes at Vitcos as late as 1565.

The war with the Spaniards was far from over, but the importance of Vitcos declined in the decades after Manco's death. Like the planned route of our expedition, the scene of the action shifted westward, into the jungles beyond the mountains. In 1572, the Indians suffered a disastrous defeat there and the fate of Inca Vilcabamba was finally sealed. The last of its rebel kings was captured, dragged off to Cuzco and dispatched according to Spanish justice. The Sons of the Sun were no more and their final refuge became a place from the past, renamed Vilcabamba the Old.

It had taken 40 years and cost thousands of lives, including those of all the principal players on both sides, but after the fall of Vilcabamba, the Europeans were undisputed masters of Peru. Vitcos lay overgrown and in ruins. Vilcabamba the Old was abandoned to the jungle and forgotten by all but the wild, forest tribesmen whose descendants, the nomadic Machiguenga, are still seen there today. For awhile, the gold and silver mines above Pampaconas, so rich in the time of Pachacuti, continued to produce, and the Spaniards worked them to their profit. As many local Indians as could be found were pressed into service and made to live in the bleak, newly founded Spanish settlement at Vilcabamba the New, high above Vitcos, close to the diggings. Within a few years, even these played out and the Spaniards lost interest and returned to the comforts of Cuzco. The otherwise poor province of Vilcabamba was left to the few locals able to wrest a living from its rough, inhospitable terrain. And so it remained for the next three hundred years.

Impatient to get moving, I downed the last of my food and started gathering up the gear I figured I'd need for my first day of real field work. Having no training or experience in archaeology, I'd brought the same gear I used at home to do site maps for my architectural clients: my feet for pacing distances, a compass for measuring directions, an altimeter for elevations and a journal and pencil for writing it all down. I slipped the last three in my pockets, where they'd be handy. In a fanny pack, I stuck a fifty foot tape, an eye level for comparing heights, two oranges, some water and a rain shell. A camera around my neck and a *machete* at my belt completed the outfit.

I've since been urged to take more advantage of the cam-corders and high-tech surveying and global positioning gadgetry that's come on the market in recent years. Maybe I should. In theory, it's a good idea. The trouble is, in practice, something always goes wrong. Just when it's needed most, anything with moving parts freezes in the high country, drowns crossing a creek or gets accidentally turned on inside a pack and dies. Sooner or later, I always end up doing things the old fashioned way anyhow, so I just do them that way all the time. To this day, I've never improved on the cheap, simple, lightweight kit I threw together that first morning, though at the time it seemed pretty amateurish. Hiram Bingham, I thought, probably had better equipment three quarters of a century earlier.

All packed up and ready to go, I saw that the others were lounging in the sun and taking their sweet time with breakfast. Damn! Didn't they understand that incredible adventures awaited us in the albeit frosty and uninviting shadows, just across the river? Maybe so, but the adventures would still be there after the shadows were gone. Silently exasperated and with time to kill, I thought back to Bingham and the rediscovery of Vitcos in modern times.

Not until the middle of the nineteenth century had men of learning begun to take an interest in the vast, uncharted *montaña*, as they called the jungle-clad eastern slope of the Andes. It was, and remains, one of the earth's last zones of Terra Incognita. The great Peruvian cartographer and naturalist, Antonio Raimondi, was the first of these early scientists to visit the upper Río Vilcabamba, ascending in about 1865 as far as Vilcabamba the New. Like other learned men of the time, he was vaguely aware of the story of Inca Vilcapampa, but at the time it was mistakenly believed that the Spaniards had never found its final capital - and that untold treasure awaited whoever did. So everyone, including Raimondi, was looking for Vilcabamba the Old. No one cared about Vitcos. The Spaniards had presumably made off with anything of value there centuries ago.

Raimondi neither encountered nor was told of any ruins during his expedition and he understandably concluded that Manco's fabled "lost city" was elsewhere. The most likely candidate, he thought, was at Choquequirau, a large Inca ruin overlooking the canyon of the Río Apurimac several days to the south. Reported some years earlier by a Frenchman named Sartiges **(4),** Choquequirau was the only important archaeological site then known in the region called Vilcabamba. Most informed opinion at the time agreed with Raimondi and the matter was considered closed for more than four decades.

Ironically, the man who would prove Raimondi wrong was himself destined to spend much of his life promoting an equally incorrect candidate for the site of Vilcabamba the Old. In 1909, an obscure young lecturer at Yale named Hiram Bingham made the arduous climb up to Choquequirau in the company of a group of Peruvian treasure seekers. Although he was impressed by grandeur of the surroundings, the American was skeptical about the prevailing opinion concerning the identity of the ruins:

"*Raimondi may be correct but, until someone shall have explored the present village of Vilcabamba (the New) and its vicinity, I am inclined to the opinion that Choquequirau was merely a fortress.*" **(5)**

For the moment, no one paid much attention to the doubts of an obscure *gringo*, untrained in archaeology and new to Peru. His challenge went unanswered. It was Bingham, himself, that was destined to explore the heart of Vilcabamba and the remainder of his life would be dominated by what he found there. On his return to New Haven after that first trip to Choquequirau, he organized the Yale Peruvian Expedition and returned to the Andes two years later, in 1911. Unlike the fortune hunters of the day, Bingham's motivation was mainly scientific. Among other things, he was determined to locate both Vitcos and Vilcabamba the Old, and had scoured the chronicles for any hint of their whereabouts. Once in the field, he headed straight down the Río Urubamba, finding several lesser ruins along the way. None seemed to be what he was looking for and he pressed on. While descending the newly cleared railroad right-of-way through the wildest part of the gorge, Bingham was shown extensive ruins at a remote place called Machu Picchu. Despite a dense overgrowth of jungle, he quickly appreciated the magnitude of the find and made plans to return. Impressive as these new ruins were, they, too, matched nothing the Spaniards had described. Still several days from his planned destination in the upper Río Vilcabamba, he continued downriver.

His next stop was at the *hacienda* at Huadquiña, then the only enclave of civilization in that part of Peru. No one there knew anything about Vitcos or Vilcabamba the Old, but they claimed "great" ruins existed nearby, nonetheless. After being taken to several minor and disappointing sites, the American bid a polite farewell and moved on. Then came his first break. He was introduced to the aging governor of a tiny village called Lucma, far up the Río Vilcabamba. From the chronicles, Bingham knew that Manco's Vitcos had been near a place called Pucyura, high in the same drainage. Asked about it, the old man confirmed that a village by that name still existed a short ride up the river from Lucma, though he knew of no ruins there. In the company of the governor, Bingham again took to the trail, stopping only to check out ruins rumored along the way. Brief investigations at Collumayu and place called Inca Huaracana in the heights above Lucma disclosed only meager remains and the expedition arrived, finally, at Pucyura. Unlike Raimondi before him, Bingham was soon told by the locals that impressive ruins could be found on the hilltop called Rosaspata, overlooking the village from the south. The American quickly hired local guides and for the second time in as many weeks climbed up to find a major Inca ruin-site, previously unknown to science. Except for the depredations of time and grazing livestock, it had remained undisturbed and forgotten for more than three centuries. Typically, Bingham's description was matter-of-fact.

"*Passing some ruins very much overgrown and of a primitive character, I found myself on a pleasant open plaza, bounded on its north side by the ruins of a large palace. The view from the plaza is a particularly extensive one on all sides. To the north and south are snow-capped mountains, and to the east and west deep beautiful valleys.*"

"*The long palace, of which we made a plan with careful measurements (has) 15 doors in front and 15 doors behind. It is divided by halls into three divisions. The front entrance to each hall is a particularly well made door, containing a re-entrant angle. These three principal doors and the other lesser doors are all of white granite, rather carefully squared and finished. The lintels of the doors are solid blocks of white granite, from six to eight feet in length.*" **(6) (Figure 19)**

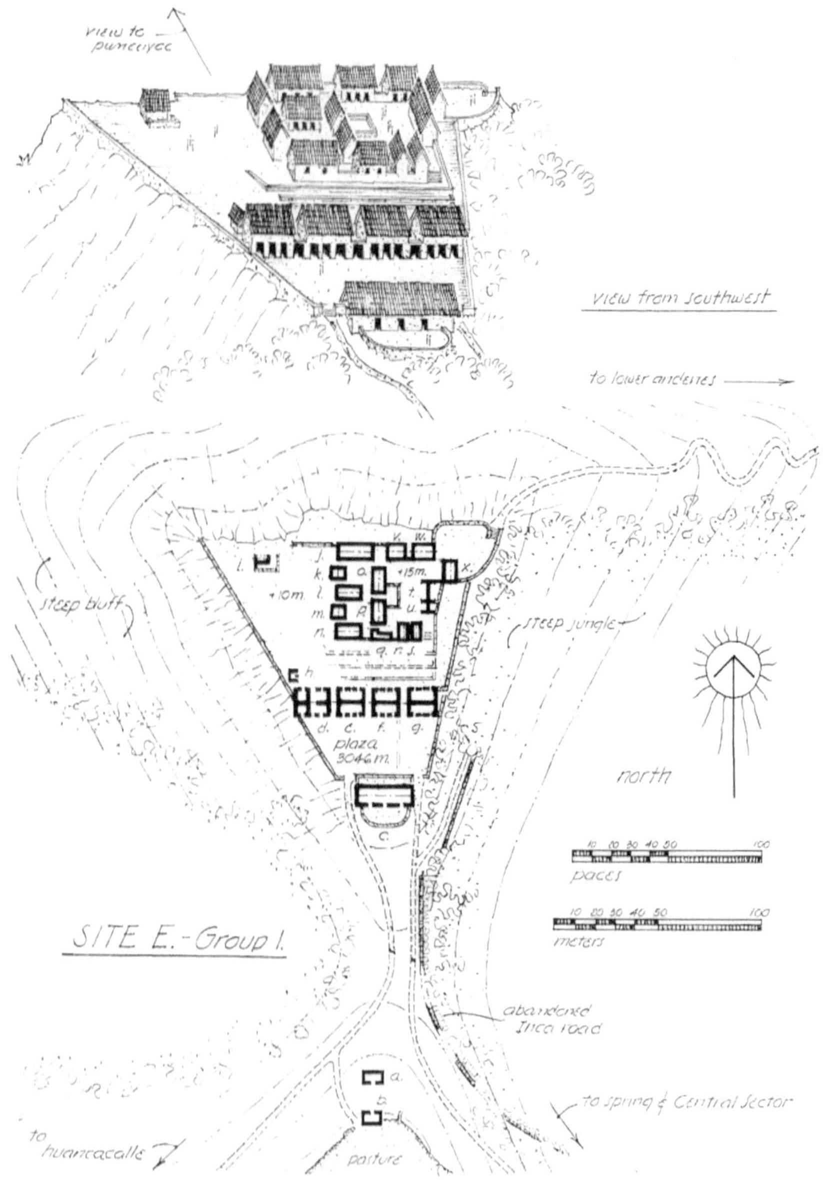

Figure 19 - Site plan of "palace" at Vitcos

The explorer's description of what he'd found was almost a word-for-word repeat of Baltasar de Ocampo's report of the appearance of Vitcos, written in 1610.

It was "...*on a very high mountain, whence the view commanded a great part of the province of Vilcapampa. Here, there was an extensive level space with very sumptuous and majestic buildings.*" *All were* "...*erected with great skill and art and all the lintels (beams above) the doors, the principle ones as well as the ordinary ones, were of marble, elaborately carved.*" **(7)**

But there was more. Bingham also recalled Father Antonio de la Calancha's 1639 report that not far from Vitcos was a sun temple called Chuquipalta, built around a great rock above a spring of water. He rightly concluded that if such a place could be found nearby, the ruins at Rosaspata had to be those of Manco's Vitcos. Sure enough, his guides said that a short walk up the valley east of the "palace" was a place they called Ñusta "Ispana," **(26)** a name the explorer rendered as Ñusta "España" - Spanish Princess - in some of his later writings. There, the locals added, was a huge, carved rock over a small, spring-fed pond. It turned out to be exactly what the American was looking for.

"*Called in early Spanish colonial times Yurak Rumi (Quechua for "white rock"), it is a white granite boulder 52 feet in length, 30 feet in width, and 25 feet high, above the level of the water and swamp that surround it on the east and south sides. About one fourth of the boulder thus overhangs a spring of clear water. Surrounding this are the ruins of houses, probably the House of the Sun.*" **(8)** **(Figures 25 and 26)**

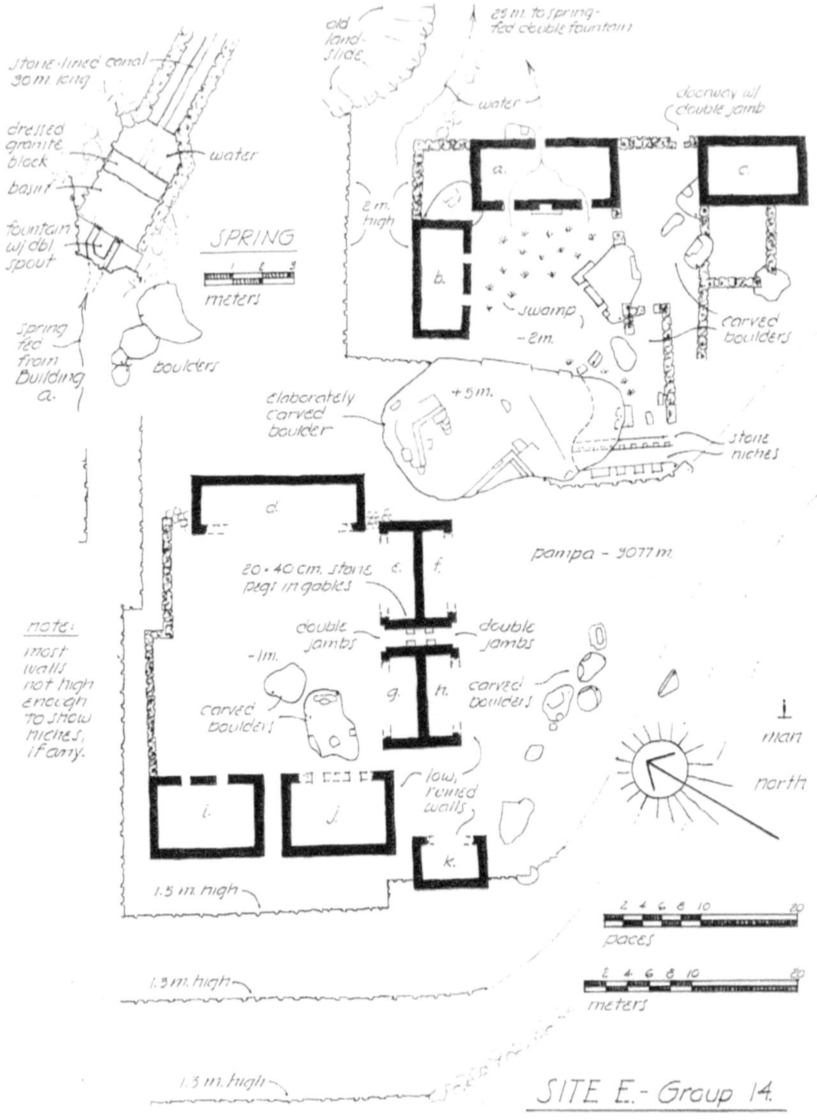

Figure 25 - Plans of sun temple and spring (Bingham's Chuquipalta)

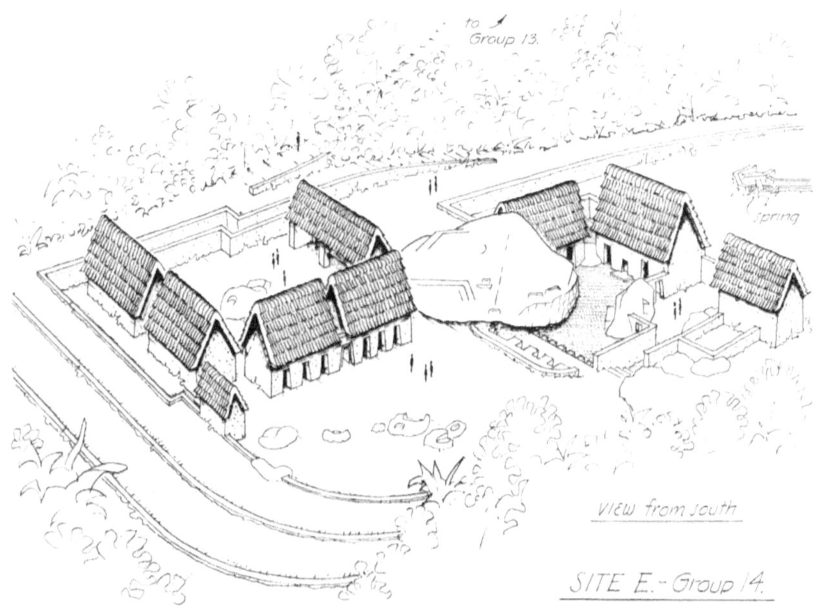

Figure 26 - View of sun temple complex

Although Bingham was shown other ruins in the vicinity, it was the boulder, laboriously hand carved into all sorts of fantastic geometric shapes and surrounded by tumbled walls, doorways and the flowing spring which, he believed, clinched his case for Vitcos. Despite occasional grumblings in the years since from other explorers intent on finding Vitcoses of their own, he was right. Ironically, however, the discovery of Vitcos didn't solve the puzzle of Vilcabamba the Old. About all that was known at the time about the relationship between the two places was that the latter was somewhere in the jungle two or three day's walk from the former. Unfortunately, Raimondi's Choquequirau fit that description quite well and, come to think of it, so did Bingham's new find at Machu Picchu - and matters were about to get even worse.

Breakfast finally done, Jill offered to wash the dishes. She wasn't feeling well and thought it best to hang around camp and rest up. The rest of us headed across the river and up the hill of Rosaspata. The day was glorious and we were all excited by the time we came in sight of the ruins. They struck me as even more interesting than

I'd remembered. Partly, I guessed, it was my new-found knowledge of the place and its turbulent history - but there was something else. For the first time, I was experiencing the thrill of field archaeology. No longer just a curious tourist, I had a purpose. The Blues Brothers would have called it a mission. From then on, I was obsessed with the ruins. For Nancy and the others, too, it was a turning point. I might be in rock-lover heaven, but in the coming weeks, my fixation would begin to wear everyone else a bit thin.

That was all in the future, though, and the group soon broke into twos and fews and roamed happily all over the site. By lunchtime, I'd put together a good plan of the complex Bingham and everyone else called "Manco's palace," the impressive plaza surrounded by buildings with fine doorways. **(Figure 19)** Just in time to join the others for the afternoon walk home, I finished the first-ever survey of the terraced valley beyond with the sun temple of Chuquipalta at its head. **(Figure 24)** It had been a great day. If this was exploring in the Andes, we all agreed, we were in for a fabulous time.

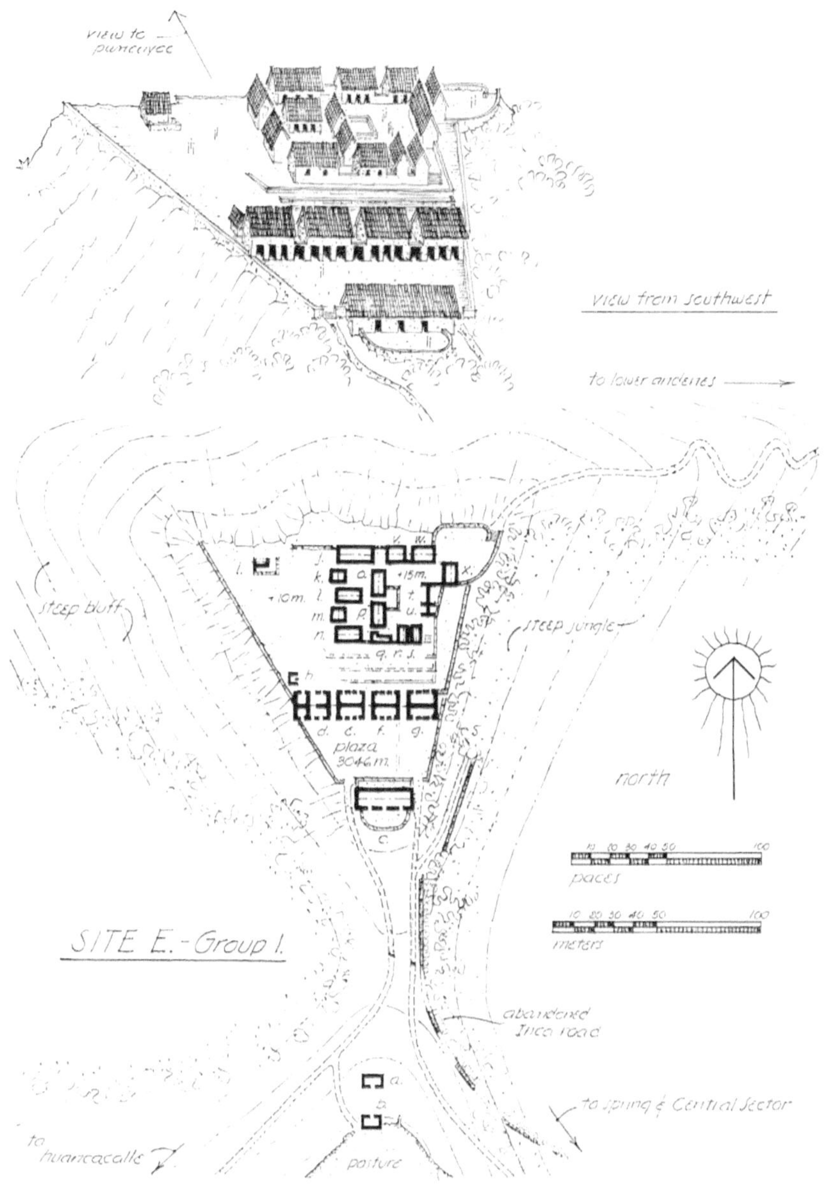

Figure 19 - Site plan of "palace" at Vitcos

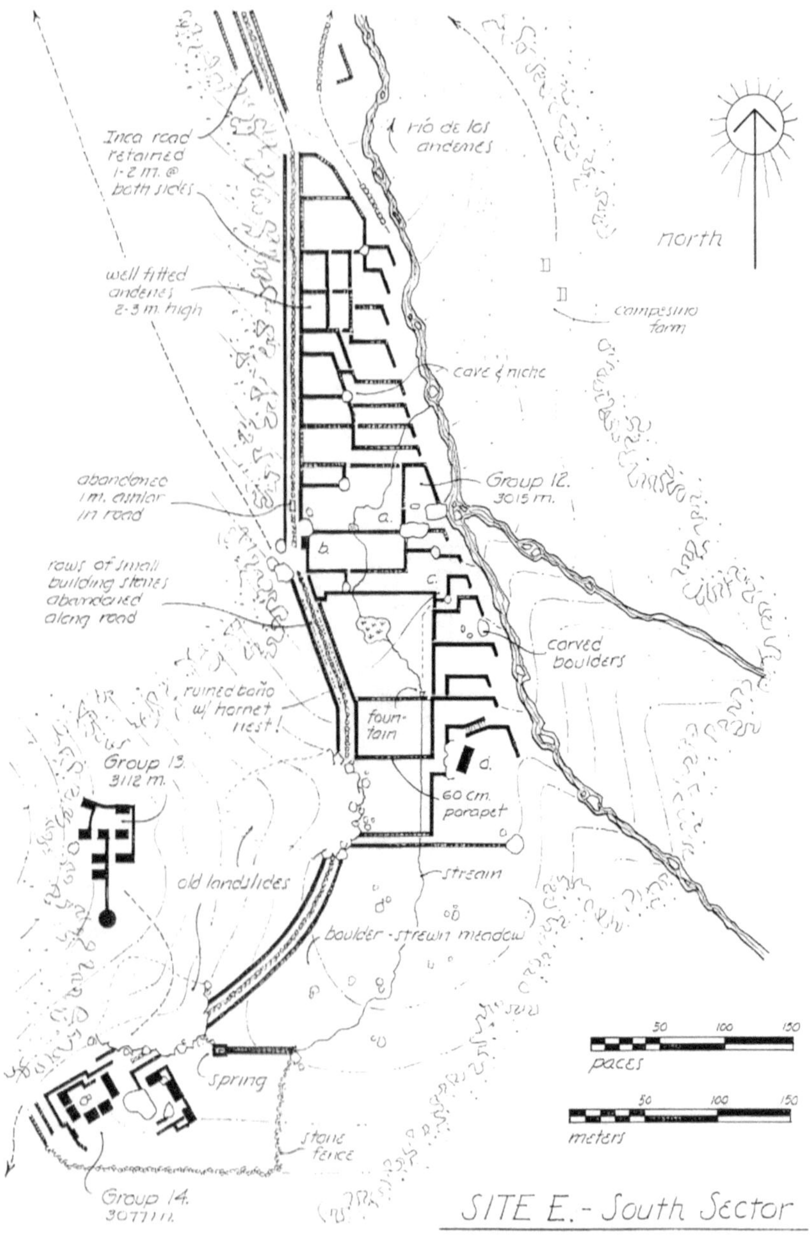

Figure 24 - "Temple" sector at Vitcos

4

Explorer Beware

As the northern sun settled strangely leftward toward the mountains in the west, we strolled down the old Inca road from Vitcos to the valley in high spirits. When we came in view of camp, however, our euphoria was shattered. Another expedition, newly arrived, was setting up nearby. The image we now had of ourselves as seasoned explorers, dozing back the frontiers of science out beyond the fringes of civilization crumbled. What were *they* doing there? Had we come all the way back to Vilcabamba only to be dogged by a bunch of silly tourists? It seemed so, until Jill came excitedly up the trail to meet us. The Italian archaeologist we'd been told about in Cuzco had just returned from five weeks in the jungle, she said, and wanted to see me. Two Indians, from Cuzco by their dress, were waiting in camp and said their leader, "*El Doctore*," had something to show me. My curiosity now fully aroused, I followed the two back to their tents and found an amiable, good-looking fellow of about forty waiting near the largest. He formally introduced himself as Renzo Francescutti, long-time student of Peruvian antiquity and resident of Trieste. Looking around, I saw he was the leader of an elaborate expedition in the classical style and, nattily dressed in a khaki safari shirt and ascot, he certainly looked the part.

From a table inside the tent, he produced a film can and handed it to me without a word. Having no idea what was going on, I cautiously opened it. Inside was the note we'd left on the summit of Icma Coya two years earlier, almost to the day. After a round of surprised chuckles, we were both struck by the almost unbelievable coincidence of our meeting within hours of the recovery of the long-abandoned little relic. The story of its finding by two of Renzo's Indians was a classic tale of petty crime and punishment. They'd been sent to the summit of Icma Coya to see if evidence of the Inca existed there and had instead found my film can. Opening it, they'd removed and pocketed the ring, but replaced the note unread, neither being able to understand English. As they later presented the can to Renzo, fully expecting a reward for their find, he'd instead demanded the ring, their little theft having been betrayed by the note. "*Gringos!* " they'd muttered, slinking away empty-handed. The ring, meanwhile, would be returned to its rightful place atop Icma Coya "on camera," I was assured, upon the Italian's return there in several weeks.

Renzo had been at Espíritu Pampa preparing to make a movie of the ruins for European television. The filming was to be "a first," he claimed, apparently unaware, as I was at the time, that an American doctor named Franklin Paddock had beat him to that honor by more than a decade. En route back upriver, he'd detoured up into the Markacocha highlands for seventeen days of exploring. They'd seen nothing of the terrorists, he said, but the expedition had been rained on much of the time. I shuddered, remembering what that was like. Despite the weather, he said, they'd searched the high country thoroughly and found one "nice *mirador*," or lookout tower, but no roads. When he learned I was planning to go up there myself, he said not to bother, assuring me that there was "nothing more to find."

Renzo was sure, he said, that Vilcabamba the Old was not at Espíritu Pampa. According to him, the ruins there were too small and not fine enough to have been an important Inca site, let alone an imperial capital. He was apparently convinced that the city was across the Cordillera Vilcabamba, in the drainage of the Río Apurimac. He produced his own map, showing a ruin there labeled "Espíritu Pampa," about twenty five airline miles, but more than a week's journey on foot, from its famous namesake. Why Renzo's alternative site should have the same name as Savoy's original candidate was unclear. I knew from my own research that few, if any, maps then in print showed Espíritu Pampa anywhere near its actual location. Without aerial surveys or global positioning technology, even the few people who'd been there didn't know exactly where it was. I guessed the Italian was being led astray by one of the many misprints that had resulted. Whether he ever actually went over into the Apurimac in search of Manco's capital, I never learned. If so, he didn't find it. Two years later, he would be looking elsewhere.

As we talked, I began to feel a growing sense of competition between us. Our expeditionary styles could hardly have been more different, yet we were there for the same reason. If there was anything more to be found in the Vilcabamba, we aimed to find it. When he learned of my relationship with Gene Savoy, there was a noticeable change in his attitude - as if I had the benefit of some sort of inside information and thus perhaps a competitive edge. Until then, I hadn't given much thought to the idea of finding anything especially important or valuable, but Renzo seemed to take the whole business very seriously. Why was he there, spending as much money in a day as we might in a month? Maybe *he* was the one with special knowledge. Increasingly wary, I wondered if he wasn't just pumping me for whatever he thought Savoy might have told me. I turned down his offer to share information and was later chastised by my own group for being so suspicious. They may have been right. I was acting a bit paranoid, remembering Savoy's advice about not trusting anyone and the hypnotherapist's warning of an unknown man I should beware of. Renzo seemed straight out of central casting for both roles.

Later that night, I invited him and his Peruvian associate, Justo Torres, to join us for some *pisco* and introduced them to the other members of Sixpac Manco II. Both men clearly enjoyed the conversation after more than a month in the hills, and we all had a good time. Renzo had to return to Cuzco the next day, but said he'd be back with his television crew about the time we planned to return up-river. With luck, he thought, we'd meet again then. Meanwhile, he mentioned, in passing, ruins his guides had told him about near a place called Tambo. He'd not gone there, he said, and didn't know exactly where it was, but there were apparently two *campesinos* living nearby, one just across the trail from the other. According to Renzo, one was named Diaz and supposedly knew the location of the ruins. It was probably unimportant, he concluded, but we might want to check it out. Finally, he added a bit patronizingly that it would be "our" find.

After two rainy days climbing up in the Cordillera, we returned to Huancacalle only to find the Army had canceled the Inti Raymi because of possible trouble with the terrorists. Frustrated by the pointless delay, we quickly got ready to leave the following morning, June 25th. Taking Renzo's advice, we decided to forget the Markacocha and head straight for the jungle. After going through the food and gear and repacking for the new itinerary, we found we'd need two horses to get everything to Espíritu Pampa, with each of us carrying a good sized backpack as well. Once downriver, we'd be okay on our own. By the time of the return trip, the food would be mostly gone and we figured we could manage what was left without help.

Don Juvenal was busy with other commitments, but promised he'd provide the horses and find us a good *arriero*, or mule-skinner. "*El mejor*," he said - the best. About dinner time, he came to our camp with one of his relatives, José Salas Cobos. At first, a typically unsmiling Indian, perhaps in his thirties, José was a man of few words and, in fact, said nothing. He gave the impression of one stuck with the unwelcome job of nurse-maiding a bunch of helpless *gringos* and I confess I was disappointed. Juvenal nevertheless insisted: José was the best man for the job. We signed duplicate handwritten contracts, scribbled on pages torn from my journal, paid half in advance and shook hands. For about seventy five dollars, we had a guide and two *betias*, literally "beasts," for two weeks. We soon found we had much more than that. We had a *compañero* , a comrade.

June 25th dawned crystal clear and after loading the horses, bidding farewell to the assembled Cobos clan, and snapping pictures of everyone arrayed in front of Gene Savoy's Andean Explorer's Club flag, we were off. In fine weather, the walk up the canyon of the Río Vilcabamba was a joy. Much of the trail was paved Inca roadway, as beautiful as it was impressive. By mid-afternoon, we arrived at San Francisco de la Vitoria de Vilcabamba, the last real village along the way. Its name, almost as long as its only street, was shortened by the locals years ago to Vilcabamba *Nueva*, the New, to distinguish it from the Incas' by then lost capital. A forlorn place, it's almost a ghost town compared to the busy *pueblocitos* down below, but unlike them it remains wonderfully picturesque. The abandoned church, with its 400 year old Spanish bell tower and enormous thatched roof is an architectural gem. Everyone was so taken with beauty of the place, we camped early and spent the afternoon visiting with the Indians and taking pictures. **(Figure 4)**

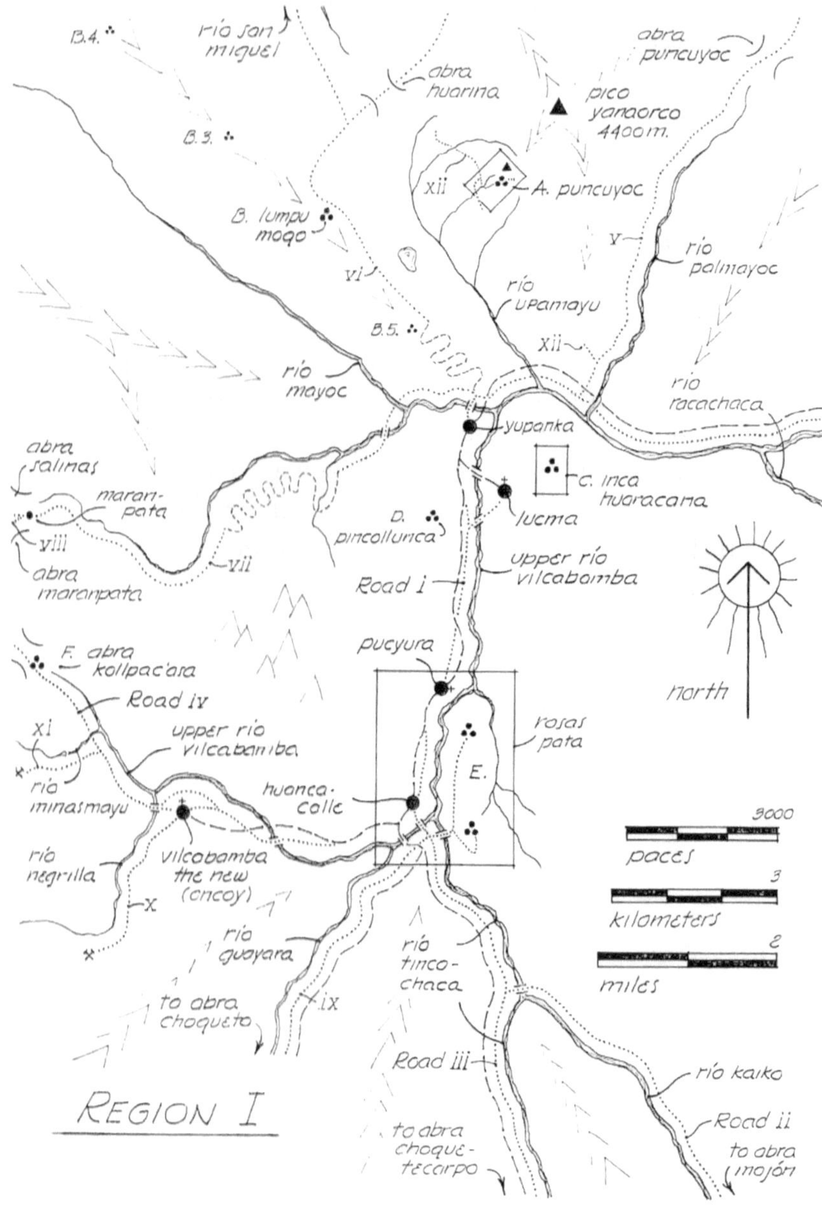

Figure 4 - Map of upper Rio Vilcabamba

The next day was again fine, and took us over the Kolpacasa, Pachacuti's Salty Pass at the head of the Río Vilcabamba.

It was the same misty gap Curtis, Brooke and I had trudged through on our way to and from Icma Coya, but we now took time to look around a bit. Just east of the pass was a level, man made plaza about the size and shape of a football field. A rustic Spanish chapel stood at the west side and a ruined shrine near the northeast corner, but overgrown stone terraces and steps all along the west edge strongly suggested Inca origins. There was no hint what use they might have made of the place, but the view of the snow-covered *cordillera* was fabulous, and sunrise seen from the plaza would have been quite a spectacle. (**Figure 31**)

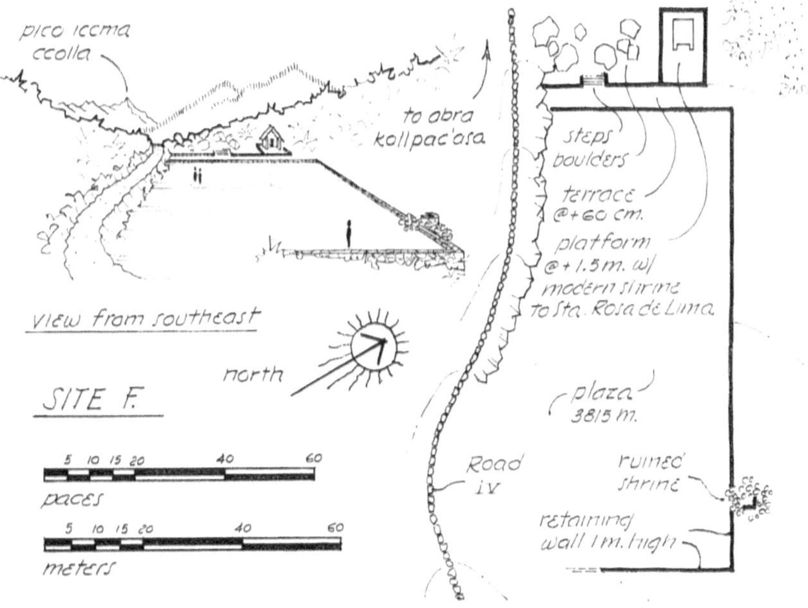

Figure 31 - Plan and view of Kollpac'asa

Beyond the pass, we descended into the head of the Río Pampaconas, the drainage that leads all the way down to Espíritu Pampa. Again, much of the road was Inca. At a place called Mollepunku, a steep section of switchbacks just above the river was staircased for several hundred yards. Its complicated intersection with three other Inca roads partway down was suggestive of a pedestrian freeway interchange. (**Figure 33**) Not far beyond, a scattering of bleak little farms perched on the last of the open *pampa* before the forest turned out to be the historic settlement of Pampaconas. Due to the fog, We'd missed it entirely two years earlier. Looking around, it was hard to believe anything important had ever happened there, but I knew that impression was deceiving.

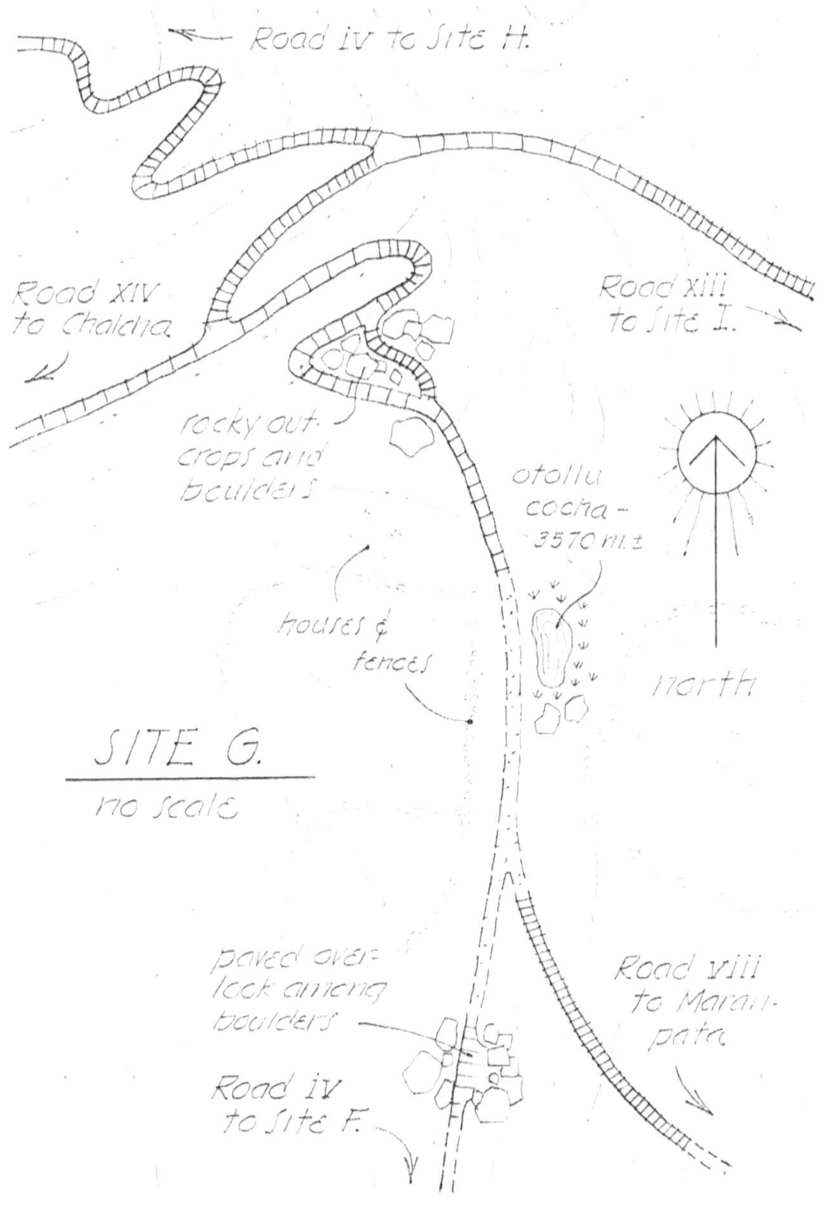

Figure 33 - Map of Mollipunku

Beginning with Bernabé Cobo's 1653 report that it was the site where the great Pachacuti Inca first took over the province in the fifteenth century, the name Pampaconas had cropped up again and again in my research. Yet, aside from the fact that it was a high, cold place that all down-river travelers passed through just before entering the forest, the chronicles didn't have much to say about the place itself, or what went on there in Inca times. A notable exception was the narrative of Diego Rodgiguez de Figueroa, a Spanish envoy sent to Vilcapampa by the Viceroy to negotiate with the rebels in 1565. He saw the native stronghold at the height of its power and the splendor he described was the culmination of two decades of peace and prosperity.

Following Manco's assassination in mid-1544, his eldest legitimate son, Sayri Tupac, ascended the throne. He was five years old at the time and it appears his father's most traditional advisors actually took command of the province. Whether they were exceptionally clever or notoriously weak is unclear, since we know relatively little of Sayri Tupac's reign except that it was long and uneventful. Unlike his father, Sayri Tupac and his elders did not continue the policy of unremitting hostility to the Spaniards and, while not surrendering Vilcabamba, they seem to have gotten on quite well with Cuzco. The young Inca was much influenced by Manco's brother, Paullu Inca, who had remained in the old city, loyal to Spanish authority throughout Manco's tenure. Now, with Paullu's encouragement, Sayri Tupac favored negotiation rather than confrontation with his father's enemies and exchanged various delegations with the Europeans. Paullu urged him to come out of exile and accept the large estates, riches and ceremonial honors the Spaniards were prepared to offer in exchange for his peaceful capitulation to their rule. Finally, upon coming of age in 1557, he agreed. Many of his captains were skeptical of the Spaniards' intentions and counseled against the Inca's decision. Wisely, they suggested he leave behind his now grown half-brother, Titu Cusi, and a younger, less experienced full-brother, Tupac Amaru, to look after Vilcabamba in his absence. To his credit, Sayri Tupac took their advice before retiring to a bucolic existence in the lush valley of the Spanish-held Vilcanota River. At first, things went well enough. He took a beautiful child-bride and established an elaborate estate at present-day Yucay. His retirement was, however, destined to be brief. Within less than three years, he was mysteriously dead and control of his estates and riches effectively reverted once again to the Viceroy. Poisoning was widely suspected, but never proved.

All the worst suspicions of the Vilcabamba Incas that the Spaniards couldn't be trusted were confirmed and widespread support for a resumption of Manco's policy of hostility was rekindled. The most legitimate heir to Sayri Tupac's throne was Manco's youngest son, Tupac Amaru, but he was politically naive and inexperienced in warfare, limitations that his older half-brother, Titu Cusi, did not share and believed the Incas could ill-afford. Tupac Amaru was thus sent into a monastic life among the nun-like Virgins of the sun, while Titu Cusi took command. Like Sayri Tupac, he continued to negotiate with the Spaniards, but unlike his predecessor, he had no intention of surrendering himself, his people or their jungle stronghold to the faithless invaders.

In many ways, Titu Cusi's reign was a return to the good old days of his illustrious father. Both favored the traditional social, political and religious values of their ancestors and neither was afraid to defy the Spaniards when they felt they had to. Since Manco's narrow escape from Gonzalo Pizarro's army in 1539, Vilcabamba had enjoyed more than a generation of freedom from foreign intrusions. Both the Incas and their forest allies had increased their numbers and strengthened their hold on a province that was no longer just a refuge. Their capital city of Vilcabamba had grown into something of a jungle metropolis and they now formally proclaimed themselves to be an independent native state, with Titu Cusi its rightful sovereign. On occasion, they even received envoys from Cuzco regarding matters of diplomacy. Figueroa's mission to Pampaconas in 1565 was perhaps the most elaborate of these and his first-hand account of what he saw captures well the wild spirit of Inca Vilcabamba at its zenith:

"*Presently, the escort of the Inca began to appear. The Inca himself came in front of all, wearing a headdress with plumes of many colors, a silver plate on his breast, a golden shield in one hand and in the other a lance all of gold. He wore garters of feathers and fastened to them were small wooden bells. On his forehead was a crown of fringe and another was around his neck. He had a gilded dagger, and he wore a mask of several colors. Arriving on the plateau where his people were gathered and his throne was set up, he gazed up at the sun, making a sort of reverence with his hand as if blowing a kiss, which they call a 'muchay,' and then went to his seat."*

"Then, two nobles carrying halberds came near the Inca, wearing crowns of plumes and dressed with much adornment of gold and silver. These two also blew kisses, first to the sun and then to the Inca, while all the rest stood near the sovereign's seat, encircling him in good order. Presently the provincial governor came with 60 or 70 attendants, all with their silver plates, lances, belts of gold and silver and similar costumes to those worn by all who came with the Inca. Finally came the Master of the Camp with the same gaily dressed following. All made a muchay, first to the sun and then to the Inca, saying 'Child of the Sun, thou art the child of the day'." **(1)**

Figueroa's purpose was to continue negotiations already begun by others with the aim of achieving the peaceful surrender of Vilcabamba to Spanish authority. It is unclear whether Titu Cusi ever really intended to go through with any such agreement, but he was astute enough to know that talking was cheap and certainly preferable to war. To further discourage the latter, he took the opportunity of the Spaniard's visit to send a subtle message back to Cuzco: if invaded, the Incas would put up a fight and had lots of men-at-arms to do it with. This suggestion was not lost on Figueroa, who's report went on to describe Titu Cusi's personal guard:

"Next, another captain named Cusi Puma entered with about 50 archers, who are Antis Indians and cannibals. Presently all these warriors took off their plumes of feathers and put down their lances. With their daggers of bronze and their shields of silver, or leather, or of feathers, each one came to do reverence to the Inca. Then there marched up about 600 or 700 more Antis, all with bows and arrows, clubs and axes. All these Indians then made an offer to the Inca that, if he wished it, they would eat me raw. They said to him 'what are you doing with this little bearded one here, who is trying to deceive you? It is better that we should eat him at once.' Then two renegade Inca orejones came straight to me with spears in their hands, flourishing their weapons and saying 'The

bearded ones! Our enemies!' I laughed at this, but at the same time commended myself to God." **(2)**

Notwithstanding the threatening tone of Figueroa's treatment by the Inca's followers, the negotiations went well. Further attacks by the Indians were averted by a peace treaty, formally signed a year later at an Inca settlement called Acobamba, across the *cordillera* , several days southwest of Vitcos. Titu Cusi thus continued to forestall any invasion of his domain by the Spaniards, and even allowed himself to be baptized a Christian in 1568. One of the priests officiating in the ceremony, an Augustinian named Fray Marcos García, remained in Vilcabamba afterward and was permitted to establish a mission at the native village of Pucyura, close under the watchful eye of the Inca, atop his nearby stronghold at Vitcos. García was soon joined by another Augustinian, Fray Diego Ortiz. Again, it seems unlikely that Titu Cusi had any serious interest in Christianity, but allowing two un-armed and harmless Europeans into his kingdom probably struck him as innocent enough at the time. Anything was worth try if it promised to hold off for awhile the decidedly more aggressive and menacing intentions of the ruthless new Viceroy, Francisco de Toledo.

It was hard to imagine great events or anything like the barbaric spectacle Figueroa witnessed as we hastened to set up camp in the failing daylight. Even the immediate threat of terrorism, so vivid among the bureaucrats of Cuzco, seemed inconceivable amidst the empty silence of latter-day Pampaconas. That impression was entirely false, of course, since we were now completely alone and beyond help of any kind in the event of trouble. The frontiers of Ayacucho, heartland of the Sendero Luminoso, were no more than a day's walk away - and nothing but a river crossing and the jungle stood between them and us.

Blissfully ignorant of all that, we'd just set about cooking dinner when an Indian boy appeared and asked sheepishly if we had any medicine that might help his mother. She had, he said, "*mucho dolor de cabeza*," a bad headache. Jim took his first aid kit and ran off down the trail with Nancy, whose bits and pieces of Quechua and serviceable Spanish had earned her the all-important job of expedition interpreter. She could take or leave the rocks, but enjoyed everyday dealings with the people - the result of, or maybe the reason for, her Peace Corps days. She and Jim returned just as we were cooking dinner and they added into the stew a handful of potatoes they'd brought back. Jim said the woman appeared to suffer from migraines and, as usual, he couldn't do much except to relieve some of her pain. She and her entire family were nevertheless on hand the next morning to see us off, this time with a whole gunny sack full of fresh potatoes.

Looking down the valley below Pampaconas, the peak of Icma Coya dominates a jumble of forested ridges and ravines. The only reasonable route through this maze is that taken by the river itself, along which winds the trail followed by all modern visitors to Espíritu Pampa. But was there another road in Inca times, since lost, as Savoy and a few others seemed to think? If so, it would have had to cross the high ridge of peaks behind Pampaconas, to the southwest. According to the satellite photo (**Figure 2**), the canyon beyond was that of the Río Zapateroyoc, itself a tributary of the Pampaconas. A road there would most likely rejoin the modern trail a few miles downstream, clearly not providing any alternative route into Espíritu Pampa. Beyond the Zapateroyoc, everything ran west, into the distant Río Apurimac and drained in the wrong direction.

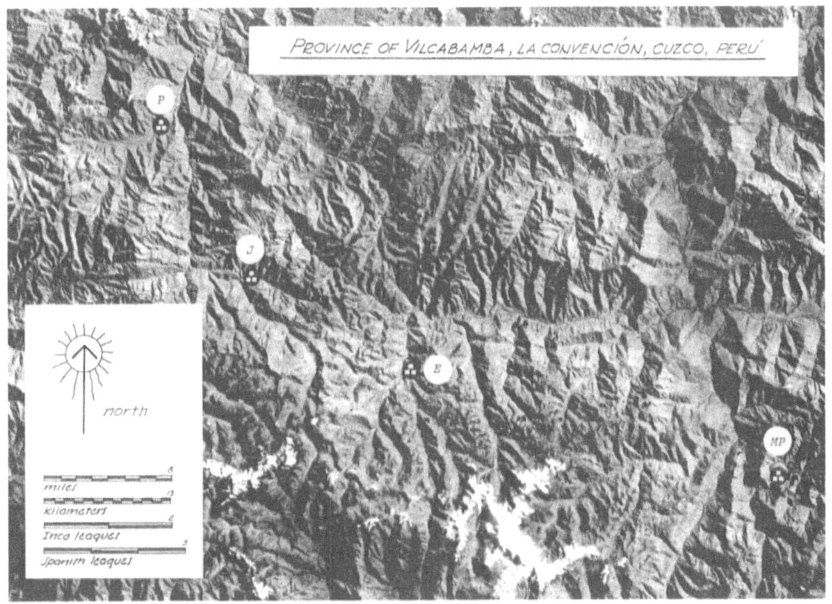

Figure 2 - Satellite Photo of Province

As we left Pampaconas and hiked down a long series of stone Inca steps through the first of the jungle, I felt confident that the Spaniards must have followed the same path in 1572. Confirmation lay at the bottom of the stairway, where the trail opened onto several large meadows along the river. According to José, the place was called Ututo, a place-name I immediately recalled from one of the Spanish accounts of the final invasion. Beyond the meadows, the trail crossed the Pampaconas via a long, double-span bridge and disappeared into thick forest on the far bank. I recalled the same bridge from our wanderings in the fog two years earlier, and realized I was back on familiar ground again.

Before crossing, Nancy, Jill and Martha decided to turn back for Cuzco, by then nearly a week away. They'd planned it all along, of course, but it was an emotional moment nonetheless. We had no doubts about their abilities on the trail, but the terrorist threat was worrisome, especially for three pretty *gringas* traveling alone in the Peruvian outback. Still, after hugs and kisses all around, they started off up a riverside footpath that bypassed Pampaconas and promised a shortcut back up to the Kolpacasa. We turned our attention downstream as they disappeared up the trail. Moments later, and unknown to us, Jill took a long, nasty slide down into the icy current as she tried to cross a washed-out gap in the trail, high above the river. Other, more serious adventures awaited them in the days ahead, but it would be nearly a month before we learned of them. Meanwhile, Chris, Jim, Paul, Barefoot, José and I crossed the bridge and headed into the jungle, eager for some real exploring at last. As it turned out, our first adventure, too, lay not far away.

5

Beginner's Luck

We were headed for Espíritu Pampa, but our first goal was to find the site of Huayna Pucara, the first of two Inca forts below Pampaconas. There, in June of 1572, the Spaniards had dealt the final blow to the Indians' defense of their capital. The site of this so-called "New Fort" had never been found, nor, to my knowledge, had anyone ever even looked for it until now. Prevailing opinion seemed to place the Spanish line of march elsewhere, lost in the jungle, so the battles they'd fought along the way were thought to be elsewhere as well. That, I now believed unlikely. All the places mentioned by the Spaniards should, I figured, be somewhere along the road we were following, below Ututo. Aside from that, whatever clues we had to the fort's location were buried in the four hundred year old descriptions of the campaign I'd found in the chronicles.

Viewed in hindsight, Titu Cusi's decision to allow the two Augustinians, García and Ortiz, into the province following his 1565 meeting with Rodriguez de Figueroa was a massive mistake. There had followed six long years of increasing tension and unrest between the Indians and their European guests, eventually leading to the violent deaths of both *padres* and the Inca, himself. Tragic as the story was for all concerned, it shed little light on the project at hand. In my early research, I'd unwisely glossed over all but its last act, the episode which resulted in the cataclysmic invasion of 1572.

Titu Cusi died in May of 1571, apparently the victim of a sudden illness after an all-night debauch at Vitcos. His successor was Tupac Amaru, the younger half-brother he'd suppressed in his own ascent to the throne eleven years earlier. Tupac Amaru's sequestered life among the Virgins of the Sun had not prepared him for command, and the control of the province immediately began to dissipate among his captains. In March of 1572, not long after Titu Cusi's death, one such captain committed a fatal error which sealed the fate of both the new Inca and his inherited empire-in-exile.

Unaware that anything exceptional had occurred in Vilcabamba and believing that Titu Cusi still reigned, the Viceroy chose that particularly inopportune moment to continue negotiations for the peaceful surrender of the province. He sent a prominent Cuzco citizen and good and trusted friend named Atilano de Anaya with messages of greeting for the Inca. Shortly after crossing the bridge at Chuquichaca, Anaya was met by a party consisting of two Inca captains and about thirty Indians, all with apparently peaceful intentions.

Although they first received the Spaniard warmly, they were nevertheless fearful that if he were allowed to proceed, Anaya would eventually return to Cuzco with news of Titu Cusi's death and worse, of the demise of García and Ortiz. Assuming this must be prevented at all cost, and acting without authority from Tupac Amaru, they surrounded Anaya's tent, dragged him out and stabbed him to death with their lances before throwing his body down a ravine into the river below. They tried also to kill all the attendants who were in Anaya's party, but one, a negro, fatefully escaped and made his way back to Cuzco with news of the massacre. Toledo immediately called a council of war. The time had come to end once and for all the treachery of the rebels. Plans were drawn for a massive invasion of the province and a rich reward was offered to whomever could capture the Inca himself.

We have several detailed accounts of the historic campaign which followed. The best are those of Martín Hurtado de Arbieto, the commander of the Spanish forces, Pedro Sarmiento de Gamboa, a soldier who took part in the action and Martín de Murúa, a historian who described the events second-hand, more than twenty years later. Taken together, these three present a vivid, if tantalizingly ambiguous, description of both the conflict itself and the country we were entering, below Pampaconas, where most of it occurred.

In preparation for the invasion, Toledo ordered two forces into the field. One, a relatively small contingent of 70 men, was sent down the nearly impassable canyon of the Apurimac River to secure the one crossing there by which the Inca might escape into the forests west of the province. The main force, meanwhile, like its predecessors in both 1537 and 1539, followed Pachacuti's old route down the Urubamba and over the Panticalla Pass to the strategic crossing at Chuquichaca. Both Murúa and Sarmiento agree that it was necessary to rebuild the bridge, but that the army met no real opposition there and crossed in good order.

At the head of a column including 250 of the most "gallant and brave residents and soldiers" of Cuzco, "all very well equipped and armed," Hurtado de Arbieto crossed the river and started up the canyon toward Vitcos. With 2000 Indian auxiliaries bringing up the rear in support, it was by far the most formidable force the Spaniards had ever sent against Vilcabamba. Surely the Incas would flee in terror once they realized what they were up against. Confident of success, the invaders thus proceeded boldly into the first of several ambushes the natives had skillfully prepared along the narrow road where the terrain effectively neutralized the Europeans' horses and superior weaponry. This opening battle probably took place at the ravine of Chuquillusca, though, as we shall see, Murúa erroneously applied that name to a subsequent engagement, many miles to the west. Wherever it occurred, everyone seems to agree that it was hard fought and nearly stopped the expedition in its tracks. Nevertheless, the Spaniards managed to prevail and, despite several similar engagements further upstream, maintained their momentum. Little by little, the Indians were driven back into the hills.

Arriving, finally, at Vitcos, Arbieto found it and the nearby village of Pucyura abandoned and the surrounding fields and flocks intact. The Incas had withdrawn with their forces, probably utilizing a shortcut through the Salinas Pass west of the Vilcabamba River (**Figure 4**) to head off the Spanish column for a final showdown in the jungles beyond the divide. Meanwhile, Arbieto called a brief halt at Vitcos to rest and nurse wounds, to gather additional food for the campaign and to search for booty. These done with considerable success, he continued on unopposed through high, open country over the Kolpacasa to Pampaconas. There, however, the newly strengthened expedition was smitten by, of all things, a measles epidemic and became bogged down in camp for thirteen days while the sickness ran its course.

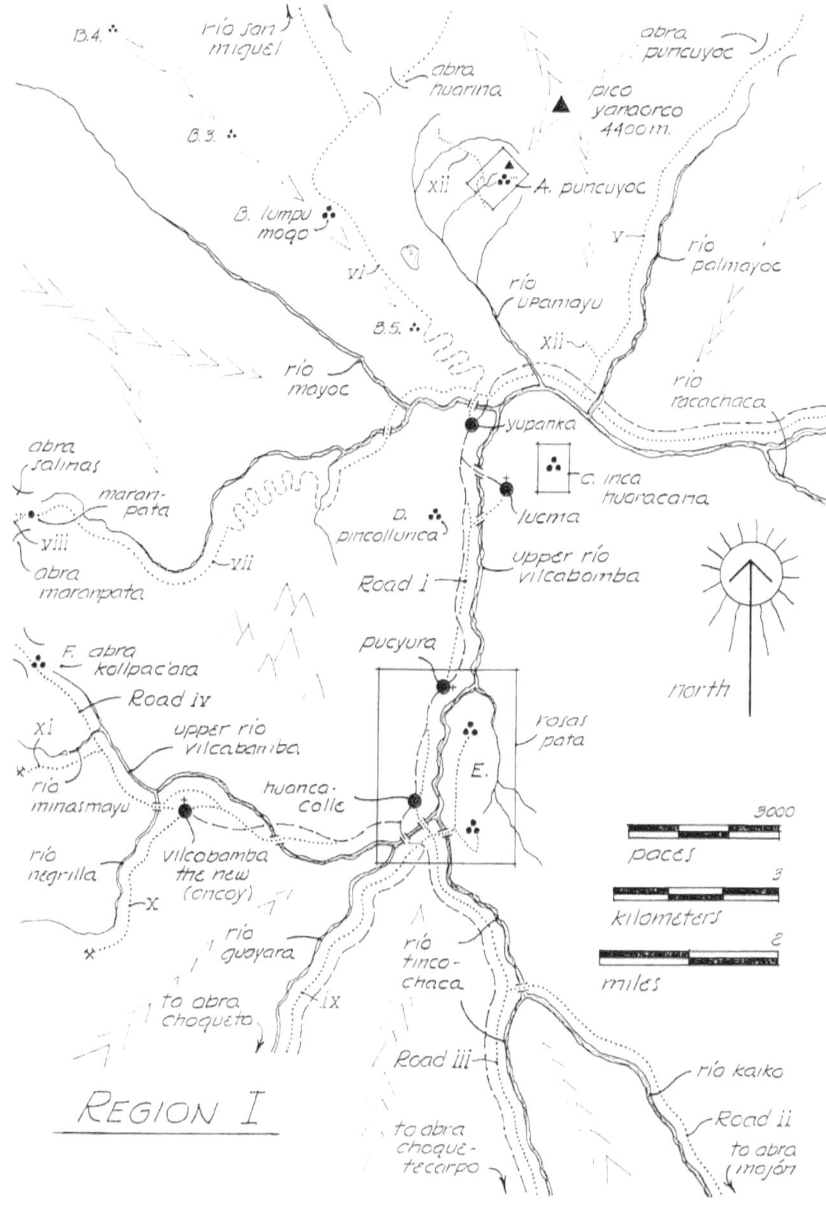

Figure 4 - Map of upper Rio Vilcabamba

Arbieto took advantage of the delay as best he could to reorganize and determine how best to proceed. His early losses were more than made up for by the unexpected return of the Apurimac contingent.

Exhausted, but still 70 strong, they straggled into camp just in time to be left behind as a rear guard. Arbieto reported leaving Pampaconas with ten days' provisions on Monday, June 16th, 1572. Not far below Pampaconas, the main body's path necessarily re-entered the forest where the Indians once again had the advantage. According to Sarmiento, there were two possible routes, the main Inca road downstream and another, leading to the native forts intended to block entry into the Inca capital at Vilcapampa. After heated discussions among his captains as to which road to follow, Arbieto decided to attack the forts directly. Hearing this, a native prisoner named Canchari tried to escape and warn the Incas, but was captured instead and hanged at a place called "Hotuto," almost certainly modern-day Ututo. **(1)**

According to José, we were continuing downstream from Ututo via the only trail he knew of. Still, there was no telling whether it was either of the ones mentioned by Sarmiento, since none of the old place-names along the Spanish line of march below Ututo remain in use. We'd just have to compare our surroundings to the descriptions in the chronicles and hope they matched. Lucky for us, the invaders left a fairly good record of their progress. Once they headed down the road to the forts, Murúa says, the going quickly got rough:

"*The camp went through the mountains and streams with excessive work by all. At the so-called Chuquillusca pass, a long split or cleft rock beside a voluminous river, one could hardly walk and both the soldiers and Indian allies went on all fours with great difficulty and risk. Seeing this, a Portuguese soldier threw a bronze cannon over his shoulder and crossed a place where 50 Indians feared to go, and many fell when they tried. Even though the Spaniards' Cañari allies were skilled with the lance, the Incas were more so, and in each difficult place, many Cañaris were wounded by the enemy's lances.*" **(2)**

Murúa's words hardly described the country we were passing through. Our trail had become a paved Inca road not long after we crossed the Pampaconas. Even though thick forest, covered with moss and draped with vines and creepers, pressed in from beyond the river bank, there were no "mountains and streams" nor any "long, cleft rocks" to negotiate. In fact, there was nothing very difficult about the hike at all. Instead, we were strolling gently downhill through a cool, pleasant tropical canyon. The others were enjoying themselves thoroughly, but I knew it was all wrong. At best, we were on Sarmiento's "Inca" road, not the one that led directly to the forts. My spirits sagged. Less than an hour into our first real search and we were already on the wrong trail.

Looking around, wondering what to do about it, I saw that the terrain across the river was exactly as Murúa described the Spaniards' route. If we'd stayed over there below Ututo, we, too, would be in the midst of a long passage through steep, rocky cliffs and jungle-choked ravines. The place called Chuquillusca might be miles away, on the lower Vilcabamba River, but everything else about Murúa's description fit perfectly. Making no mention of Chuquillusca, Arbieto agreed that the terrain beyond Ututo was difficult and went on to describe ambushes that the Indians had prepared there, confirming the substance of Murúa's account. Antonio de la Calancha, describing different events altogether, called the same patch of country "Chuquiago". **(3)** Maybe Murúa, I thought, writing long after the fact about events he'd not taken part in, just got the name wrong. No one knows, but it's a classic example of the kind of problem explorers often face.

By the time I had all this sorted out, it was much too late to turn back, so I made a mental note to check out the other side of the river for old roads on our way back upstream. Meanwhile, I comforted myself with the unlikely idea that the trails might converge somewhere further down and get us back on track. One way or another, we were trying to find Huayna Pucara, the New Fort. Arbieto claimed it took four days to get there from Pampaconas. (**28**, 146) That was a problem because I knew from my own experience in 1982 that a strong hiker could almost make it to Espíritu Pampa in two or three. What could account for such a big difference? Renzo took it as proof that Manco's lost capital was somewhere else, much deeper in the bush, and Juvenal said the Italian wasn't the only one who thought so. On the other hand, the Spaniards' progress below Pampaconas was a lot slower than ours by all accounts. They had over two thousand people and all their gear to deal with, and had to fight every foot of the way. Besides that, Arbieto reported the "tongues were cut" from several guides who "took the wrong passes" (**28**, 148), suggesting that time was wasted on false trails. As a result, it's quite unclear how far the expedition traveled to the next stop mentioned in Murúa's account, a place he called Anonay:

"*The following day, an Inca captain named Puma Inca surrendered peaceably to the Spaniards. He said that the Incas wanted a truce; that he was not to blame for the death of Atilano de Anaya, but that certain other captains were. The camp arrived at Anonay and halted with much care and precaution, as they found many palm tips driven into the ground with poisonous herbs on the points to kill anyone who stepped on them. This Puma Inca told of how the captains had built a fort, well fortified and called Huayna Pucara. He gave the design and told how the storming of the fort could be done without any danger.*" (**4**)

Sarmiento agrees that the next stop was at Anonay, but claims that a battle was fought there during which Puma Inca was captured. Arbieto makes no mention of the incident, so which version is correct will never be known. Neither Sarmiento nor Murúa offers any hint as to where Anonay was. The only place with a similar name today is the *pampa* of Ayunay. Near a tiny settlement called Vista Alegre, it is many miles downstream where the canyon of the Pampaconas makes a huge, right-angle bend to the north. (**Figures 2 & 44**) Murúa continues:

"*The next day the camp advanced two leagues toward Huayna Pucara and stopped at a place called Panti Pampa to plan the attack. It (the fort) was a league and a half, almost two leagues long, and at a distance looked like a half moon or crescent. The road was very narrow, in very mountainous and rocky terrain with a wide, voluminous river running alongside. Everything was dangerous and fearful. In the heights was a sharp, knife edged ridge where the Indians had made a wide fort from stone and mud, with mounds of rocks ready to be thrown down by hand or with slings. Along the entire ridge were also mounds of very large boulders balanced with levers. The Spanish column seemed trapped in the crescent or half moon of the mountain ridge. Had the Indians succeeded in their plan, not a living soul would remain, as the boulders would have killed everyone, and any who'd tried to escape by jumping into the river would have drowned or been shot by Chuncho archers hidden on the other side.*" **(5)**

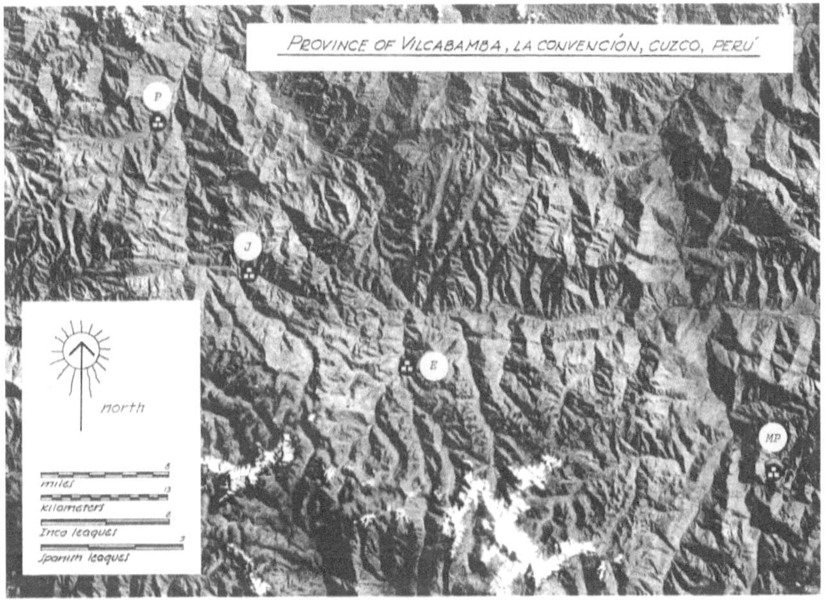

Figure 2 - Satellite Photo of Province

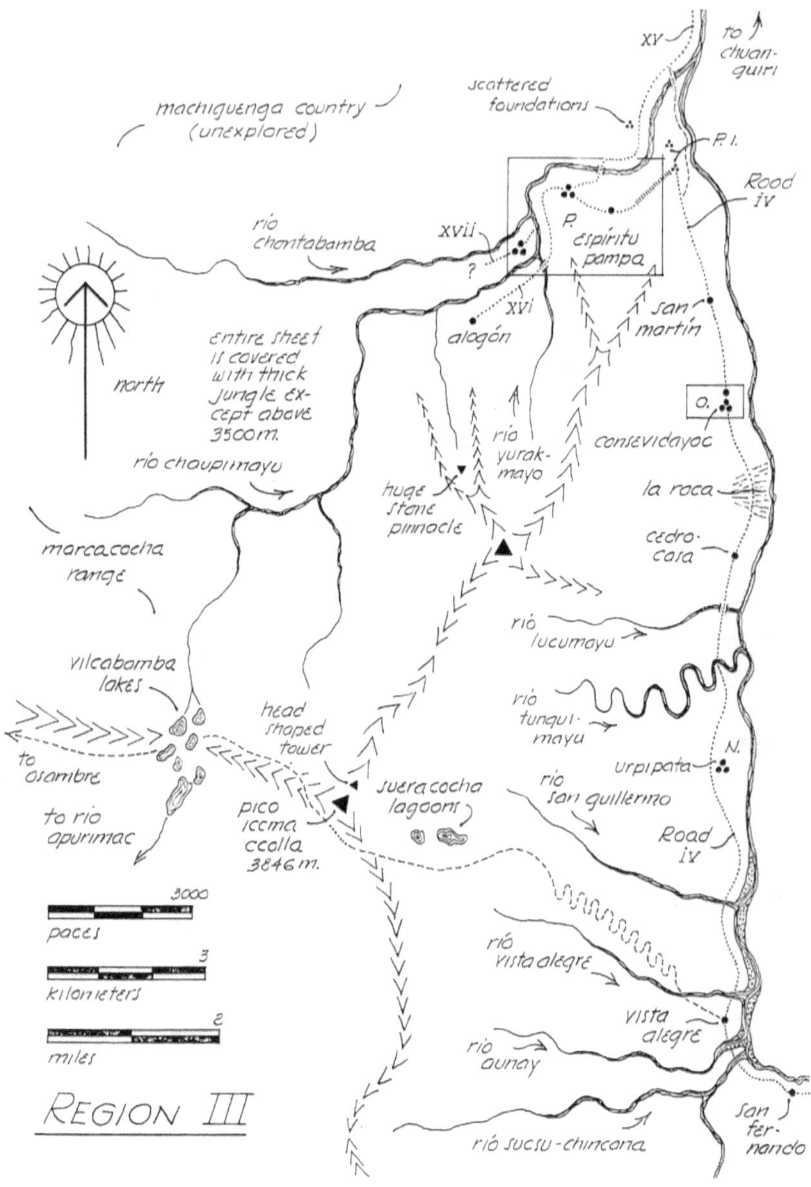

Figure 44 - Map of lower Rio Pampaconas

The name Panti Pampa no longer exists and appears only in Murúa's account as the place from which the Spaniards first saw Huayna Pucara. Again, there is no way to know where it was. The "two leagues" between Anonay and Panti Pampa isn't as helpful as it might seem. In those days, a nautical league was 1/20th of a degree of latitude, or about three English miles. On land, where latitude didn't count for much, a league was about an hour's walking, also about three miles. Because the Indians walked faster, an "Inca league" was longer, about four miles. A terrestrial league thus ended up being more a matter of time than distance and Murúa's "two leagues" may just mean a two hour walk. Wherever the fort was, there's little doubt as to its design. Arbieto's description echoes much of Murúa's, but adds architectural detail:

"*The Indians of the Inca had fortified three quarters of a league (about half Murúa's estimate) in some very narrow passages with many boulders. At the end, on a knife-edge ridge they had built a fort with a wall 200 paces long and two wide, with a single, narrow door where only one man could enter at a time.. It was crowned with merlons in order to defend itself from arquebus (gun) fire and had four small towers and a large quantity of rocks to be thrown by hand down onto the road, which ran along a stream. And for an arquebus-shot's distance in front of the fort, they had placed many palm stakes rubbed with herbs.*" **(6)**

Benefitting from Puma Inca's advice and their own reconnaissance from Panti Pampa, the Spaniards pressed the attack Saturday morning, June 21st, 1572. It was to be the decisive battle of the war, and Arbieto threw his full force into the action. Though the fort was on high ground, dominating the road passing below, there was apparently an even higher ridge from which fire could be directed into the Inca positions. Just at first light, "after six in the morning", an assault force was sent up onto this ridge. After seven hours of un-opposed but difficult climbing through steep, thick cloud forest "on all fours, some grasping others", according to Murúa, the Spaniards reached the top and showed themselves to the enemy below. Quickly realizing their vulnerability, the Indians began an orderly retreat out along the knife edge toward Huayna Pucara, abandoning in place the many boulders and piles of rocks that had threatened the main Spanish force, waiting on the hillside below. Seeing this, Arbieto began advancing out onto the slope, firing off cannon shots as he went. Thus caught in a crossfire from both above and below, the Inca captains abandoned the fort and withdrew downstream. Tupac Amaru was already gone, having retreated to Vilcapampa the day before. With surprising ease, the invaders had thus triumphed where, but for the help of the defector, Puma Inca, they might have suffered disaster. It was a death blow from which the natives never recovered.

After a couple of hours, our trail crossed another bridge back to the Pampaconas side of the stream and began a long traverse up the canyon wall. It occurred to me that the only reason our easy, paved road had detoured across the river was to avoid the five-mile stretch of cliffs and ravines, now behind us. That the Incas might have concealed this detour from their enemies and lead them instead into a wilderness ambush seemed altogether likely, I thought, trying to keep my mind off the the trail, itself. Increasingly annoyed by the fact that we were trudging uphill in order to go downstream, I was relieved when an hour later we rounded an exposed ridge several hundred feet above the water and were met with a cool, refreshing breeze.

A huge vista opened before us. The trail now began a long, descending traverse along a sweeping, right-hand bend in the canyon. The result was several miles of road visible ahead of us and running alongside the river in the form of a giant crescent - exactly the word Murúa had used to describe the road as it passed under Huayna Pucara. About halfway down the hill were two farms, one on either side of the trail. **(Figure 40)** It must be Tambo, I thought, recalling Renzo's tip about ruins. I looked everywhere for them, but there was nothing. Then, I saw it: not a ruin, but a hilltop dominating the trail, steep on all sides except one, where a long knife edge ridge connected it to easier ground. The terrain towering above Tambo was exactly as the Spaniards had described the site of the New Fort. **(Figure 39)** From a Far Eastern tour with the Marines many years earlier, I knew a little about the defensive use of terrain, and the hilltop was a very strong position, well chosen for control of the road. A glance at the satellite photo showed that the Río Zapateroyoc flowed below the far side, so that all possible routes downstream from Pampaconas were covered.

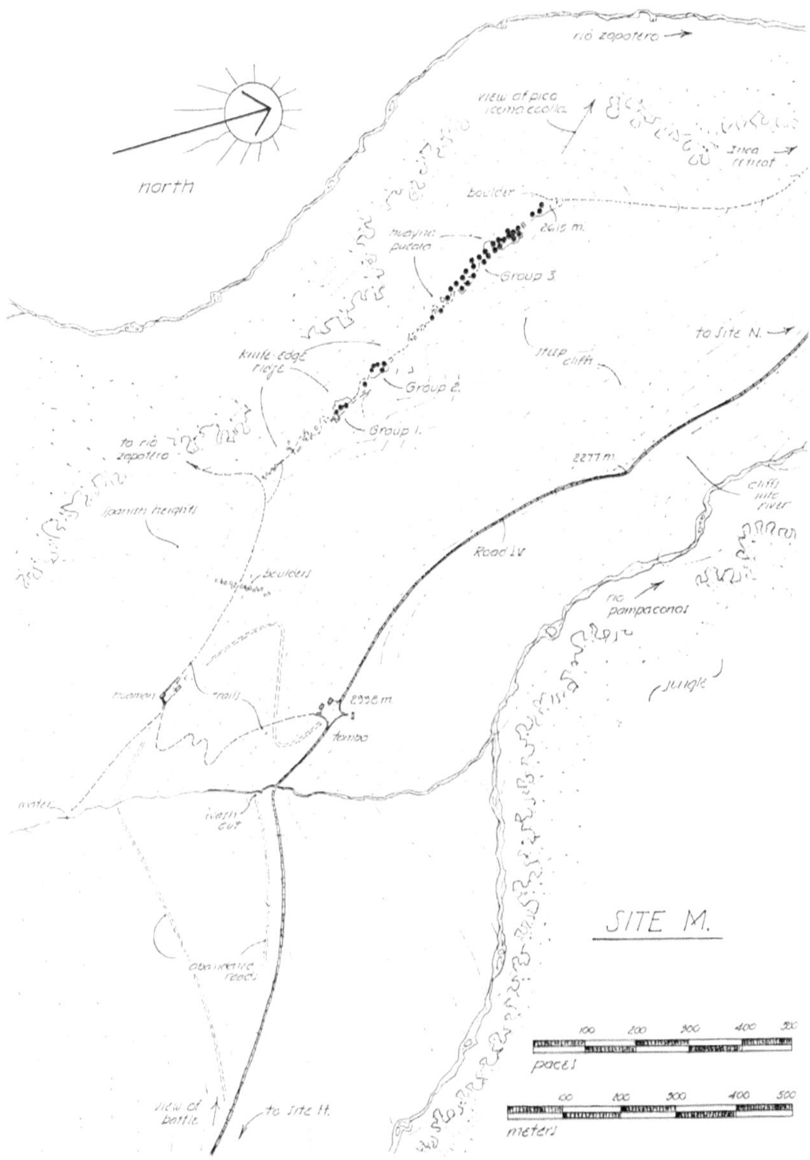

Figure 40 - Map of Tambo and vicinity

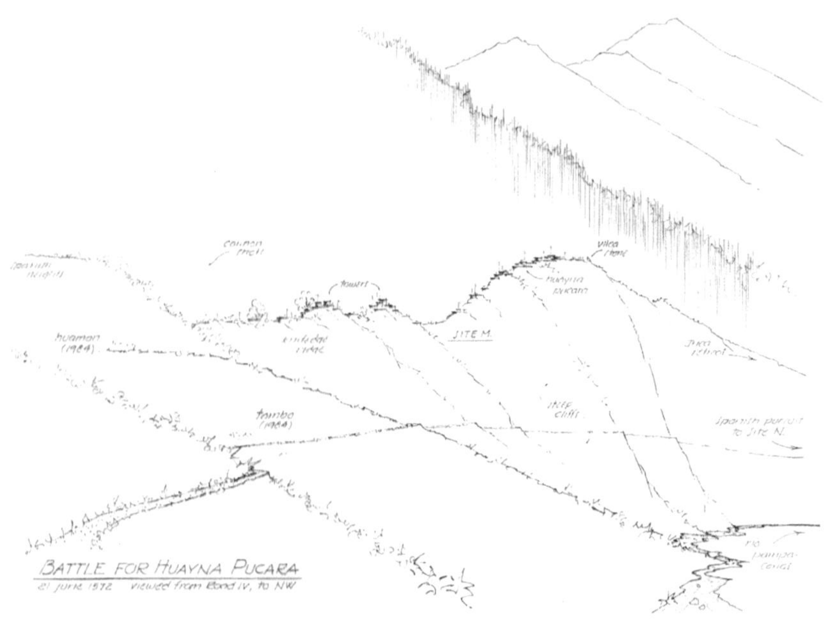

Figure 39 - View of Tambo and vicinity

We practically ran down to the farm houses, anxious to find Señor Diaz and learn the location of the ruins. I felt sure we'd find the fort atop that hill, but the jungle looked thick and Diaz would know best how to get up there. Several youngsters at one of the farms told us their parents were all downriver. Questioned further, they said they knew no one named Diaz and had never seen any ruins in that area. How could that possibly be, I wondered? The place matched the Spanish descriptions word for word. Discouraged, we took a break and discussed what to do. It was at least 500 feet up to the ridge, but it looked like there was a faint trail cut through the brush. José looked at me and said, "*Vamos arriba?*" - "Are we going up?"

I thought for a moment. Even though it was mid-winter in Peru, the equatorial sun seemed almost directly overhead and out in the open it was blistering hot. The hillside above was steep and covered with *bosque*, as the natives called especially nasty undergrowth, thick enough to make for tedious going, but too low to offer any real shade. Surely, the kids would have known if there'd been anything up there. To José, it was all in a day's work either way. Like all the *campesinos* , he saw no difference between going up and coming down, a lifetime in the Andes having taught him they were both sides of the same coin. Sorely tempted to pass, for some reason I heard myself say "*Sí, vamos!* " And up we went.

The path led up to a third farm, perched on a small bench not far from the beginning of the knife edge and invisible from below. Everyone was off working, but the path seemed to continue beyond the farm towards a notch leading over into the Zapateroyoc. It was only a short scramble up steep rocks from the notch onto the crest of the knife edge. José was in the lead as we climbed the moss-covered ledges. Near the top, he paused to clear away some moss and vines. "*Construido!* " he shouted and continued excitedly to the ridge. When I reached the cleared place, I understood. It was a carefully built stone wall.

As we reached the crest of the narrow ridge and began traversing out towards the hilltop, we encountered more walls, stairways and platforms, all buried under 412 years of rotted vegetation. To either side, the ground fell away so steeply that the crest presented the only feasible approach to the hill. Excitedly, I looked for the fortifications the Spaniards had noted along the ridge and, one by one, they appeared. The boulders the defenders had planned to roll down onto the Spanish column were still there, scores of them the size of refrigerators. (**Figure 43**) About 200 yards out, a long stairway ascended to a minor summit covered with terraces and walls. The latter seemed to be the remains of circular buildings. (**Figure 41**) I wondered if they were the towers Arbieto had reported along the ridge. A hundred yards farther on was a second peak, even more elaborately fortified and crowned by more of the circular constructions (**Figure 42**). Everywhere we looked, we found ruins.

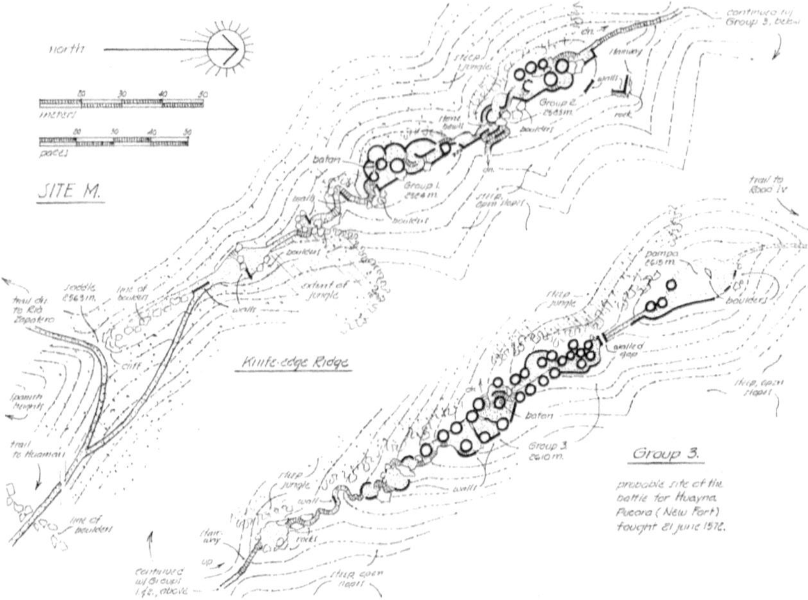

Figure 43 - Site plan of Tambo (probable site of Huayna Pucara)

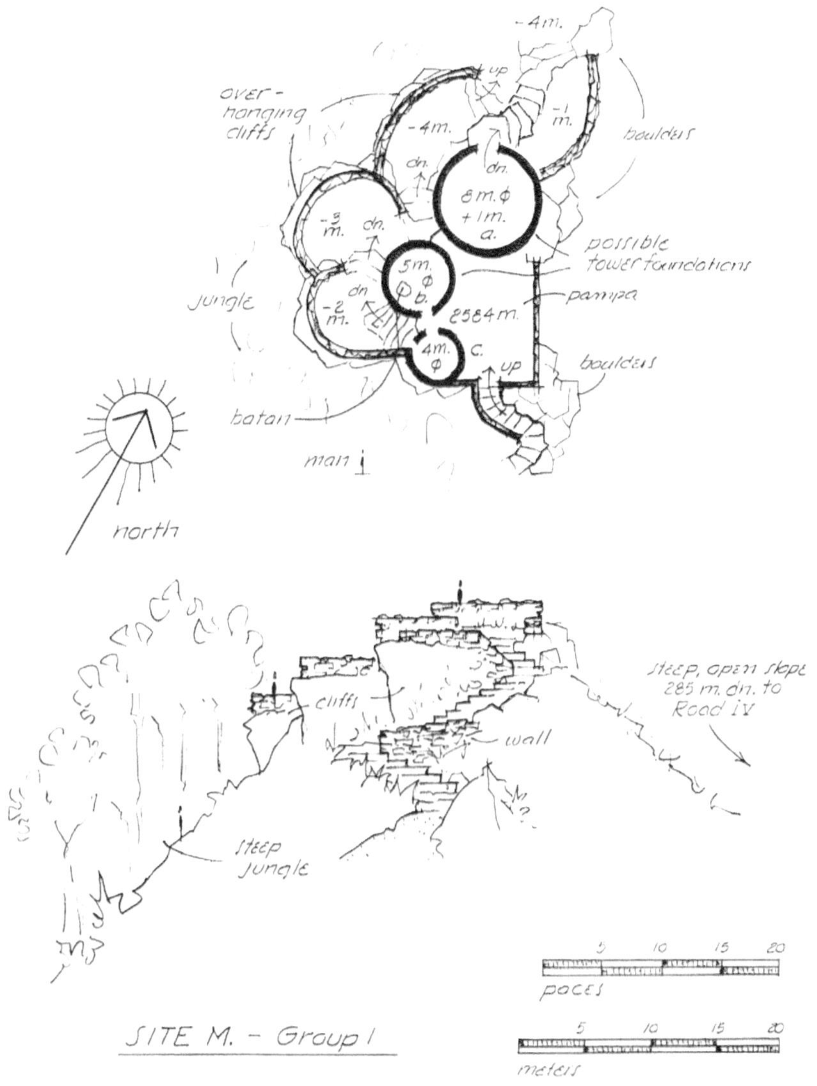

Figure 41 - Plan and view of first platform

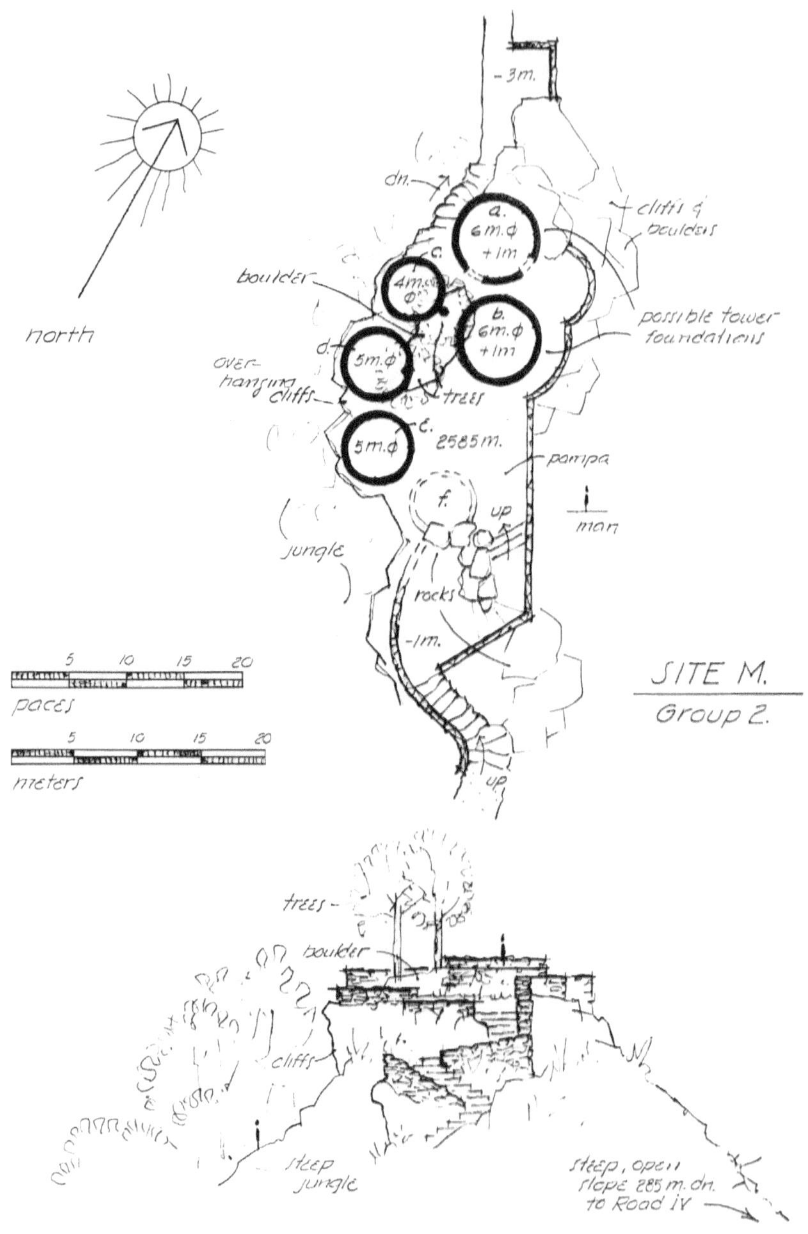

Figure 42 - Plan and view of second platform

Barefoot and Jim Little continued down to a rocky gap separating the knife edge from the main hilltop beyond and disappeared into the jungle. José, Chris and I explored the two platforms already encountered. At one point, José nearly stepped on a small, yellow snake. He turned with a smile and said, "*Cuidado, amigos - es muy peligroso.*" "Watch out - it's deadly." From then on we were all eyes in the bush, imagining poisonous fangs hidden under every rock - even though José, un-fazed and bare-legged, kept on rooting around in the thickets without a care. The masonry was crude rubble work, apparently set in mud that had mostly washed away. Not much was standing above ground level and many of the retaining walls had collapsed. I made rough sketches of the best preserved work and decided to devote several days to clearing and mapping the whole site on our way back upriver.

Barefoot called down from the hilltop that they'd found more ruins and we should come up for a look. The crest ran a hundred yards beyond the second platform and was topped with more of the perched boulders, but hardly any constructed work. Then, as the angle steepened up the final slope, we found almost continuous stairs, walls, terraces and boulders. Reaching the top, circular foundations - 28 in all - flanked the crest on both sides. (**Figure 43**, Group 3) Unlike the ones we'd found lower down, these were packed tightly together. The slope down to the main trail was steep, rocky and open, such that the defenders had a great advantage over anyone attempting to pass below. The other slope, down towards the Zapateroyoc, was equally steep, but covered with thick cloud forest. At the very top of the hill was a small, flat meadow, edged with a low retaining wall and interrupted only by three more circular constructions and a large, uncarved boulder. The latter appeared to be a *huaca* stone - an object of worship.

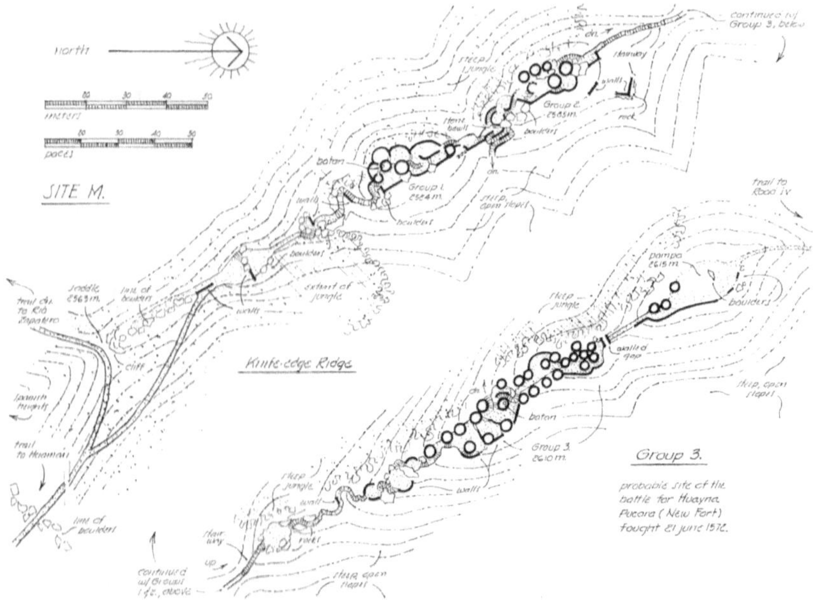

Figure 43 - Site plan of Tambo (probable site of Huayna Pucara)

The hour was late and we planned to spend the night in Vista Alegre, so we reluctantly backtracked towards the path down to the main road. Along the way, I noticed a number of carved stone utensils and José found several pieces of broken stone bowls and some primitive pot shards built into a crumbling retaining wall. It began to look as though the site pre-dated the Incas, but had been rebuilt and fortified by them in the face of the Spanish invasion. That might explain why it had been called the "New" Fort. As we reached the end of the knife edge and scrambled down towards the path, I saw that the high ground across the notch would have been a threat to the Incas if occupied by long-range weapons. Cannon shots fired from there would have raked the knife edge along its axis all the way out to the towers - a favored maneuver of sixteenth century naval gunners called "crossing the T" - and could hardly have failed to find targets. It was the final clue suggesting the identity of the ruins. According to one of his captains, Arbieto had surprised the Indians and won the day by placing 50 arquebus gunners and one of his cannons on heights commanding the approach to the fort.

Back on the main trail, we hurried down into the gathering darkness in hopes of finding a good campsite by the river before nightfall. As we passed under the fortified hilltop high above, the trail crossed slopes so steep that anything dropped from the fort would have carried us with it down into the river, a hundred or so feet below. José had been impressed that I'd known where to look for the ruins with no help from Diaz. I explained to him that the Spaniards had written of the place and I'd recognized many of the features mentioned in their accounts of the battle. From that moment on, there was a subtle change in our relationship, as if José was beginning to think we weren't just a bunch of helpless tourists after all.

Late in the day, the trail crossed the Rio Zapateroyoc, coming in from the south. A farm just across the creek turned out to be that of Señor Diaz. He wasn't there, but when we asked about ruins, his children pointed to a path climbing straight up the ridge separating the Pampaconas from the Zapateroyoc. **(Figure 32)** It figured. Following it would no doubt have lead up along the spine of the divide to the small meadow with the boulder at the highest point of the fort. Viewed from the standpoint of the defenders, it had provided a ready-made escape route when the battle turned against them - an desirable feature, I knew, of any good defensive position.

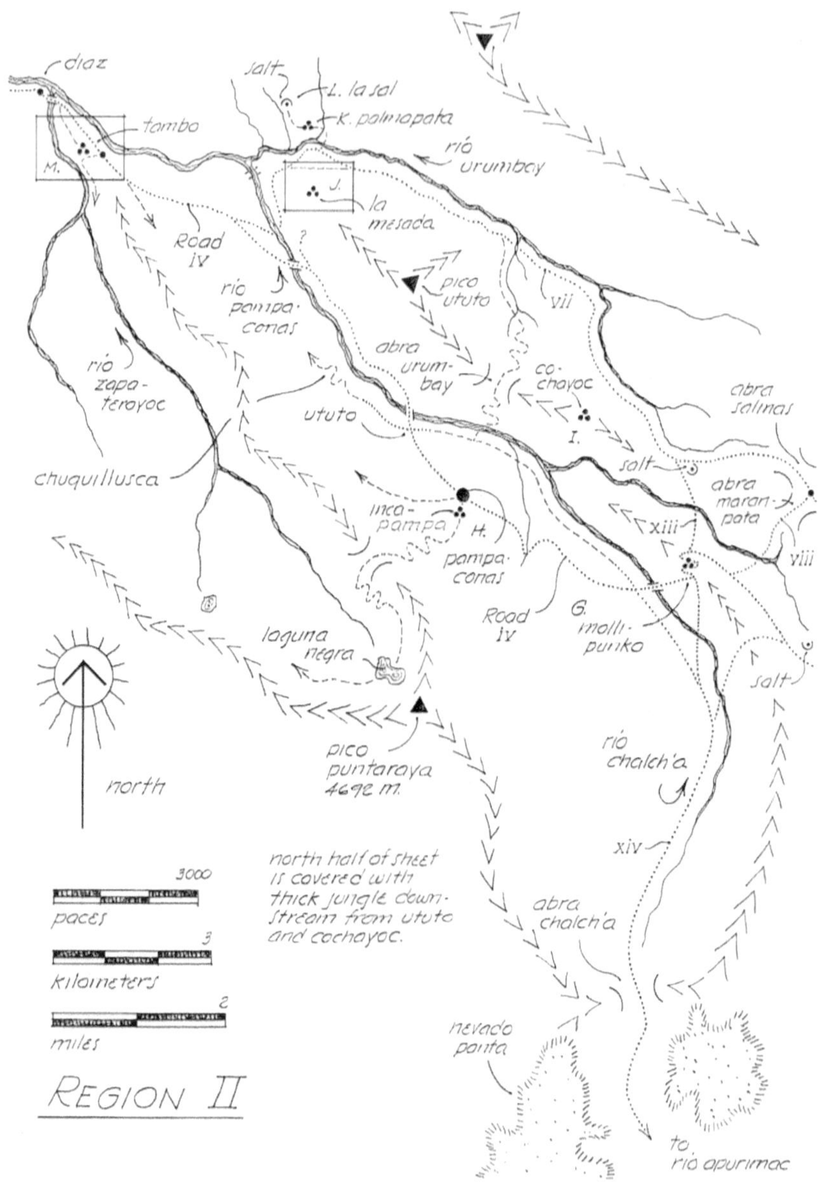

Figure 32 - Map of upper Rio Pampaconas

Just at dusk, we passed a cluster of huts called San Fernando. **(Figure 44)** A strange flag was flying nearby and a group of men with guns were talking loudly in one of the yards. They paid us no heed, but when I asked José who they were, he just said, "*Vamos.*" We did. Being alongside the river again, we camped at the first good place, a large gravel bar near the big bend of the Pampaconas near Vista Alegre. My barometer read 6500 feet and the air was warm, heavy and moist. We'd lost more than a mile of elevation since crossing the Kolpacasa, and jungle sounds and smells enveloped us. The tropical night closed in with startling suddenness. Reflecting around the fire, we could scarcely believe our luck. There we were, a bunch of neophytes not yet an entire day into the exploration phase of our trip, and we'd already found something important, a major ruin that had eluded all our predecessors. Huayna Pucara, the long-lost New Fort, was back on the map.

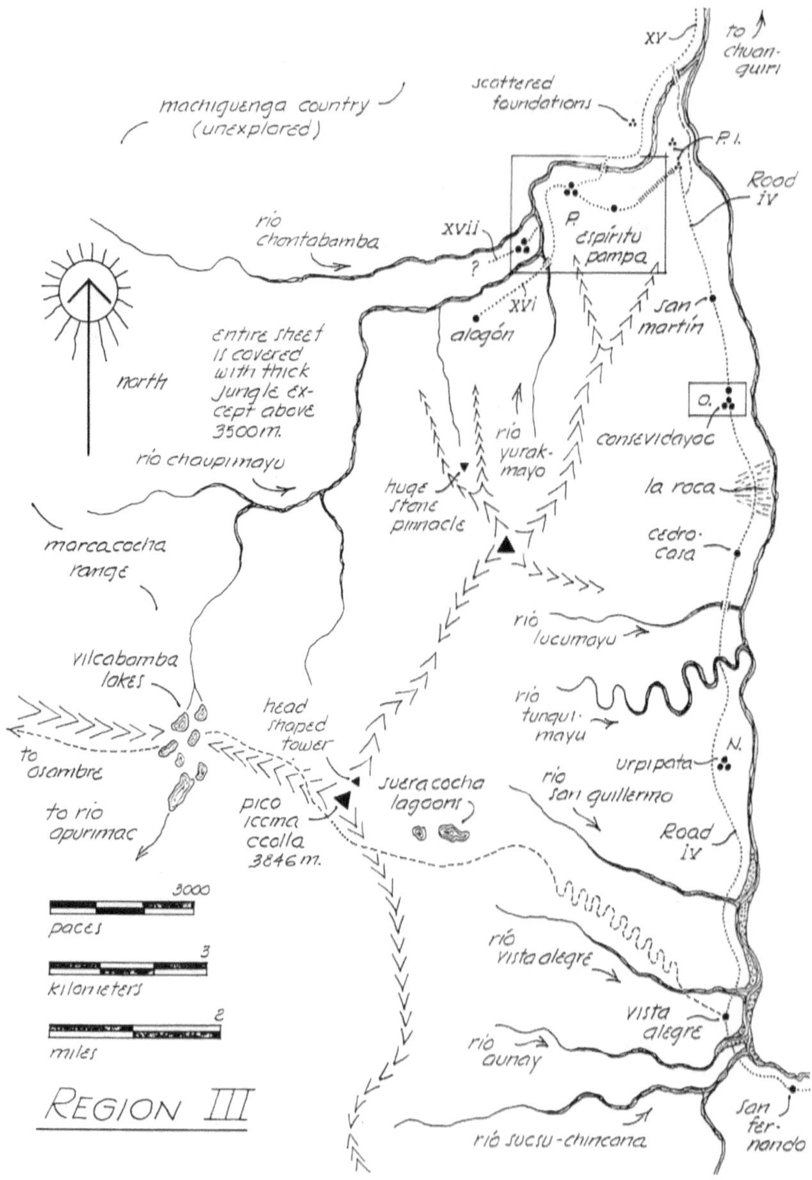

Figure 44 - Map of lower Rio Pampaconas

6

The Plain Of Ghosts

In the morning, we stopped in Vista Alegre to see Zacarias Luque, an old friend of Juvenal's that had showed Curtis, Brooke and me the nearby trail up into the Markacocha, but he was away on a trip downriver. His wife thought we might meet him on the trail, as we later did. With our discovery of the New Fort, I now felt certain we were back on the road followed by the Spaniards in 1572. That meant the next stop on their route to Vilcabamba was our next objective as well. The trouble was, not much is known about the place and what little there is is far from clear.

On account of their orderly retreat after the fall of the New Fort, the Inca's forces remained more or less intact, but they were thoroughly demoralized. Sarmiento reports that the column advanced the following day to a fort called Samaua and the day after that to "Hatun Pucara," the Big Fort, but notes no action at either place. Neither of the other chroniclers even mentions Samaua, but Arbieto agrees that they advanced unopposed to what he calls only the "second fort" and found it abandoned. Murúa, on the other hand, claims they advanced to "Machu Pucara", the Old Fort, "*...where Manco Inca had defeated Gonzalo Pizarro* (in 1539, due to the stone in Pizarro's shoe) *and found the Indians waiting there in force.*" **(1)**

Most researchers have accepted Murúa's account, ignored Samaua and agreed that Arbieto's second fort was at Hatun or Machu Pucara. On the theory that the words "big" and "old" had arguably similar connotations among the Incas, both names are assumed to refer to the same place - with "Old" Fort being favored, probably, because it contrasts so nicely with the "New" Fort, just upstream. Assuming Murúa's claim that Machu Pucara was the scene of the action in 1539 is correct, then according to Titu Cusi's description of that battle **(2)**, it would have been in dense forest, about "three leagues" (3 hours? 9 miles? 12 miles?) upstream from the capital at Vilcabamba. Also, it would be found near a river, since Manco escaped capture there by swimming to safety as the tide of battle turned against him. The last point is reinforced by Murúa's report that in 1572 one of the Spaniards had to jump into a river to avoid being burned when his padded armor caught fire during the skirmish there. **(3)** Of the fortress itself, we know nothing, except that Arbieto thought its defenses "good." **(4)**

As we bid *adiós* to Señora Luque and continued downstream, reference to the satellite photo showed that only a few places met all of those requirements and they were all in the next mile or two of the canyon. Cocky from our instant success the day before, we strutted off down the trail from Vista Alegre confident we'd be having lunch in the ruins of Machu Pucara. Several places along the way seemed promising, but we spent all morning bashing about in the jungle to no avail. José had never heard of ruins in that part of the canyon, but gamely led off with his *machete* every time I thought the terrain looked right. More searching after lunch turned up nothing. By mid-afternoon, we were hot, tired, and badly dehydrated. No one had seen José for awhile, so we flopped down and waited for him to catch up. As we lounged alongside the trail, a pack string appeared, headed upriver. It turned out to be Zacarias Luque, as his wife had predicted. He and several of his sons were bringing coffee beans up from the warmer country downstream for transport, eventually, over the mountains to Cuzco. The climate where we were headed might be friendly, but the situation was not, he cautioned. Looking like a trapper from the Rocky Mountain fur trade, Luque carried a huge shotgun across his saddle. Its barrel was so rusted he'd wrapped it with copper wire to prevent its bursting on discharge. "*Por los diablos*," he said, patting the weapon and spurring his horse on up the trail. "For the devils," the terrorists, we guessed, peering nervously off into the increasingly dark forest.

Finally, José appeared with his *manta*, a sort of backpack made from a folded blanket tied around one shoulder. It was filled to capacity. We couldn't imagine what he'd picked up. When he reached us, he unfolded the blanket and out rolled thirty huge grapefruits. We ate them all, five apiece, right then and there. Our thirst thus quenched, our minds were freed to focus on lesser annoyances and we realized how cruddy and bug-bitten we were from the day of clawing around in the jungle. So we ended the day's work with a quick dip in the Río Tunquimayo, a strangely serpentine creek flowing into the Pampaconas from the mist-shrouded slopes of Icma Coya, far above. **(Figure 44)**

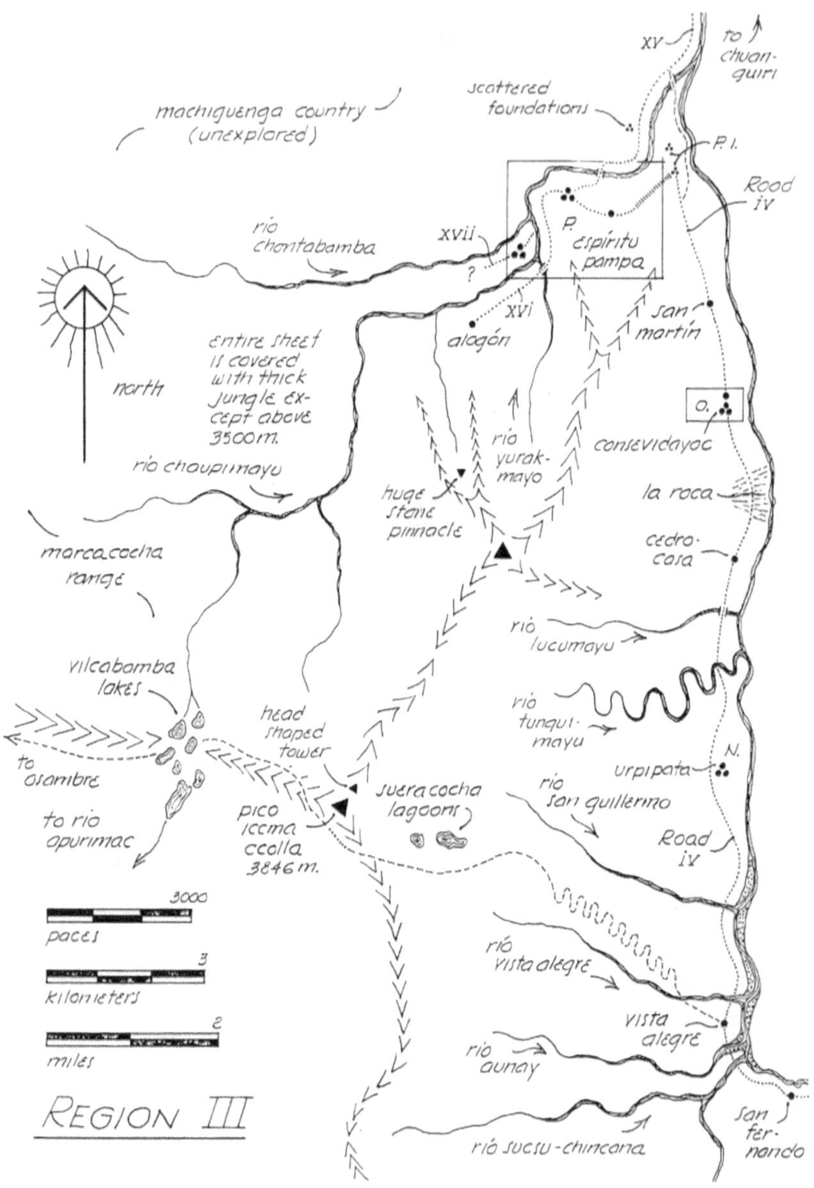

Figure 44 - Map of lower Rio Pampaconas

By nightfall, we were too close to Espíritu Pampa to expect to find the fort. We must have passed it somewhere during the day, but with so little to go on, there was no telling where. We'd just have look again on our way upriver. José unloaded the horses at Cedrocasa, a tiny, isolated clearing in the midst of the now impenetrable forest. Dense vegetation pressed hard from all sides and made for a gloomy, claustrophobic camp. Our goal in the morning would be the site of Marcanay, the village all visitors to Vilcabamba the Old passed through shortly before reaching the city. Gene Savoy had thought it up the wild Río Chaupimayo above Espíritu Pampa, beyond the mountains to our west (**Figure 44**), but that didn't square with our discovery of the New Fort. It was clear we were approaching the city from the right direction, and Marcanay had to be along our route somewhere. As with Machu Pucara, though, the Spanish records had precious little to say about the place.

Despite what Murúa calls "much disturbance" upon the column's arrival at the Old Fort, the Indians soon retreated in the face of the Spanish onslaught and he claims the invaders moved on to the town of Marcanay the very same day. Sarmiento says they reached Marcanay the next day, Monday, June 23rd, and Arbieto seems to agree. At this point, another chronicler enters the picture; Antonio de la Calancha, the Augustinian priest whose 1639 tome was Bingham's major source of information about Vilcabamba. In my hasty research, I'd paid little attention to what I mistakenly dismissed as his long, tedious and irrelevant account of the martyrdom of Diego Ortiz. I knew the basic outline of the story, though. Prior to his execution, the Indians had dragged the hapless *padre* before Tupac Amaru, Titu Cusi's successor and the last of the Incas, for sentencing at the town called Marcanay. Like everyone else, Calancha placed it "two leagues" from Vilcabamba, or about an hour's walk below Machu Pucara. Passing through Marcanay en route downstream, according to Murúa, the Spaniards hadn't yet learned of Ortiz fate, nor of the part the town had supposedly played in his demise. They were to learn of both from captives some days later and would vent their rage by completely obliterating the village on their way back upriver. Other than this, all we know of the place is that Murúa claimed the invaders "*...found fields full of corn, ready to harvest, and plantations of yuca and guava which delighted the men, as they were hungry and in need of supplies. The camp master restrained the soldiers from falling out of line to help themselves to the sugar cane, fearing a* *possible ambush*". (**5**) Whatever the town may have looked like, it was clearly a lush, tropical and productive farming community.

The night at Cedrocasa was long, damp and cold, but the morning dawned clear, making it five in a row. José was amazed, noting that, for *gringos* , we were having strangely good luck with the weather. From camp, the road rose steadily until we were nearly a thousand feet above the river. The jungle was thick and the ground steep and craggy - no place for a town, I thought. Finally, the trail traversed a huge cliff called La Roca, "The Rock," and a spectacular vista opened down the canyon. Suddenly, the scene was one of pastoral beauty. The terrain spread below was gentle and cultivated in all sorts of crops. Off in the distance, we could see the cluster of buildings the Indians called Conservidayoc. A tiny settlement, it crowned a flattened ridge-top between two rivers, the Pumachaca and the Sarahuasi. Both tumbled eastward into the deep canyon of the Río Consevidayoc, as the Pampaconas is nowadays called below La Roca.

José said we were only a couple of hours from Espíritu Pampa, so we should have been very close to the site of Marcanay. The obvious answer was that Consevidayoc *was* Marcanay. Could it possibly be that simple? The location was right. The Spaniards said the fields around Marcanay were rich in crops, including sugar cane and corn. Consevidayoc was certainly the only place we'd come to that met that description. The invaders had ended up completely destroying the village when they found out about Ortiz. Did that mean there was absolutely nothing left of the original buildings - no ruins whatsoever? José said the locals were quite sure there were none in the area, but I wondered about that.

Hiram Bingham had written that a man called Saavedra, the *campesino* he found living at Consevidayoc in 1911, had numerous Inca artifacts in and near his house. Where had they come from, I wondered? As we finally arrived among the buildings, I noticed a large, flat rock lying discarded by the trail. A six inch hole had been laboriously hand-drilled through its center. A lot of work to just throw away unless, of course, it was an artifact of some sort. Then it hit me. It was the very same stone Bingham had reported 71 years earlier. Saavedra told him he'd found it atop an old tomb with a plate of solid silver covering the hole. **(6)**

Finally, we filled our canteens from a canal running down the middle of the ridge through the several houses into a crude stone basin, not unlike those I'd seen at minor Inca sites elsewhere. Though it had been patched with cement in recent times, there was no telling how old the stonework was. The whole water system seemed strangely elaborate for such an otherwise poor place, especially since there was a natural stream no more than a minute's walk away. I decided to look the whole place over more carefully on our return upriver.

Continuing below Consevidayoc, the east facing slope traversed by the trail became increasingly dry and open, reminding us of Wyoming. It was hard to believe we'd soon be in the thick rain forest described so oppressively by Bingham and Savoy. The only hint that we were still in the tropics was the tiny settlement of San Martín, where water from a small, spring-fed creek supported a small, but lush patch of growth and crops. Consevidayoc, it seemed, was the only place in the lower valley hospitable enough to support a population of any size. Upstream was La roca and the steep, dense forest and now, downstream, we found land too dry to farm.

Across the river, there was more moisture and we saw a few small farms, but the slopes were steeper and received no sun until midday. We knew from our own experience picking campsites that the best exposure was northeast in this country of cold nights and warm days. The morning sun quickly cut the chill from the land except on shaded west-facing slopes. That the Incas had agreed seemed plain. Every known site from Machu Picchu to Vilcabamba the Old was situated to receive morning sun, likely for spiritual as well as practical reasons.

As our road reached the crest of the ridgeline separating the gorge of the Conservidayoc from the valley of Espíritu Pampa to the west, we saw that just over the top, the forest once again prevailed. I'd often noticed the same thing in the Rockies - the shady side of a ridge held its moisture and supported more growth. In the gap where the trail crossed over and began its descent into the valley beyond, there was a small rectangular platform with stone steps leading up to what appeared to be the foundation of an even smaller ruined building, possibly an old guard station of some sort. **(Figure 48)** Those being the first ruins we'd seen since leaving Tambo, we pressed on excitedly to a nearby overlook, anxious to see what lay beyond. It was June 29th.

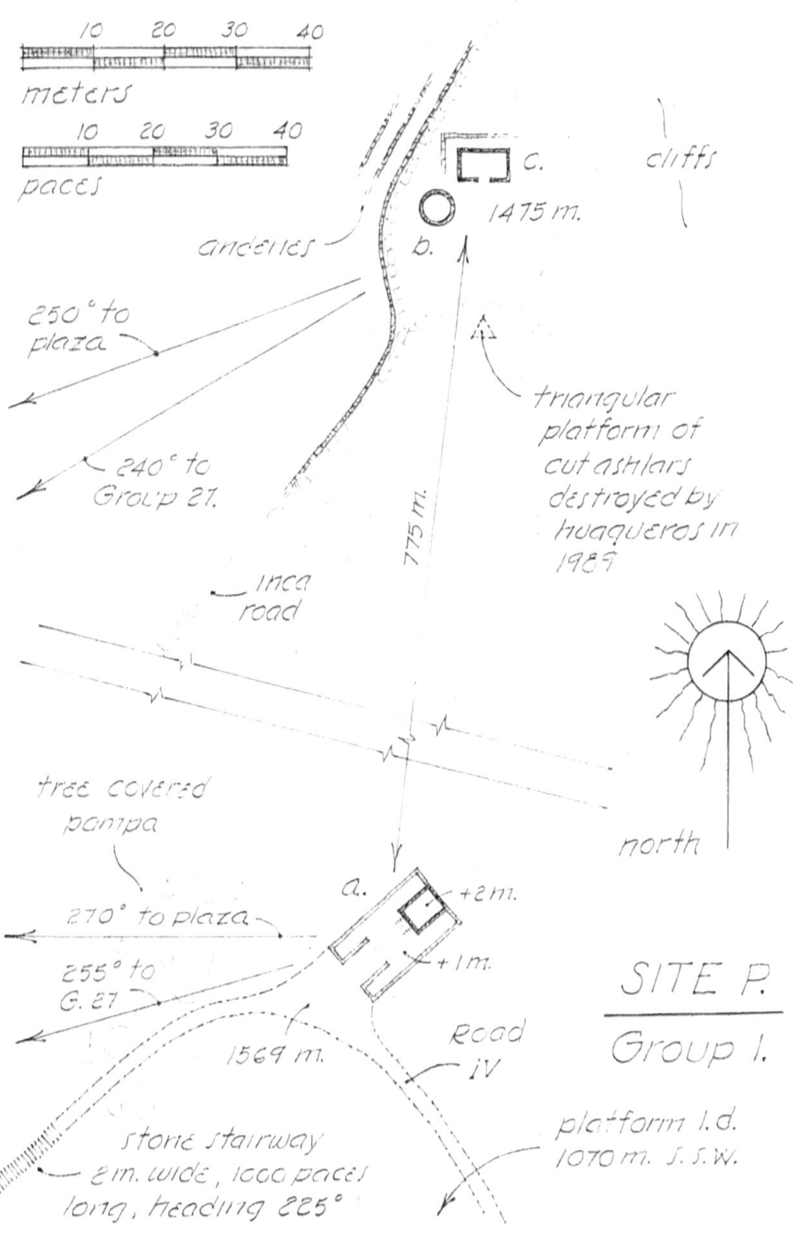

Figure 48 - Group at top of stone stairway

Four hundred and twelve years earlier, almost to the day, the Spaniards had stood at precisely the same spot, gazing down upon their long sought after prize - the fabled jungle stronghold of the Incas. It was June 24th, 1572, "the day of Saint John the Baptist," according to Murúa. The Europeans had marched non-stop from Marcanay after an uneventful bivouac there during which no Indians had shown themselves. Continuing on into the city below our vantage point, they found it abandoned and ransacked. The thatch of its most important buildings was still smoldering, the city having been put to the torch by the fleeing natives. Calancha later noted that the city had been the "largest in the province" and Arbieto counted at least 400 houses among the ruins. It was Murúa, though, that left us the best description of the place. His words are all that future explorers would have to go on in their latter-day attempts to identify the site:

"*The town was half a league wide as one approaches from Cuzco and a huge distance in length. They used to raise parrots, chickens, ducks, rabbits, turkeys, pheasants, peacocks, and macaws there, and 1000 other species of colorful birds, very beautiful to see. There were also many guava, peanuts, pecans, papayas, pineapples, avocados and other diverse fruits and wild trees. The bees made honeycombs such as those in Spain, and the corn was harvested three times a year. The good disposition of the land and the water with which they irrigated gave forth crops in great abundance: coca, sugar cane, yuca, sweet potatoes and cotton.*"

"*The houses were covered with good thatch, although the Inca's house was on different levels and covered with roof tiles. They had painted the entire palace with a great variety of beautiful pictures, as was their fashion, and its doors were of very aromatic cedar, which is abundant thereabouts. The town had a square sufficient for many people, where they used to run horses and rejoice in merriments. The Incas, therefore, had nearly the luxuries, greatness and splendor of Cuzco in that distant, or rather exiled, land - and they enjoyed life there.*" **(7)**

None of that was apparent from our overlook. Instead, spread below was a large, gently sloping valley surrounded by steep, forested mountains. Two or three huts dotted a patchwork of cleared fields toward the lower end, but beyond these, the upper reaches of the drainage were clothed in a dark, unbroken mantle of rain forest. There was no hint that beneath all those trees lay the ruins of a once great metropolis - a long lost jungle paradise, of sorts, in which an entire generation of Indians had lived in peace and plenty, far from the insults of their would-be masters from another world. There was an overwhelming sadness about the thought, especially in view of the aftermath of the fall of their final capital.

The Incas, having fled with all they could carry, seem to have left little of value behind to reward the invaders' victory. Nevertheless, the Spaniards set up headquarters in the "same house of the Inca" (the one on different levels with roofs of tile), according to Murúa, and began combing the city and surrounding hills for fugitives and booty. Among the latter were the mummified remains of Manco Inca and Titu Cusi, both of whom had avoided capture in life only to be thus humiliated in death. Pursuing leads extracted from prisoners, Arbieto sent detachments deep into the surrounding jungle to round up the surviving Incas. Especially important were Tupac Amaru and the only legitimate heir to his throne, Titu Cusi's son, Quispe Titu. The Spanish general was determined not to repeat the mistake of his predecessors a generation earlier, who'd won all the battles, but failed to capture the Inca and thus lost the war.

Quispe Titu was captured first, following a six day ordeal in which his pursuers climbed without food or water through steep cloud forests infested by rattlesnakes. Another party, dispatched to hunt down Tupac Amaru, instead came upon a treasure trove of gold, silver and emeralds which had been cached with some Chunchos, deep in the jungle. Included in the find was a golden image of the sun, a particularly sacred object which Murúa thought worthy of some respect. The idol and all the other spoils were nevertheless immediately and indiscriminately pocketed by the soldiers, much to his disgust. Murúa's description of the fateful capture of the Inca, too, shows a certain regard for the Indians which was shared by precious few of his countrymen.

"*General Arbieto wanted very much to capture Tupac Amaru in order to finish the war and he commanded García de Loyola to go in search of the Inca with forty soldiers. They walked forty leagues* (more than 120 miles!) *from*

Vilcabamba the Old before finding the Inca's trail. Some fearful forest Indians told the Spaniards it had been five days since the Inca had departed their camp, and that Tupac Amaru's wife had gone with him sad and afraid, as she was ready to give birth. The Inca loved her so much, they said, he himself looked after her and helped her carry her apparel, walking bit by bit."

"*Loyola continued fifteen leagues (almost 50 miles further) until he came upon Tupac Amaru and his wife, warming themselves by a fire. They had paused next to a large river, the pregnant lady being terrified of going out onto such a huge body of water. The Inca showed himself to be a very kind, discreet man and exceptionally well-spoken. He was firm and serious, but nothing bothered him - nor did he demonstrate any appreciation or concern for all that he had lost.*" **(8)**

The Spaniards occupied Vilcabamba for some months, fortifying the ruins of a sun temple in a pass above the city as a defense against incursions by the hostile jungle tribes still holding sway in the interminable forests downstream. A new voice, that of Gabriel de Oviedo, a prominent cleric of Cuzco, reported that the expedition finally returned to that city in September of 1572. Along with the mummies of Manco and Titu Cusi, the captive Incas and their families and retainers were paraded triumphantly through the streets in chains. All were imprisoned and divided among the monks to be taught the Holy Catholic faith. Oviedo marveled "*that heathens should show such intelligence in understanding it.*" **(9)** Tupac Amaru, especially, was apparently a quick study and was ready for baptism after only three days of instruction. Thus catechized, he was hastily tried and falsely found guilty of a long list of trumped up capital offenses. With the pre-determined verdict thus in, and over the strenuous objections of more than a few of his closest advisors, Toledo summarily condemned the Inca to death. He was, the viceroy decreed, to be beheaded without delay.

The execution was set for the 24th day of September, exactly three months after the fall of Vilcabamba. For the conquering Incas, exalted Sons of the Sun and builders of the greatest empire the New World had ever seen, it was to be the last day of history. The roar of the enormous crowd was deafening as tens of thousands of Indians chanted their shock, disbelief, anger and sorrow at what they were about to witness. Even the uneasy and heavily armed Spaniards and their grossly outnumbered Indian allies were well aware that a terrible thing was about to happen. Despite four decades of iron-fisted rule in the sprawling and still magnificent Inca capital that climbed the slopes all around them, the *conquistadores* would soon be reminded of who still ruled the hearts and minds of Cuzco.

Tupac Amaru Inca led through Cuzco in chains, 1572; from Guaman Poma de Ayala, ca. 1613.

A great scaffold had been erected in the midst of the old Inca plaza of Haucaypata and onto this Tupac Amaru presently climbed, together with his guards and several priests. By simply raising his hand, he commanded a silence so profound that Oviedo said all present "*stood as if they were stone.*" **(10)** He then delivered a brief farewell, unexpectedly extolling the virtues of Christianity and denouncing the pagan ways of his forefathers. Likely, he was simply embracing the age old idea that the religion of the winner in a clash of cultures was by definition superior to that of the loser. Although the stunned Europeans were delighted, they nevertheless hacked off his head promptly when he was finished and stuck the grisly trophy proudly on a pole for all to see. Oviedo noted that thousands of Indians hovered around that pole throughout that night, "*mourning the loss of their Inca.*" **(11)** In the morning, Toledo ordered it taken down, there being no other way to disperse the crowd.

The Spaniards abandoned the ruins of Vilcabamba to the jungle, where they laid forgotten and undisturbed for the next three centuries. The site disappeared, literally, beneath a dense, green blanket of vegetation. Having established their own provincial capital in the highlands, at Vilcabamba the New, they came to call the old Inca city Vilcabamba the Old - but no one ever went there except nomadic, forest tribesmen in search of game. In time, lost Vilcapampa vanished from the map and, like Atlantis, Camelot and El Dorado, continued to live only in legend. It was this legend that had captured the imagination of young Hiram Bingham during his first experience with the Incas, at Choquequirau, in 1909 - and led two years later to his discoveries of both Machu Picchu and Vitcos. Despite such stellar successes, when Bingham heard rumors at Vitcos of even more spectacular ruins, deeper in the jungle, he left immediately to check them out. From his encampment at Rosaspata, the American proceeded up to Vilcabamba the New and learned there of a large Inca city, far down the lower Río Pampaconas, two more days to the northwest. The expedition crossed the Kolpacasa and, passing through Pampaconas en route, plunged into the forested canyons beyond. Where today a good trail continues downstream, there was then next to nothing except mud and jungle. It was an horrendous trek, but Bingham finally arrived at his destination.

"*At the end of a difficult journey in a country where there is extremely little flat land, we found, at an elevation of 3300 feet, a small alluvial plain. It is called Espíritu Pampa, or Pampa of Ghosts, and was covered with dense forest and jungle. (At) a place called Eromboni Pampa, there are several terraces and a long rectangular building with twelve doors in front and twelve behind. Near here was a fountain with three spouts. About 200 yards away was the most important group. The present Indians call this group of houses Tendi Pampa and evidently they were the houses of the chief people of the place.*" **(12) (Figures 52, 55 and 56)**

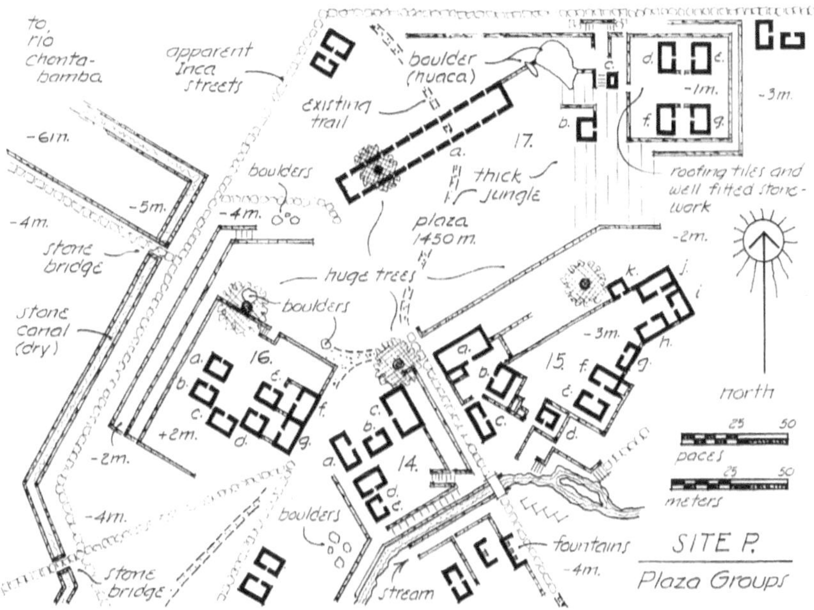

Figure 52 - Plan of the main plaza (Bingham's Eromboni Pampa)

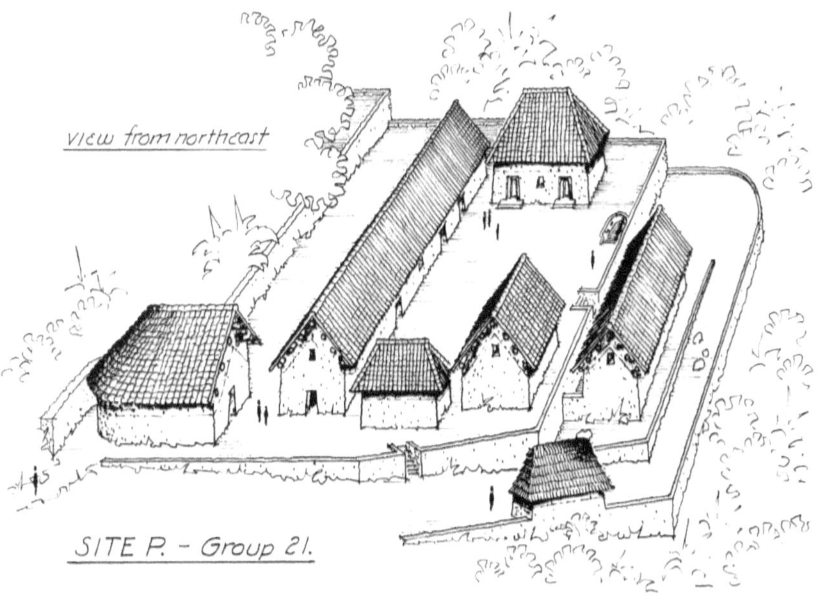

Figure 55 - View of two story group (Bingham's Tendi Pampa)

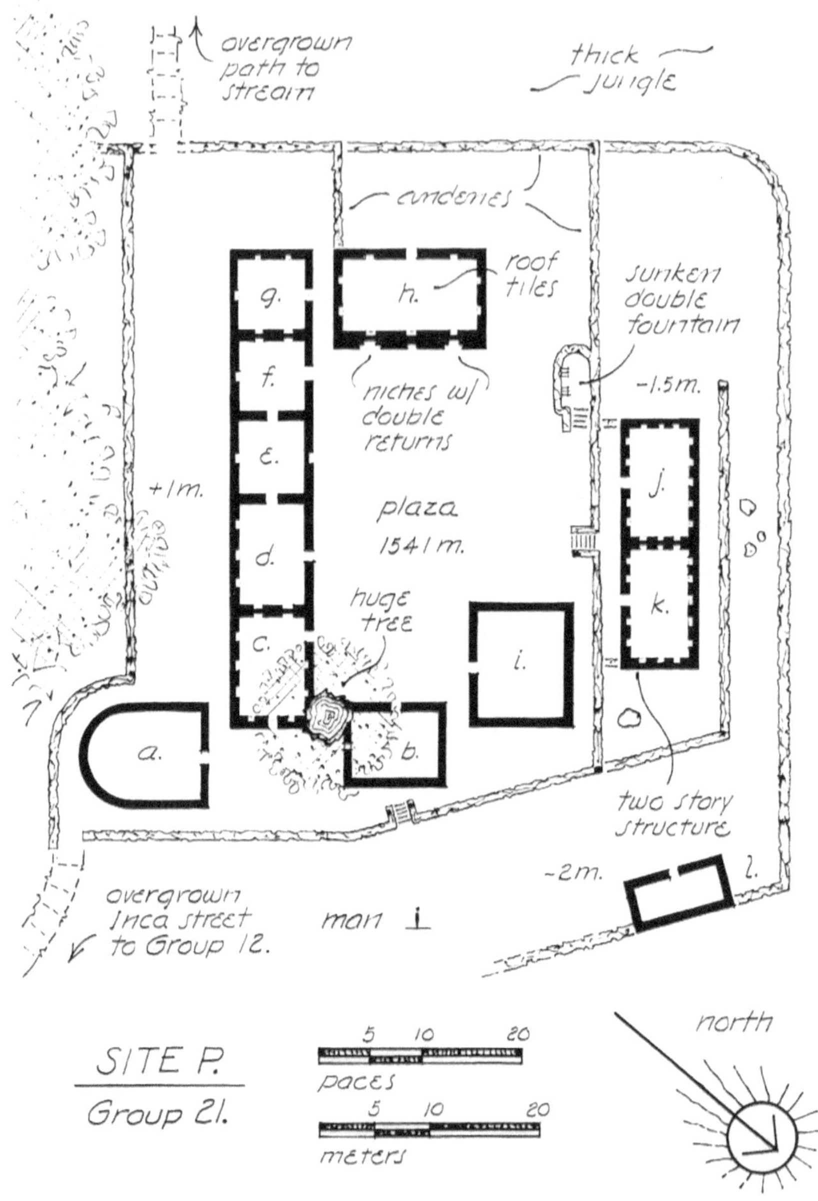

Figure 56 - Plan of two story group

Incredibly, Bingham had walked through the midst of more than three hundred ruined buildings yet seen only a score due to the thick and tangled vegetation under which they lay concealed. Even the

Indians who lived there knew no better. The few buildings he saw were badly tumbled and had not been especially fine when standing. He pronounced the site undoubtedly Inca, but dismissed it as unimportant. Possibly, he thought, it had been one of Titu Cusi's several residences. Only one unusual detail caught his eye.

"*This exception was the presence of a dozen or fifteen roughly made Spanish roofing tiles of varying sizes. The Indians could offer no explanation of the mystery. Apparently none of the houses ever had tile roofs, as the number of fragments was not enough to cover more than a few square feet and nearly all were outside the buildings.*" **(13)**

Bingham's primary source was the chronicle of *Padre* Calancha, and so he was unaware of Martín de Murúa's report that the Spaniards had found Vilcabamba the Old in a long, low, tropical valley and that they had been surprised to discover some of the buildings roofed with tiles. Otherwise he might have paid more heed to the note, scribbled in his own hand on page 100 of the expedition journal **(14)**, that the local Campa Indians also called Espíritu Pampa "Vilcapampa" - and he might have stayed long enough to ferret out the truth of the matter. But, he did not. Beset by his highland guides, who were miserable and afraid in the wet, intimidating forests, he abandoned Espíritu Pampa, never to return.

The expedition backtracked to Machu Picchu, unquestionably the most spectacular of the many sites it had uncovered. In comparison, the Plain of Ghosts must have seemed a poor find. Even if one included it among the three possible candidates for the "lost city" Bingham had set out to find - Choquequirau and Machu Picchu being the other two - Espíritu Pampa was by far the least impressive. Despite some initial ambivalence, the explorer finally concluded that, of the three, Machu Picchu was indeed Vilcabamba the Old, and he suppressed any nagging reservations throughout the remainder of his life. It was, as far as he knew, the "largest town" in the province, just as Calancha had described the Inca's final capital, and was about the right distance from Vitcos. Few knew, and fewer still cared, that it was in exactly the wrong direction.

Troublesome details aside, Bingham's arguments proved convincing to almost everyone, including several generations of popular writers, guides, tourists and Peruvian politicians interested in promoting travel to his admittedly magnificent "lost city". It would be decades before anyone was to retrace the explorer's steps, review the pertinent chronicles or otherwise be in a position to reassess his analysis critically. Even then, Bingham's prestige and the momentum of the past would be hard to overcome. Despite massive evidence to the contrary in John Hemming's monumental The Conquest of the Incas, published in 1970, and Alfred M. Bingham's revelation of his father's own doubts in his 1989 biography, Portrait of an Explorer, confusion persists still. The caption below a photograph of Machu Picchu in the recently completed Hall of South American Indians at the Denver Museum of Natural History indicates that the city was a "fortress" abandoned by the Incas in 1572 - a cautious, but clear reference to its erroneous identification with Vilcabamba the Old.

Except for the wanderings of Christian Bües, a retired Swiss agricultural engineer and amateur map maker who roamed the province between 1915 and 1920, the ruins of Vilcabamba lay forgotten and undisturbed for more than 40 years after Bingham's departure in 1911. Although Bües eventually compiled the first and, for many years, only map of the region, it included little country west of Rosaspata, omitted Espíritu Pampa altogether and thus cast neither light nor shadows across Bingham's increasingly accepted claim that Vilcabamba the Old and Machu Picchu were one in the same.

Meanwhile, the clearing, excavation and restoration of what had come to be called the "Lost City of the Incas" proceeded apace with considerable financial backing from the prestigious National Geographic Society. There was little doubt that Machu Picchu was among the finest archaeological finds of all time and the story of its discovery became an enduring classic of exploration. **(15)** Bingham's early surmises that the city's precipitous location had been chosen for defense and its relatively friendly southeastern approaches blocked by a "dry moat" and wall fit nicely with the idea that it had been Manco's final "fortress". Likewise, the absence of Spanish artifacts in any of the various digs conducted there suggested the site had eluded discovery by the *conquistadores*, then a widely accepted myth about Vilcabamba, since no documents to the contrary had yet come to light. In time both ideas would be discredited, but for the moment, Raimondi's old ideas about Choquequirau were eclipsed. The Incas' final redoubt had been found at Machu Picchu and, for the second time, the matter was erroneously considered closed.

One of the earliest to doubt Bingham's identification of Machu Picchu as Manco's final capital in print was Victor Wolfgang von Hagen, an outspoken expatriate American explorer and writer who would become a well-known fixture in Latin American archaeological circles. During a visit to Machu Picchu in the course of his "Highway of the Sun" expedition in 1953, he observed that the site was ill suited for a resident population of "more than a hundred people" and was far too small to have been the Inca capital. Vilcabamba the Old, he concluded, must still be out there, yet undiscovered. **(16)**

In July of that year, he visited Pucyura and, like Bingham before him, was shown the ruins of Rosaspata. His notes record nothing new about the site, but reflect instead his preoccupation with the Inca road network he and his group were determined to explore. Julio Cobos, Juvenal's father and a long-time resident of the area, told von Hagen of old roads leading to Machu Picchu, Choquequirau and Espíritu Pampa. Cobos said he had a *hacienda* at the latter and that there were ruins in the nearby jungle from which the Machiguengas had taken gold earrings and nosepieces. They called the place "Orinbone" (Bingham's Eromboni), Hatun Vilcapampa or Vilcabamba Grande. The last two, meaning "Vilcabamba the Great" in Quechua and Spanish respectively, should have been highly suggestive of Manco's lost capital.

Despite such tantalizing leads and Cobos's offer to take him to Espíritu Pampa, von Hagen didn't go there. Instead, his papers indicate that he sent assistants into the surrounding countryside in search of the Inca roads Cobos had promised. Being, at the time uninterested in that, I prematurely shifted my attention to the next player - like Bingham, a giant in the search for Vilcabamba the Old. Had I but read on, I'd have learned of a seemingly insignificant discovery by one of von Hagen's teams that was to loom large in our own explorations of the same area, thirty one years later.

It was less than eleven years, however, until an explorer arrived at Julio Cobos' farm near Rosaspata willing to revisit Bingham's ruins at Espíritu Pampa and verify Cobos' stories of a great stone city in the jungle guarded by Machiguenga tribesmen sporting Inca jewelry. Enter Gene Savoy, a flamboyant American then living in Peru; a man with lots of money, even more energy and a weakness for publicity; a prototype Indiana Jones. Like Bingham before him, Savoy's principle source was Calancha (Murúa's work was only just then becoming available) but he thought the old explorer was wrong about Machu Picchu. The Spaniards, he knew, had passed through Vitcos and continued northwest into the forests beyond Pampaconas in search of Vilcabamba the Old during both of their successful invasions of the province, just as Bingham had in 1911. Machu Picchu was almost 30 miles southeast of Vitcos - exactly the wrong direction - and thus several days *closer* to Cuzco. It just didn't fit, and Savoy was certain that Espíritu Pampa had to be the site of the lost capital. Bingham, he figured, must have seen only the outskirts of the large ruins rumored by Cobos and the Machiguengas.

There was only one way to find out for sure, of course, and in July of 1964, Savoy, his Canadian assistant Doug Sharon and two Peruvian associates, Cuzco archaeologist Antonio Santander and Victor Ardilles, set out with Cobos for his hacienda at Espíritu Pampa. They were greeted there by two of Julio's sons, Flavio and the eldest, Benjamín, who agreed to serve as their guide. The first day, they were taken to see all of the same ruins Bingham had reported over half a century earlier. Even the roof tiles remained strewn about, exactly as Bingham had described them. Savoy, however, found many more and, though equally ignorant of their significance, he correctly concluded that some of the buildings had likely been roofed with tiles, rather than the native thatch. As Hemming would show six years later, it was a critical piece of evidence. For the moment, though, it seemed only a modest accomplishment and

Savoy retreated to camp disappointed. He was sure that they were missing something important, hidden still in the surrounding jungle.

After a discouraging and wasted day of heavy rains, Savoy returned to the forest determined to see for himself. The growth was so thick and wet that the going was slow and the visibility nil. Benjamín and Flavio had lined up some friends to help with the cutting and Savoy sent them off into the bush for a look. Almost immediately, and not twenty feet off the trail, they stumbled on a completely overgrown, but well worked stone fountain that even the guides had never before seen. It turned out that the locals, by and large practical and incurious people, hardly ever strayed off the trails. The lesson struck Savoy like a thunderbolt: no one knew what was in there!

Hastily, he devised a plan to find out. Everyone would fan out from a common starting point until someone found something. Then, they'd all reassemble at the find and fan out again. It worked. Within minutes they'd uncovered two previously unknown building groups, one elevated on a terrace above a walled avenue and the other clustered inside a sunken enclosure nearly 300 feet long. Then, strangely, there was nothing. Finally, a hundred yards to the north, several more house groups and a huge boulder turned up near the long building with 24 doorways that Bingham had reported in 1911. Savoy didn't yet know it, but he'd found the heart of the city. The empty expanse of forest between the building groups wasn't evidence of a small, sparsely populated settlement at all. It was the large, main plaza of a sprawling, jungle metropolis. **(Figure 52)**

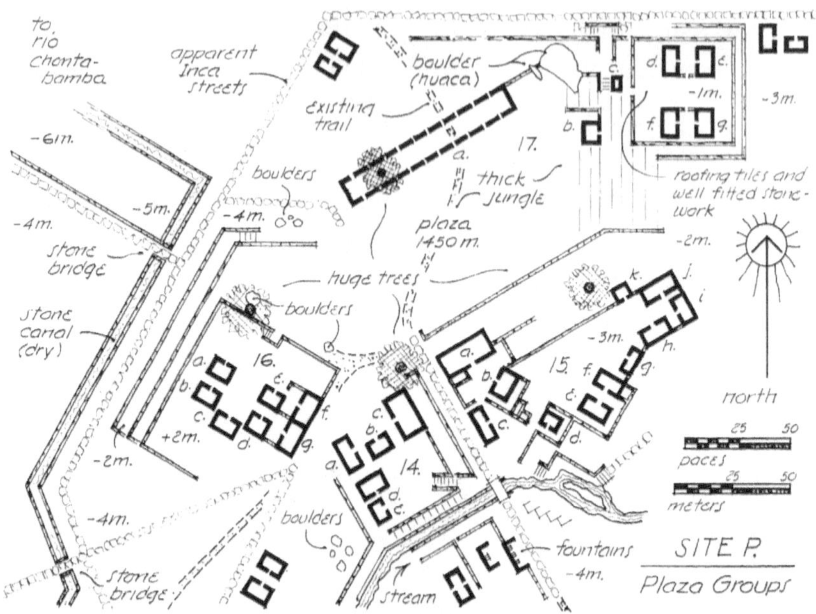

Figure 52 - Plan of the main plaza (Bingham's Eromboni Pampa)

Throughout the remainder of that day and several more, group after group of ruined buildings were hacked out of the all but impenetrable *bosque*. Before it was over, Savoy had found several hundred structures which he estimated covered more than 500 acres of rain forest, all apparently undisturbed for centuries. Though many of the ruins were circular, a feature more characteristic of other cultures, some seemed typically Incan. Satisfied that he'd found a large Inca city, albeit one with a large non-Inca population, he speculated with uncharacteristic caution:

"*Is this Manco's Vilcabamba - the lost city of the Incas?*" he asks rhetorically in Antisuyo. "*I am certain we are in parts of it,*" comes the answer, despite a dearth of what would nowadays be called hard evidence. **(17)**

Next, he put his men to the considerable task of clearing the best work for photographs and began organizing his notes in anticipation of mapping what he'd found. The results in both cases were disappointing. The photos he eventually published were few in number and failed to convey either the significance or the magnitude of his find. The sad truth was that his city wasn't very photogenic. The difficulties of jungle photography, the common style of most of the architecture and its generally poor state of preservation all conspired to project a rather pitiful image of Savoy's hard won prize. With accurate and detailed maps and drawings of the ruins, he might have turned that impression around and left a valuable record of his finds for the future. Unfortunately, he did not. His best documentation, not published until 1978, was done by the then noted Peruvian architect, Emilio Harth-terré. Not among those who had visited the site, Harth-terré was totally dependent on Savoy's notes - a very difficult situation, judging from my own experience, since field notes are seldom complete and memory inevitably comes into play when trying to plot a site back in the drafting room. Harth-terré's plan of the groups around the plaza was fairly detailed and the layout looked convincingly Incan, but his sketchy depiction of the remainder of the city showed a random scattering of buildings that seemed much less so. Savoy chose to show only one group, dubbed the "Palace of the Platforms," in detail. Harth Terré's plan and perspective views had it on a low, Mexican-looking pyramid which hardly seemed Incan at all. **(18)**

Much as Bingham had sensed the need to confirm his identification of Rosaspata as Manco's Vitcos by finding the nearby Sun Temple of Chuquipalta, Savoy now sought to corroborate his candidate for Vilcabamba the Old by locating Marcanay, the town all the chroniclers agreed was two leagues, or about six miles, away. Less clear was the supposed proximity of a place called Mananhuañunca, where the Augustinian, Ortiz, had been put to death. Savoy believed it to be very close to Marcanay. After a brief trip out to Lima for supplies and consultations with various experts, he returned to Espíritu Pampa in September of 1964 determined to find both sites. For some reason, he assumed them to be in the unexplored jungle upstream and southwest of the city - opposite from the direction to Consevidayoc - and there he began his search. It was horrible country, thick and wet, teeming with insects and cut by three raging torrents draining from the steep cloud forests all around. Crossing into the confluence of the two largest rivers, he quickly found some modest oval foundations which encouraged him to press on. Eventually, his men uncovered two significant buildings further upstream, one round but apparently Inca and another long and narrow, about 200 yards away. The first, Savoy pronounced to be Mananhuañunca, the site of Ortiz' demise, and the other, he claimed, must therefore be Marcanay. If the evidence for his identification of the main city was thin, for these two "corroborating" sites it was nonexistent. Nevertheless, the explorer was satisfied.

"There can be no question about it," he concludes in Antisuyo. "We have recovered two legendary sites. The key to Vilcabamba." **(19)**

Savoy's confident conclusion turned out to be premature. The considerable media attention given to his discoveries was long on adventure but short on science. Had he returned for a second season, as planned, he might have changed that, but a guerrilla uprising, instigated in 1965 by a leftist champion of *campesino* rights named Hugo Blanco, intervened and Savoy never went back. The professionals were suspicious. Who was this adventurous American? What were his credentials? Where was the solid documentation of his finds? The explorer's cases for Marcanay and Mananhuañunca, especially, seemed weak. Absent accurate maps and plans, how was anyone to evaluate any of Savoy's claims without going all the way to Espíritu Pampa to check them out, and who would bother to do that? And so, the academic community withheld its judgement and greeted his material with skeptical indifference, a far cry from the acclaim he believed it deserved. Savoy was outraged. It was a snubbing he neither forgave nor forgot.

Attracted partly by the media blitz that accompanied Savoy's claims, two English adventurers on assignment for the BBC visited Espíritu Pampa shortly after the explorer's departure in 1964. They noticed an apparently minor but significant detail that had eluded both Bingham and Savoy. Mark Howell had written a book about his travels throughout the old Inca empire two years earlier. Since then, he'd been exploring the cloud forests of the upper Amazon with Tony Morrison, a zoologist who in time would become a noted Andean traveler, author and film maker.

Benefiting from several freshly opened pits they found in the floor of one of the buildings, probably dug and abandoned by Savoy's crew, they noticed a layer of ash about a meter beneath the accumulated sediments of vegetation that blanketed the site. In their book about the trip, they speculated that the city must once have been burned and, ironically, took this as evidence that Espíritu Pampa was not, therefore, the site of Vilcabamba the Old after all. **(20)** In fact, their discovery added strong support to Savoy's claim. Just as neither Savoy nor Bingham had known the significance of the roofing tiles, Howell and Morrison were unaware that in describing the Spaniards' entry into the city 394 years earlier, Martín de Murúa had reported exactly what the two Englishmen had found.

"*The Indians had gone, putting fire to all they could not carry.*" **(21)**

7

A Promise To The Inca

Ever since the day I gazed down from the summit of Icma Coya, I'd wondered what Savoy's city was like. Now I was about to find out. José had gone ahead with the horses while I filled the others in on what I'd learned about the place in the intervening two years. Moving on, we immediately arrived at the top of a carefully laid stone stairway about two meters wide traversing down the slope arrow-straight for at least a thousand yards. Both Bingham and Savoy had been impressed with this grand entrance to whatever lay below. Though the centuries had washed out many of the steps, there was no doubt it had once been a broad avenue, built to accommodate two-way traffic of *llamas* and pedestrians in and out of the valley.

The lower end of the stair and the original paving stones beyond had long since disappeared into two creeks now flowing in deep ravines filled with dense jungle. Just beyond the second, the land had been cleared for crops and there were several thatched roof houses. It was the farm originally built by Julio Cobos, but since leased to tenants. A delightfully pleasant, scenic location, it was our base camp for the next week. **(Figure 47)** José had lived there with his family until two years earlier and knew the surrounding valley and its handful of residents well. They, in turn, accepted us immediately, any friend of José's apparently being theirs also. As a result, our camp at the Plain of Ghosts was one of the most enjoyable of the entire expedition - quite the opposite of the snake-infested, green hell we'd been led to expect by the hypnotherapist and his strange partner in Cuzco.

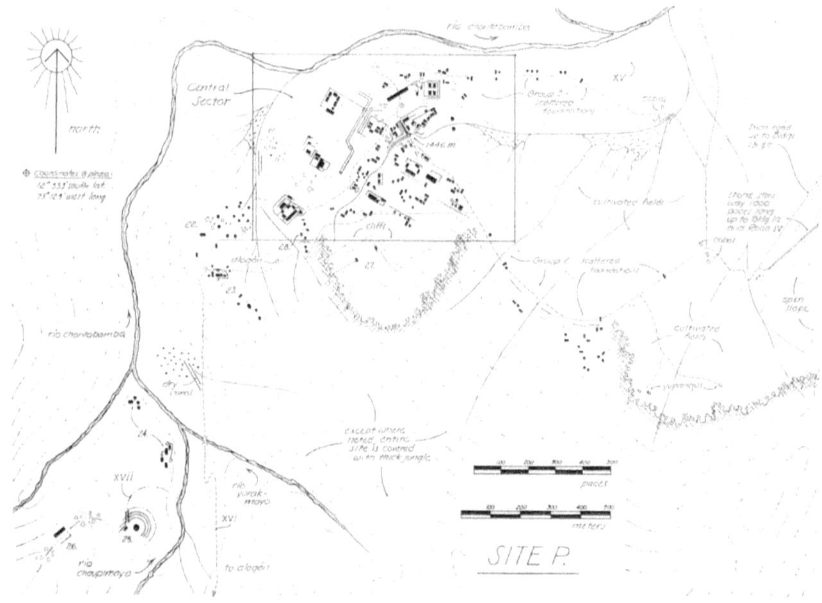

Figure 47 - Map of Espiritu Pampa (Vilcabamba the Old)

We had two projects in mind. In addition to exploring the ruins, we wanted to visit a strangely-formed mountaintop that our satellite photo showed not far from the city. The very summit looked like a volcanic crater with a dark spot near its center, possibly a small lake. According to <u>Antisuyo</u>, an old Machiguenga woman had told Savoy of "*great stone ruins at a lake atop a high, cold mountain near the city*" **(1)** and looking at our photo, I was sure I knew exactly where they were. Our original plan would have gotten us there coming down from the Markacocha highlands, but now that was out. Instead, we'd have to look for old roads leading up to the peak from the city or, finding none, bushwhack up through the forest.

Since the ruins were nearby and well known to José, but none of us had any idea how difficult it might be to reach the peak, we decided to try the climb first. The morning after our arrival again dawned clear, so we were up early and off to the mountaintop, or so we thought. The route to where we planned to start up took us through the outskirts of the city, so we got a brief look at Manco's lost capital along the way. It was a marvelous place, completely covered with vines and lush tropical growth, all beneath a green canopy of huge trees a hundred feet overhead. The opening scenes of "Raiders of the Lost Ark" came inescapably to mind. It was exactly the kind of thing we'd all hoped for. An occasional bird or monkey chattering high above was the only sound other than the ring of our machetes. Everywhere, there were stone terraces, walls and tumbled buildings, but the dense brush allowed no sense at all of the relationships between them. Without using a compass, I had no feeling for direction - even the sun being difficult to see most of the time - and distances were meaningless unless carefully paced off and noted. I was struck by how difficult it was going to be to make a decent map of the place, and began to understand why no one yet had.

Leaving the ruins behind, we continued on along a good trail ascending the valley of the Río Chaupimayo beyond the city towards the Markacocha crest, off to the southwest. José said the trail led to the farm of a family named Aragón about a mile up the river, but ended there. He was unaware of any road or trail further upstream, or of any ruins beyond the site Savoy had called Marcanay, in the jungle covered hills across the river from the farm.

Aragón was a delightful place, the exact edge of inhabited Peru as nearly as we could tell. The two thatched huts sat at one end of a large plantation of coffee trees surrounded by dark rain forest. Near the main house was a huge orange tree, heavy with fruit. Sitting in the shade of the porch, watching his pigs eat the fallen oranges, was Señor Aragón, the aged family patriarch. He spoke only Quechua, and after exchanging brief greetings with José, said in all his life he'd never been up our mountain, but he doubted there was anything up there. Wishing us luck, he nevertheless gave us all the oranges we could carry, shook his head and waved goodbye with a wide, toothless grin.

The base of the ridge we planned to climb was a mile farther up the valley and, as José had predicted, there was no sign of a road. Once we started up, the going was steep, buggy and thick, with no water and no breeze. Within minutes, we were soaked with sweat and covered with insect bites and scratches. By late afternoon, we were climbing through the treetops, exhausted and unsure even of where the ground was. The barometer said we'd gained half a mile of altitude, but wherever we looked we saw only green. Not wanting to be caught out in the forest at night, we had no choice and turned back doubly discouraged by how fast we lost all our hard won elevation, slipping and sliding down the cleared track. Back to our tents by dark, we cleaned up, ate a big dinner and decided to give it one more day.

In the morning, we got another early start under cloudless skies and quickly reached our previous high point. We attacked the demonic wall of tangled growth with renewed vigor, but were immediately slowed to a crawl. If anything, it was worse than the day before. None of us had ever seen anything like it and even José was barely getting through. Hours later we'd gained less than 500 feet toward our still unseen goal and realized it was hopeless. Thoroughly beaten, we straggled back into camp with daylight to spare and dampened our defeat with a couple of rounds of *pisco*. By dinnertime, our spirits had returned and we found we were of two minds regarding just how important getting up our mountain really was. A new theory emerged as to how it might be done and Jim Little, Chris, José and one of the locals decided to give it a try. Not wanting to waste any more time, I opted for getting to work in the ruins and Barefoot and Burghard agreed to help.

We all walked to the city together in the morning, again clear, and there the two teams split up. Paul, Barefoot and I spent the morning cutting trails through the buildings, making notes as we went, and trying to get a feel for the place. By lunchtime, it was a lot less intimidating than it had seemed the first day. We'd located several distinct ruin-groups and decided to map each independently, then later relate them to one another. The trail into the city arrived first at a series of fountains by an elaborately channelized creek spanned by a stone bridge, still intact. The principal avenue had apparently crossed the bridge and climbed a gentle slope up into the midst of our groups **(Figure 52)**. We established this avenue as a baseline and related everything to it, cutting only as much brush as was needed to run compass lines and pace them off. The work went quickly and we turned out to be pretty good surveyors.

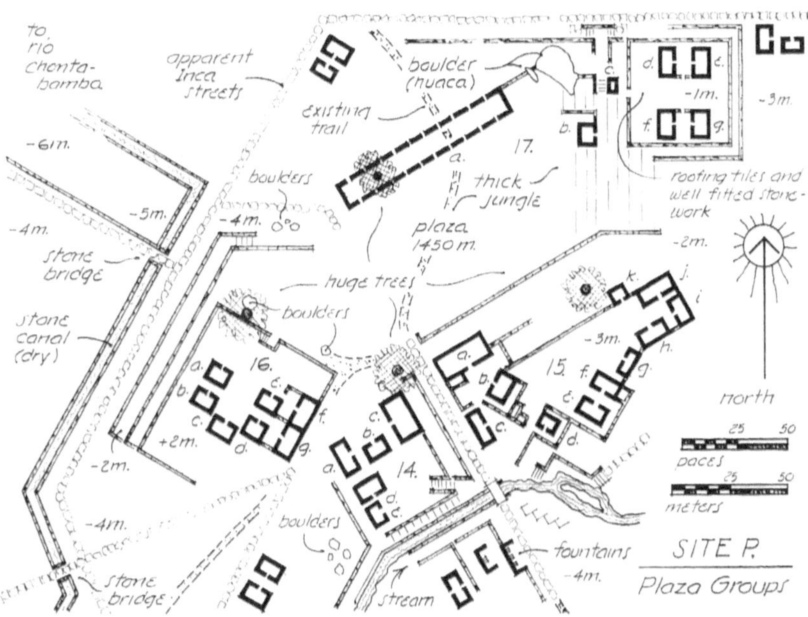

Figure 52 - Plan of the main plaza (Bingham's Eromboni Pampa)

That night, I felt I had a fair idea of the center of the city, though it was little more than a mass of numbers and rough, unrelated sketches in my journal. By flashlight in my tent, I began to piece together the whole on paper. Slowly, the plan of the city emerged and showed itself to be laid out around a large, trapezoidal plaza. **(Figures 49 and 50)** It was a sophisticated arrangement intent on creating an urban center for the apparently sprawling complex. The plaza was entered via the avenue up from the bridge and its far side, some 75 yards away, was defined by the single, large building noted by Bingham and Savoy. At first we'd thought it a long street between two rows of houses, but once cleared, we saw it was one enormous room, 88 yards long and 10 yards wide, with doorways 8 yards apart all the way down both long sides. To the right, at the plaza's north end stood a great isolated boulder of white granite and nearby was a walled-in platform 50 yards square, with four buildings of carefully cut masonry arranged symmetrically about its center. About 170 yards to the south, forming the other end of the plaza, was a raised platform about 50 x 78 yards, with a stairway leading up to a horseshoe-shaped cluster of five buildings still standing head-high. **(Figure 52)** Beyond these large and presumably important structures, other less imposing groups seemed to be scattered in all directions.

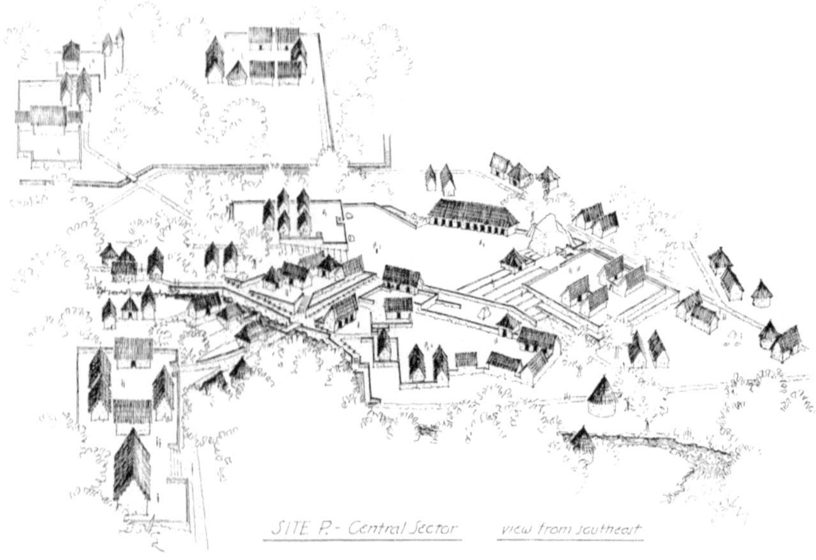

Figure 49 - View of city center

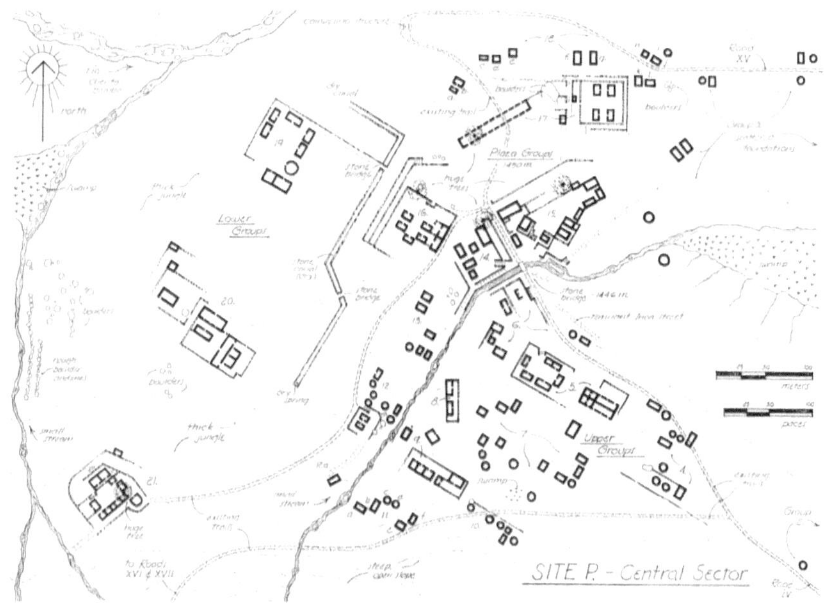

Figure 50 - Site plan of city center

Mapping those outlying areas was our next day's project. We'd figured out a radial search pattern centered on the bridge, knowing that the further we got from the plaza, the more we were likely to miss. What we didn't know was that the site was much bigger than it seemed and there was a lot of stuff out there. We had two more days to do what amounted to a week's work. There was still no sign of Jim's team as I put away my notes and blew out the candle around ten PM. No doubt, they'd not quite reached the top and decided to avoid the long trip back to camp by staying up on the mountain overnight. Surely, I thought, they'd succeed in the morning and bring back a full report the next afternoon.

The fourth of July was yet another beautiful day, and although we missed some important areas, our scheme for exploring the rest of the city turned up scores of new ruins. The good weather was a big factor. Everything we were doing would have been ten times harder slogging around in the rain and mud. Also, the jungle seemed less and less intimidating. At first, all three of us had crept timidly through the growth, imagining a snake under every bush. José had laughed, assuring us *serpientes* were "*no problema*," and whether it was true or not, we were starting to believe it.

By late afternoon, we were mapping Bingham's Tendi Pampa, a compact group more than a quarter mile from the plaza. The roof tiles reported by Bingham and Savoy were scattered around, as they were at several other places in the city. Still standing nearly full height was a two story building with neat rows of pockets inside, where upper floor beams had once rested. Except for the spreading roots of an enormous tree that had swallowed parts of two other structures, the whole place was in pretty good shape. A lovely, sunken fountain with two spouts still graced the open side of a small courtyard near a wall decorated with the only niches in the city showing double jambs, a classically Incan detail reserved for especially important circumstances. **(Figures 55 and 56)**

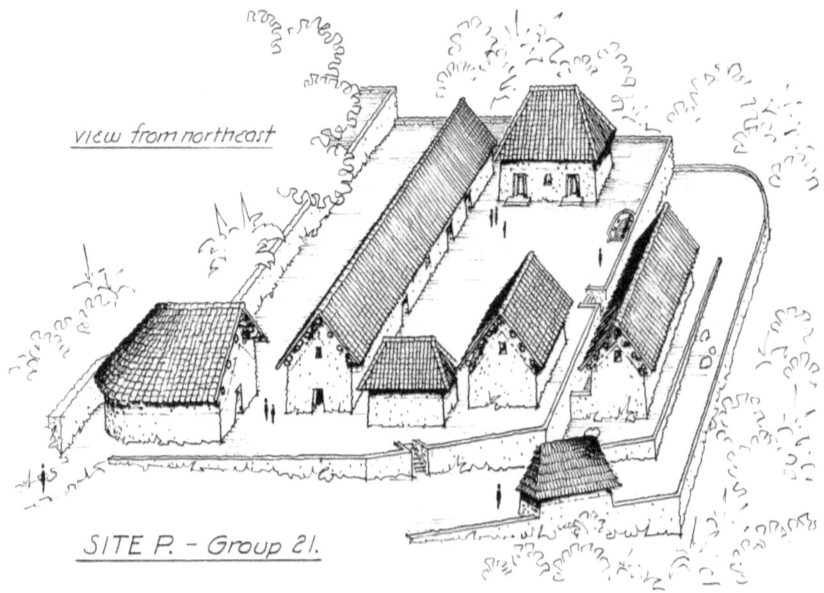

Figure 55 - View of two-story group (Bingham's Tendi Pampa)

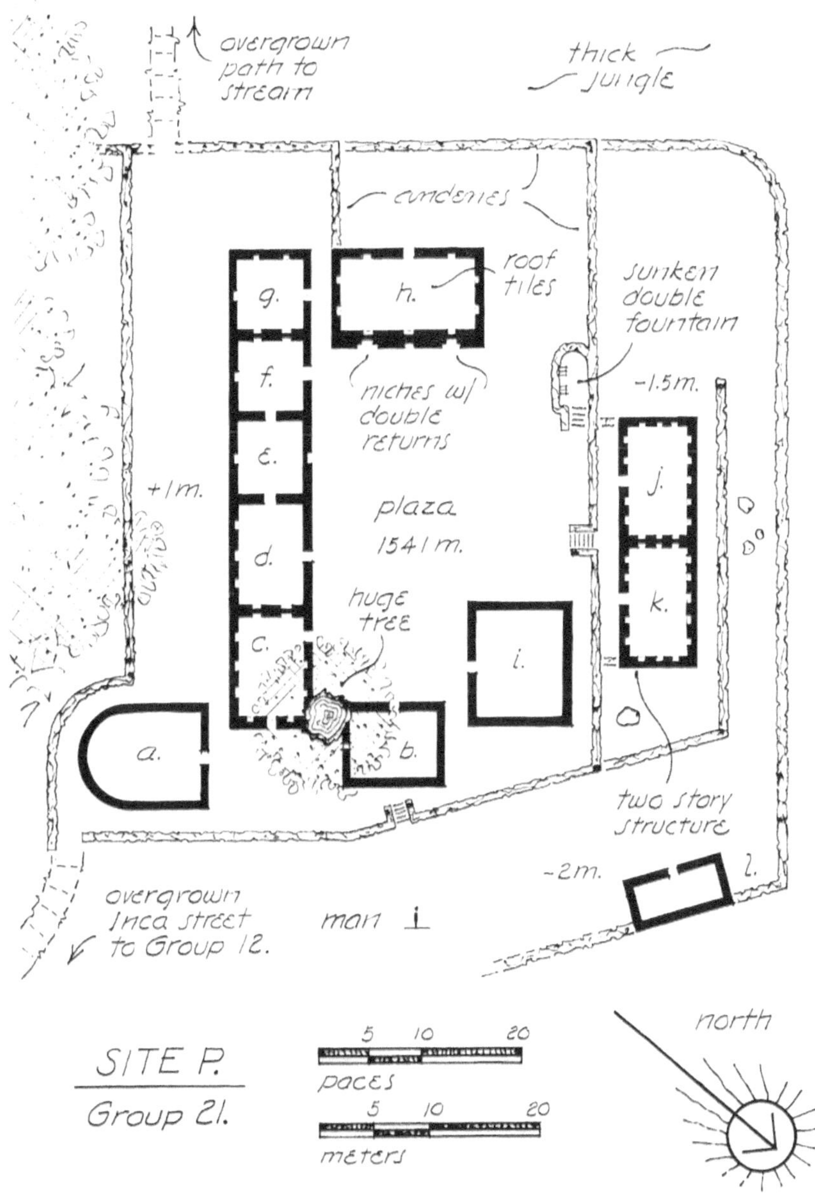

Figure 56 - Plan of two-story group

Back at the plaza, we decided to work our way home by a new route paralleling the Río Chontabamba along the northern edge of the site. Tumbled houses were scattered here and there as much as half a mile from the city center. Murúa described Vilcabamba as long and narrow, exactly as we were finding it. He reported that many crops were grown there, and I thought that probably explained the dispersed ruins throughout the gently sloping forest. In Inca times, it must have been cleared farmland punctuated occasionally by the homes of the workers. Some of those original structures may well have been built entirely of wood and thatch, long since decomposed. If so, many of the "400 houses" counted by Arbieto would never be found unless the whole valley were someday cleared and excavated, a hugely expensive and unlikely prospect.

Jim and his group were waiting when we got back to camp. They looked awful. As we suspected, they'd not gotten to the top the day before, nor, they said, at all. Their new plan was a total bust. Completely spent, they'd sat out the cold mid-winter night just below the ridge at about 8,000 feet, almost a mile above the valley. After what Chris described as "the longest twelve hours of his life," and warmed by the rising sun, they resumed the ascent only to find the top still impossibly far above. There was no way they could get through another night out up there, and at 8,600 feet they turned back with just enough time to get home by nightfall. Sixpac Manco II had been dealt a "cruel blow," as I wrote in my journal that night, but no one could say we hadn't given it our best shot. "*Un dia mas*," said José, by that time as sure as we were that some fabulous lost city lay hidden somewhere up there, just one more day beyond our reach. I thought of the story of Jack and the Beanstalk as I dozed off to sleep.

Lying in the dark, waiting for daylight a few hours later, my thoughts wandered to the aftermath of Savoy's pioneering work in the 60s. Where Bingham had closed the book on further explorations in the Vilcabamba for nearly half a century, Gene had reopened it and stimulated a renewal of interest in the region. Howell and Morrison turned out to be only the first of what was to become a steady stream of outsiders bent on braving the jungle and the guerrillas in search of adventures of their own. Meanwhile, the eye of the media briefly followed Savoy north to Chachapoyas and refocused on his claimed discoveries there. In the Vilcabamba,

Hugo Blanco's rebellion was eventually put down. Unrest nevertheless persisted, culminating in 1968 with the overthrow of the government in Lima by a military *coup* hostile to, among other things, Savoy's many well-heeled friends in the capital. The explorer himself, meanwhile, became implicated in various intrigues and was effectively run out of the country in late 1970. Interest in his city remained, however, and as the new *junta* settled in and conditions in the country normalized, another American expedition arrived on the scene, this one intent on shooting the first movies of the Vilcabamba ever made.

It was 1970, and Frank Paddock, an adventurous Massachusetts doctor, led a small group of friends and family up the Río Vilcabamba just to have a look around - and thus became the first of many tour guides that would in time be drawn to the region. His films of Rosaspata and the surrounding mountains were the earliest hints of the spectacular sights which awaited travelers there. But at Espíritu Pampa, the same problems that had plagued Savoy's still photography limited Paddock's cinematic efforts even more. The ruins came off as dark, dreary, uninteresting piles of overgrown rocks - hardly the stuff of a travel agent's dreams and quite the opposite of the by then vastly popular Machu Picchu.

Paddock's films thus had little impact on visitation to Savoy's city. Before going home, however, the doctor did manage to add something new to the picture. He ascended the Río Guayara from Cobos's farm in Huancacalle and crossed the Choqueto Pass into the drainage of the lower Apurimac River to the southwest. **(Figures 3 and 4)** Aside from a 1959 SWiss mountaineering expedition that had mapped the peaks of the Nevada Panta in and around the pass, **(2)** he was probably the first *gringo* explorer to do so since Christian Bües, half a century earlier. All the way up to the pass, he encountered patches of Inca roadway and at the settlement of Arma, several hours beyond, he found unmistakably Inca ruins . It was the first hint since von Hagen's visit in the 50s that yet another major thoroughfare had radiated from Vitcos in Inca times and further strengthened the idea that the ruined citadel atop Rosaspata had been the early center of Manco's post-Conquest world.

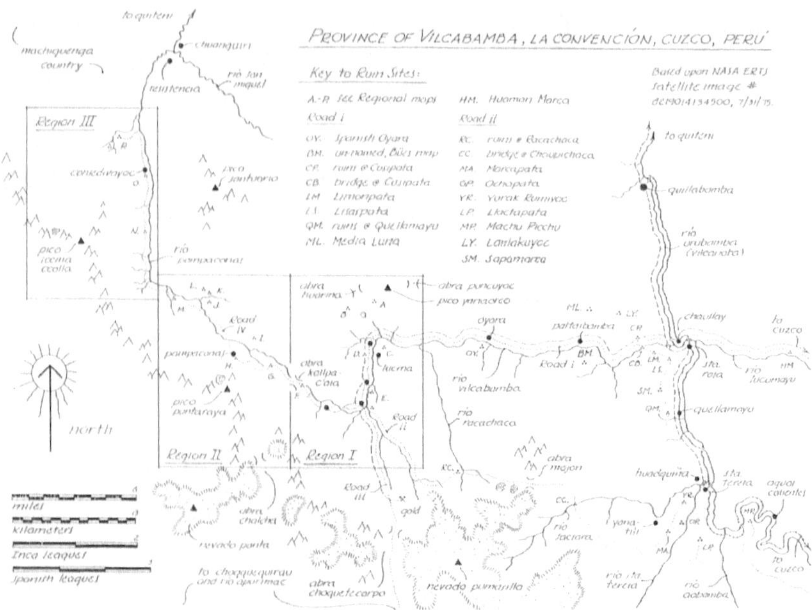

Figure 3 - Map of Province

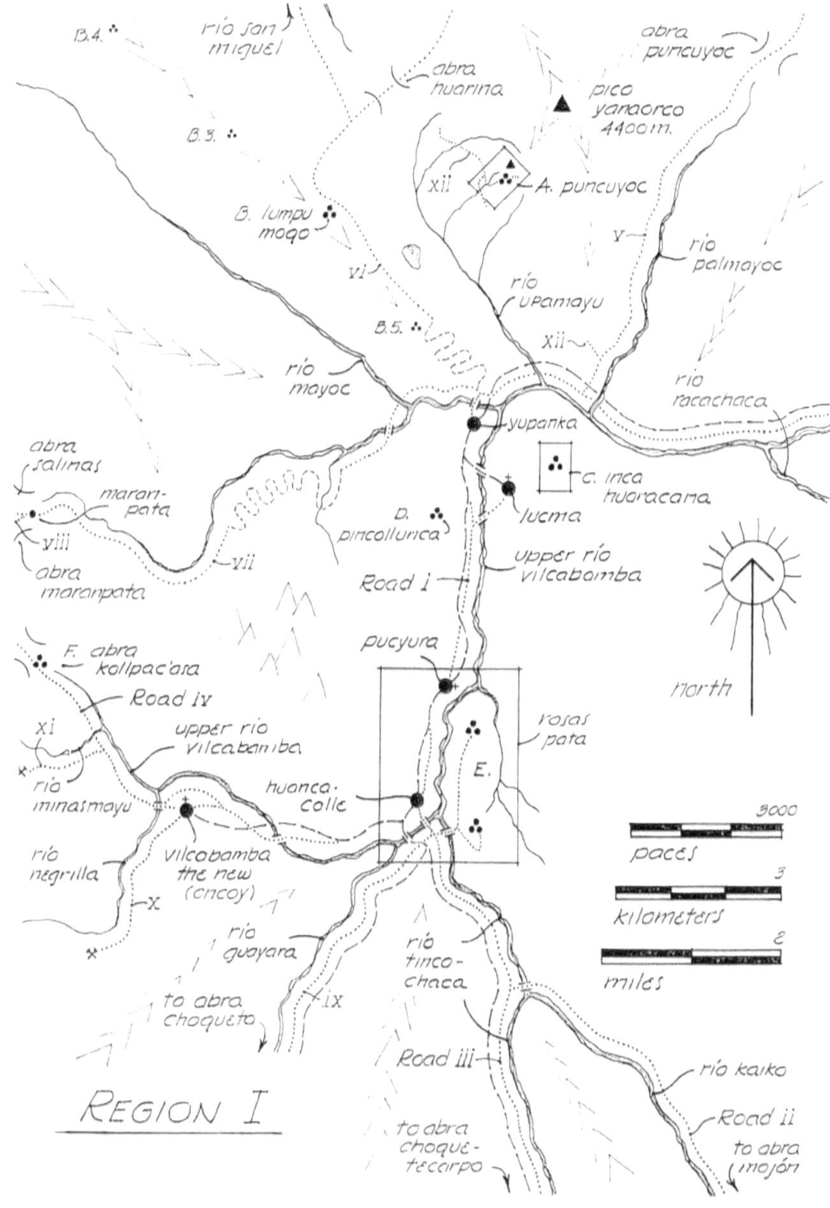

Figure 4 - Map of upper Rio Vilcabamba

At the same time Paddock was wandering the high passes of the remote Andes, John Hemming's publication of The Conquest of the Incas in both London and New York changed everything.

Overnight, everyone with any interest at all in the Incas knew all about Vilcabamba and the efforts of Bingham and, particularly, Savoy to uncover its secrets. Savoy's book, Antisuyo, was released at about the same time, but to a much smaller readership. It struck most scholars as an adventure story of dubious scientific merit and didn't cause much of a stir except among Savoy's fellow explorers. Hemming was another matter. Future Director of the Royal Geographical Society in London, he was a respected historian; a man to be taken seriously. Never mind that, unlike Savoy, he had little first hand knowledge of Vilcabamba. His research, though largely academic, was exhaustive and impeccable. It was he, after all, that turned up the passage in Murúa's then newly available chronicle describing the tile roofs at Vilcabamba the Old - to this day the only bombproof evidence linking the ruins at Espíritu Pampa with the Incas' lost capital. And so, despite his best efforts to give credit where credit was due, it was Hemming, not Savoy, that put Vilcabamba on the map and caused professionals around the world to question Bingham's entrenched notion that Machu Picchu had been the Incas final capital.

Motivated by this and, at least in part, by the irksome publicity Savoy was receiving, Peruvian scholars began to show a belated interest in the final refuge of their illustrious ancestors. Though not, strictly speaking, an explorer at all, since he probably never set foot in Vilcabamba, Peruvian anthropologist Luis A. Pardo was among the earliest of these. Pardo's brief but excellent 1972 summary (in Spanish) of the history of Inca Vilcabamba and its exploration in more recent times added little that was new to the growing store of knowledge about the region. It did, however, bring the story to the attention of a wider audience among his own Spanish-speaking countrymen, several of whom would soon embark upon exploratory expeditions of their own. Regarding Vitcos, his text supported Bingham, but his narrative was illustrated with a quaint and grossly inaccurate 1907 map that showed "Pitcos" (sic) many miles from the historic village of Pucyura. This, in turn, stirred some debate as to the validity of Bingham's long accepted claim that Vitcos had been at Rosaspata. Nearly everyone finally concluded that the old map was simply wrong. Much more interesting was the Peruvian challenger Pardo presented to question Savoy's claim as the discoverer of the lost city at Espíritu Pampa.

"*We received personal information from the Professor Antonio Santander Caselli, who claims to be the rightful discoverer of Vilcabamba the Old,*" he wrote. "*He* (Santander) *exhibits that the 14th of July, 1964, he discovered the mysterious Vilcabamba.*" **(3)**

Santander, we should recall, was a member of Savoy's 1964 expedition and, by his own account, seems to have entered the ruins two days after Savoy. He nevertheless maintained that he had "initiated his explorations five years before" in some unspecified way and thus believed himself due credit for the find. The truth of his claim was never determined, but it would not be the last time Savoy found himself embroiled in controversy as to exactly who went where first.

Most prominent, or at least widely published, of the Peruvians to follow up on Pardo's writings was Victor Angles Vargas, a prolific historian, scholar, author and traveler. During the decade of the 1970s, Angles personally assembled a vast amount of data describing the numerous Inca ruins in and around Cuzco, the Inca heartland. This Spanish language work was first published in 1978 and re-issued ten years later in three large volumes. Copiously illustrated with maps, drawings and photographs, it is probably the most encyclopedic single source of this information currently in print. Others may offer more recent or detailed material regarding particular sites, but Angles covered the entire region, and included a brief section on Vilcabamba.

He ventured as far as Espíritu Pampa and accurately recorded various features there and at Rosaspata along the way. Of the many other ruins in the province, he visited and described only Choquequirau, an interesting but peripheral site which played no known part in the history of Inca Vilcabamba. Though he tended to simply confirm and restate previously established ideas, Angles nevertheless approached the task with a much better understanding of Quechua, the old Inca language, than any of his predecessors. He was also more interested in the role played by the natives in reclaiming the province from the jungle and acting as guides for its increasingly numerous visitors. Through his writings, their contribution came alive, really for the first time.

Angles, for example, properly translated the name of the place Bingham had called "Ñusta España," the big white rock surrounded with ruins and apparently named for a "Spanish princess." Not so, said the locals. Half a century after the famous American had been told essentially the same thing by their grandfathers, they assured the Peruvian that the correct name was Ñusta "Ispanan," Quechua for "the place where the princess urinates." An entirely different matter, this gave possible meaning to a shallow but prominent drainage channel cut into the top of the elaborately carved rock. In his description of Bingham's Chuquipalta, the pious *Padre* Calancha complained that various "abominations" had occurred atop that very same rock in Inca times, (**15**, 796) and Angles' revelation suggested he might have been right. Regardless, it was a good example of how important the meaning of a single word could be in trying to correlate ruins in the field with local traditions and the written record.

But, by far, Angles' most significant insight into the exploration of Inca Vilcapampa was his recognition that the province in general and the city in particular were "extraordinary archaeological repositories," deserving of the same kinds of government protection and study then becoming commonplace at various other, less remote sites. He even advocated building a *carretera*, or auto road, to Espíritu Pampa so that public access to the ruins might be easier and scientific research there encouraged.

Although no such road has yet been built, the years following Angles' Vilcabamba visit were to see great improvements in access to the region. The road up to Huancacalle greatly simplified travel to and from the railroad, and thus Cuzco and the world. From Quillabamba, a similar route was hacked from the jungle down the Urubamba to an outpost shanty town called Quiteni, and from there up the tributary Río Cosireni to the tiny settlement at Chuanguiri, a single day's walk down the Río Consevidayoc from Espíritu Pampa. (**Figure 1**)

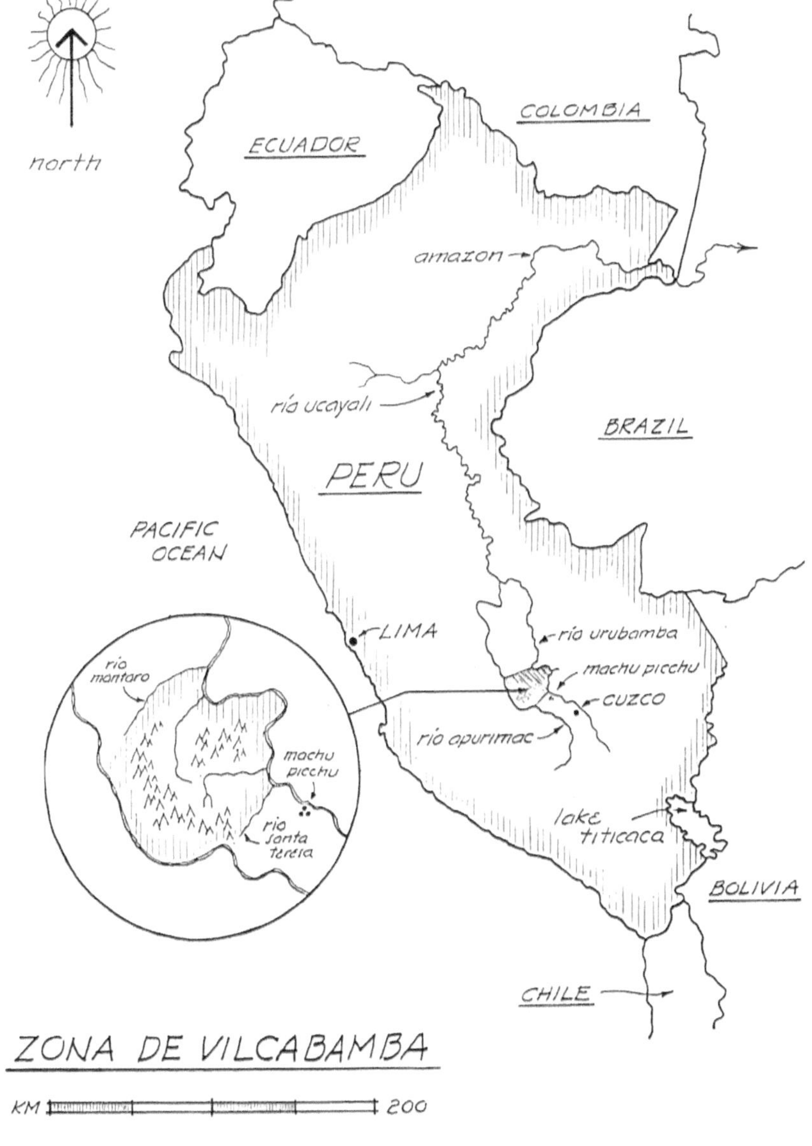

Figure 1 - Location Map

All that road building might have precipitated a flood of visitors and immigrants to the region but for one thing; fear. Despite a decade of relative tranquility, the old grievances of Hugo Blanco and others had never really gone away. The country was still run by an oligarchy with little interest in the common people. By the early 1980s, the fanatics of the Shining Path had begun their Maoist campaign to bring down the old order. Their headquarters in the Department of Ayacucho was just across the yawning chasm of the Apurimac River from Vilcabamba. Few trails crossed from one side to the other, but the *guerrillas* controlled them all. Roving Sendero Patrols began causing enough trouble that the government sent in the Army. The *campesinos* laid low, hoping the whole thing would blow over and both unwanted intruders would go home. Neither did, and the locals were tragically caught in the middle. Most travelers wisely vacationed elsewhere - all, that was, except the crazy ones like Sixpac Manco.

Crazy ones there were, though, and all through the late 70s and early 80s a scattering of *gringos* showed up at Cobos's farm in search of - what? Adventure, mostly, but there were notable exceptions, as I learned to my considerable dismay. Despite my best efforts to find out everything there was to know about Vilcabamba before coming back, the work of several key players escaped me completely - Francescutti, for example. Unknown to me or any of the others, our paths were on collision courses and it was only a matter of time until we were to meet, head-on. Much as it first looked like the field was all mine, I was fated to have lots of interesting company as I delved deeper into the mysteries of the Incas' last stronghold.

By the mid-1980s a few of these new players would appear, but like everyone else who'd gone to Vilcabamba since Raimondi, they'd be handicapped by the lack of any solid documentation from those who'd gone before. Despite all the effort that had gone into discovering the elusive lost city and all the hoopla and controversy over the years about who'd found what, no one - not even everyone taken together - had bothered to keep, let alone publish, a complete, accurate record of what they'd found. Bingham came closest, but he understandably became preoccupied with Machu Picchu. The best of his Vilcabamba material remained unfinished and buried in the archives at Yale. After more than a century of exploration, there still wasn't an accurate map of the province. Aside from Bingham's material, Harth-terré's second-hand drawings for Savoy and a couple of sketches by Victor Angles Vargas, there were no drawings of the ruins at all. Yet anyone serious about piecing together the bewildering jigsaw puzzle that was Inca Vilcabamba needed to have all the pieces, or at least all those that were known, laid out on the table. It couldn't be done. Theories abounded, but no one was playing with a full deck. Lying there in the dark, waiting for dawn, I told myself - that, at least, was about to change.

It was our last day at Espíritu Pampa. The horses were needed up-river and José had to leave right after breakfast. We figured to take a leisurely trip back to Huancacalle on our own, continuing the search for Marcanay and the Old Fort as we went. Glancing up into the clear sky as he turned to leave, José shook his head and said, only half joking, that Tupac Amaru Inca must surely be watching over us. Never in his memory had *gringos* enjoyed so much good weather in the Vilcabamba. In fact, his experience was quite the opposite. Outsiders, he said, generally brought rain as the Incas tried to hide their secrets from prying, alien eyes. To us, it sounded like just another quaint myth, but José and his fellow *campesinos* took such things seriously and, lucky for us, saw our good fortune as a sign that the spirits approved of our efforts.

Jim and Chris slept in and planned to wander down to the ruins later in the day, after a much-needed rest. Paul decided to hike back to Huancacalle by himself to see some additional sights and work on his Spanish. Barefoot and I, meanwhile, had one more area to search and headed back into the ruins for one last day of exploring. We headed straight out the trail to Alogón, bypassing the plaza area. As always, we were noting distance and direction and looking for ruins along the way. About a half-mile beyond the city, our path rounded a high, open corner before plunging down into the forest again. We'd recalled some rocks strewn about the bend in the trail as we'd passed several days earlier and decided to have a look around. Not more than ten feet into the bush was a large building with two doorways, still six feet high and made of well cut granite blocks. Nearby, we found seven other buildings and several walls and terraces. (**Figure 57**, Buildings 23a-i) This group was more than a mile from the buildings we'd mapped the previous afternoon - additional evidence that Vilcabamba really was the "metropolis of the jungle" the Spaniards claimed.

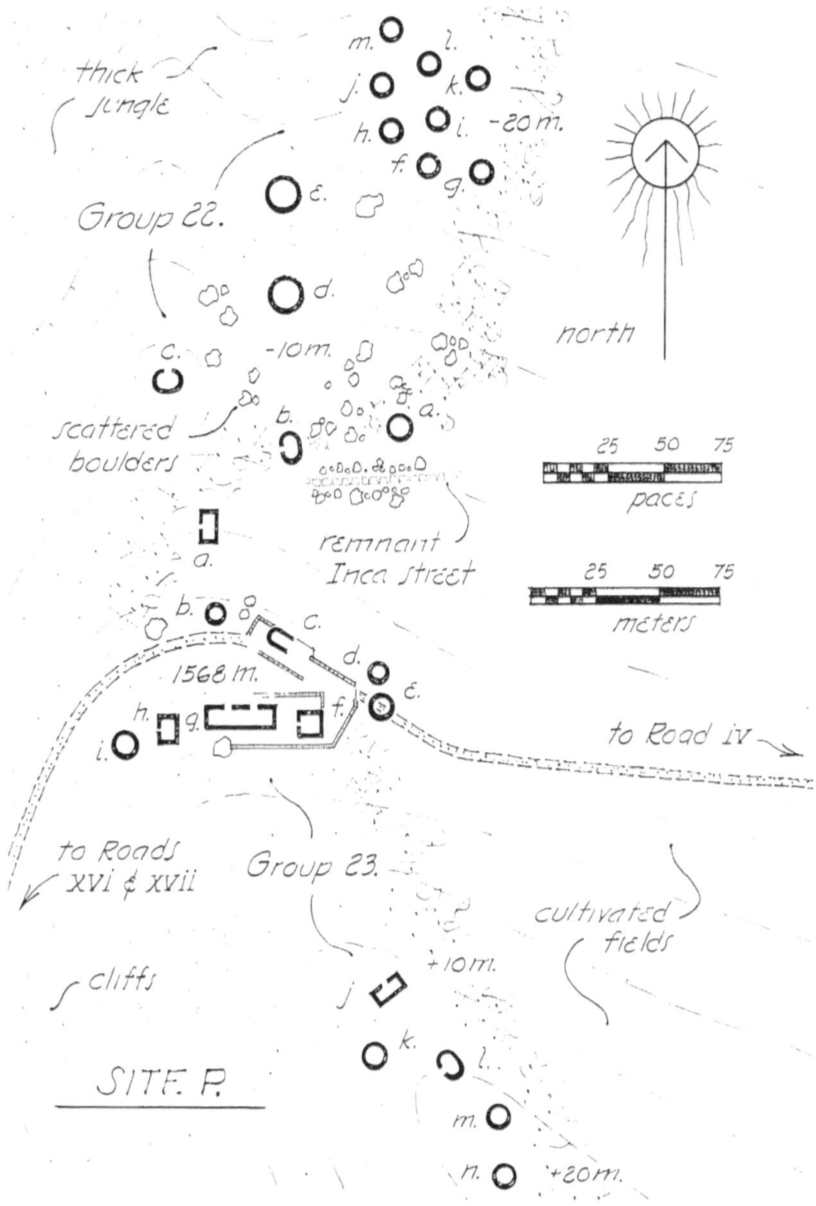

Figure 57 - Site plan of outlying groups

The site Savoy called Marcanay, at least a half-mile farther on and across the Chaupimayo, was our next destination. We weren't sure how to get there, but José had nodded towards the far side of the river when we'd asked him about it on the first day. Neither of us could remember the exact place, but thought it had been somewhere downstream from the Río Yurakmayo, a swift, turbulent tributary coming down from the heights to the east. We dropped off the trail and searched the swampy bank of the Chaupimayo for signs of a path or crossing of some sort, but found nothing. Continuing upstream, we crossed the mouth of the Yurakmayo on huge boulders deposited there by past floods. Not far beyond, the main trail switched back down from a cliff and passed within a few yards of the river. The place seemed familiar and both of us realized it was where José had said to cross.

After fording the icy, waist-deep current, we began searching the far bank for the site. Above a steep bluff rising 25 feet out of the water, the country was flat and the vegetation less thick than along the shoreline. Almost immediately, we came onto a cluster of strangely oval-shaped foundations, with walls connecting them to several large boulders. (**Figure 58**, Buildings 24a-e) We assumed it was the same place Savoy had found on the way to Marcanay and Mananhuañunca and if so, we were short on time. He said it was another hour, at least, up to the ruins. Together with the time it would take us to check them out and backtrack home, it was an hour more than we had. Much as I wanted to go anyway and take our chances with the daylight, Barefoot pointed out that Savoy's hour assumed you knew where the ruins were. We didn't, and might well spend the time plus some and still not find anything. I had to admit he was right, so we hastily cleared and mapped the buildings at hand and headed reluctantly back to camp.

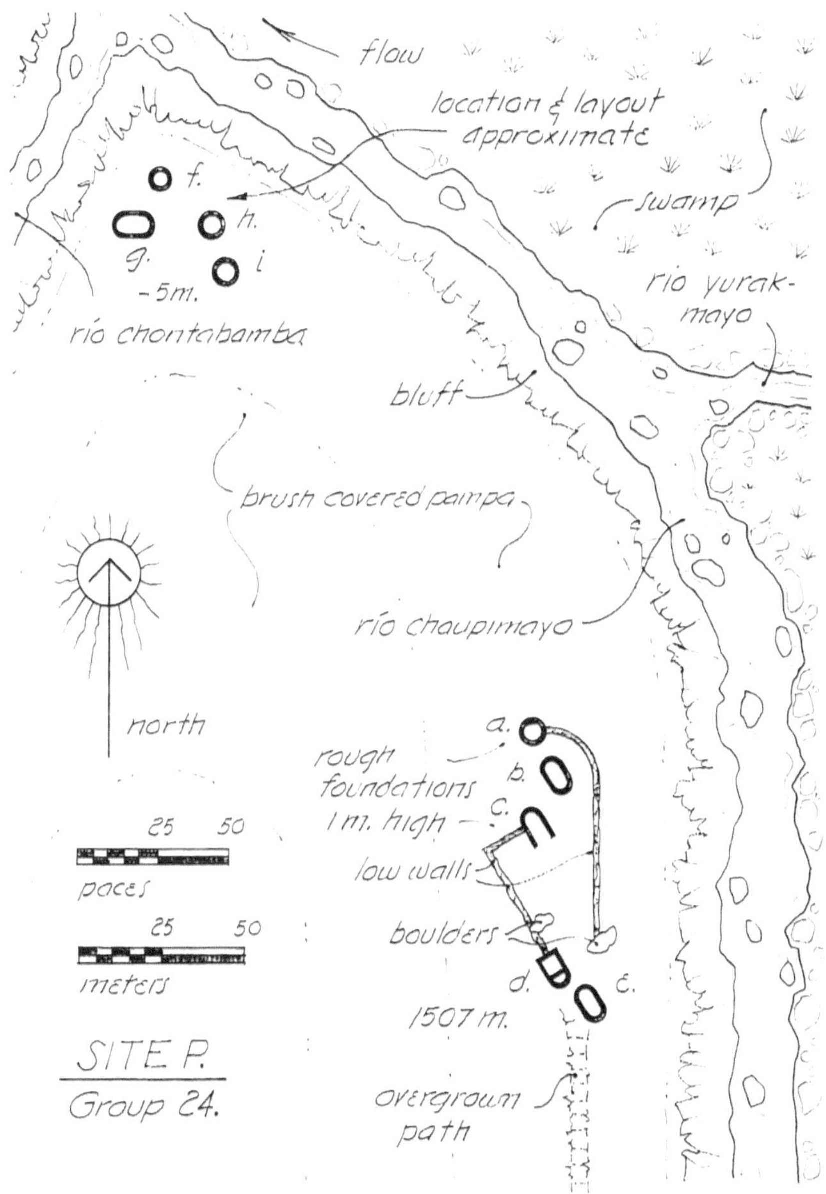

Figure 58 - Non-Inca groups across river

Inevitably, the return trip went much faster than expected and we arrived at the tents with almost an hour of daylight to spare. I was fuming, certain that we could have gotten to Savoy's sites after all. I was about to launch into a tirade when Jim and Chris appeared. They told how they'd gone into the city and, among other things, cleared every scrap of moss and vegetation from the giant boulder or *huaca* stone at the north end of the plaza. It was uncarved, they said, but beautiful nonetheless, and impressive in its prominent situation. Hold on, I thought. Maybe there was a way to salvage the day, after all. By then, there wasn't more than a half hour of light left, but I couldn't resist the idea of running back down there to have a look for myself. Fifteen minutes later, I stood panting before the rock. It gleamed white in the premature dusk of the forest and was indeed majestic. The side facing the plaza curved slightly, like a shallow orchestra shell, and was angled so that a speaker standing before it would be heard clearly by an assembled crowd. I was reminded of the so-called "sacred rock" at Machu Picchu, which some experts thought a backdrop for orators or story tellers. The silence was total in the forest twilight, and I wondered when powerful words had last echoed there. It was easy to imagine the spirits of the Incas, gathered still, waiting for the speaker to begin. The Plain of Ghosts, indeed.

There's something about an abandoned city, especially one overgrown and in ruins, that forces even the most superficial tourist to contemplate mortality. All around are reminders of people who thought their world would go on forever, just like we do. They were wrong, just as we'll be, one day. It ought to be depressing, or sobering, at least, but it somehow isn't. Instead, it is liberating and encourages a long, no nonsense view of life. Something similar accounts, I think, for the appeal of distant galaxies, dinosaurs and high-risk sports.

Moved by it all, I climbed up on top of the house-sized boulder and deposited another tell-tale film can - this one containing a Sixpac Manco logo imprinted on a scrap of cloth, a large Peruvian coin and a written promise to Tupac Amaru Inca that, with plans and sketches, I'd do my best to bring his forgotten city back to life. Crouching atop the rock, I was already considering how to make good on that pledge when an eerie screech somewhere off in the near-darkness jolted me back to a more immediate problem -

getting out of there. I slid down and started picking my way nervously back through the ruins, my eyes gazing ahead without focusing - letting the rods and cones do their jobs, just like they taught me in the Marines.

Since our group had been split up on July 4th, we decided to celebrate a day late even though paul and José were already gone. We asked some of José's friends to join us, cracked open the *pisco* and boiled up several pots full of freeze-dried cheese *enchiladas*. The kerosene stove had given out, so we sat around an open fire, took turns stirring the pot and nipped on the bottle. Later, we "struck the colors," folded Gene Savoy's flag and shot off one of our red emergency flares - not a bad way to wrap things up.

8

A Star In The Forest

We left for Consevidayoc early the next morning, hoping to have most of the day to pursue the several leads we'd turned up there coming downstream. By mid-morning we were camped in the school yard, next to the canal, chatting with the locals. They were interested in our theories about Marcanay, but they insisted there were no ruins nearby. Chris and I decided to trace the little watercourse upstream to its source, while Jim Little and Barefoot stayed in camp. At first, the canal was just a ditch dug into the hillside, but as we followed it further, it became a carefully built channel cut from the living rock of a sheer cliff. At one point, the face of the cut was at least 40 feet high and entirely chiseled from solid bedrock. We continued on to the Río Sarahuasi where the canal began, but found no evidence of constructed work. Any that might once have existed there had long since washed away. Still, it was clear that someone had once provided Consevidayoc with an elaborate water supply system. We hurried back to camp, eager to share our find with the others

Barefoot greeted us with even more exciting news. He'd gone into the jungle just below the soccer field to relieve himself and accidentally fallen into a pit filled with brush. As he tried to climb out, he noticed it was actually a stone ruin of some sort. Once he'd cleared away some of the growth, he found it was an oval-shaped foundation about 20 by 30 feet, built of field stones set in clay. So, there were ruins after all. I was glad, but not overly surprised. The *bosque* was incredibly thick and covered with sharp thorns. We eventually found two more buildings, but they were so tumbled and overgrown, they were all but invisible in the uninviting gloom of the thickets. Without careful clearing and study, they seemed no more than natural outcrops of loose fieldstones. It was no wonder they'd gone unappreciated by the *campesinos*.

After clearing away enough foliage to take a few photos in the rapidly failing daylight, we did a quick search around the school yard for additional signs of ruins. Here and there were suggestive mounds of scattered rocks and lines of half-buried stones, but nothing conclusive. It seemed as if an earlier town-site had been obliterated by the clearing and leveling of the school yard and soccer field, which together covered a large area exactly between the canal and the ruins **(Figure 46)**. We turned in sure that there'd once been a larger settlement all around us. If so, its tropical climate, agricultural aspect and location, two hours upstream from Vilcabamba, all matched closely the Spaniards' descriptions of Marcanay. What else could it have been?

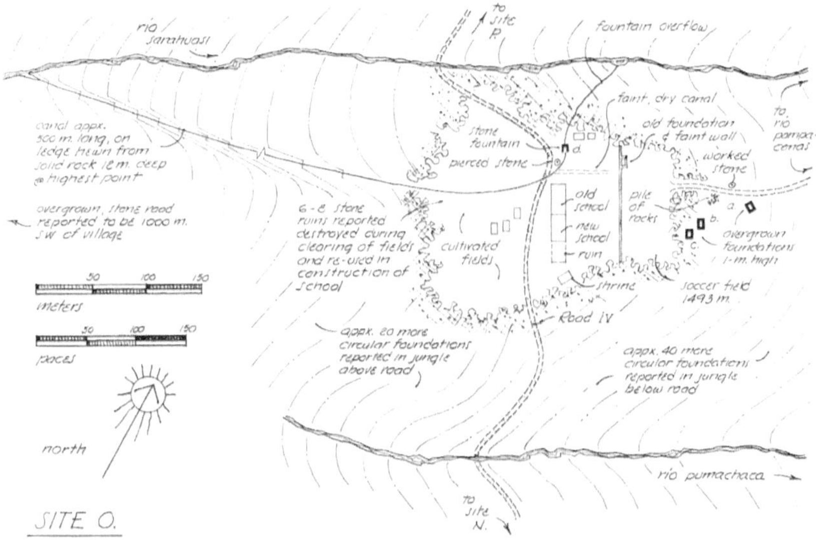

Figure 46 - Map of Consevidayoc (probable site of Marcanay)

Unbelievably, the next morning dawned clear for the twelfth consecutive day. Even the high peaks were open, revealing a spectacular view of Icma Coya directly up the Río Pumachaca behind town. The head-shaped profile of its summit crag stood in bold relief, like a thousand-foot-high granite bust of some primitive mountain god - which, of course, is exactly what it was. It seemed a final bit of evidence in support of our idea that the village had been an important place in Inca times. The *pampa* of Consevidayoc is the only place along the road below Tambo from which the *apu*, or sacred peak, of Icma Coya can be seen. It was hard to believe the Indians wouldn't have made some use of the vantage point it provided.

Our next objective was Machu Pucara - the Old Fort. I still thought it had to be somewhere between the serpentine Río Tunquimayo and Vista Alegre, probably closer to the former. **(Figure 44)** We must have missed it, somehow, on our way downriver. By noon, we'd set up camp in a tiny clearing near the Río San Guillermo, about an hour below Vista Alegre, and were methodically checking every defensible terrain feature in the area. We found nothing. Then, late in the day, one place, especially, struck me as the perfect site for an ambush. For 50 or 60 yards, the trail squeezed along a narrow ledge between steep bluffs into the river and cliffs rising vertically to a craggy hilltop, smothered in jungle. This has got to be the place, I thought, thrashing up through the rocks and tangled growth toward the summit. Every foot of hard won elevation got me more excited. By the time I reached the crest, I fully expected to find the lost fortress - but, instead, I nearly fell off the other side. What looked from below like a level area on top, turned out to be a long, thin flake of stone, horizontal in profile, but so narrow there was no place even to stand, let alone build a fort. Disappointed, I went home in the dark for the second time in three days - something I was starting to get good at.

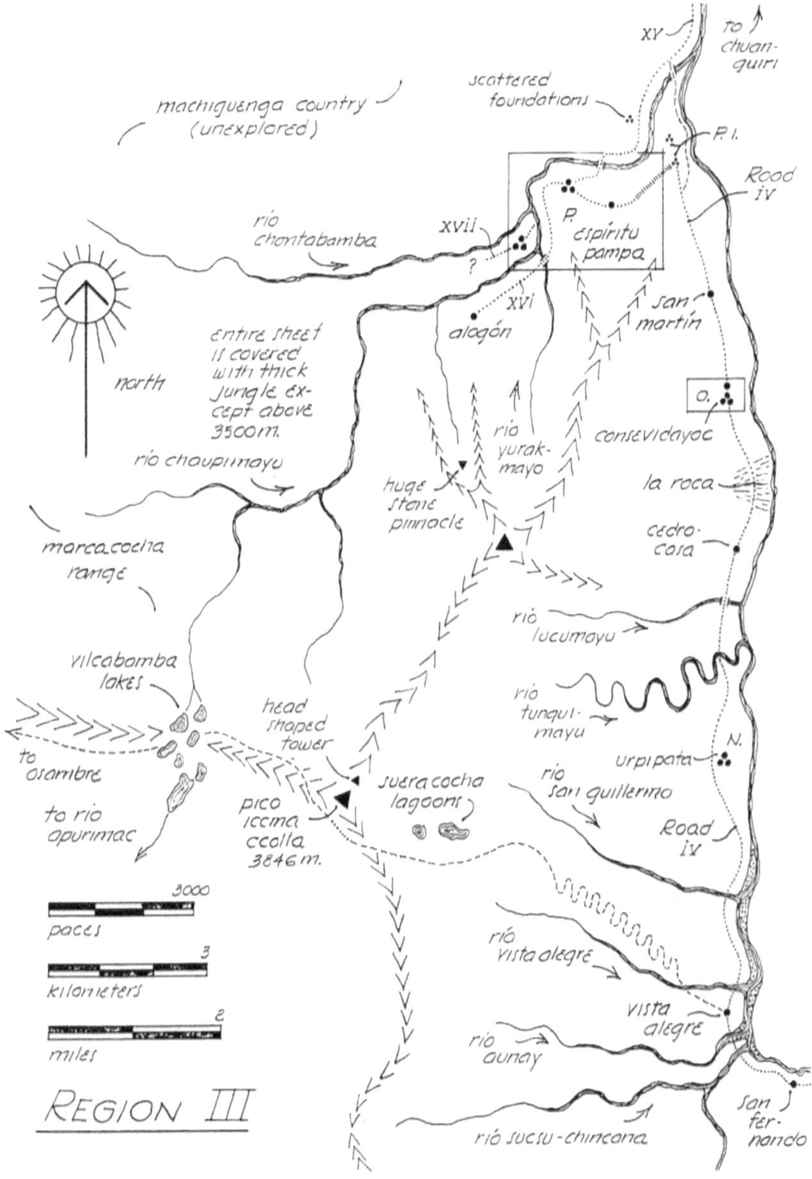

Figure 44 - Map of lower Rio Pampaconas

All the next day, we kept looking, but still found nothing. As we sat drinking coffee by the fire the second night, I was depressed - actually angry. Scarcely four days of food remained in our packs and we had to leave for Tambo the next morning. I didn't want to go home without all three of the missing sites identified. Walking into the darkness up the trail to work off my frustrations, I felt betrayed by Tupac Amaru, our guardian angel. He'd allowed us to find all his secrets but this one. How, I thought, was I to make good on my promise to bring his world back to life if I couldn't find it all? Machu Pucara had to be somewhere nearby, if only the Inca would drop me a hint as to where. Half expecting a star to fall in the forest and show me the way, I went to bed even more irritated when no such sign was given.

While we were getting ready to leave in the morning, a large pack string passed through our camp en route upriver. Some of the horses shied from our partly disassembled tents and strange *gringo* gear and there was a bit of a rodeo as the *campesinos* tried to coax them on towards Vista Alegre. One of the latter, a youngster, stopped at our fire and lingered while his companions disappeared up the trail. After an awkward moment of wondering what he wanted, I left my packing and struck up a conversation. He was a relative of my friend Luque, he said, and lived nearby. Why were we there, he asked? I explained that we were looking for ruins and asked if he knew of any thereabouts. "*No*," he said. "*No hay*," there aren't any. Again disappointed, I was about to bid him *ciao* and get back to my packing when he added that the only ruins he knew of were at a place called Urpipata, about a mile back down the trail.

That was it! The Old Fort must be at Urpipata! The boy couldn't delay long enough to take us there, but described the ridge on which the fort stood and told how to get there before hurrying off to join his friends. Why had he lingered at our camp? Was his the clue I'd asked Tupac Amaru to provide? It was incredible! Excited, we abandoned our packing, grabbed our *machetes* and ran back down the trail in search of Urpipata. Jim Little thought it was down the first ridge we came to that fit the boy's description, and down he went. Chris and I thought it might be the second, but ended up going down the third. Expecting instant success, we'd brought no food or water and, after several hours of cutting down a steep, brushy ridge, we realized our mistake. We were badly dehydrated and the nearest water was the Río Pampaconas, still far below. We'd found no ruins.

Success, it seemed, had slipped through our fingers. Exasperated, we continued to the river, slithering down jungle covered cliffs for the last hundred feet or so.

Refreshed by a swim, a rest, and lots to drink, we began to backtrack up the hill. My altimeter said we'd lost nearly 1,000 feet, but we made good time on our cleared trail. We looked everywhere for ruins, old roads or any sign at all of human activity, but found nothing. It was late when we regained the trail. Hungry, tired and thoroughly disgusted, we headed back toward camp. As we approached the second ridge, the one we'd by-passed in the morning, we both wondered if maybe it was the one we should have taken. Chris said maybe so, but he was going on to camp. He was beat. Me too, but I was even more obsessed with finding the damned fort, if there was any chance at all. I figured I had at most one hour of daylight left. I promised Chris I'd go no more than half an hour off the trail before turning back and crashed off into the bush alone.

After twenty minutes of hard cutting, there it was! Completely buried under tons of vines, creepers and rotted vegetation were two 15 by 30 foot buildings inside a walled compound 12 paces wide and 43 long. The ruins crowned a steep hilltop, accessible only by a sharp, 150-yard long crest running back toward the road. **(Figure 45)** The effect was a bit like that of a little rectangular castle with two towers and only one, very restrictive approach. All that was missing was a drawbridge. On the theory that there might be more, I cut a line several hundred feet down each face of the hill but found nothing else. Back up on the ridge, it was nearly dusk and visibility was fading fast, so I sketched a quick plan of the fort in my journal and hurried back out to the trail. Less than 50 yards on towards camp, a small creek gurgled across the path. It was dark by the time I got there, but who cared? I was so thirsty, I gulped drink after drink, sight unseen. It must have been the water supply for the fort, I guessed, but it was hardly the "river" the chronicles had led me to expect. Never mind that. I'd found the last of the missing sites, and that was what counted. Picking my way back to camp by starlight, I was a happy camper.

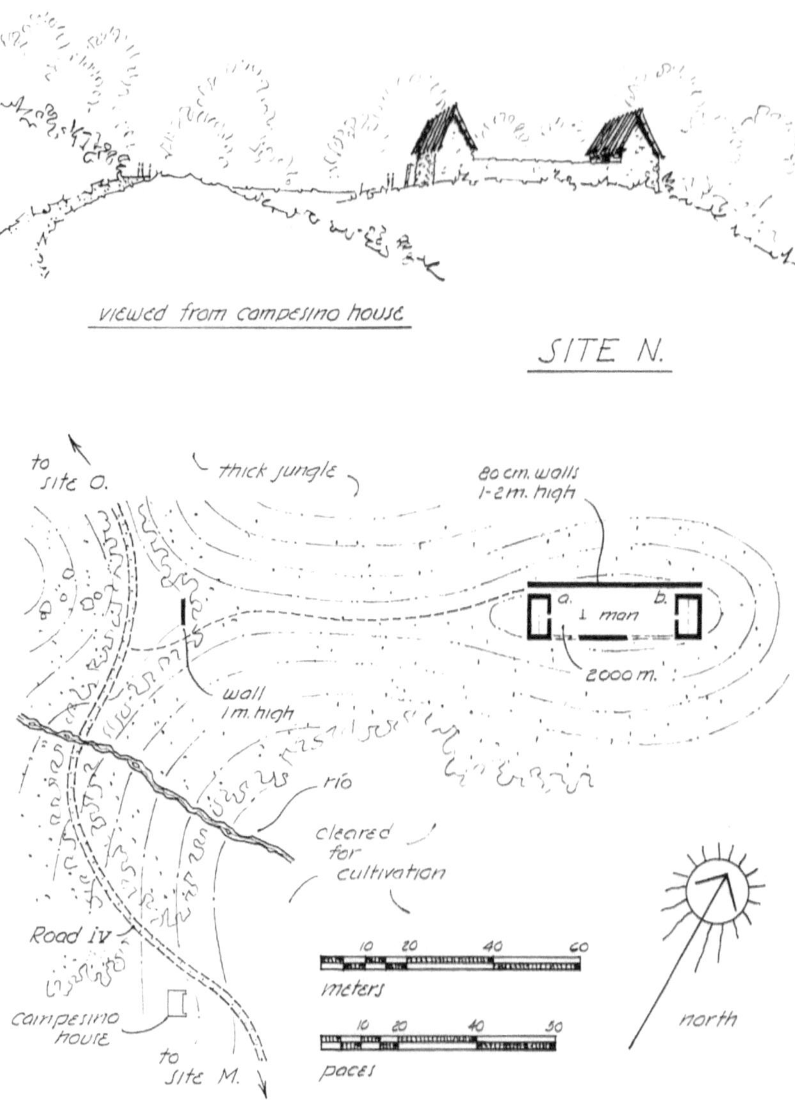

Figure 45 - Site plan and view of Urpipata (probable site of Machu Pucara)

Hiking up the trail towards Tambo the next morning, I thought how everything about the Old Fort seemed to fit. It was a strong position, well sited for defense. On the down side, it had no secure water supply and was too small to accommodate a very large garrison. Not surprisingly, it had been taken easily in 1572 by the Spaniards' overwhelming force. Probably built as a fortified *tampu*, a sort of way-station used by the Incas to accommodate and control traffic along their roads **(1)**, it was likely never intended to withstand a concerted siege. Unlike the ruins at Tambo, its classically Incan design and construction suggested it had been built long before the final Spanish invasion. Possibly, that accounted for its name, the "Old" Fort.

As we approached Tambo, I realized that, despite their many differences, both sites used the terrain in much the same way. Both were on hilltops accessible only via long, narrow crests, steep on both sides. That way, few attackers could easily get close enough to do damage at any one time. No doubt it was a scheme that worked well in the face of arrows and sling-stones, but long-range firearms would have been another matter, entirely. Just as steel swords, armor and horses had beaten the Incas on the battlefield, cannon and arquebus fire had made their fortifications obsolete. Even so, I was glad no enemies held the heights towering above the narrowest part of the trail as we edged beneath Huayna Pucara. Slogging up the final slope to the farm nearest the fort, we were greeted by its owners, Señor Huaman and his wife. They showed us where there was water and offered us the flattest part of their little farmyard for our camp.

A spectacular place, it commanded a view of the entire lower Pampaconas Canyon, with Pico Icma Coya floating on a cloud layer high above. We even erected a flagpole and ran up Gene Savoy's colors just at sundown. While I was fiddling with the flag, the rest of the crew lined up at mock attention and saluted. The Huamans loved it and were proud, they said, that their ruins were so important. They showed us some walls being used to house their pigs and explained that they'd been uncovered when the land was being cleared for cultivation, years earlier. Interestingly, they were the remains of typically Incan houses, unlike anything at Huayna Pucara, just across the slope.

Maybe Huaman's farmyard had once been an Inca *tampu*, I thought, like the Old Fort. It was in the right place, about midway between

Pampaconas and Urpipata, and an easy day's walk from either. It had good water and pasture for llamas and, after four centuries, wasn't the place still called Tambo? Of course! The whole layout of the old thoroughfare between Vitcos and Vilcabamba the Old was suddenly clear. Except in wartime, the Incas liked to travel at a leisurely pace, moving only half a day between stop-overs. Their way stations, or *tampus*, were typically laid out with that in mind **(2)** - just as they seemed to be between Rosaspata and Espíritu Pampa. Then as now, travelers had likely stopped at the sites of Vilcabamba the New, Pampaconas and Conservidayoc - and Tambo and Urpipata, I now realized, exactly filled the gap between the last two. **(Figure 1)**

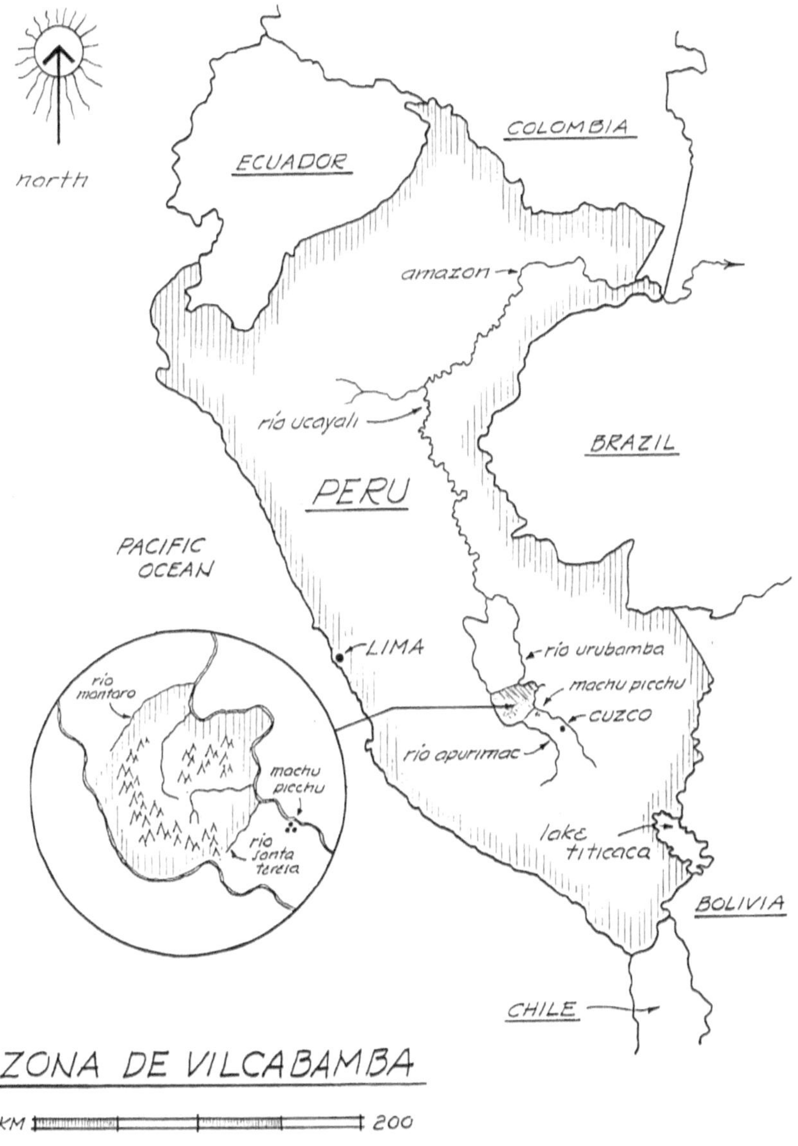

Figure 1 - Location Map

We slept late the next day, cooked the last of our breakfasts and set out for the ruins about noon, again in bright sunshine. Barefoot and I decided to clear both of the platforms in order to get accurate measurements and see if we could find evidence that the "four small towers" reported by General Arbieto had been located there. Chris and Jim Little went on up to the hilltop to study the ruins there in detail. After several hours, we'd completed work on the platforms and found many walls and foundations, stairways and terraces. Some of the foundations might have been circular towers, but nothing much was still standing above ground level and it was hard to be sure. Probably the Spaniards, mindful that their only line of retreat lay directly below the fort, destroyed it utterly after their victory. Whatever the explanation, we found none of the debris piles commonly caused by the natural deterioration of a site.

The ruins up on the hilltop were more of the same and I spent the rest of the day mapping the entire ridge. A detail associated with the little meadow at the very summit caught my eye. The approach to the meadow from the cluster of houses below followed a narrow crest for about 25 yards. Partway out, it had been cut with a shallow moat, only a few feet wide and carefully lined with stones. The gap wasn't big enough to be a physical barrier, but instead must have had some social or religious purpose. Across the gap, only three foundations fronted onto the meadow, near the center of which stood the isolated boulder. (**Figure 43**, Group 3) The whole arrangement had about it the feel of a sacred precinct, reserved for the chiefs, priests or important activities or occasions. Despite the fact that everything about the site suggested non-Inca origins, the prominent boulder was featured in much the same way as its larger counterparts at both Vitcos and Vilcabamba the Old. As a rock lover, I felt among kindred spirits at all three places.

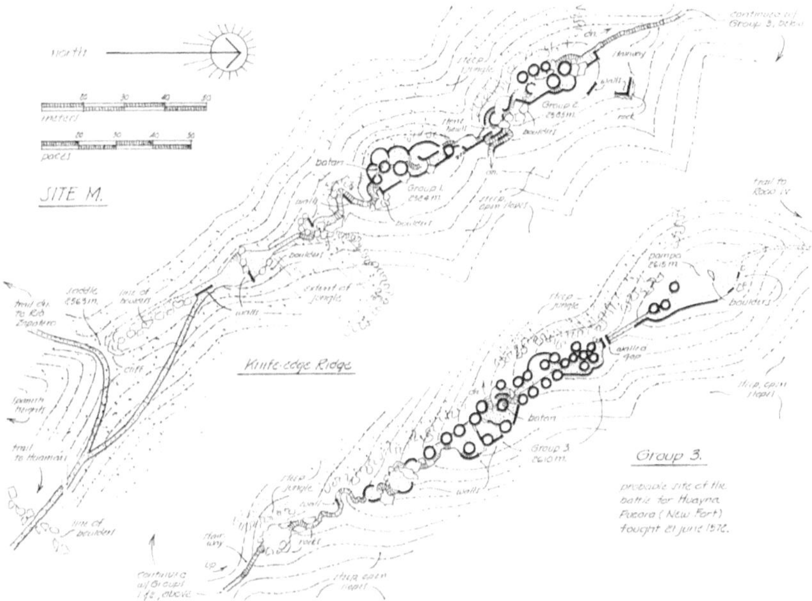

Figure 43 - Site plan of Tambo (probable site of Huayna Pucara)

What is it about rocks, I wonder? In my own vaguely pagan way, I think of stone as much more than just an old fashioned building material. In the high mountains, or among the desert canyons of the American southwest, it reveals itself as the eternal substance of the Earth, a skeleton barely draped with a thin, fleeting veneer of life. No one knows exactly what the Incas and their neighbors thought about it, but my guess is they felt pretty much the same way. The proud glacial erratics scattered all through the Andes were revered as reminders of Pacha Mama, Mother Earth - literally the mother-of-all boulders - their (and our) home, after all.

The meaning of the carvings is harder to imagine. Clearly, at the many sites like Ñusta Ispanan, they had great, if enigmatic, significance. Elsewhere, in more rustic surroundings, they may have been no more than the leavings of apprentice masons, aspirants to a trade likely regarded as a proud calling among their elders. The great white monolith featured so prominently at Espíritu Pampa, however, must have seemed truly a gift from the gods. Like the Incas themselves, he was a highland wanderer come to rest in the forest, many miles from his origins in the distant crags. His choice of a home may have inspired theirs as well and possibly gave rise to its name, Vilcapampa, the sacred plain.

The next day, July 11th, we returned to the ruins to tie up a few loose ends before heading upriver. By noon, we were packed up and getting ready to go when Señora Huaman greeted us with a pot of coffee and a large bowl of steaming *yuca.* We looked so thin, she said, she'd taken pity on us and fixed us a treat. She was right. We'd been low on food since leaving Espíritu Pampa and were a scraggly looking outfit, each of us having shed a good 20 pounds since leaving Cuzco. The coffee was wonderful, but hungry as we were, it was all we could do to choke down the *yuca.* Called *cassava* or *manioc* down in the jungle, it is a nutritious but bland root, boiled to a pulpy consistency before serving. Unseasoned, it is a bit like eating lumps of wet paper and a little bit goes a long way. Nevertheless, we finished it all, thanked the Huamans and their enormous family for their generosity, and slogged off down the hill to the trail.

After crossing the lower bridge to the far bank of the Pampaconas, I began studying the terrain on the Tambo side of the river. I was looking for evidence that the Incas might have destroyed the upper bridge and tricked the Spaniards into remaining over there during their difficult and lengthy march from Ututo to the New Fort. The country looked exactly as the invaders had described it; blocked everywhere by jungle choked, north facing cliffs and ravines. The river had found a plane of weakness or discontinuity in the substrata, such that the two sides of the canyon were totally unalike. The topography was such, however, that the difference was hardly noticeable viewed from upstream. Coming down the canyon from Ututo, the Spaniards would have seen no reason to cross over.

We Arrived at the upper bridge by late afternoon, crossed back to the meadows of Ututo and camped not far from where the ladies had left us 15 days earlier. While the other guys got set up, I scouted the Pampaconas side of the canyon below the bridge for any signs of an old road there. Sure enough, a seldom-used trail, occasionally showing Inca paving stones, continued downstream for a mile or more, passing through meadows dotted with old *campesino* houses, mostly abandoned. Finally, the rocky hills I'd seen from the far bank closed in against the gorge of the river, by then several hundred feet deep. The trail disappeared into a jumble of huge, overgrown boulders. It was pretty much what I'd expected. Upon reaching the boulders, the Spaniards could easily have been deceived by a false trail into the forest beyond. They'd complained that the Indians had cut down trees to block the road and perhaps, I thought, to conceal the fact that it was the wrong road - the easy one by then hidden from view in the forest across the deep gorge of the Pampaconas. Such a scenario might, I thought, explain the four days it took Arbieto to reach Tambo, a place from which we'd just come in four or five hours.

There was a chill in the air that night and the fire felt good. Even better was the feeling that we'd found everything we'd come looking for. Whether we'd done something right or just been lucky wasn't clear. Partly, it was the latter. Unlike all our predecessors, we discovered early on that we were following the same road the Spaniards had used in 1572. Finding the New Fort on the first day had proven that conclusively. But without Renzo's lucky tip, we'd have walked right past the place like he and everyone else had. Once there, I'd known what to look for, though, and maybe that was the bottom line. Successful exploration was basically a matter of informed luck.

We had another week before going out to Cuzco, and talk around the fire turned to the remainder of the trip. Having come steadily uphill, we were now near the edge of the high, cold *pampa* at about 9500 feet. The kerosene stove had begun to leak badly at Espíritu Pampa and now burst into flames whenever we tried to use it. With the leftover fuel, we'd had no trouble starting fires but higher up, firewood would be scarce. Our plan for the rest of the trip had called for a week of climbing in the high peaks, but above the snow line, there'd be no wood at all. Much as we all wanted to get out of the woods and up into the glaciers, a plan change looked unavoidable. After considering our options, a compromise emerged. Barefoot and Chris had had it with the *selva*, as the locals called the interminable forest, in much the same way we might refer to the "sea" or the "desert". Now that they were out, the two of them said they weren't gong back and remembering my rainy week on Icma Coya, I knew the feeling. They decided to go up to timberline at the base of the *cordillera,* wander around for a few days and enjoy the open air. Jungle or no jungle, Jim Little and I had caught the exploring bug and wanted to find more ruins. The only other one I knew of was the two story building somewhere up in the Puncuyoc Mountains that Savoy had mentioned before we left the States. "That's where I'd go," he'd said. I told Jim the story and asked if he wanted to line up José again and give it a try. "Why not?" he said. "Maybe there's another Machu Picchu up there."

9

Icing On The Cake

We pulled into Huancacalle late the next day and found several surprises waiting. Paul was back in camp, having been all the way to Cuzco since we'd last seen him at Espíritu Pampa. The ladies, he said, had gotten out pretty much as planned and were now scattered all over the map. Nancy was already back in Jackson Hole, Martha was traveling alone down at Lake Titicaca and Jill, who'd been somewhat taken by Renzo's continental charms, was visiting him down in Lima. Getting to Cuzco, however, had been an ordeal all three would remember awhile. Their attempts to get from Pucyura to Yupanka on the first night had been met by a bunch of drunken, trigger happy soldiers shooting their weapons into the air and trying to frighten and impress the three pretty *gringas* in true *macho* style. The friendly *teniente* we'd met on the way in was still there, but his authority was eclipsed by a hostile *capitán* so drunk he'd vomited all over himself. When the three finally got a lift down the road in an army jeep, the driver, also drunk, had so terrified them with his crazy driving, they'd jumped out partway along and run for their lives, only to be pelted by a bunch of stone throwing kids. For awhile, they'd told Paul, the whole thing had been pretty scary. It didn't bode too well for the Peruvian Army's chances of whipping the *terroristas* either, I thought, listening to the story.

Little and I tried not to think about our wives negotiating their way through a bunch of armed, bored, horny and boozed up *federales*, but weren't surprised that they'd handled it well. No doubt the details would make for quite a saga when we got home. Meanwhile, we were headed into harm's way, ourselves. To get up into the Puncuyoc Range, we'd have to deal with the same outfit to get past Pucyura and I wondered what was in store. Figuring José would come in handy if there was trouble, we were relieved when he said he could go with us. Paul, too, decided to join in, strengthening our team to a party of four.

Don Juvenal wanted to go, but couldn't. He was waiting for Renzo and his film crew and was committed to work for them whenever they got back. He'd not seen the Puncuyoc ruins, but had heard about them from old timers who had. As we planned the trip, he passed along to José what he'd been told, since José had never been there either. While we talked, a loud roar echoed up the canyon. It was Renzo, this time in a big, twin rotor army helicopter. With him was an *entourage* of strutting troops, slick Italian film makers, and posturing government officials - all looking very anxious to get back to the city. The Italian waved me over to the chopper and shouted to borrow my satellite photo for a couple of hours. Remembering the rebuke my crew had handed me for not sharing information last time, I ducked under the rotors and tossed it up as he lifted off to Quillabamba for more fuel.

The local kids loved it of course, but the ominous "whump-whump-whump" as he disappeared down the valley momentarily took me back twenty years to my own helicopter days in the Far East. The kids could have my share of all that, I thought, walking back to camp. In fact, hard as I tried to be fair and open minded, the whole scene with Renzo bothered me. Jim and Paul, too, felt there was something wrong with the picture. We hadn't realized how accustomed we'd become to the quiet pace of life in the *montaña* until then. We'd begun to see the world through Indian eyes and viewed that way, Renzo's arrival and departure in clouds of dust, noise and comic activity seemed absurd and alien. Sadly, most contact the Indians had with their government and with *gringos* was like that. It was little wonder they'd become suspicious of everything outside their valleys.

Later, Renzo returned with my photo, having looked for several sites but seen "nothing," he said, from the air. That was hardly news to us, since we'd had some trouble identifying what we'd found on foot. Off he flew to the comforts of Cuzco for the night, while we three went up to José's for coffee and quiet returned to the Vilcabamba. José said Puncuyoc wasn't the only ruin we hadn't yet seen. He claimed there were a number of sites nearby that were out of the way and seldom visited, especially by *gringos*. We told him we wanted to see them all and for the first time I started thinking about a booklet that might include everything in the region under one cover. In addition to Vitcos and Vilcabamba the Old, we'd mapped all the missing sites over in the Río Pampaconas. Why not record everything in the upper Vilcabamba as well? We agreed that our first job was to find Puncuyoc, but if there was time left over we'd try to get to all of José's other sites, too.

Passing through Pucyura the next morning, no one stirred at the army post. Bottles lying all around said everyone was probably still hung over from the night's partying. We didn't stop to check. On our way down to Yupanka, a road-side shanty town where the trail to the Puncuyoc began, we decided to detour across the river to Lucma, the tiny but picturesque provincial capital. I'd heard about a ruin near there in 1982 and José said it was in the heights above the village. Along the way, we stopped at the old church, a wonderfully picturesque structure recalling the one at Vilcabamba the New, but partly built with recycled Inca stones. Legend had it that anyone entering the ancient Spanish bell tower next door would soon die from some horrible respiratory disease. Looking up the mountain, we decided to save our lungs for the climb. From the churchyard, the trail switch-backed steeply up to a saddle between two high hills, then continued up the northerly one to a summit standing directly in a hairpin bend of the Río Vilcabamba, at least a thousand feet below.

Just under the top was a large, grassy plaza with low stone retaining walls at three sides **(Figure 13)**. José called the place Inca Huaracana, *huaraca* being the name of the famous Inca sling. There was a local tradition that from there, the Inca - no one seemed to know which one - had once slung a huge stone northward across the river to thwart the escape of a faithless wife. The stone had supposedly smashed the deep gap called Abra Puncuyoc into the distant skyline, and the wife had been turned into the jagged stone pillar still standing partway up the pass, forever unable to join her lover on the other side. **(Figure 14)**

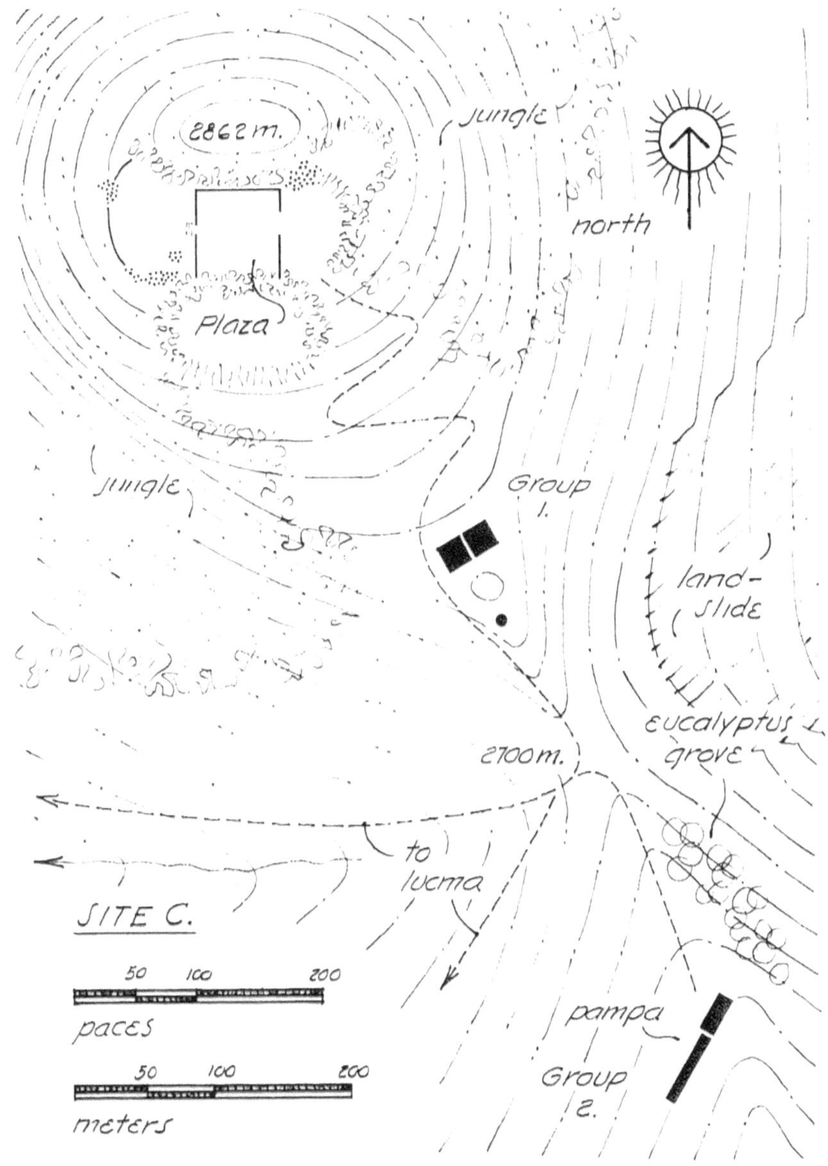

Figure 13 - Map of Inca Huaracana

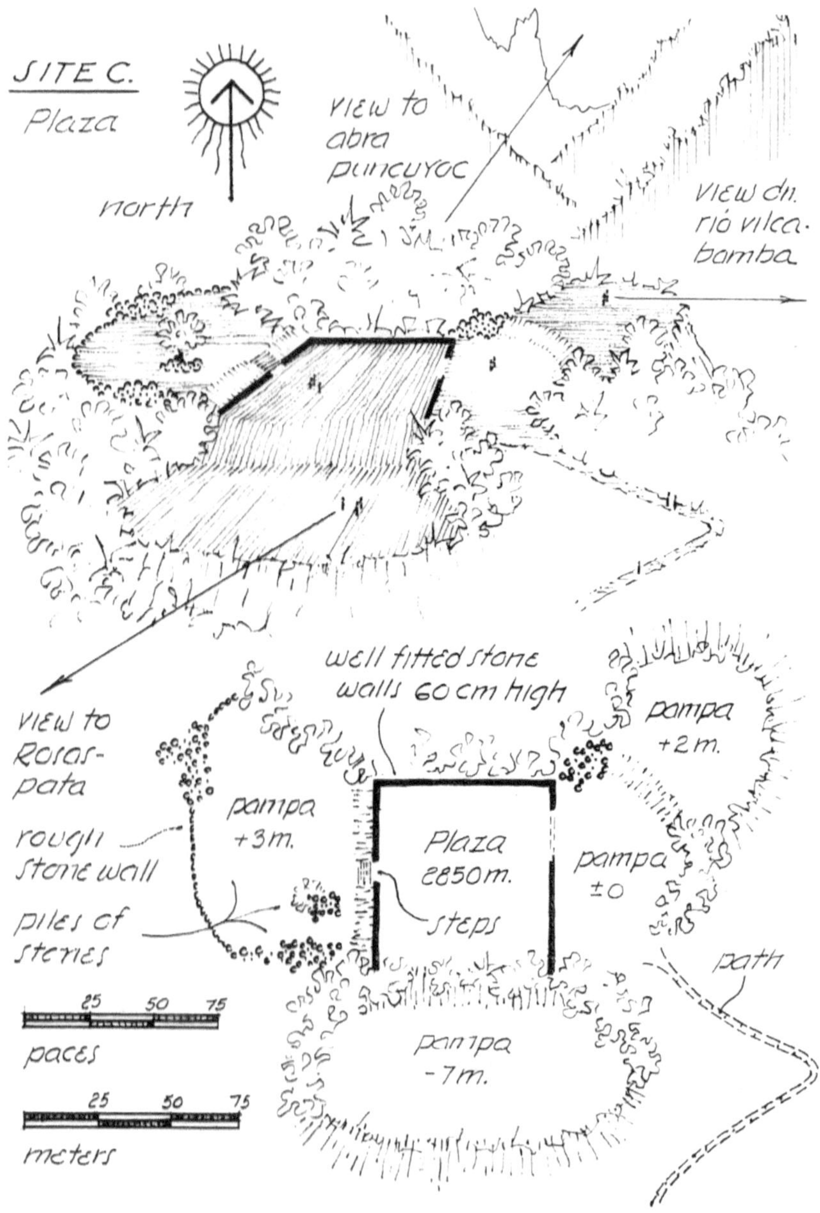

Figure 14 - Site plan and view of plaza

I mapped the plaza and several apparently related *pampas* nearby, and then checked out the hilltop. The views all around were fabulous. The Puncuyoc Range marched across the entire horizon to the north. José said the ruins we sought were hidden somewhere among the highest and wildest peaks forming the western ramparts of the pass. Despite the fine weather, their jungle choked gullies were shrouded in mist and new snow plastered the dark granite of their craggy ridges. There was no avoiding the impression that we were headed into serious country. Back to the south, the ruins of Vitcos could just be seen atop Rosaspata, standing alone amidst the head-water canyons of the Río Vilcabamba. Flowing around the foot of the hill on which we stood, the river turned sharply eastward and ran down a deep canyon towards the Urubamba. The *carretera* was plainly visible, winding downstream alongside the watercourse for miles. As we watched, a truck inched its way up the road toward Yupanka, still an hour or more away. As a vantage point, the plaza commanded views over at least 300 degrees of the surrounding country. It is known that the Incas regularly communicated over great distances by simple line-of-sight methods: smoke and reflected sunlight by day and watchfires by night. Whatever other purposes the site may have served, Inca Huaracana may well have been an important hub in such a signaling network.

Strangely, there were no ruins at the summit, not even a platform from which to take in the view - nothing, in fact, but thick, thorny brush. This was to become even more of a mystery months later as I drew a plan of the site from my notes. It was laid out in the shape of a huge bird, flying due north toward Puncuyoc Pass. **(Figure 14)** The only part of the bird no longer apparent was the head, which must have sat squarely on the highest, seemingly undeveloped point. Possibly, the bird-like plan of the site was just a coincidence, though I doubt it. More likely, the peak had ritual significance in Inca times and was the scene of ceremonial activities of some sort. Possibly it was preserved as the actual place from which the king had hurled his mythical sling-stone.

Either way, the apparent lack of any constructed work was surprising. In fact, the only structures I could find anywhere were well down the hill, near the saddle between the peaks. Two heavily overgrown but otherwise intact buildings still stood there, nine or ten feet high and classically Incan in their design and construction. **(Figure**

15, Group 1) Hiram Bingham had reported two structures at a site above Lucma he also called Inca Huaracana, but his sketches looked nothing at all like what I'd found. (**Figure 15**, Group 2) Turning back down the steep trail toward Lucma, I was puzzling over that when a faint, circular foundation turned up in the midst of a plowed field, much of the hillside having been cleared for cultivation. It had been 73 years since Bingham's visit. Maybe his finds had since been trashed by the farmers, I thought, but why hadn't he found the plaza or the two big houses still standing? Was there more to the site than José knew about?

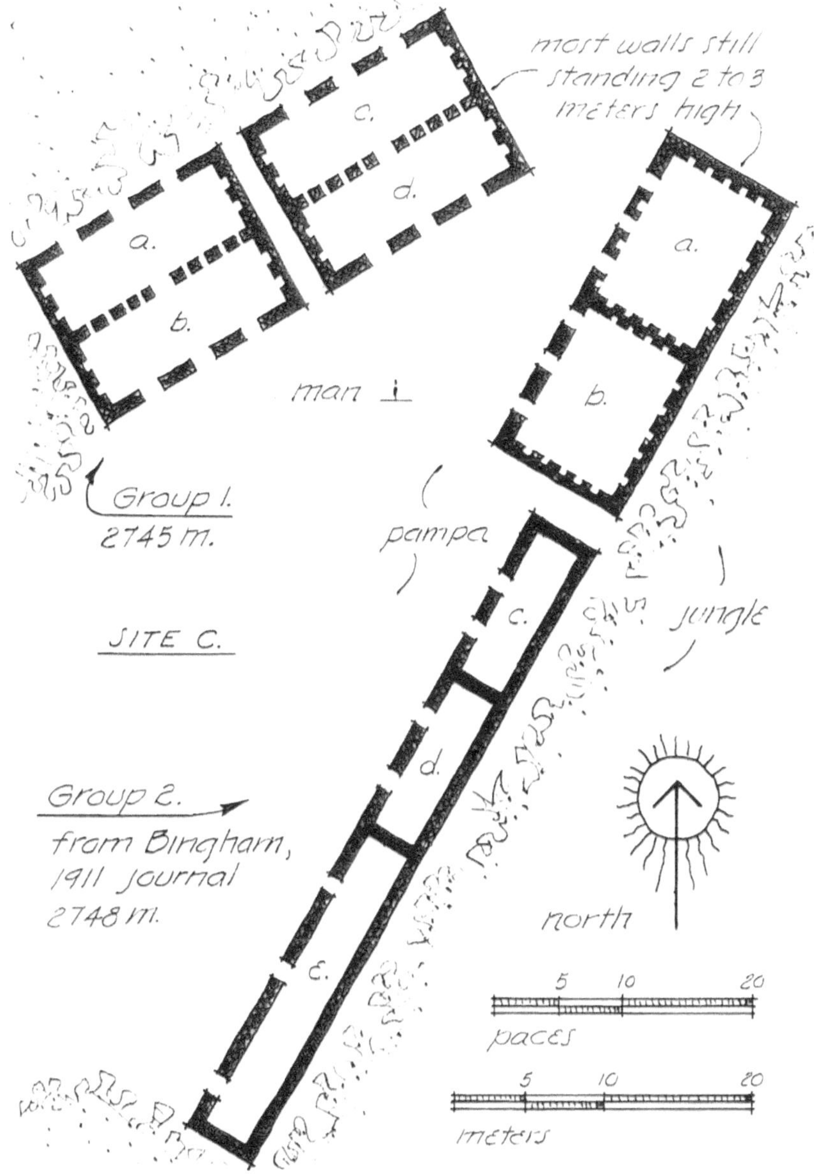

Figure 15 - Floor plan of structures

In Yupanka that night, we ran into no hostility at all. Rather, we drank beer with the mayor and several policemen well into the wee hours. José found a young man who'd been to the Puncuyoc ruins some years earlier with his father and thought he could find his way back. He called himself Ausavio Rivera, and we welcomed him aboard with another round of beers. Later, there was sporadic gunfire and the sound of exploding grenades, but we hardly noticed - or cared. The bored *soldados* up at Pucyura had to kill time somehow, and I knew from my Marine Corp days how much fun it is to play with guns and things that blow up. The idea that they might actually be firing at terrorists never even occurred to us.

The trail up into the Puncuyoc began right across the Río Salinas, a tributary that flowed into the Vilcabamba just below Yupanka. **(Figure 4)** A narrow bridge crossed to the first of what turned out to be countless switch-backs up the relentlessly steep, forested slope on the far bank. José said the trail led to the 12,500 foot Huarina Pass and, eventually, down into the jungle on the other side. Our ruins were supposed to be up near the top, somewhere. As we began the climb, our partying of the night before weighed heavily. Worse, the weather was finally starting to turn. We plodded up into the clouds with our heads down and our spirits turned off, oblivious to everything but the trail underfoot. By the time we reached the pass, it was blowing hard and starting to rain, so we looked for a sheltered place to camp. Finding none, we bivouacked on a soggy bench just beyond the pass minutes before it began to really pour. Forcibly reminded of how little fun exploring is in the rain, I thanked Tupac Amaru for the three weeks of sunshine we'd already enjoyed. Paradise lost, or so it felt.

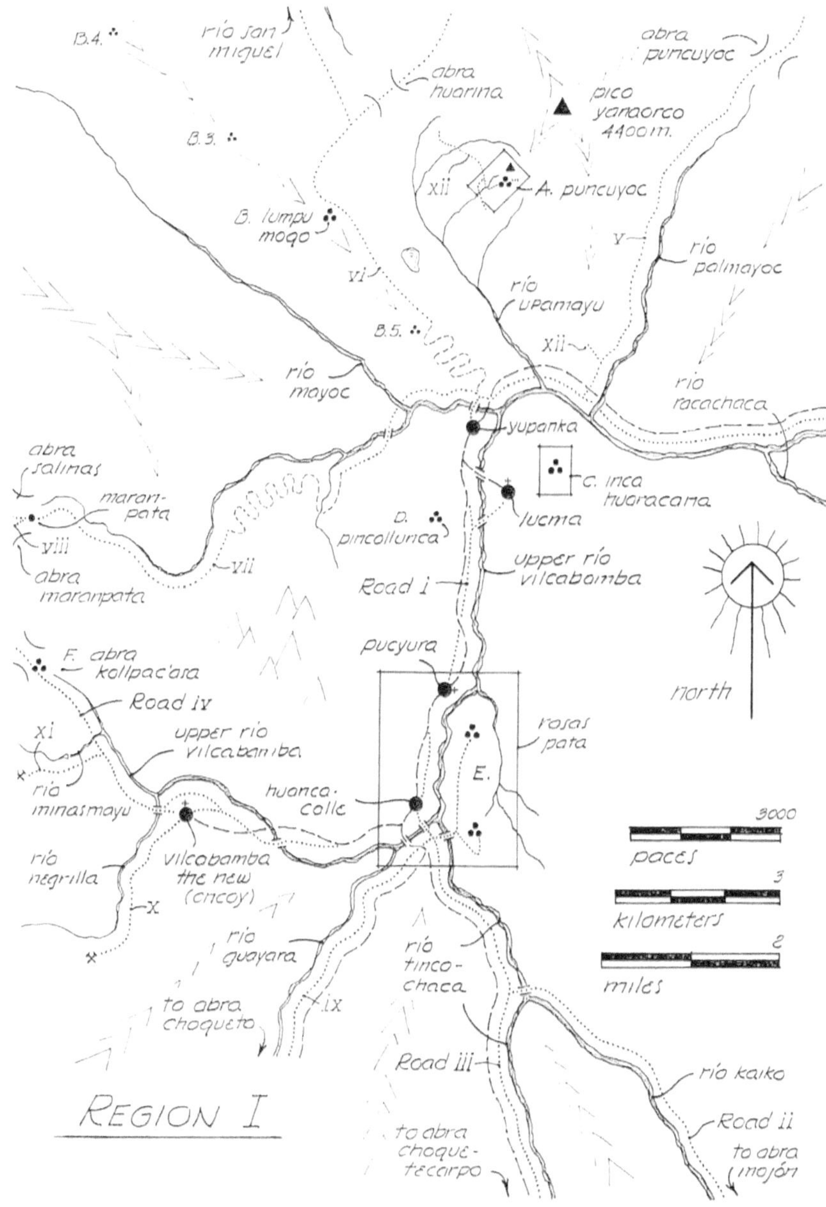

Figure 4 - Map of upper Rio Vilcabamba

The pass separated the Puncuyoc Range from a long ridge running westward toward the Santuario, or "Sanctuary", another unexplored massif with an intriguing name. Ausavio claimed the ruins were nearby, actually visible from the trail in clear weather. Exactly how to get there was another matter. The entire ridge was blanketed with fog so thick we had to stay close so as not to become separated. José and Ausavio had brought no shelter of any kind, so we gave them our large Visqueen ground sheet and they fashioned a make-shift tent. After a sorry dinner cooked slowly over a smokey fire in a steady downpour, we crept into soggy sleeping bags, soaked to the skin, and began to think twice about how badly we wanted to find the ruins.

The rain ended in the night, but the fog persisted such that we wandered around most of the next day in the clouds finding nothing. I was beginning to think Ausavio was a fake when José stopped at an overhanging rock and set fire to some dry *ichu* grass under the sheltering ledge. Into it he carefully fed some of the green *coca* leaves he, like all the Indians, always carried to chew on. We looked on in silence, wondering what was going on. Ausavio's matter-of-fact attitude suggested it was all in a day's work, so we didn't ask. Just then, there was a lucky break in the weather and we moved on. Ausavio now led off with more confidence, the terrain being more or less visible for the first time in two days.

We crossed a ridge line into a beautiful glacial *cirque* just as the clouds closed in once more. Again, José went through the ritual. Again, the sky opened and revealed the route. It was now obvious that he'd intended that the first time, also. Jim, Paul and I looked at each other in disbelief. Surely, all that hocus-pocus wasn't having any effect on the weather. When I asked José about it, he became a bit sheepish, admitting that it sounded far fetched. He said it was an old legend that the Incas sacrificed *coca* leaves whenever clouds obscured their way in the mountains. He'd tried it from time to time, he said, usually with good success. Suffice it to say that he made such offerings on six occasions in the Puncuyoc and the weather cleared within minutes all six times.

Later that day, Ausavio thought we were getting close. We were no more than 300 yards from our miserable bivouac of the previous night, but this time the surroundings were visible and, to him, familiar. The weather was definitely improving, so we decided to stop for the night and continue the search in the morning. Still skeptical, we were suddenly encouraged when Jim Little stumbled onto a stone roadway hidden in the thick *ichu* grass while looking for a place to set up his tent.

"Let's go!" I hollered, rushing over to have a look. "Savoy said to follow roads, and now we've got one to follow."

José was excited because it was clear no one had been that way for years. The paving was completely overgrown and all but disappeared as it passed through occasional patches of *bosque*. Whatever it led to had been undisturbed for a very long time. Fully revitalized, we decided to use the last of the daylight to scout the route beyond camp. Almost immediately, it rounded a ridge into the next *cirque*, passing a badly tumbled foundation of some sort on the crest. Not far beyond, we lost it. After cutting a steep, nasty patch of jungle into the valley below, José and Ausavio took off up a long, open slope on the far side. I found a continuation of the paving, but it effectively dead-ended in thick cloud forest several hundred yards later. There was nothing to do but head back to camp, but I was sure that our ruin lay somewhere beyond that wall of thick growth. The next day, we'd know for sure. An hour later, we heard the two *campesinos* returning in the dark, talking excitedly. At the top of the big hill they'd climbed, they said, was a sharp ridge overlooking the next valley. The descent was cut off by cliffs, but across the gorge, in a high gap between two craggy peaks, they'd spotted a stone building that seemed to be in perfect condition. I was excited, but not surprised. The road must have continued through the jungle where I'd turned back, around the ridge beyond and into the same canyon they'd seen from the ridgetop. No doubt it then ascended the drainage to the building among the peaks at its head.

Sure enough, the road lead us straight to the ruins in the morning, passing a raised platform as it crossed the last ridge along the way. The valley beyond was a spectacular place, hanging above a high waterfall and surrounded by jagged rock towers. The road crossed the creek just above the falls, stone abutments still testifying to the bridge that had once spanned there. Beyond, was a staircase, perhaps half a mile long and retained with a well built stone wall a meter or two above the slope all along its downhill side. Just below the building in the notch, the stairs deposited us on a small *pampa* with a tiny, isolated lagoon near its center. The road ran out to the shoreline, then turned abruptly up more stone steps to the ruins. **(Figure 5)** Near the lagoon, I almost tripped over a pile of cut but unused stone cylinders hidden in the grass. In 1911, when Bingham found many of the buildings at Machu Picchu nearly intact, a common feature of the the tall gables still standing was a row of cylindrical, wine bottle-sized stones projecting to the exterior, just below the roof line. He'd called them "pegs," and assumed they'd been used to tie down the roof. The fifty or so in the pile at my feet had apparently been abandoned there en route to some yet unfinished building project, since there was no sign of quarrying anywhere nearby. It gave me an eerie feeling, as though a gang of workmen might return any moment, pick them up and continue on their way.

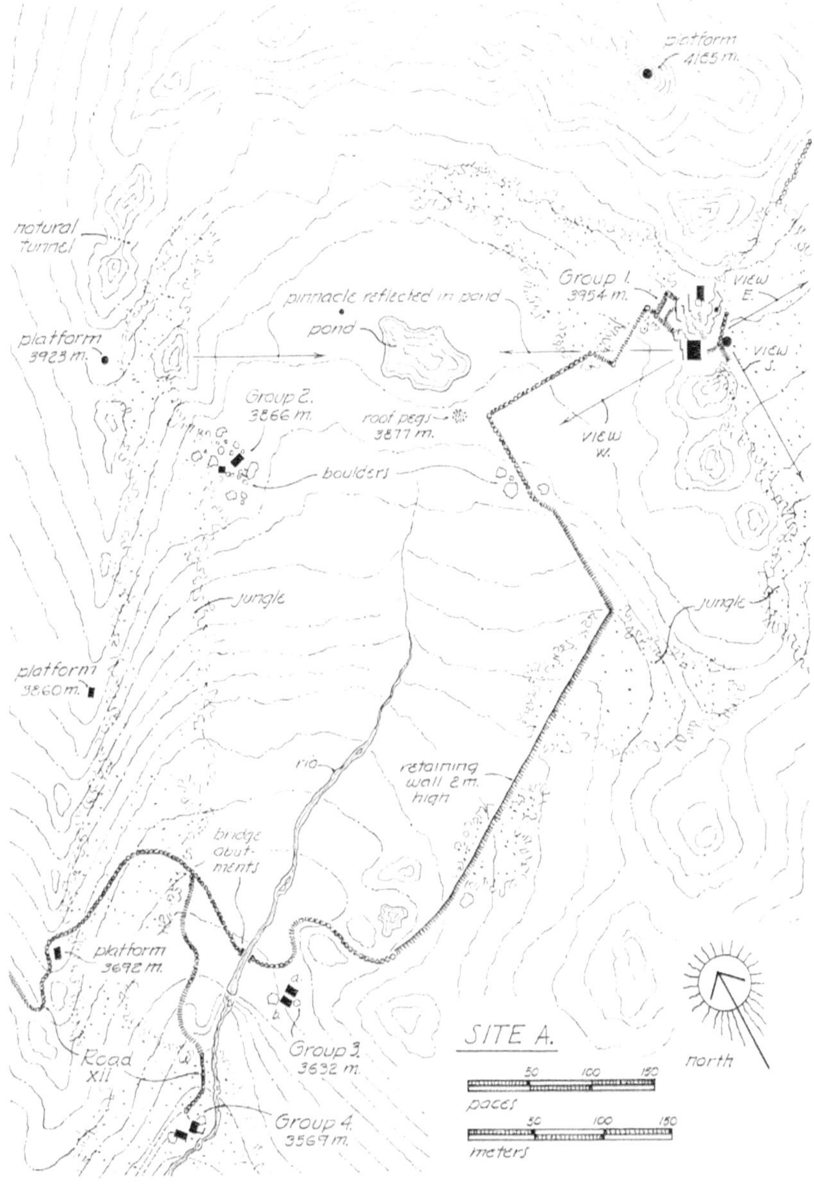

Figure 5 - Map of Puncuyoc

Continuing up the final stairway through a dense grove of tangled, moss covered trees, we arrived at the object of our search and found all our efforts of the past few days repaid several times over. The building before us was one of the finest any of us had ever seen.

(Figure 6) A terrace, retained by a fine wall with nine niches, made a small plaza in front of the entrance and overlooked the *pampa* and lagoon several hundred feet below. Across the *cirque* stood a large rocky crag with an enormous white spot near its summit. In the surface of the pond, the reflection of the spot was neatly centered. At each compass point was something special. Vitcos was plainly visible, half a mile below us and six or seven miles off to the south. Looking west, an overgrown stone platform could be seen through the binoculars, high on the ridge we'd crossed coming from camp. Due east was a sharp granite spire, standing tall and slender on the skyline, high in the Puncuyoc peaks. Near the main building were various retaining walls, stairways and fountains, together with the ruined, circular form of at least one other structure - all built of rough *pirca*, or fieldstones set in clay mortar.

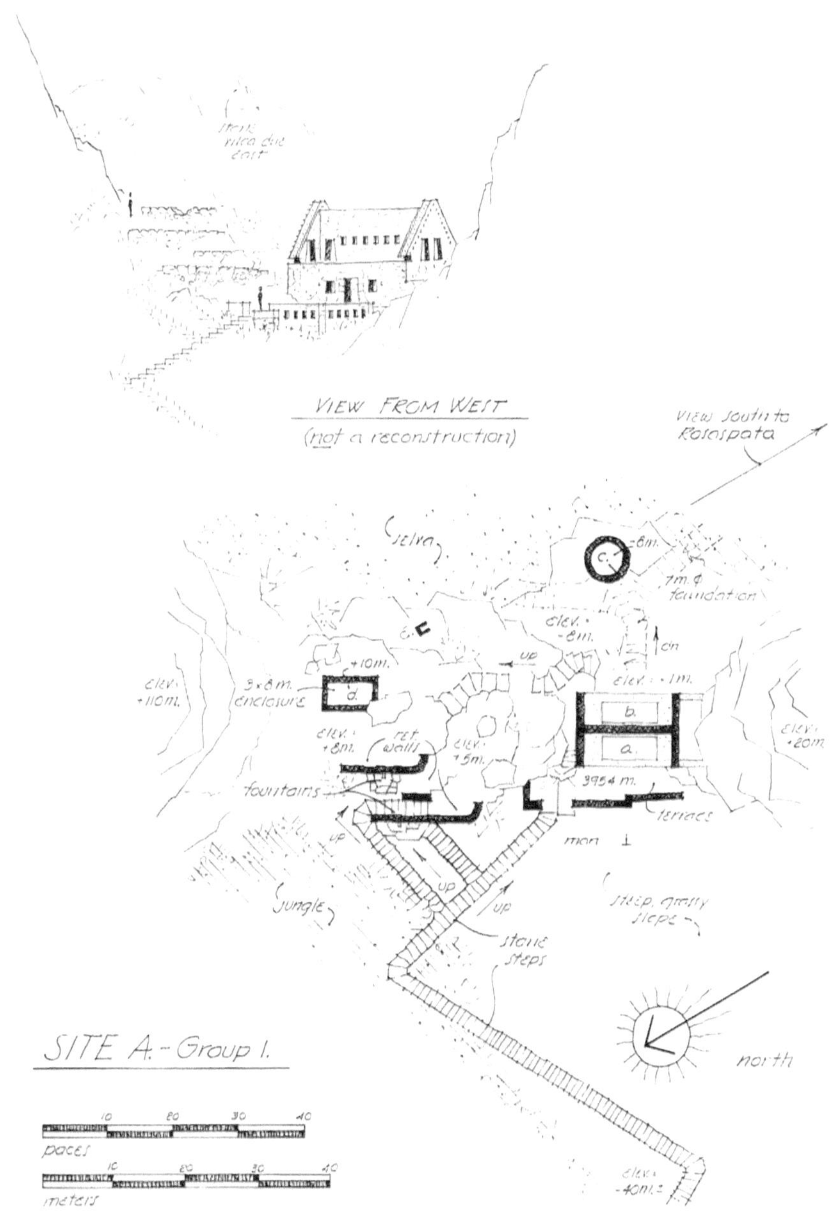

Figure 6 - Site plan and view of Incahuasi

In spectacular contrast, the masonry of the main building itself was all well fitted, with large, finely cut blocks framing the many openings. There'd been two stories with two rooms on each floor, the whole laid out with eight doors, five windows and twenty-six niches. Of these, the fourteen in the lower level rooms were man-sized and had carved stone rings Bingham had called "eye bonders" recessed in the centers of their rear walls. The steep gables were fitted with more eye bonders and many more of the projecting stone pegs than any building at Machu Picchu - or anywhere else I knew of, for that matter. The entire structure was detailed in a totally unique way none of us had ever seen before, and hardly a stone seemed out of place. We had found one of the most elaborate, best preserved examples of Inca architecture in existence. **(Figures 7-9)**

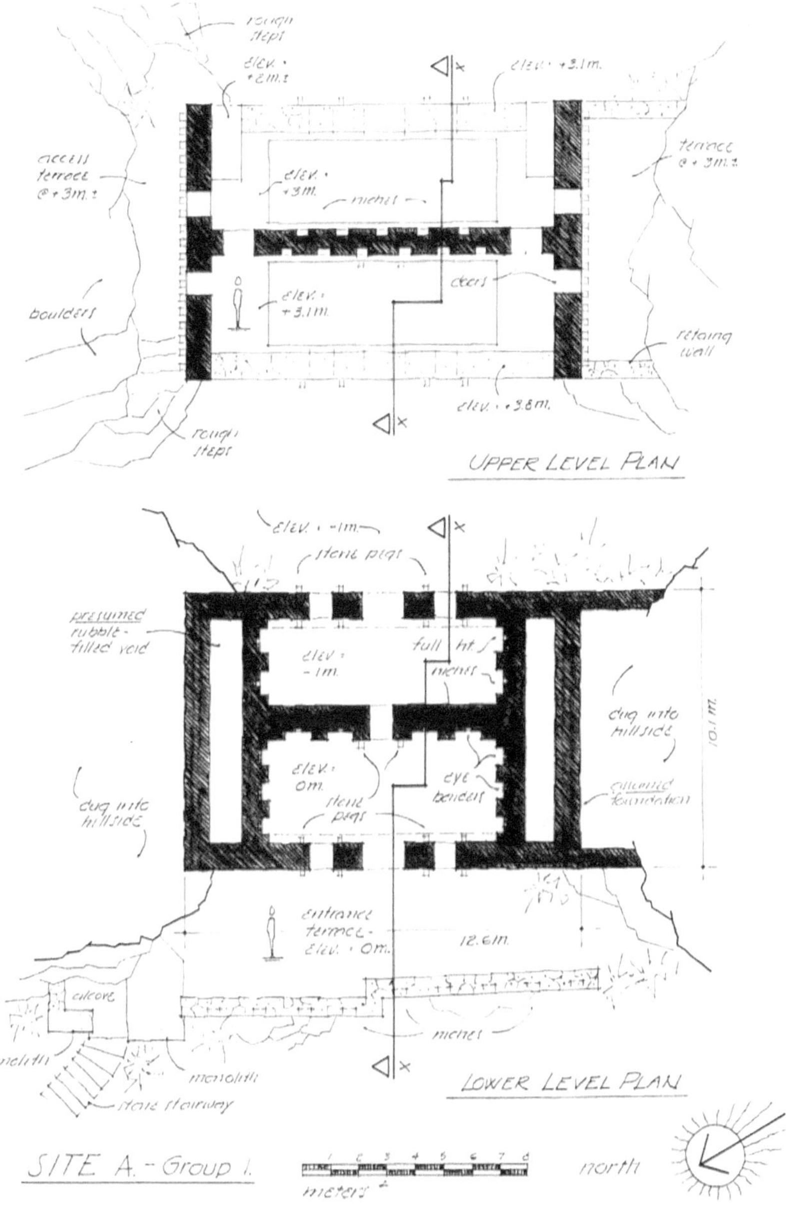

Figure 7 - Floor plans of Incahuasi

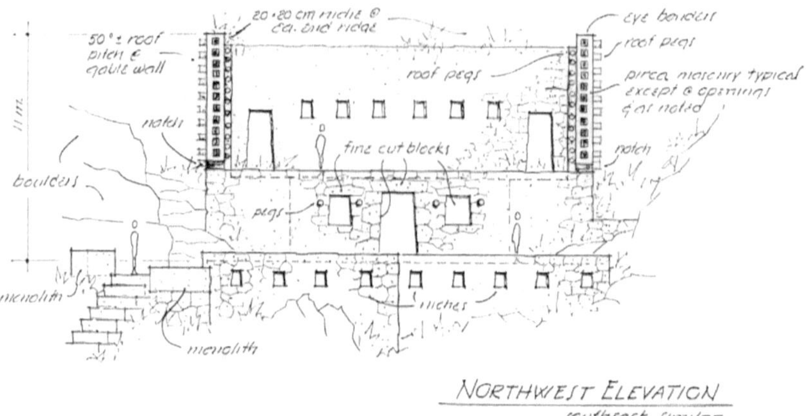

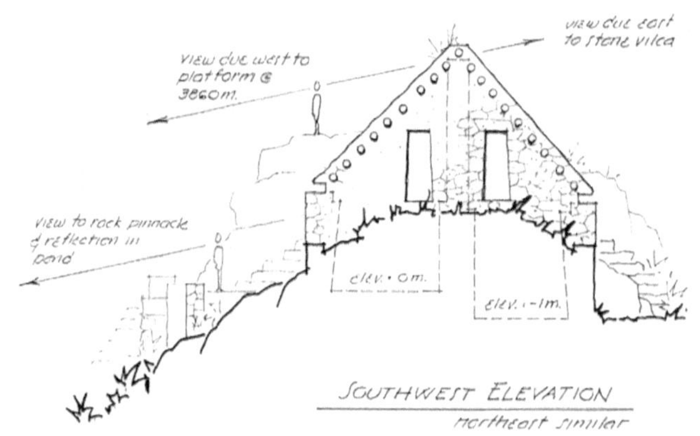

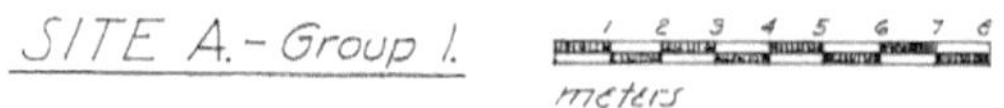

Figure 8 - Exterior elevations of Incahuasi

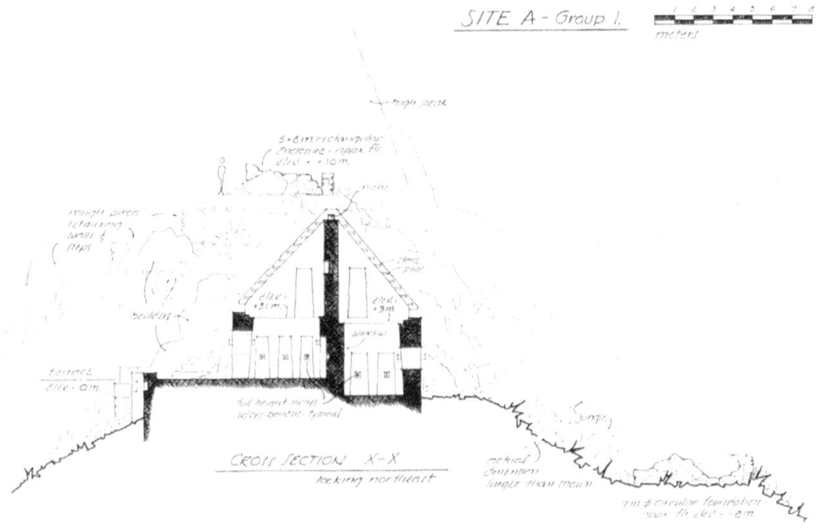

Figure 9 - Cross section of Incahuasi

As Paul and I set about sketching and measuring the building and its surroundings, Jim, José and Ausavio took off to search the head of the rugged, partly jungle filled canyon beyond the 12,850 foot high notch in which the ruins lay. Eventually, they found a brief continuation of the road there, but nothing more, and returned several hours later to find us about finished. The weather, which had let up for a few hours, was again turning sour, so we headed down with just barely enough daylight to make camp before dark. As it turned out, we misjudged by a half hour or so and ended up in a downpour, clawing our way home through the wet jungle at night. It made for a thoroughly unpleasant end to an otherwise spectacular day.

The weather had improved again the next morning, so we went back up to the site to make sure we hadn't missed anything important. The clearing sky turned out to be short-lived, though, and the main building was completely socked in by the time we got up there. A quick look around in a cold fog and increasing drizzle failed to turn up anything new and wishfully thinking we'd gotten it all, we turned and headed back down. After a fast lunch shivering in a rising wind , we broke camp and slipped and skidded down the steep, muddy trail to Yupanka in what had become an icy, driving rain. A thoroughly miserable retreat, it went quickly, at least, and we arrived in time for a big dinner and more than a few beers under the dry, sheltering thatch of the lone *cantina* there - paradise regained!

Huddling around the table, joking and laughing at the rain outside, it struck me that our "discovery" of Puncuyoc was exactly the unexpected surprise I'd dreamed of, the ever-so-sweet icing on the cake I'd hoped for months earlier while planning the trip. The sting of failing to reach the strange mountaintop above Espíritu Pampa was forgotten. Puncuyoc, I realized, was a truly magnificent find. Unlike the historic but tumbled ruins we'd found along the trail to Vilcabamba the Old, the significance of Puncuyoc was its architecture. Like Machu Picchu, Puncuyoc seemed to have no known history but was instead a virtually undisturbed relic from the world of the Incas. From my reading, I knew that made it an almost incredible rarity. Better yet, its near-perfect state of preservation - more pristine, in fact, than anything at Machu Picchu - and its complex design made it a veritable laboratory for the study of Incan building techniques. With the expedition all but over, it looked like we'd hit the jackpot. Like Bingham, seven decades earlier, we'd been blessed with unbelievable good luck. What else could we possibly hope for?

Gunfire and grenades again punctuated the long night in Yupanka, but we were due to leave for Cuzco the very next day and didn't much care. The police claimed they were firing at terrorists, but José and the locals didn't seem at all concerned, so we weren't either. As before, we camped in the midst of the village garbage dump on a flat, low-lying *pampa* alongside the river that Brooke, Curtis and I had used in 1982. Each rainy season, the river would rise and wash everything downstream, an example of solid waste disposal, Peruvian style. Between floods, the dogs, chickens and pigs picked over the worst of the trash and the shoreline made a surprisingly pleasant campsite. We called the place Playa Yupanka, or "Yupanka Beach."

Strolling back up the road toward Huancacalle in the morning, José said there was one more site we might as well see. Located atop a high ridge across the river from Lucma, it was a bit of a grunt to get to, he said, and there wouldn't be much to see once we got there. No matter; by that time, I was obsessed with ruins and wanted to see them all. Not so enthusiastic, Paul was feeling a bit weary after our cold, wet tour in the Puncuyoc. He decided to take a break and wait for us down by the road. Jim Little, always game, joined José and me as we started up a steep, rocky rib. About twenty minutes above the road, the crest leveled off, but the terrain still dropped off sharply on both sides. Presently, ruins began to appear along the top. Though less overgrown and half as long, the site was not unlike Tambo. José called it Pincollunca after the Inca flute, or *pincuyllu*, but didn't say why. **(Figure 16)**

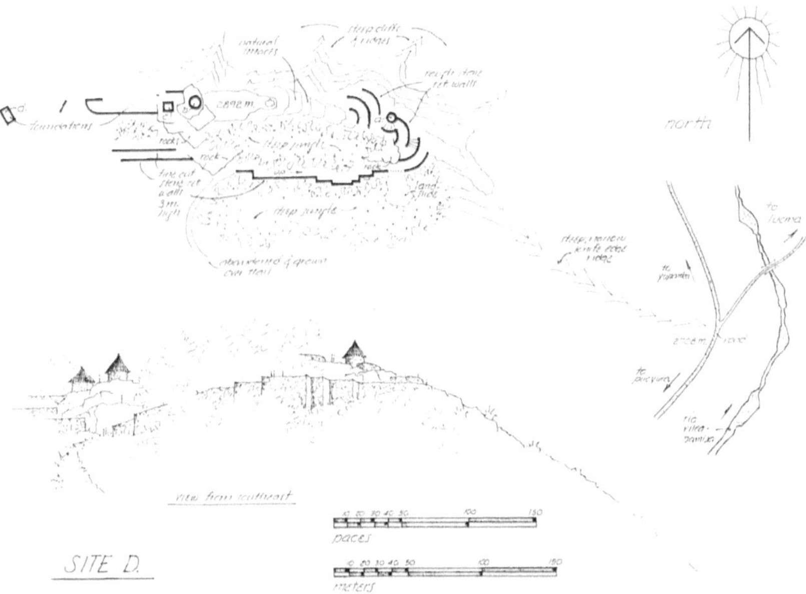

Figure 16 - Site plan and view of Pinccollunca

As he'd predicted, the site wasn't much to look at. The stonework visible was rough and generally laid out in curved shapes. Stone steps and terraces led up to a small summit, where stood the now inevitable boulder at one end of a tiny *pampa*. Beyond were the foundations of two buildings, more walls and a short slope leading down to the main hillside beyond. According to my altimeter, we'd gained almost 700 feet of elevation and there were panoramic views all around. The archaeology may have been a let down, but the situation was well worth the climb.

After a quick break, we headed back the way we'd come. Just where the descent turned steep, an unusually well built wall disappeared into the thick jungle of the shady, south side of the ridge. While I paused to do some sketching, Jim disappeared into the bush with José, following the wall. Almost immediately, they came to a steep landslide which had destroyed about 30 feet of the structure and discouraged further progress. Pressing on, they discovered that the wall resumed across the slide and continued for more than 200 yards down the slope. Unlike the rough walls above, this was fine Inca work, well fitted, and ten feet high in places. José was amazed. In all the years he'd traveled that area, he'd neither seen nor heard about that wall. At its lower end, it gave onto a pleasant little side valley, leading gently back down to the road. In Inca times, it appeared to have been a grand ramp of sorts leading up to the hilltop site, though centuries of erosion and vegetation had long since combined to render it all but impassable and practically invisible.

Back at the road, Paul was feeling a bit better and we continued on up to Huancacalle, planning to spend the rest of the afternoon packing for our departure the following day. Chris and Barefoot slogged back into camp just in time to pitch in, and we filled one another in on our respective adventures while we worked. Not surprisingly, the rain we'd experienced had been snow higher up. Nevertheless, they'd gone about as high as they could without climbing gear and said there was a whole world of spectacular alpine challenges not a day and a half above camp. Best of all, there was no jungle - just clean granite and ice. I made a mental note to come back one day properly outfitted to slip up there and do some climbing. Much as I was enjoying my newfound love affair with exploration, the mountaineer in me was still alive and well. I'd often imagined how exhilarating it would be to look down on the

Vilcabamba from a 20,000 foot peak. For the moment, though, the project at hand was wrapping up the expedition we were on.

Before leaving Yupanka, we'd made a deal with a truck driver to pick us up in Huancacalle at four P.M. the next day, so there was still time in the morning to visit the other sites José wanted to show us. He invited us up to his house for dinner that night and his wife did *choclo* and roast *cuy*, the ever-present guinea pigs that scurry underfoot in every Andean household. Once cooked on a spit, the little rodents look disconcertingly like tail-less rats, but done properly, they can be quite tasty. José's wife knew her stuff, and the whole dinner was delicious, especially washed down with the cheap Peruvian wine we'd picked up at the tiny *tienda*, or store, down in Pucyura and brought along for the occasion. It's difficult to appreciate how much a simple bottle of wine - any wine - means to people for whom five dollars is a respectable day's wage, but José left little doubt it was a rare treat. Everyone seemed to have a great evening and, with a little help from the booze, we were struck by how much we were going to miss our two months in the Vilcabamba.

José said we'd need at least half a day to see every other ruin he knew of in the area, so we were up early, just in time to see him appear out of the darkness with a huge pot of hot coffee. We were out of almost everything by that time and coffee seemed to be what we missed the most. Nothing could have pleased us more and we quickly wolfed down a quick breakfast of stale, week-old *pancitas*, or bread cakes, brought back to life by repeated dunking in José's sweet, rich brew.

The first site we visited was at the very summit of Rosaspata, which we reached just at sunrise. In 1982, I'd wondered what was up there, but hadn't had time to find out. Now we saw that the entire crest had been terraced and ringed by a well built retaining wall, at places ten feet high. A three foot parapet along much of its length suggested that the enclosure might have been intended for defense. Three small buildings still stood overgrown with brush, and piles of rocks, faint walls and old terraces spread over the rest of the enclosure - an incredible 700 feet east to west and 1200 feet north to south. **(Figure 29)** To the north we could just make out Puncuyoc, Inca Huaracana and Pincollunca floating on distant ridgelines above Manco's palace. **(Figure 30)**

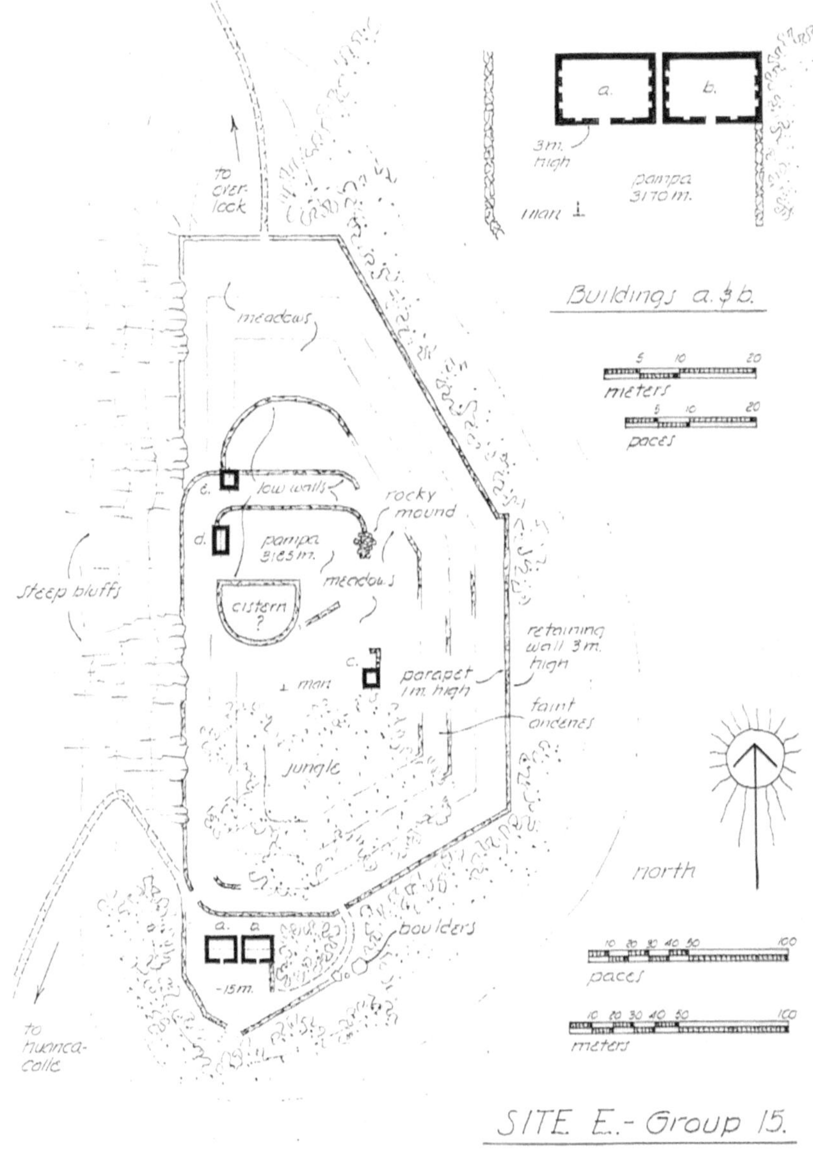

Figure 29 - Plan of "fortress" at Vitcos

Figure 30 - View of "fortress"

Off to the east and far below, the valley was filled with *andenes* cascading artfully down from the ruins surrounding the great white boulder, the famed Yurak Rumi. Between us and them, however, the hillside was covered with tangled growth, quite the opposite of the west slope, where cliffs and steep, open terrain plunged all the way down to Huancacalle. The best of the ruins were just below the south end of the enclosure, where a small terrace, also retained, surrounded two large, overgrown but intact buildings apparently intended to guard the entrance to the larger platform above.

Next, we dropped into the thick *bosque*, of the east slope. About halfway down to the *andenes*, spread along the hillside between the Yurak Rumi and Manco's palace were three building groups, all well preserved but choked with thorny vegetation. Each was quite different from the others. One included among its nine simple, but formally spaced structures a large circular building, the only one of its kind at Vitcos, set off from the others at the end of a long retaining wall. (**Figure 28**, Group 13) The second group showed fine stonework and had ten doorways in two large, elaborate buildings with steep gables still standing. The structures faced each other across a small, walled-in courtyard. (**Figure 22**) Quite unlike the first two, the last was a cluster of nine modest foundations packed tightly together and walled about its perimeter. (**Figure 28**, Group 9) After mapping each in turn, we continued our tour, traversing across the slope northwards towards Manco's Palace.

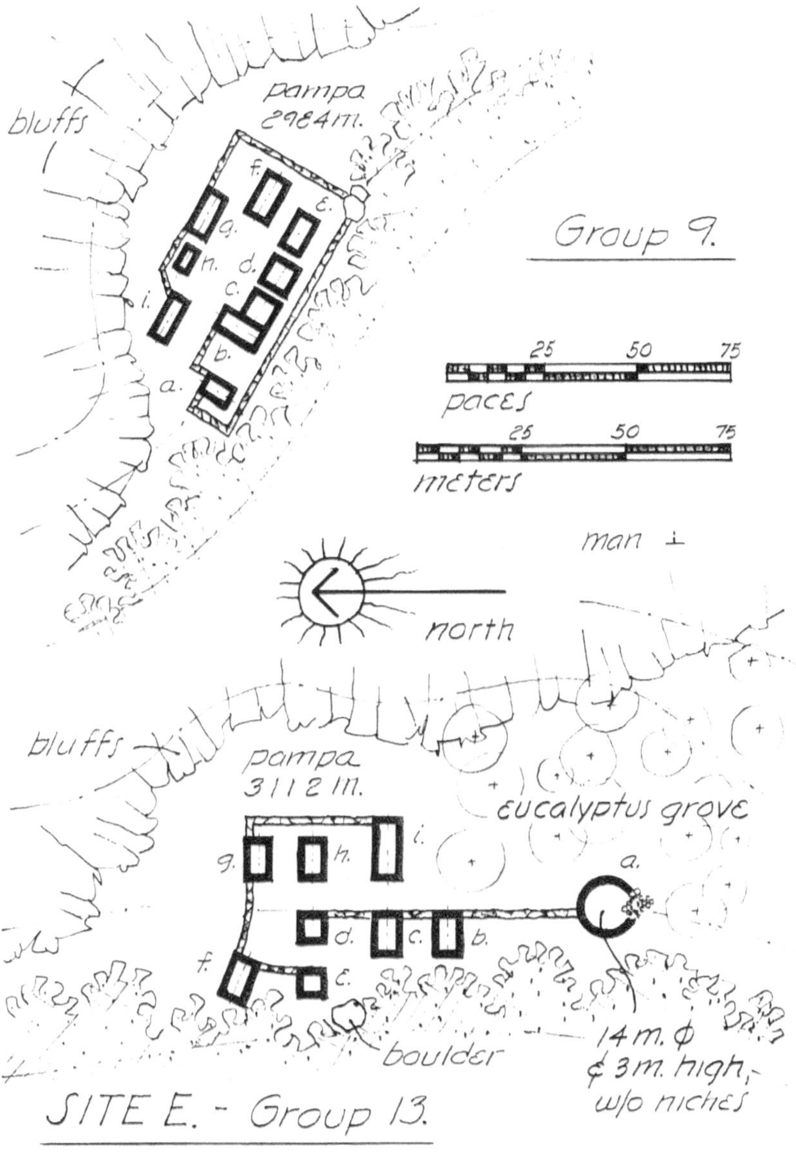

Figure 28 - Site plans of house groups

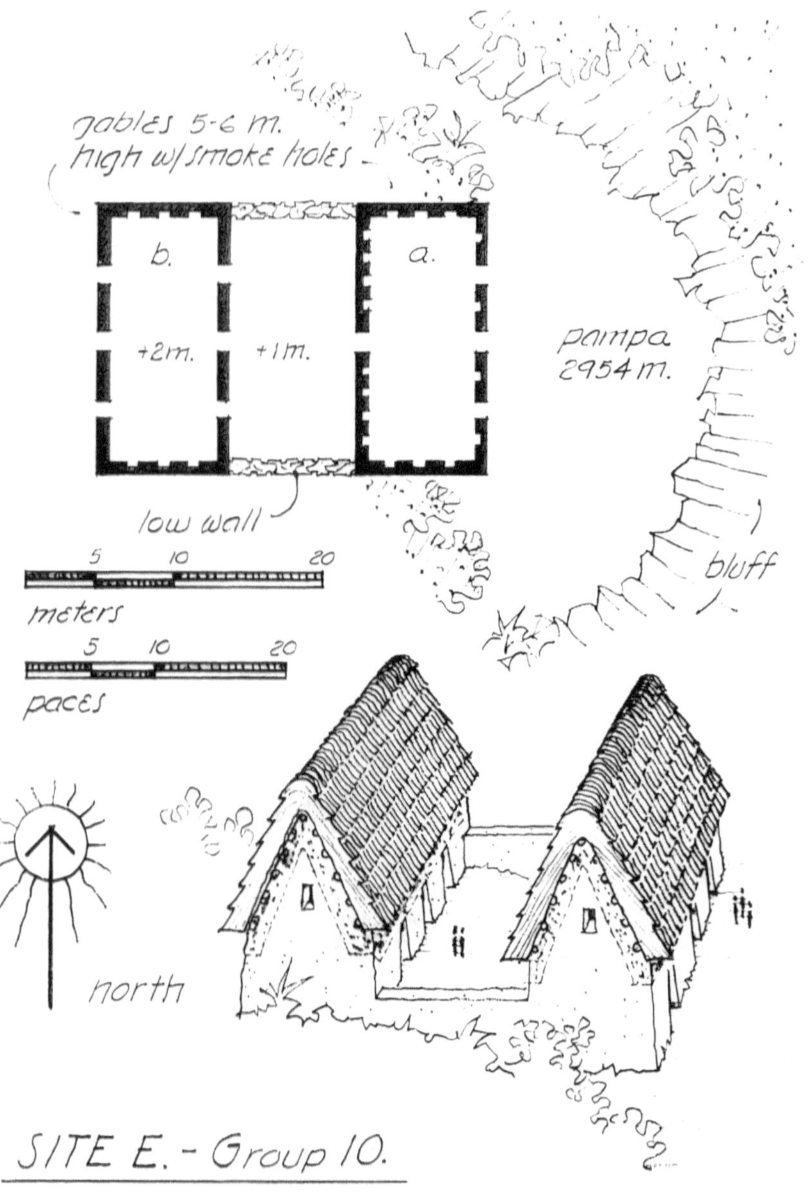

Figure 22 - Plan and view of double building

That name is an outgrowth of the local legend that it is the place where the famous Inca was murdered, since the plaza amidst its tumbled buildings seems the only place at Vitcos appropriate for a game of quoits. Who actually built the place or lived there, or whether it was a palace at all, is not really known. Of all the house-groups at Rosaspata, it certainly occupies the most prominent and commanding terrain and has about it the most palatial aspect, but the fine quality of its masonry strongly suggests origins earlier than Manco's post-Conquest occupation. My guess is that Manco lived elsewhere, possibly in the big, double buildings with the courtyard in between, and that the so-called palace dates from the time of Pachacuti. Its best stonework is actually very fine. Large, beautifully fitted granite blocks surround the many doorways into the main building, a long structure facing onto the plaza from the north. (**Figure 19**, Building 1d-g) Most Inca sites of consequence seem to have had one or more such "great halls", called *kallankas* by some writers, and the large one facing the plaza at Espíritu Pampa is a classic example. The experts have long been puzzled by the long building at Rosaspata, though. Its multi-roomed layout is quite unlike that of other known *kallankas*, which, like the one at Espíritu Pampa, typically contain only a single, long, narrow room.

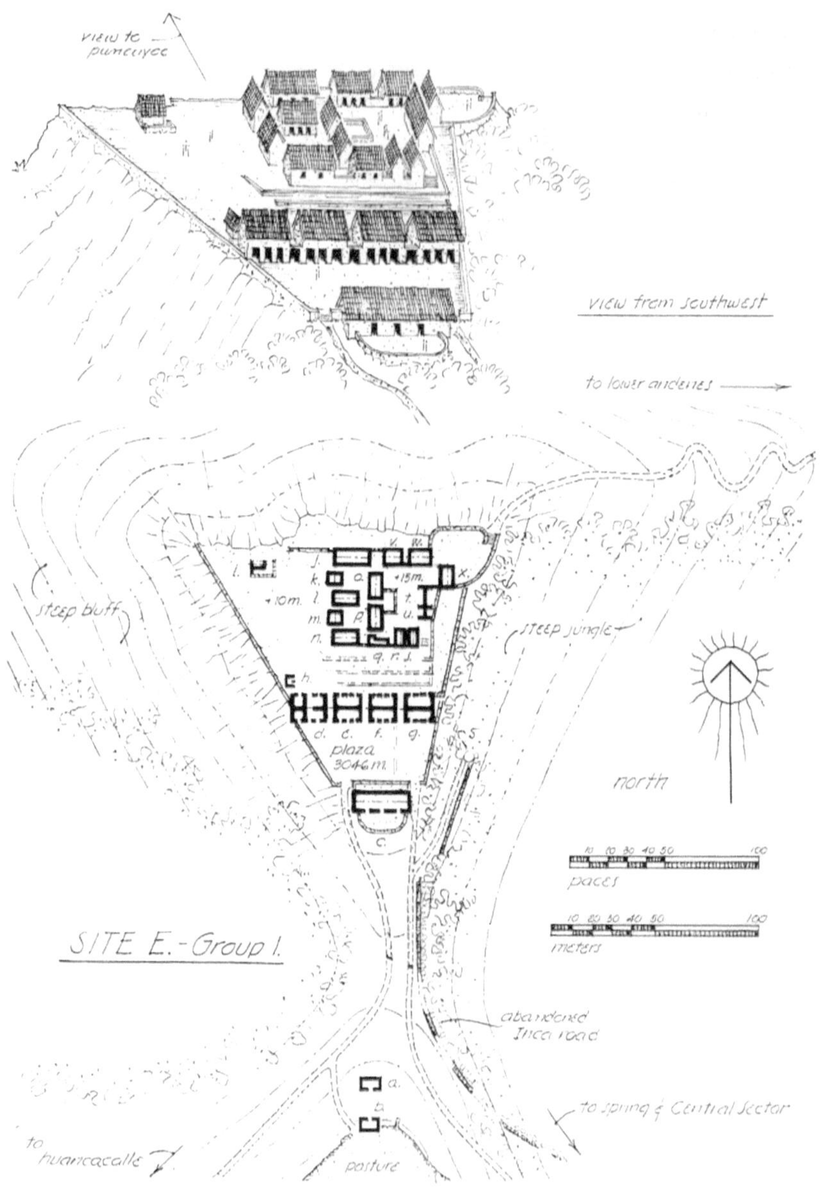

Figure 19 - Site plan of "palace" at Vitcos

For some reason, I was thinking about that very problem when, less than three hundred yards from the palace, we came to an overgrown rock wall, almost 60 yards long. At first, it seemed to have no openings at all, but a closer look showed the outlines of trapezoidal doorways every eight paces, apparently walled up by the Indians in recent times, probably to create a pen or corral for their animals. Recalling that the great hall at Espíritu Pampa, too, had doorways at intervals of about eight paces, we stopped to investigate. The wall turned out to be the front of a large, one-room structure, the real *kallanka* of Vitcos. Its six doorways had once opened northeast, onto a small *pampa* overlooking the valley of *andenes*, and the interior walls were fitted with continuous niches on all sides. Both features closely matched those of a ruin called Unca Pampa that Bingham's guides showed him in 1911 **(1)**. **(Figure 21)** It had since become so filled with debris and brush, the badly tumbled back wall was nearly invisible. To the casual passerby, the place would hardly have looked like a building at all.

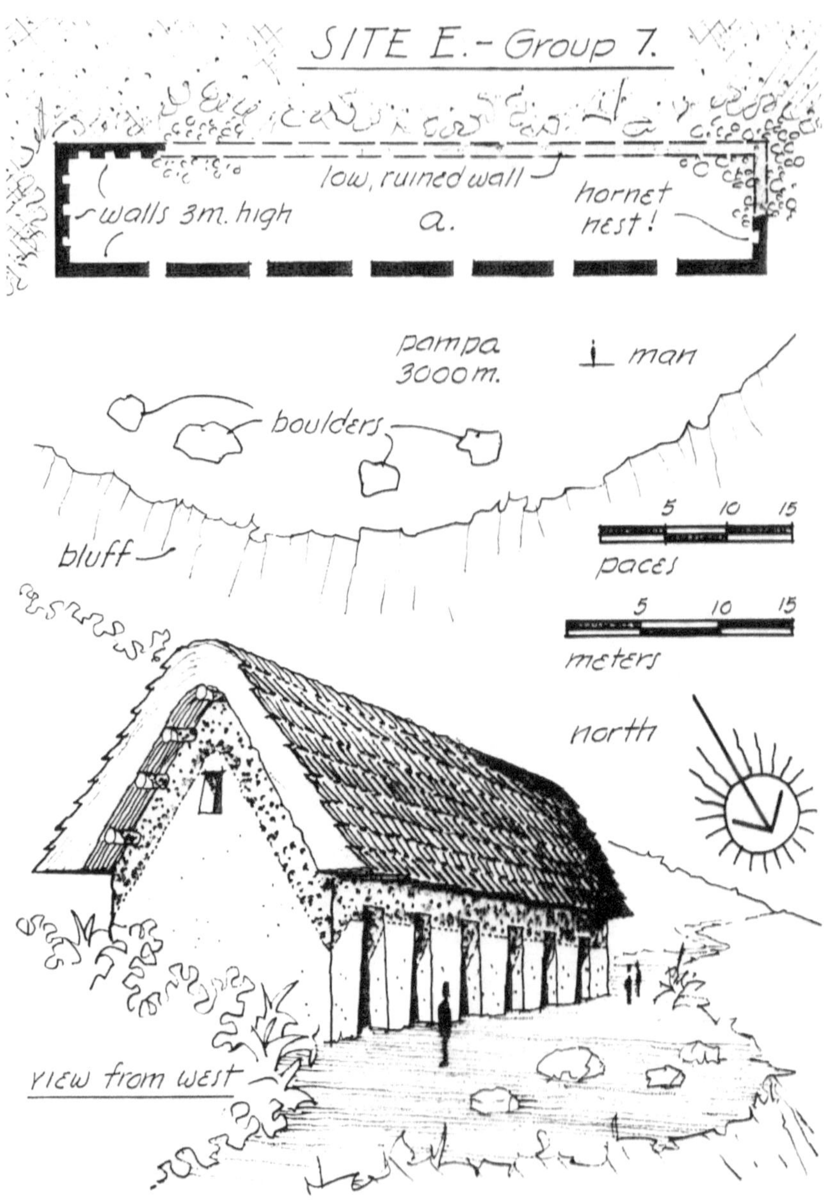

Figure 21 - Plan and view of kallanka (Bingham's Inca Pampa)

That being the last stop on José's tour, the others took a shortcut around the north end of the hill and cut the trail back to camp. I continued on to the palace for one last look around and then doubled back through the *andenes* to Bingham's sun temple, with its strangely carved boulder, spring and enigmatic surrounding ruins. What little literature there was seemed to treat the latter and all the other remains at Rosaspata as so many isolated sites, unrelated to one another. From what I'd seen, that wasn't true at all. It seemed to me they all added up to metropolitan Vitcos. I decided to map everything there on a single sheet and, for ease of comparison, do a similar map of the ruins at Espíritu Pampa at the same scale. With luck, I could then superimpose the plans of both cities onto terrain maps made from satellite enlargements and end up with fairly accurate aerial views of both of the Incas' final capitals - something no one else had ever done. **(Figures 17 and 47)**

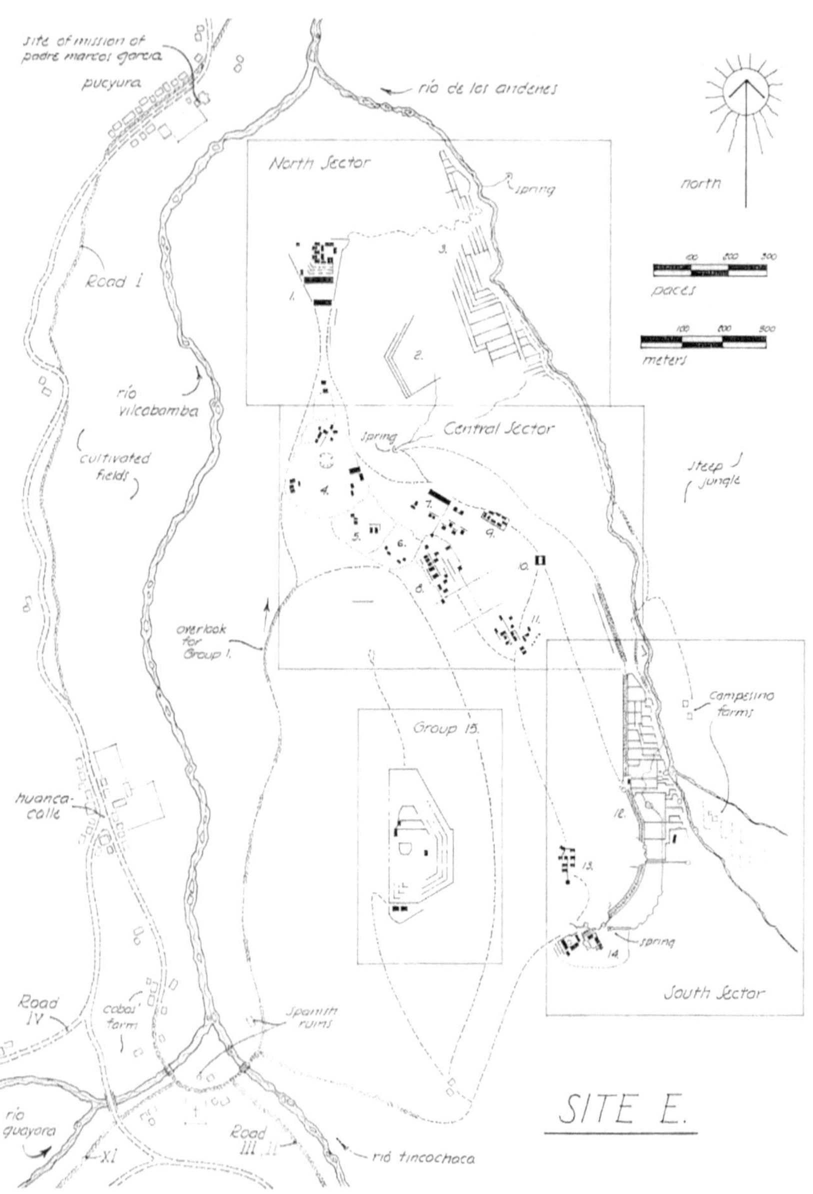
site of mission of padre marcos garcia
pucyura
río de los andenes
North Sector
spring
north
paces
meters
Road I
río vilcabamba
cultivated fields
Central Sector
spring
steep jungle
overlook for Group I.
campesino farms
Group 15.
huanca-calle
South Sector
spring
Road IV
cabos' farm
Spanish ruins
río guayara
XI
Road III, II
río tincochaca
SITE E.

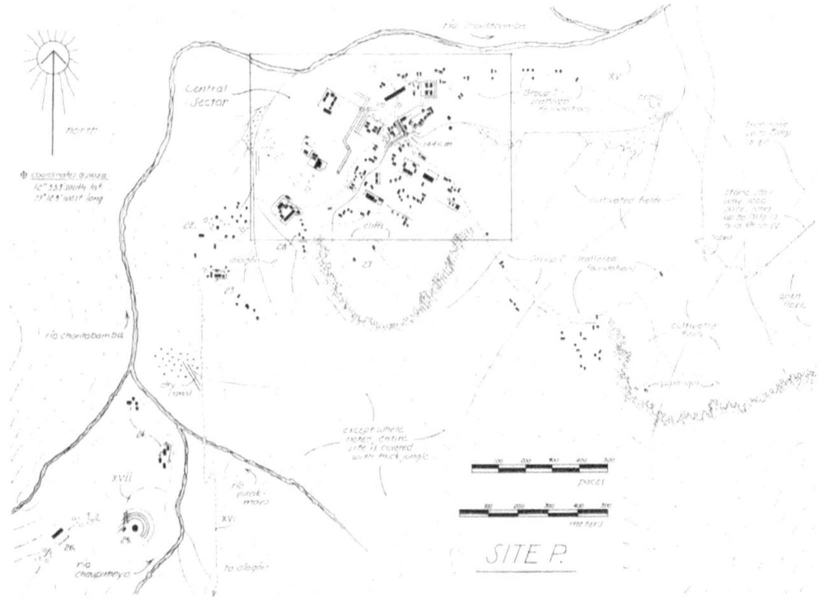

Figure 17 - Map of Rosas Pata and vicinity

In light of all we'd seen, found and done, there wasn't much doubt in my mind that Savoy was right about Vilcabamba the Old. Never mind his erroneous sites for Marcanay and the place called Mananhuañunca. Marcanay and both of the forts reported by the Spaniards had turned up along the only reasonable route between Pampaconas and the city, all pretty much according to the chronicles. The city itself was easily big enough, spreading for at least two miles through the forest. Arbieto had counted 400 houses, of which we'd found 116. Many others were doubtless still hidden in the bush, and others yet may have been built of adobe or wood, now long gone. The same thing was probably true at Vitcos, long accepted site of the first Inca capital-in-exile, where we'd found only 56 buildings - not very many for such a once-important place.

Also interesting, because they raised new questions rather than answering old ones, were sites like Tambo and Pincollunca. Were they the homes of the pre-Inca inhabitants of Vilcapampa or of the Incas' allies in their 35-year war with the Spaniards - or both? And, in any case, who were they? Were more of their villages lost in the forest, waiting to be found? If so, there were lots of places - like the entire Puncuyoc and Santuario Ranges - to look. All sorts of exciting work remained to be done, and as we packed up to leave, I was already thinking about coming back.

After an emotional farewell to José, Don Juvenal, his brother Flavio, and their respective families, we hiked reluctantly up the hill to await the truck. As I sat on my backpack, watching the crowd of kids gather for the great event - the arrival of a truck - I wondered what it all meant. We had accomplished what we'd set out to and much more. Our luck with the weather, the Indians, the terrorists, and the Incas had been uncannily good. Everyone had performed well and enjoyed the kind of experience that doesn't come along every day. As usual, the locals had taught us a great deal about simplicity without really trying. We, meanwhile, had made few converts to the world of complexity, our hearts likely not in it.

It would have made little difference. The *campesinos* would continue to plow the ruins under as their families grew and the markets for their crops increased. Their kids would learn Spanish, and even English, in school - while the old Quechua slowly died out. The road up the Vilcabamba River would be improved, year by year, until the 20th century finally came up to stay, rather than just visit. There'd even been talk in Cuzco about creating a national park in the region to safeguard the archaeological sites and make them more accessible to outsiders. What all this might mean to the locals wasn't clear, but the resulting changes would be many and rapid - almost never good news for traditional societies. Unless the terrorists won, I thought, some kind of government program was probably inevitable, sooner or later. But for the moment, the old ways remained unchanged in the Vilcabamba, and it was something fine to see.

Part II

10

Second Thoughts

A lifelong skeptic in all matters supernatural, I've never paid much attention to the New Age Peru of Shirley MacLaine and company. Still, there's no denying the spiritual power of the place, nor of the age-old beliefs of its millions of long-suffering Indians. By the end of the expedition, constant exposure to the ghost of greatness lost had begun to grow on me. Reflecting back on the eerie good fortune that had greeted us at virtually every turn, I realized I'd become convinced that Tupac Amaru, himself, was taking a personal interest in our affairs. Maybe it was just his insurance that I'd make good on my promise to bring Vilcabamba back to life, but for whatever reason, his attentions seemed to follow me all the way home - and beyond.

Once we were out of the mountains, even I could see how driven I'd become during the trip. Now that the pressure was off and a sense of detachment was possible, it was clear that our early successes had lured me into an almost maniacal compulsion to get it all, to find every ruin and solve every problem. At long last, I was done, and the relief was overwhelming. The expression on Nancy's face when she saw me get off the plane in Jackson Hole said it all. I'd lost 30 pounds since we'd parted company below Pampaconas nearly a month earlier and, after traveling for 44 hours straight, must have looked like a zombie. I certainly felt like one. She and I tried to fill each other in on all that had happened, both at home and in the jungle, but the adrenalin that had kept me going for weeks finally wore off and I crashed. Within minutes of pulling away from the airport I was sound asleep - and so ended Sixpac Manco II.

When I woke up the next day, my first call was to Savoy, since his Andean Explorers Club had co-sponsored our trip. After all that we'd found, I felt I had exciting news to report. He was gratifyingly excited to hear it, but thinking back, there was a tinge of something else in his reaction. When I told him about Puncuyoc, especially, it was as if he'd known about it all along and I was simply confirming what he, somehow, already knew. He'd been planning a re-do of Antisuyo for some time, he said, and thought what I'd found would be perfect for inclusion along with some other new material he'd received from another explorer named "Culp," or so it sounded. When I had all of my maps ready, Savoy concluded, Nancy and I should come to Reno and make a presentation to his local Club membership. Several times he emphasized that they would only be interested in new and previously unpublished material. That was hardly a problem from my point of view, since at that early stage I naively assumed I was lucky to be getting published at all, let alone in more than one place.

Meanwhile, Jill had been seeing Renzo, off and on, ever since they'd first met that day at Rosaspata. She was even planning a trip to his home in Trieste. Still feeling a bit ashamed about the suspicious way I'd dealt with the Italian during the trip, I decided to send along a thick packet of informally copyrighted material about what we'd found. I knew he'd be especially interested in Puncuyoc, since we found it after we'd last seen him at Huancacalle. Shortly after dropping his package in the mail to Jill, I mentioned it in passing to Savoy during one of our by then frequent phone conversations. "Really?" In that case, he said, he probably wouldn't want my material for his book after all. My do-it-yourself copyright wouldn't cut much ice in Europe, he thought, and there was thus no telling what Francescutti might do with the information. I knew in an instant he was right. I'd just given away the farm! Panicked, I hung up and and quickly called Jill to ask that she send everything back - which, bless her, she did. Savoy's warnings - highly ironic, as things turned out - had me so paranoid that I worried she might make copies and take them to Italy anyway, playing the part of a double agent, perhaps unwittingly recruited by Renzo for just that purpose. It sounds crazy, I know, but I'd been home less than a week and the intrigue was so thick, it was as if I'd brought a treasure map back from Peru.

The deed to the farm safely back in my hands, I set about documenting what we'd found. The winter of '84-5 arrived early in the Wyoming Rockies and the late autumn days were short, cold and snowy. It was a perfect season for working indoors and making finished maps and plans from the many pages of notes and sketches in my journals. Like the jungle-choked ruins they represented, the data made no sense at all until plotted onto large sheets of drafting paper. It was a fascinating process, like watching photographs take shape in a tray of developer. Slowly, as each new bit of information was added, the essence of sites completely unintelligible in the field re-emerged after four hundred years of obscurity. By early November everything we'd seen of Inca Vilcabama was shown on eleven large blue-line print sheets and I'd put together several hundred of our best slides to augment the drawings. I felt we were finally ready for Savoy's experts, so off we went to Reno.

Seeing Gene again, both Nancy and I were reminded of our first visit with him back in 1983. On that occasion, he'd been a courteous host, but wary and suspicious. Intentionally, he'd positioned himself in front of a brightly back-lighted window so as to appear no more than a silhouette to our squinting eyes. He exuded a certain unsettling charisma, but at the same time struck us both as a bit humorless and self-important. Since then, we'd learned more about the man and could better appreciate why.

His first-born son, Jamil, had died in the aftermath of the huge avalanche and landslide that in 1962 had swept down from Peru's highest mountain, 22,198 foot Huascarán. It had completely obliterated the village of Ranrahirca not far from Savoy's home in Yungay, beneath the towering peaks of the Cordillera Blanca. Thousands had died, and in the chaos which followed, disease had spread quickly among the survivors, including poor little Jamil. Though only a toddler at the time, the boy had somehow nonetheless revealed the secrets of the New Testament to his father before succumbing to cholera. Savoy thus believed Jamil was nothing less than the reincarnation of the child-Christ, and on that foundation, he'd created his own considerable following. Called the International Community of Christ, his church was eventually headquartered in Reno - though it claimed members from around the world. Maybe a bit of stand-offishness was to be expected of someone who'd literally fathered his own religion - but Nancy and I had both come away from that first meeting feeling awkward and uncomfortable.

Since then, things had warmed up. I'd come to like the man and even sympathized with what I began to imagine was his predicament. He seemed to have become trapped by the success of his church and bound to a lifestyle almost the antithesis of adventure. I knew how important my three or four months away from everyday life each year were to me and found it hard to believe anyone who'd become accustomed to that sort of thing could ever give it up for a year-round, sedentary, city routine - let alone one ruled by the obligations of a church leader. By the time of our second meeting, just before the expedition, Savoy had mellowed considerably and talked more easily of his own adventures - and tragedies - in Peru. Though he still maintained he'd never go back, it was obvious he missed at least the better parts of his previous life as an explorer.

Arriving, now, for our third visit, we found him courteous, but again cold and formal. He'd assembled a dozen or so people for the occasion, including his own family, and I chalked his distant demeanor up to the need to perform for this group of what could only be called his followers. To his credit, he shared the spotlight graciously though, and I doubt that it came easily. Dinner and my slide show went well enough, but the response to the latter was both a surprise and a let-down. No one except Savoy seemed to know anything at all about what I was talking about. Members of his Club the others apparently were, but experts on Peru they certainly were not. Where I'd hoped to learn something new about what we'd found, instead I was greeted with polite interest and little more.

Savoy, meanwhile, wanted to know about everything, but seemed especially fascinated by Puncuyoc. It was surely the most photogenic ruin we'd found - no doubt about that - and was, after all, the site Savoy said he'd have gone looking for in our place. But of all we'd found, Puncuyoc was the least significant, historically. As far as I knew, in fact, it had no history at all, and Savoy didn't appear to know any more about it than I did. Naively, I expected him to be more interested in the forts and Marcanay. They were the finds that clinched once and for all his claim that Espíritu Pampa was Manco's capital, but he didn't seem to care. Historic or not, they had zero media appeal.

The main outcome of our stay in Reno was that Savoy and I finally had a chance to talk seriously about his new book and my involvement in the project. My drawings, photos and a written manuscript were to be submitted to him by June 1st of the following year, 1985, for editorial review. Inasmuch as there was "no money" in a project like this, according to Savoy, my payment for whatever he decided to use was to be 50 copies of the resulting book, to do with as I pleased. In retrospect, it wasn't much of a deal, but at the time, I agreed and returned home eager to begin writing up our experiences. In appreciation for the pleasant evening at his home, I left Savoy a set of duplicates of my drawings. It would prove to be a mistake.

Back in Wyoming, I found that a large ranch house I'd designed for Don Kendall, then Chairman and CEO of Pepsico, had to be completely reworked and re-drawn in time for a previously scheduled construction start, then only four months away - and Don hadn't gotten where he was by missing deadlines. So, the crunch was on. I worked on his house about ten hours a day and tried to write for another three or four. Never having done any serious writing before, I was surprised by how difficult it was, yet how satisfying when words went together well. I caught myself mulling over passages in my mind as I sat drafting the final design of Don's house by day and mentally working out the details of that design while pecking away at my word processor after hours. Nancy and I ended up discussing some aspect of one project or the other - or both - almost every chance we got. It was exhilarating in a way, but intense. By New Year's day, I'd begun to fade, and by early February, we realized we were both badly burned out. We needed some warm sunshine and a change of pace.

Neither of us had ever been to the famous Anasazi ruins at Chaco Canyon and we figured a week or so in the desert might be just the thing. Our plan was to have some fun in Santa Fe for a few days before heading out to the ruins. While in town, we thought we'd look up Ed Ranney, the well-known photographer there who'd recently collaborated with John Hemming on a beautifully crafted, large format book about the Incas. **(1)** The trip figured to be a perfect get-away until the day before we left, when the frigid jet stream, which had been stalled over Wyoming for weeks, began dropping further and further south. By the time we stepped out of our rental car at La Posada, six inches of wet snow blanketed Santa Fe. Everyone there was quite excited. Disgusted, we got a room with a fireplace and called room service for a basket of juniper logs and two very tall drinks.

Under other circumstances, it might have been romantic. As it was, we wanted out. In the morning, we went directly to a travel agent, told him to get us the "cheapest seats available on the next plane to anyplace with warm, sunny weather," turned without another word and left for a luncheon date with Ranney at a nearby cafe. Once in from the cold, we found that the wine was good and the conversation stimulating. In a short time we began to cheer up in spite of ourselves. Ed turned out to be a great guy and thoroughly enjoyed the story of our adventures the previous summer. He thought my drawings would be of great interest to the experts, but he was quick to add that he wasn't really one of them. The man I should see, he said was someone named Rowe who apparently taught archaeology at Berkeley. Although I wrote it down, the name meant absolutely nothing to me. It should have, and, if my research hadn't been so myopically focused on Vilcabamba, it would have. A little disappointed, I thanked Ed for the tip and said I'd follow it up for sure. Since I hardly ever had occasion to visit the Bay Area, I knew it might be years before I could make good on the promise, but figured I'd drop his friend a line, at least, when we got home. Lunch done, we invited Ed to stop in on us next time he was in Jackson and slogged back through the snow to the ticket office hoping we might get a plane out that very same day.

"I checked out every destination in the sun belt. They're all socked in," the agent said. "But there's a great fare on the afternoon flight to San Francisco and, believe it or not, the computer says the weather out there is fabulous!"

Nancy and I exchanged glances of mock astonishment. It wasn't at all what we'd had in mind, of course, but Tupac Amaru was at it again. Clearly, the Inca wanted us to see this Professor Rowe and just to be sure we got the message had placed him squarely beneath the other end of our new-found rainbow. A quick call to Berkeley confirmed that the weather was indeed good and the archaeologist was available to see us. We took the seats without another thought, loaded up our unused camping gear and sped off down I-25 toward Albuquerque International. Chaco Canyon would have to wait. Uneasily, we were both aware that the thick roll drawings that lay on the back seat of our rental car was instead pulling us deeper and deeper into the far off jungles of Vilcabamba.

Dr. John· Howland Rowe turned out to be a highly distinguished professor of archaeology at the University of California and the founder and long-time President of the Institute of Andean Studies there. He has been doing pioneering work in Cuzco and elsewhere in Peru ever since the 1940s and is one of the world's pre-eminent authorities on the Incas and their imperial capital. **(2 & 3)** Despite his esteemed position in the front rank of Andean scholars, he was delighted to hear from us again when we called upon arrival in California. He cordially invited us both - complete unknowns - to join him, his wife, Patricia J. Lyon, a renowned anthropologist in her own right, and several friends from the Institute for coffee and a discussion of what he called "our work" in the Vilcabamba.

We met at the home of Jean-Pierre Protzen, a Swiss-born architect who was then chairman of the huge architecture school at Berkeley. Besides Protzen and the Rowes, two of Rowe's former students, Susan Niles and Margaret MacLean, were on hand and I soon had my maps and drawings spread out all over the floor. In contrast to Savoy's group, it was immediately obvious that everyone present had long experience in Peru and knew a great deal about the Incas. They all showed genuine interest in and considerable insight about what we'd found and done. Though impressed with Puncuyoc, they fully appreciated the historic significance of the other sites, as well.

Rowe was convinced, he said, that Rosaspata and Espíritu Pampa were indeed the sites of Vitcos and Vilcabamba the Old, but he wanted to know more about them. Aside from pre-Hispanic Cuzco and Tomebamba - the latter buried beneath the modern city of Cuenca, Ecuador, and both now largely destroyed by centuries of human occupation - the only other capitals the Incas had ever ruled from were the two cities we'd mapped in the Vilcabamba. While neither was pristine, both had lain more or less undisturbed since their abandonment in the sixteenth century and Rowe was certain that much of interest remained to be learned there. I was flattered by his praise of our work as a needed first step in what he clearly thought an important direction. Only in hindsight, I saw that he'd cleverly put the ball squarely back into my court. From that day on, it was inevitable that we'd return to the Vilcabamba and finish what we'd apparently only just begun.

In place of the open hostility Savoy had led us to expect from what he termed "the professionals," we instead sensed an immediate camaraderie. Modern archaeology works overtime to off-set the curse of its romantic and not altogether savory past, with the result that to amateurs like myself its more scientific practitioners sometimes seem inclined toward scientism, instead. The romance, adventure and excitement are still there, though, and there was no mistaking the strong appeal of those qualities among our new-found friends from Berkeley.

Mention of my doubts about Renzo brought unequivocal nods of agreement from several present who'd apparently dealt with him in the past. They claimed he wasn't really an archaeologist at all and thought of him more as a promoter trying to make a name for himself in archaeology. Others were more interested in my relationship with Savoy, but no one seemed to think I needed him or his book to legitimize what I was doing. When I protested that my drawings probably weren't up to academic snuff, Rowe laughed.

"Who else is doing what you are, let alone doing it better? Just make a clear distinction between fact and speculation," he said, "and you'll be okay."

In time, I heard complaints that the professor was more supportive of newcomers like me than he was to his fellow academics. I have no idea about that. Andean archaeology seems divided into two camps, those whose focus is on hard evidence and others, called structuralist, more inclined to fill the gaps in the historical record with informed suppositions. Rowe is a long-time advocate, actually one of the founders, of the former group. Some of his colleagues, feeling that the factual material has been pretty well mined out, sift through the tailings in search of new ideas - a more theoretical approach he sometimes greets with undisguised skepticism. All that aside, it was clear that Nancy and I had accidentally blundered up into the Board room and unwittingly gotten the attention of the Chairman. I've since wondered many times whether Savoy's dire predictions might have been more accurate if we'd shown up at the downstairs employment office instead, looking for work.

Before we left California, Rowe treated us to a tour of the vaults beneath the University anthropology museum. The public seldom gets to see the iceberg of stored artifacts in such places, of which the items on display are typically no more than the tip. In one drawer was the perfectly preserved mummy of a Peruvian girl with brightly colored ribbons beautifully braided into her long, black hair. In another was a meter-long, bronze crowbar still showing fresh scrape marks as if the Incas had used it moments before. I thought of the stockpiled roof pegs laying concealed in the mists of Puncuyoc, a quarter of a world away. The same spooky feeling that the workers were somewhere nearby returned as we continued our tour.

Finally, John asked us up to his office. There was something he wanted to show me, he said. Taped to the door was a plan of the pre-Incan, Peruvian ruins at Gran Pajatén, done in the late 60s by Duccio Bonavía, a Peruvian archaeologist. I got the point immediately. Some months earlier, a group from the University of Colorado had visited Gran Pajatén and initiated a media blitz describing their "discovery" of the site afterwards. Savoy, who'd included photographs and a description of the ruins in Antisuyo, published in 1970, cried "foul!" and claimed that he'd first spotted the site even before Bonavía. The subsequent scramble for credit made it all the way to Time, Newsweek and People and everyone involved came off looking a little silly. Smugly, I thought that was one mistake I'd never make.

But it wasn't the plan of Pajatén that John wanted me to see. Instead, he handed me a file once we were inside the office. Enclosed, he said, were some sketches and photos recently sent to him by a fellow named Stuart White, an expatriate American geographer who'd apparently lived in the Vilcabamba for two years in the late 70s and done some exploring there. Rats! I'd never even heard of the guy and my first reaction was disappointment that another *gringo* had so recently beaten me into the area. It was like finding out about a new girlfriend's former lover. That she'd had one wasn't all that shocking - you just didn't want to hear about it. White and his wife, Lynn Hirschkind, with whom he'd first gone to Vilcabamba, had since built up a good sized llama and alpaca ranch in the Andes northeast of Cuenca. We were all eventually to become a good friends, at first through a lengthy correspondence and later during visits and shared adventures in both Ecuador and Wyoming. In fact, Nancy ended up buying me a llama of my own as a 50th birthday present in late '88 and I got his half brother for her that same Christmas. From then on, Stu was to be our *compañero*, fellow explorer and visiting llama expert - but at the time, that was all years in the future.

I flipped to the first photo in Rowe's file and my heart sank. It was Puncuyoc. The sketches weren't as pretty as mine, but it was all there. If anything, his notes were more detailed and the measurements shown were more accurate than my own. With a knowing smile, John said White's report would appear in the next edition of his Institute's journal, Ñawpa Pacha. Far more detailed than anything done by Bingham, von Hagen or Savoy, White's would be the first really scholarly documentation ever published in English about Inca Vilcabamba. It is still among the best **(4)**. So much for my fame and fortune as the "discoverer" of Puncuyoc. How many of our other "finds" were already well known, I wondered.

It was coming home from Berkeley that we got our second shock. The switchboard operator at our motel in Fort Collins, Colorado rang our room to say we had a long-distance call. Assuming it was my son, Chris, the only one who knew where we were, I was instead surprised to hear Savoy. He was excited. Having called us at home and gotten our number, he had big news that just couldn't wait. "Just returned from an expedition to Puncuyoc," he said. "Quite a place!" This, from the man who had just three months earlier assured us he would "never go back" to Peru. It was obvious he'd begun planning the expedition before we'd even left Reno and had the drawings I'd left behind to show him the way. With the help of the local *campesinos*, he said, he'd taken his family up there for a few days to look around and photograph the ruins. I was stunned! In a matter of seconds, it looked like my mentor had turned into a competitor, and a formidable one at that.

While I was still reeling from the news, he switched to Gran Pajatén and his manner changed abruptly from enthusiasm to anger. He complained bitterly about the treatment he'd gotten - or, rather, failed to get - in the media coverage of the University of Colorado's expedition. He was, he said, "setting the record straight, once and for all." Tom Lennon, the archaeologist in charge of the Colorado group was, according to Savoy, yet another "professional" trying to steal his thunder. "You can't trust anybody in this business," he concluded, echoing once again his advice to me the previous spring. I began to wonder if I shouldn't include Savoy, himself, in the warning.

Mainly, I felt angered that yet another *gringo* explorer was now muscling in on what I'd come to think of as my territory. I worried who else would turn up next? Worst of all, there wasn't a damned thing I could do about it, so I listened on in silence. On a more positive note, Savoy switched back to his Puncuyoc trip and said something that recalled our visit with Rowe. He thanked me for my drawings and said his guides had found the maps and plans "excellent" and "especially useful." For the first time, I realized that was what separated me from the many other "adventurers," as the experts liked to call them, who hovered at the periphery of Andean archaeology. They wrote entertaining, if sometimes exaggerated, accounts of their travels. Some speculated wildly on various "mysteries" encountered along the way, but few produced anything useful to serious researchers - and therein lay their sin. Had I turned up at Berkeley with nothing more than a good story and some pretty slides, our reception might not have been so warm. Instead, Rowe had invited us to attend the next annual meeting of his Institute and insisted that I give a paper describing our 1984 expedition. He thought the entire membership would be interested in what we'd done.

Fortunately, the Institute meeting was still nearly a year away. My immediate problem was finishing up the description of our travels in time for Savoy's June 1st editorial deadline. Still uneasy with his abrupt about face and the surprise trip to Puncuyoc, I figured I'd better get back to it and complete my manuscript as quickly as possible. Then came the third shocker. Late in February, Carl Kriegeskotte, an old friend and adventure film-maker in New York, sent me a copy of a letter he'd gotten from Savoy soliciting advance purchases of the new book, available at "$250.00" each! Savoy's comment that there would be "no money" in the project leapt immediately to mind. Featured, was to be a description of the "Sun Temple of Pitcos" (Pardo's spelling for Vitcos), a fabulous two story structure that sounded a lot like Puncuyoc to me. According to his letter, Savoy had managed to "locate" it in the course of a hair-raising adventure in the company of "fellow members" of his Club. The part about the "Sun Temple" went on to say that the book would include "maps and architectural renderings of the ruins, all previously unpublished." I wondered how I could have been so dumb as to leave all that stuff in Reno. The punch line was near the end: a limited edition was to be mailed out "just as soon as it comes off the press, estimated to be June, possibly earlier." **(5)** Although Savoy sent the letter out to a long list of potential buyers for "our" new book, I never got one. I would have never even seen a copy but for my friend, Carl, in New York.

It didn't take Sherlock Holmes to see that the material he'd asked me to submit by June 1st would arrive too late to be included in the $250 book. Savoy had gotten all he needed from me back in November, when I'd foolishly left my drawings behind. Galvanized into action, I went back to my word processor, double-time. By the end of March, the manuscript was finished and I decided to publish it myself, desk-top style, as SIXPAC MANCO: Travels Among the INCAS. **(6)** I was careful to include all the maps and drawings we'd left with Savoy and I registered the copyright through the Library of Congress. With a certain poetic justice, I sent a copy of the finished product to Savoy on April Fool's day, 1985, with a letter suggesting he let me know if he wanted to use any of its contents in his new book. I also enclosed a copy of the incriminating letter with Kriegeskotte's name blocked out to keep him from being involved if there was trouble. My only comment: "You've told me from the start that I should 'trust no one' and I guess you really meant no one."

Author's logo and 1985 book cover design.

Savoy never responded nor, to my knowledge, was his new book ever published. Almost a year later, I passed through Reno on my way home from Rowe's Institute meeting and decided to drop in on him, unannounced, for a cup of coffee. Why not? I should have been angry at the man, but I was mainly just curious about what he'd have to say for himself. As might be expected, the atmosphere at his place was a bit tense until we descended several floors into the basement and he closed the door to his study. No apology was expected, and none was given. He'd "misjudged" me, he said. He had thought all along that I was "his man" in the Vilcabamba - but he could now see that I was "my own man." "Baloney," I thought, but decided to let it go. I was older and wiser, but there was no real harm done. As Gene talked, I even saw the bright side. In his own way he'd taught me yet another valuable lesson: copyright everything. I chalked the whole thing up to experience and changed the subject.

Despite the circumstances, he was more relaxed than I'd ever seen him and, surprisingly, we both enjoyed the visit. Partly, I think, it was the fact that we were alone for the first time and he felt no pressure to perform for an audience. Also, once we'd managed to more or less clear the air between us, the fact remained that, for better or worse, we had a lot in common. His work at Espíritu Pampa, after all, had inspired me to go to Peru in the first place. Having done so, it was my work at Puncuyoc that had inspired him to go back, after twenty years of self-imposed exile. Tom Lennon got the credit - or blame - for putting Savoy back on the front page, but the explorer's return to the jungle was, to some extent, my doing.

Once there, however, he quickly returned to his old ways. According to my friend Juvenal, who participated as a horse packer and guide, Savoy's Puncuyoc expedition was an elaborate affair attended by much hoop-la and publicity. With him in addition to his family were various dignitaries and more than a few armed policemen to discourage trouble with the terrorists. A large crew was hired to open the old Inca road up to the site and they completely cleared the jungle from the main building and a nearby, but previously overgrown and unreported Inca *baño*, or bath. Savoy then photographed everything exhaustively for inclusion in the $250-a-copy book. The workers, meanwhile, were apparently well provided with imported beer, as the number of discarded aluminum cans we found there some months later confirmed. Everyone involved seems to have regarded the expedition as a return to the good-old-days of Savoy's grand adventures in the sixties. But, it was not to be, at least not in the Vilcabamba.

History was, in fact, about to repeat itself. Though he has continued his explorations in Peru, to my knowledge Savoy never went back to Vilcabamba after that first trip in early 1985. Just as he'd done twenty years earlier, he shifted his attentions to the northern region of Chachapoyas, where Lennon had unwisely slighted his work at Gran Pajatén. The inflated media blitz which attended the Colorado group's return from the site had failed even to mention Savoy, let alone honor his twenty year old, though widely disputed, claim as the "discoverer" of the place. From Gene's point of view, the villains were the same kind of "experts" who'd ignored his accomplishments at Espíritu Pampa two decades before and now they were trying to take credit for his work just as the Peruvian, Santander, had then. His response was vintage Savoy. He counterattacked. In July of 1985, he announced the even more startling and news-worthy "discovery" of a vast complex of sites he called Gran Vilaya, **(7)** a hundred or so miles north of Gran Pajatén. Where the latter was comprised of a score of buildings, Savoy's new finds included, he said, more than twenty thousand! How much of all this was really new and how much just a re-hash of earlier work by himself and others remained unclear, but the media loved it. The Coloradans were effectively eclipsed and the spotlight was once again squarely on Gene Savoy. For how long, remains to be seen, but one thing is certain: "Indiana" Savoy is back, and we've not yet heard anything like the last of him.

11

Back To Square One

Savoy wasn't the only one who got a first-run copy of my book, of course, and I gave one to each of the members of Sixpac Manco I and II as well. Jim Little, especially, had gotten interested in the whole project and when I stopped by his office to drop one off, it turned out he'd been doing some reading on his own. In fact, he was just then finishing up Victor von Hagen's Highway of the Sun, the story of the expedition that had led the explorer to Vitcos in search of Inca roads. There was a brief passage about a ruin not far from Rosaspata that von Hagen called "Puncuyoc". The place, Jim said, sounded awfully familiar. Back home, I grabbed my copy and, sure enough, there it was, a few pages beyond where I'd lost interest the previous year. **(1)** So much for selective research. von Hagen's description of the site differed in a few strangely significant details from what we'd found, but it was the same place, all right. Though he hadn't gone there himself, von Hagen dismissed the ruins as "Spanish inspired," based on what his people told him. No wonder nobody had bothered to follow up on the discovery for nearly a quarter of a century, until White's visit in 1978. "Tough luck, Stu," I thought, consoling myself with the fact that he hadn't discovered the place either.

The whole thing was beginning to remind me of the meaningless but lingering controversy about the "discovery" of Machu Picchu by Hiram Bingham **(2)**. The Indians increasingly claimed they'd known about his "lost city" all along. The *campesinos* pointed out that they were already living in the ruins when they took him there. Various European and Peruvian explorers said they'd heard about Machu Picchu long before Bingham's visit and one complained that he'd actually told the American where it was. Despite all such carping, however, the world had long ago decided to give credit where it was due and there was little doubt in the popular mind about who'd found the magnificent site above the clouds. Even the professionals identified the place with Bingham - he'd done most of the work there, after all - and that brought the matter close to home. The only real casualty had been the word "discovery." It would never again be used in quite the same way. I'm often reminded of a joke I once saw in the New Yorker showing Balboa gazing out over the Pacific, with raised sword and Spanish flag unfurled. One of his Indian guides has turned to another and says, "I think he's right. There *is* an ocean out there." And so it was with Puncuyoc. I couldn't help wondering: who'd been up there before von Hagen's group?

With Savoy's silence after my April Fool's surprise, it looked for a time like the cast of characters in the Vilcabamba had finally revealed itself and the plot had ceased to thicken. That impression was short-lived. On May 14th, I received a thick package of Xeroxed correspondence addressed to Savoy, but sent to me by someone named Robert von Kaupp - no doubt, I assumed, the "Culp" Gene had mentioned in passing at the dinner in Reno. The copy of Sixpac Manco I'd sent to him on April 1st had apparently been forwarded on to von Kaupp shortly thereafter. According to the cover letter that came with the correspondence file, von Kaupp thought my book a fine piece of work with, however, one small reservation: it was "all wrong." Despite our differences, I'd written that Savoy was right; that the ruins at Espíritu Pampa were without doubt those of the Incas' final capital at Vilcabamba the Old. von Kaupp's letter claimed there was no way that could be true. It was just what I needed: Puncuyoc, the crown jewel of our expedition, had been reported decades earlier by von Hagen, was to be published by White and was being claimed after the fact by Savoy. Now someone new was saying I was all wet about Espíritu Pampa! Thoroughly depressed, I opened the file and began to read.

Robert von Kaupp turned out to be a crusty Washington, D.C., real estate investor, trained in anthropology and fluent in both Spanish and Quechua. All this, I learned some months later when we met and bonded over more than a few beers in Cuzco. Despite our differences, we got on well and Nancy and I even visited him at his home in the capital during a subsequent trip east. He lived not far from the Library of Congress, with easy access to and a broad knowledge of the chronicles of Inca Vilcapampa. In 1978, he uncovered a mystery which neither he nor anyone else has been able to solve in all the years since.

The personal notes of both Bingham and von Hagen tell of a place called Mananhuañunca in the forest beyond Pampaconas where the locals believed a Spanish priest had been killed and/or buried - which, was not entirely clear - in Inca times. **(3** & **4)** Neither explorer ever went there or bothered to publish the reports. Strangely, Savoy failed even to mention the legend during his search for Marcanay and Mananhuañunca in the jungles above Espíritu Pampa. His guides were, after all, the sons of Julio Cobos, the very man who'd advised von Hagen. With Savoy as his primary source, von Kaupp was thus unaware of the story until he learned of it from the locals during a visit to Yupanka in 1978. Unlike his predecessors, he was also told of an obscure ruin site, not far from Mananhuañunca, called La Mesada. No *gringo* had ever been there, and even the *campesinos* knew little about the place. From his reading of Calancha, von Kaupp knew immediately that the Spanish priest must have been Ortiz, the fellow who'd died so slowly that the Indians had come to call the place of his execution Mananhuañunca - "he-would-not-die." If so, then the ruined town had to be Marcanay, the supposedly nearby village where the unfortunate *padre* had been sentenced to death by Tupac Amaru Inca.

Like Savoy and everyone since, von Kaupp understood that locating Marcanay was one of the keys to clinching once and for all the site of Vilcabamba the Old, so he immediately demanded to see Mananhuañunca and the nearby ruins of La Mesada. Pancho Quispicusi, a colorful and well-known Yupanka guide, agreed to take him there in the poor conditions of an especially rainy March. Then came the bombshell. According to Pancho, neither site was anywhere near Savoy's ruined city. Instead, both were in the remote canyon of the Río Urumbay, about mid-way between Rosaspata and Espíritu Pampa and thus more than twenty miles, or nearly seven leagues, from the place the world had come to accept as Manco's lost capital. For von Kaupp, the message was clear: Savoy and his supporters were dead wrong. The chronicles were unequivocal: Marcanay was no more than a scant "two leagues" - six miles - from the city. The Inca's final refuge couldn't possibly be at Espíritu Pampa. It was still out there, hidden somewhere in the forest near La Mesada, waiting to be discovered.

In support of this revisionist - actually revolutionary - new theory, von Kaupp wrote a brief report of his Urumbay visit five years later, in 1983 **(5)**, but it was never published. It's not easy to imagine why, since he was the first explorer to go there and, if he was right about the place, it was a major find. Even harder to understand, was his failure to take photographs or even make sketches of what he saw. At Mananhuañunca, he described a "recently opened tomb" marked with "radiating lines of stones." Across the canyon to the south, he said, was a "large Inca ruin" with "a central nucleus" surrounded by more than "eighty four houses on different levels, like *andenes.*"

According to his voluminous correspondence with Savoy, von Kaupp and Quispicusi had been scouring the jungle for the "real" Vilcabamba the Old ever since, but without success. Still, if the locals were right about Mananhuañunca and La Mesada was, in fact, Marcanay, the search for Vilcapampa had been set back to square one. Just when almost everyone had come to accept Savoy's claims - and, perhaps more to the point, Hemming's endorsement - hard evidence directly to the contrary lay there in the wild, jungle choked canyon of the Río Urumbay. The catch was, no one but von Kaupp knew about it. He'd tried to convince Savoy, and apparently gotten nowhere. Now it was my turn. The question was what, if anything, should I do about it? Though he'd gone there by a completely different route, it turned out his sites were no more than a couple of miles - less than a league - from Tambo, the hilltop ruin I'd identified as the New Fort. I realized I had no choice. The only way to deal with von Kaupp's counter-theory and complete my inventory of all the sites in the province was to go there and check them out for myself. Ever since the meeting in Berkeley, Nancy and I had known we weren't quite done with the Vilcabamba. Now, I knew exactly where to go and what to do. The decision was easy. Come July and August of the following season, 1986, Sixpac Manco III would be back in the jungle.

Meanwhile, all through the summer of 1985, von Kaupp kept on sending me a steady stream of material, most of it contrary to some aspect or other of the ideas I'd so confidently advanced in Sixpac Manco. Ours was the classic conflict between scholar and field man. Bob would build 20 and 30 page treatises on the turn of some obscure phrase in the chronicles or some passage quoted from Bingham, Savoy or Hemming. For him, the fact that something had been written down made it so. I had found ample evidence to the contrary. Again and again, I'd found things on the ground that contradicted the written record, and had come to the conclusion that one pile of rocks in the field was worth ten old books in the library. For me, research was a means to an end - finding sites - not an end in itself.

It should have been no surprise, then, that one of von Kaupp's favorite sources was the work of Edmundo Guillén Guillén. Guillén is a noted Peruvian ethnohistorian, not an explorer. Yet, in the years following publication of The Conquest of the Incas, Guillén decided to retrace the route of the Spanish invasion of 1572 and compare what he found on the ground to the descriptions in the chronicles. He especially favored the reports of Arbieto, the Spanish commander, and Sarmiento de Gamboa, since both had actually witnessed the action. Hemming had given a detailed account of the campaign based on these and other sources, but his handling of the geography was necessarily vague since in 1970, none of the forts or battlegrounds involved had ever been positively located. No one had ever even looked. Like Angles Vargas before him, Guillén decided it was high time a Peruvian got into the picture and in 1976 he set out for Vilcabamba.

Almost immediately, he stumbled upon an apparent contradiction between Hemming's interpretation of the chronicles and the actual terrain. A few kilometers up the Río Vilcabamba from the famous bridge at Chuquichaca, Guillén came to a steep gorge or ravine called "*Choquellusca*" which, he said, was "*remembered for the ambush of the Spaniards in 1539*," **(6)** the rout described by Pedro Pizarro in which disaster had nearly resulted from a pebble in Gonzalo Pizarro's shoe. Murúa, in his account of the invasion of 1572, identified the same stretch of rough country as the pass of "*Chuquillusca*" **(7)** and Guillén understandably assumed that the scene of the action in both cases must therefore have been the rocky canyon he'd found that still bears essentially the same name. The contradiction arises when one recalls that both Pizarro and Murúa were clearly talking about a place in the forest beyond Pampaconas, more than fifty kilometers to the west of Guillén's ravine. **(Figure 32)** Further complicating matters, Calancha, talking about the country beyond Pampaconas, had called it "*Chuquiago*." **(8)** Guillén solved the problem by moving the scene of both battles eastward, although it was much more likely Murúa's misuse of the name Chuquillusca to describe the place actually called Chuquiago that caused all the trouble. **(9)**

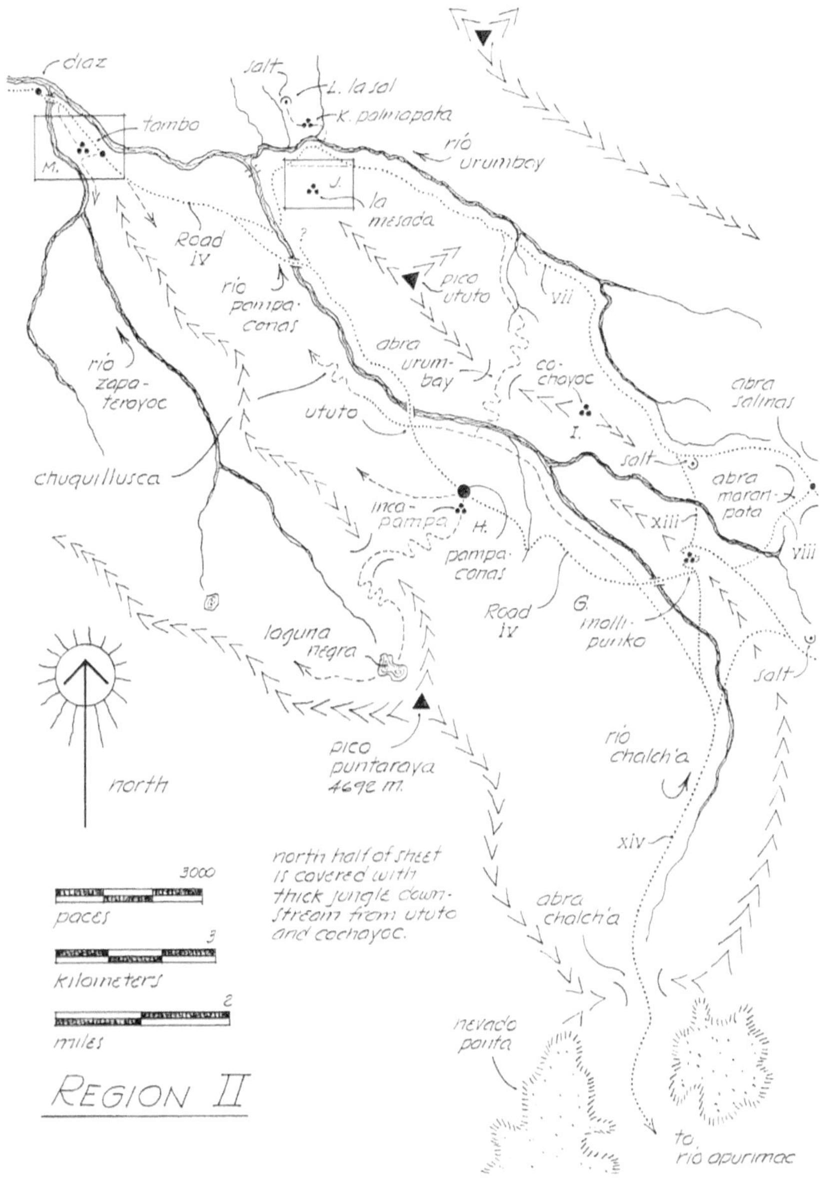

Figure 32 - Map of upper Rio Pampaconas

Proceeding on up into the highlands, Guillén soon found what he believed to be another discrepancy in the long accepted record. Baltasar de Ocampo had described Vitcos as "*...on a very high mountain whence the view commanded a great part of the Province of Vilcapampa.*"

(10) Rodriguez de Figueroa, en route to his fateful meeting with Titu Cusi in 1565, found Vitcos between a village called "*...Arancalla, in a very rough country near the snows, where there was a large fort..,*" **(11)** and his destination at Pampaconas. Guillén had problems reconciling Bingham's Vitcos with both reports and concluded that "*Rosaspata does not correspond to these descriptions.*" **(12)**

The Peruvian agreed that Vitcos must be nearby but, like all researchers up to that time, he was unaware of the true extent of the ruins at and near Rosaspata. Also, he was misled by the turn of a single word in Figueroa's narrative. Guillén assumed the fortress named "Arancalla" must have been the cluster of huts the locals still call "Layangalla", several kilometers up the canyon, beyond Rosaspata, on the road to Pampaconas. It followed that Vitcos must therefore lie hidden, yet undiscovered, somewhere in the hills between Layangalla and Pampaconas - in any case a long way from Bingham's ruined "palace" at Rosaspata. Very much in character, Guillén didn't bother to actually look for his new Vitcos. He would have been disappointed if he had. The country in question is high, open and well known to the *campesinos*. There's nothing there. If, instead, he'd looked for Arancalla *below* Rosaspata, he might have found Pincollunca, **(Figure 16)** a site which matches Figueroa's description quite well. Finally, had he but ventured to the very summit of the hill of Rosaspata, he would have found there the immense, terraced "fortress" which commands precisely the panoramic views Ocampo described. **(Figures 29 and 30)**

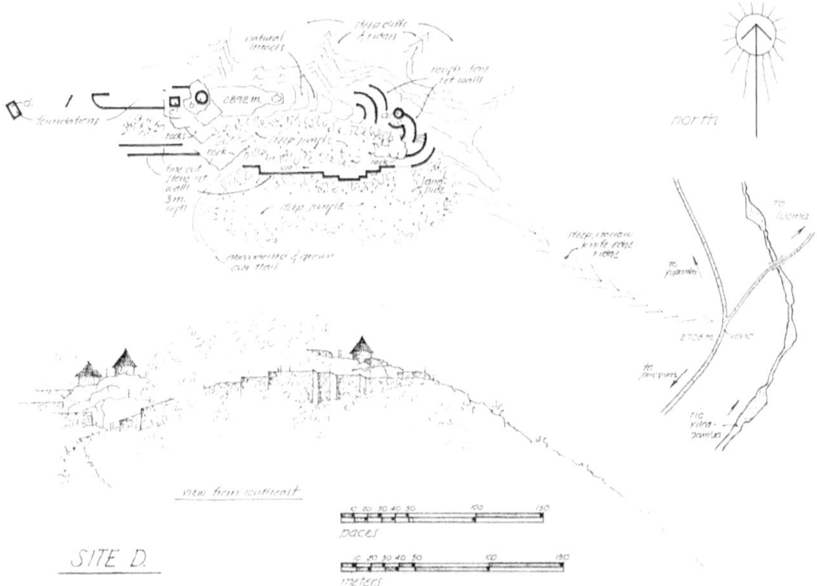

Figure 16 - Site plan and view of Pinccollunca

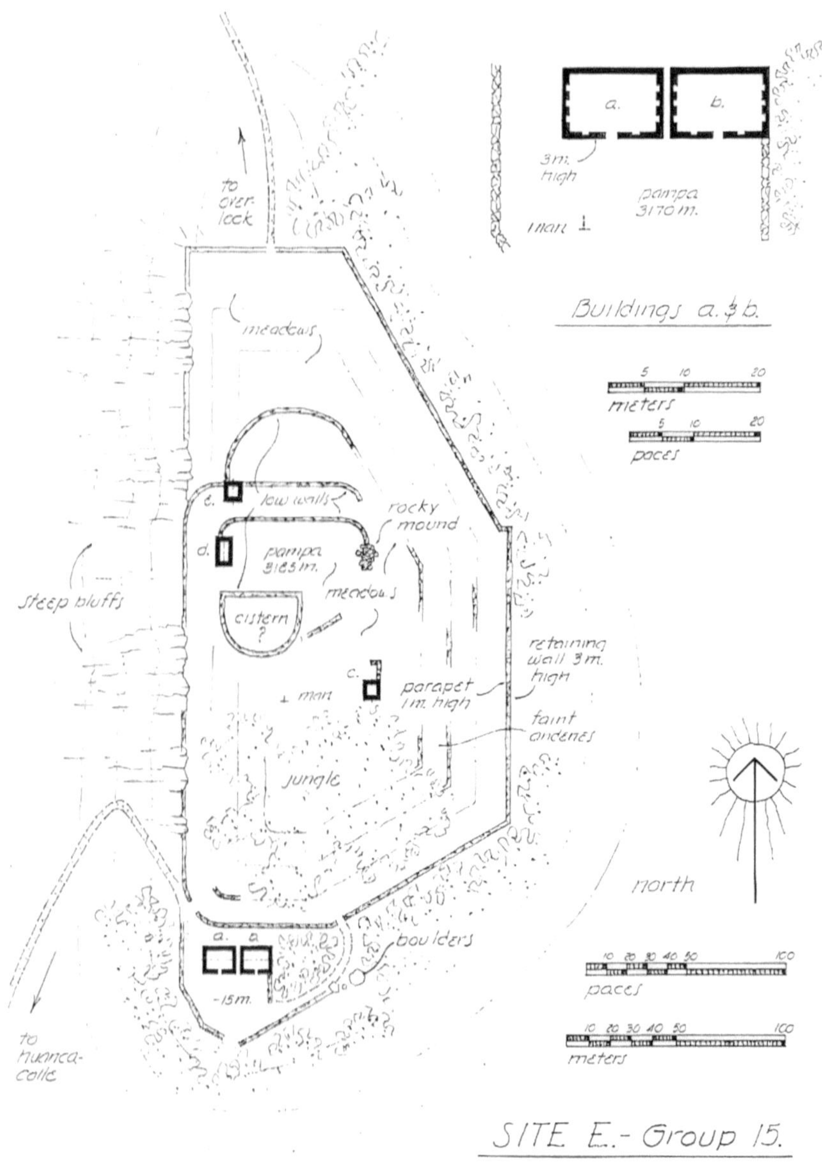

Figure 29 - Plan of “fortress” at Vitcos

Figure 30 - View of "fortress"

Rather, he hastened over the pass of Kolpacasa and dropped into the forest below Pampaconas. At first, there wasn't much to go on because beyond Ututo, the big meadow along the river, none of the old place-names seemed still in use. Again, his analysis of the terrain hinged on a single word. The Spaniards said they'd camped at "Anonay" two days before the battle for the New Fort. Just above Vista Alegre, Guillén noted that the trail crossed the Río "Ayunay,"

(Figure 44) and determined it must have been the scene of the Spanish bivouac. Assuming so, he predicted locations downstream from there for both forts. Again, he didn't actually look very hard for either site, but simply deduced where they would someday be found.

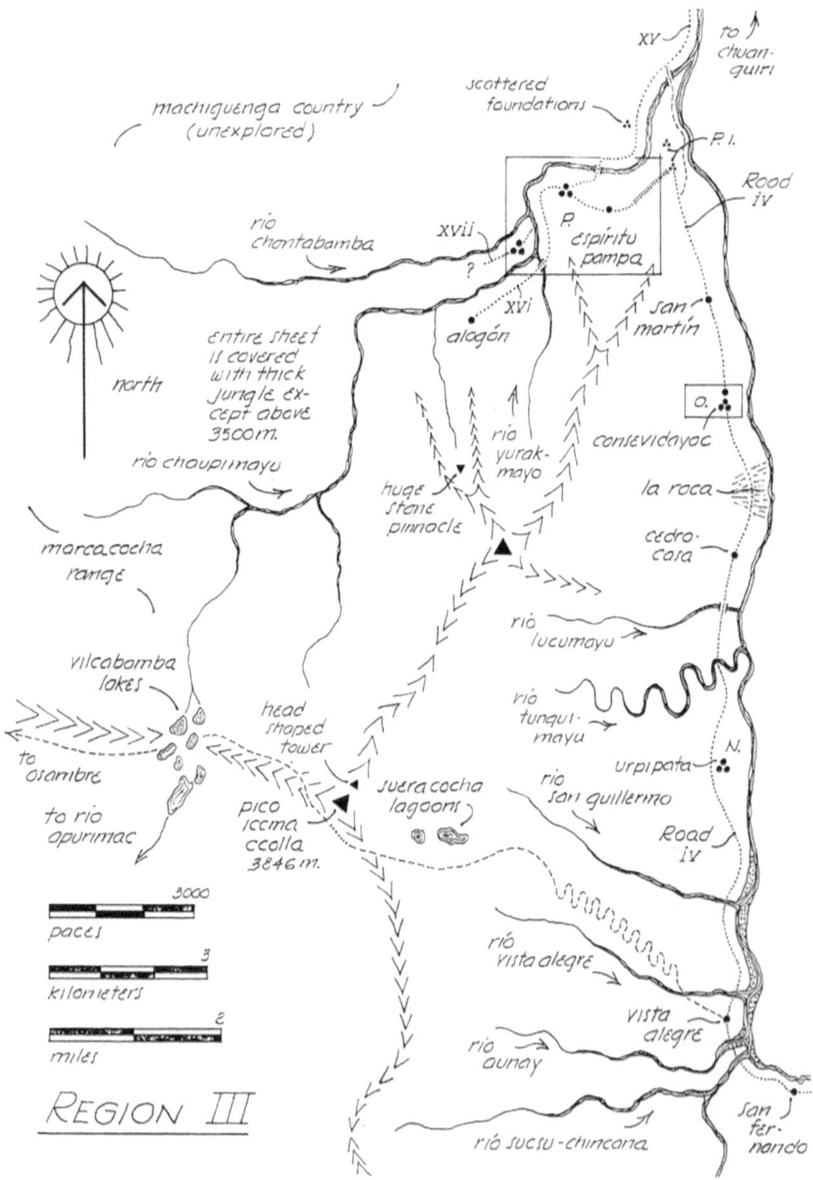

Figure 44 - Map of lower Rio Pampaconas

As might be expected of a renowned historian and academician, Guillén tended to emphasize research and the written record in favor of exhaustive field work. Juvenal Cobos, one of his guides in 1976, told me that "Dr. Larga Vista," as they affectionately called him, was well liked by the men since they never had to cut trails very far into the bush. Instead, from astride his horse, Guillén would peer off into the forest with his binoculars - *larga vistas* - and explain to the men what ought to be found there. Still, like Hemming, his research is thorough and some of his arguments are theoretically sound. In the years since von Kaupp first introduced me to Guillén's work, Edmundo and I have become well acquainted. Despite lengthy arguments over many rounds of *cervezas*, neither of us has convinced the other of anything - except that the "Vilcabamba Club" is a small, select group of crazies, whether *gringos* or *Peruanos*. Regarding the forts, we've pretty much agreed to disagree. As this is written, in fact, Guillén's new book describing the 1572 campaign goes to press in Peru and, with my blessings, uses a few of my own maps and drawings to once again make his case. **(13)**

A final player von Kaupp put me onto presented no challenge to my ideas, but filled instead an important niche none of the rest of us had paid much attention to. Just as von Kaupp and Quispicusi began combing the heart of Vilcabamba for the real lost city of the Incas, an Englishman named John Beauclerk was among a group of his countrymen - and women - busily exploring the fringes of the province. Beauclerk was particularly interested in the Apurimac slope of the Cordillera Vilcabamba where Paddock had reported an Inca road and ruins near the highland village of Arma in 1970. A second Inca road bypassed Arma and crossed into the headwaters of the Río Huacaraquina or Mapillo, a major tributary of the Apurimac. On the assumption that Paddock's ruins probably weren't the only ones in the region, Beauclerk checked out the lower reaches of the Mapillo in 1979.

He found evidence there of Inca occupation in several places, most importantly at Acobamba, **(14)** a name recalling the peace treaty with the Spaniards signed by Titu Cusi in 1566. Heavily overgrown ruins there turned out to be an Inca palace or country estate of some sort. Beauclerk thought it almost certainly the location where the historic negotiations and signing had taken place. Since the Viceroy's delegation must surely have approached Acobamba from Spanish occupied Peru, across the Apurimac, the road along which Beauclerk's, ruins were found must therefore have been a major route into and out of the province in Inca times. Titu Cusi's father, Manco, and prior to the treaty, Titu Cusi himself, had periodically raided the country west of Cuzco, no doubt utilizing the same road to and from their stronghold at Vitcos. I'd often noticed Inca paving stones ascending the Río Guayara behind Cobos' house **(Figures 4 and 17)** and wondered where they led. Now I knew.

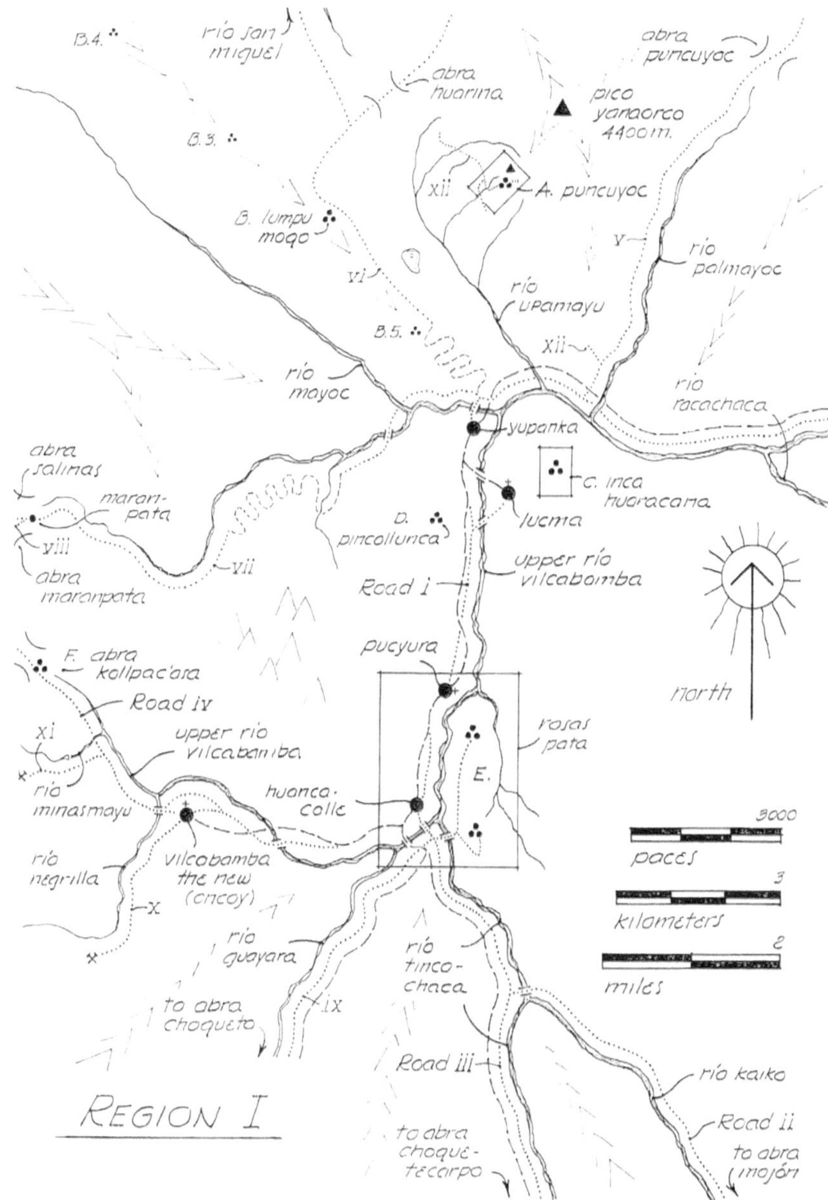

Figure 4 - Map of upper Rio Vilcabamba

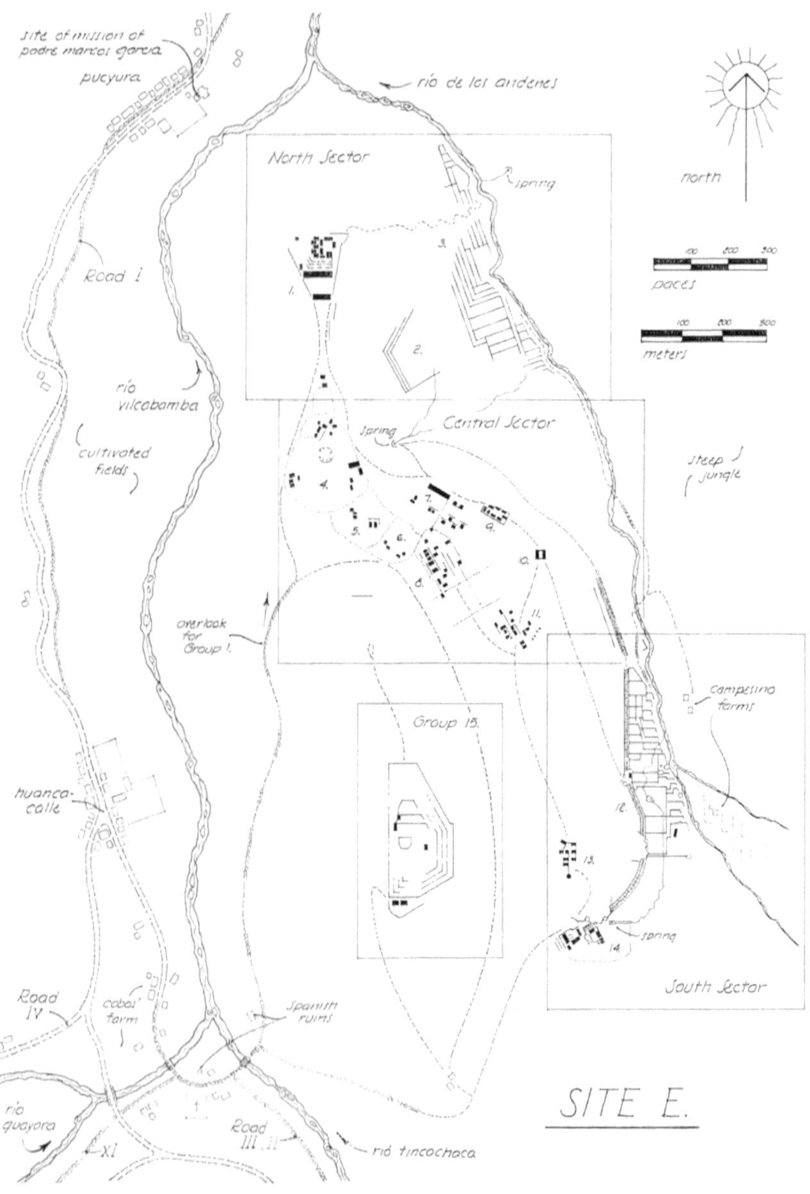

Figure 17 - Map of Rosas Pata and vicinity

In addition to Inca sites and roads, both Beauclerk and his *compañeros* working the eastern edge of Vilcabamba found evidence there of indigenous, non-Incaic populations. **(15 & 16).** Their villages were typically clusters of round houses, either of fieldstone or set at least on stone foundations. They seemed to be pre-Inca but ceramics found at many of the sites suggested they'd survived well into the Inca period as well. Probably, Beauclerk thought, they were among the native tribes of "Antis" and "Chunchos" subjugated by Pachacuti Inca in 1440. Prior to that, he believed they'd been allied with the Chancas, Cuzco's arch enemies that the "Over-turner of the Earth" had trounced back in 1438 - so it was no accident that the pacification of Vilcabamba had been an early priority of the famous Inca's reign.

A century and a quarter later, Rodriguez de Figueroa witnessed the hordes of jungle tribesmen that supported Titu Cusi in his defiance of Spanish authority. Apparently, they were descendants of the same people Pachacuti had brought into the fold. Assuming so, where, had they all lived? If they'd built stone villages, the remains should still be out there someplace. The only non-Inca site we'd seen was Tambo, with its 36 or so houses. Even though I had it figured as the site of the New Fort, it might also have been the home of a few of the Incas' allies. Beauclerk's message was that there had to be more - probably a lot more - similar groupings of stone circles scattered here and there around the province. For the first time, I saw that to be really complete, my inventory of Inca Vilcapampa would have to include not just the Incas, but the tribes they shared the province with as well.

Through the fall of '85 I busied myself putting together my presentation for Professor Rowe's Institute meeting, scheduled for early January. When the time came to step up on the stage I was one very nervous amateur, but it was comforting to see the faces of our Berkeley friends scattered here and there around the hall. My only ace in the hole was that my topic was one about which even the impressive array of experts in the audience knew very little. Mercifully, their attitude was thus more one of curiosity than critical scrutiny. I gave a sweeping summary of our survey work in the Vilcabamba - pretty light-weight stuff compared to the highly technical material that otherwise dominated the program - but it was well received and I was encouraged to keep at it. Although the maps and drawings were the meat of my paper, the slides of Vilcabamba were gorgeous and more than a few people told me afterwards that the images of our explorations reminded them of why they'd gotten into archaeology in the first place. Without really trying, I'd apparently inspired them to get back out into the field and kick a few rocks themselves. As an added extra, I sold 40 copies of Sixpac Manco, already by then in its second printing - the first edition having been mostly given away by a fledgling author who couldn't imagine that anyone would actually buy one of his books.

That was in January of 1986. I gave another paper in 1987 and was subsequently voted a member and Research Associate of the Institute. Nancy and I have been back every year since and I've given papers almost every year on a variety of subjects. Best of all, we've developed lots of interesting contacts and friendships among Andeanists all over the world. It's a small, colorful group and - contrary to Savoy's warnings - there's room in it for anyone doing serious work and willing to lay it open to the scrutiny of the scientific community.

Back home from Berkeley, we began preparations for the upcoming expedition in earnest. With the benefit of our experience in 1984 and all that had happened since, we had a pretty good idea what this new trip was all about. Savoy's maps of Espíritu Pampa showed ruins in places I hadn't yet been. We had to go back down there, verify his findings, and look for anything even he might have missed. Then there were von Kaupp's sites in the Urumbay. What if he were right about Marcanay? There might be a whole new city in there, yet undocumented. La Mesada sounded interesting in its own right, and needed to be added to my inventory in any case. Guillén's reservations about Vitcos and my fort sites had to be dealt with. Even if I was right and he was wrong, the only way to prove it was to check out his theory on the ground. And finally there were Beauclerk's non-Incaic tribesmen and their lost villages. I'd assumed they'd been built entirely of wood - now long gone - but if they were on stone foundations, we had to find them. Altogether, it was a full agenda, so we again allowed for six full weeks of solid field work.

It was during this period, too, that responses to Sixpac Manco began to come in from an astonishing variety of people. In addition to those copies I'd sold myself or given away, Don Montague had sold quite a few through his South American Explorers Club catalog and hardly a day went by that didn't bring at least one letter from an enthusiastic supporter - or critic. In contrast to my frequent and demoralizing exchanges with von Kaupp, I corresponded often with John Hemming in London and John Rowe in California. Both were enormously helpful and supportive. I was much encouraged to have such giants in my corner. It was a heady time. Everything seemed to be going our way and it was hard to see what could possibly spoil our up-coming adventure. Surely, Tupac Amaru was still there, watching over us, as he so often had in the past. Then came the final shocker. Less than a week before our departure, a bomb exploded on the Machu Picchu tourist train while it stood waiting to leave the station in Cuzco. Many people were injured and a number were killed, including an entire family of Austrian vacationers. They'd been touring South America on their way to a reunion with relatives in - of all places - Jackson Hole, Wyoming.

12

Fitting The Stones

By the time we reached Cuzco, news of the bombing had been widely reported - although the follow-up revelation that it had been a mistake, was not. The targeted coach had been intended for a party of delegates to a political convention, but got switched into the tourist train at the last minute. Travel agents and vacationers all over the world nevertheless crossed Machu Picchu off their lists, at least for the time being. Consequently, the old Inca capital, normally teeming with activity in early July, seemed something of a ghost town instead. As we stepped out of the normally littered and odoriferous, but now oddly clean and fresh-smelling Calle Loreto, the apparent emptiness of the Plaza de Armas struck me as illusory and unsettling. Absent the noise and clutter of the present, it was as though the restless spirits of all those whose life-blood had drained away into that tragically historic little patch of the New World were pressing all around me, felt but unseen. Whatever the reason, I was uncomfortable. Tupac Amaru was still there, but perhaps we'd lost his favor, or worse, the bill was coming due for his many favors in the past. It was a feeling that would dog me throughout the coming weeks. Though I said nothing to the others, I knew from day one that Sixpac Manco III was headed into hard times.

With Nancy and me were several new players. Susan Akers, an artist and weaver from Maine, had become a close friend during several summers in Wyoming. Young, pretty and athletic, she was an avid hiker in the mountains around Jackson Hole and was enthusiastic about a trek in the Andes. Susan was always easy to spot in the crowd, her blonde hair standing out among the cluster of dark heads that always seemed to surround her. To the Indians she must have seemed the typical, fair-haired *gringa*. But an average *tourista*, she was not. Susan had a special reason for being there. As a weaver, she'd always been fascinated by the extraordinary textiles - both pre-Columbian and contemporary - for which Peru is justly famous and she jumped at the opportunity to see these wonders first hand. That she actually knew something about how they were made, heightened her appreciation for what the rest of us superficially thought merely pretty. Fortunately, some of her insights eventually rubbed off on each of us and we all came away richer, to varying degrees, for the experience.

Equally knowledgeable in an entirely different way was Ben Giles. Ben and I had taught mountain climbing together in Wyoming years earlier, but he'd long since married and become a farmer in eastern Oregon. Unlike most of today's farmers, at least in the United States, he worked his land with a team of draft horses, utilizing methods centuries old. All had gone well until early one morning a year or so prior to our trip. An uninsured teenager had nearly killed him in an early morning head-on and he'd been many months recovering in the hospital. Medical bills and legal fees quickly became overwhelming and he lost his farm, his horses and finally his wife. His health was shot. Broke, alone and bitter, he needed to get away and we both thought some time in the high country might be just the ticket. It was and it wasn't, as things turned out. But once among the *campesinos*, it was truly amazing to see how much he understood and admired their livestock and farming practices. Again, his special interest in things the rest of us knew little about stimulated new curiosities in all of us.

Finally, there was Bruce Davis, a landscaping and masonry contractor from Denver who specialized in dry-laid stone retaining walls - *andenes*, in other words, not unlike those of the Incas. I'd been introduced to Bruce by Tom Lennon, the archaeologist directing the University of Colorado's Gran Pajatén dig, then underway despite the flap with Savoy. Bruce was interested in ancient construction techniques on the chance they might be applicable to his work in Denver and Tom thought I might be able to help him out. At first, Bruce wanted to sponsor our expedition in exchange for some research beneficial to his business, but despite his apparent lack of outdoor and adventure travel experience I saw in him a kindred spirit and suggested he come along with us and do his own research instead. My friends have long - and accurately - accused me of being a "rock" person. While their slide shows are inevitably filled with colorful scenes of village life, lovable children and aged faces beaming with character, mine show only rocks. When Bruce not only lasted through several such shows, but asked good questions, it was clear to both of us that Sixpac Manco III was going to be his kind of trip and he signed on.

None of our new companions had ever been to Cuzco before, so we made the mandatory circuit of the shops filling the arcades bordering the plaza. The empty restaurants and trinket shops reminded me of Jackson Hole in the off-season. Rounding the corner into the steep, narrow alley of Calle Procuradores, however, visions of home were replaced by stark evidence of the moderate earthquake which had jarred the city several months earlier. Piles of debris littered the old stone paving and many of the buildings leaned precariously out over the street, collapse being apparently prevented only by temporary log shoring angling crazily in all directions. It was easy to see why the death toll was so often high when severe quakes struck such places. Jagged cracks everywhere snaked across the plastered rubble walls of the old Spanish colonial buildings. Only the Inca foundations of fitted stones seemed sound and untouched.

While the others continued on up the hill to Sacsawaman, Nancy and I decided to check in with the I.N.C. and begin the process, once again, of obtaining a permit to enter the Vilcabamba. We knew that terrorism was still very much an issue despite the much-reduced police presence in the streets and around the public buildings - likely the result of newly elected President Alan Garcia's then popular attempts at dismantling the old military oligarchy. If the train bombing was any indication, the situation had gotten even worse since '84. Recalling the nervous reception our plans had received last time we visited the I.N.C., we paused for a beer in the nearly deserted Plaza Regocijo to consider our prospects.

Since the 1984 trip, we'd learned of Renzo's efforts to obtain an exclusive, 5-year contract with COPESCO, the Peruvian tourism and development agency, to do archaeological and development work in the Vilcabamba. If such a deal had been struck, we might not be permitted even to enter the region, let alone work there. There seemed little doubt that Renzo regarded us as unwanted competitors and there was the possibility that he might have attempted to discredit us in some way among his many apparently powerful friends in the government. Paranoid as that idea seemS, such intrigue is by no means unheard of in Latin American archaeology. There was the off chance we might walk into the I.N.C. office and find ourselves in trouble for some trumped-up offense in 1984. This "GRINGO TREASURE HUNTERS JAILED!" scenario was reinforced somewhat by the fact that the officials we'd be dealing with were probably all new appointees of President García, a leader not then among Washington's best pals in South America.

There being no alternative, we nevertheless crept meekly up the stairs to the Director's office in the wonderful old colonial structure that housed the Instituto. The building had been nicely restored with gleaming white stucco which, unfortunately, only emphasized the large cracks which everywhere recalled the recent earthquake. For an architect already a bit on edge, the prospect of a cataclysmic structural failure was an unneeded distraction. As we presented our credentials to the Director's secretary, I noticed that she was the same lady I'd dealt with two years earlier. She was even wearing the same heavy wool sweater against the chill of the mid-winter day, the glass having long ago been broken out of her office windows. As in the U.S., the bosses might come and go, but the people who actually ran the country were too valuable to replace.

Upon being ushered into the Director's office, we realized immediately how foolish had been our Machiavellian concerns. At the cluttered desk sat a small, amiable man of, perhaps, 65 peering at us through glasses fully half an inch thick. He was Dr. Oscar Nuñez del Prado, an accomplished and widely respected anthropologist recently put in charge of the Instituto's complex operations in Cuzco. What with the earthquake, bombing of the Machu Picchu train and change of government, it was immediately obvious that the last thing he had time for was a hassle with a bunch of crazy *gringos* willing to spend good money for a vacation in what the Peruvian military regarded as an "Emergency Zone." By this, they apparently meant that their control of the province was in doubt and tended to evaporate after dark. The specter of Vietnam came unavoidably to mind. Despite his cautionary tone, Nuñez quickly signed our permit, cordially but disinterestedly accepted two copies of Sixpac Manco on behalf of the Instituto and sent us on our way.

On our way back to Alicia's, we ran into the others coming down from Sacsawaman. They were all dazzled by what they'd seen, but Bruce, especially, was intrigued. There was no denying the place was impressive, but for a specialist like him the real question was: how was it done? The same thing had nagged me ever since my first visit with Curtis and Brooke, and the answer was anything but clear. While everyone else continued on to Alicia's, Bruce and I went back up the hill for another look, determined to formulate a scheme of construction to account for the perfectly fitted, Cyclopean stonework. Although every observer since the Conquest has been astonished by the results, no one had ever devised a plausible method for achieving them.

Conventional wisdom held that the fit had been accomplished by so-called "trial and error", a method requiring many movements of each stone. Vito's company in Denver had lots of experience handling big rocks, and he had grave doubts about trial and error with 50 or 100 ton stones. Many of my clients in Wyoming built old fashioned log houses, and it occurred to me that the "scribing" technique the carpenters used to notch the irregular logs perfectly together in a single, straightforward operation might somehow have been used by the Incas to fit stones. Vito knew the accepted theory wouldn't work and I thought I knew an alternative that would. Walking through the ruins together that afternoon, we began to come up with some good ideas, but we left at dusk still a long way from having solved the problem. It couldn't be "rocket science," we laughed, but the fact was, unlike the project before us, we know how to build rockets.

That night, we celebrated our arrival over dinner with several of our Berkeley friends, including John Rowe and Susan Niles. John had been spending his summers in Cuzco since the 40s and was still at it. Though he had a great deal of important field work to his credit, one of his specialties was pouring through the mountain of old documents and records of sixteenth century Cuzco stored there and largely unread ever since. Uninteresting as such material might be to the untrained eye, John often found there important clues to life and events in and around the Inca capital in the years following the Conquest. Susan and he formed a good team, with John bringing his encyclopedic knowledge of the written record to bear on research and Susan following up in the field. Together, they were finding new and important sites right in and around Cuzco, as well as going back over many of the well known but poorly studied sites in the surrounding countryside.

Also present was Sara Steck. A guide for Mountain Travel, the world-famous adventure tour company co-founded by her father, Alan Steck, Sara had just returned from a visit to Vitcos. She'd gone there with several of our other Berkeley friends, Bernard and Linda Bell, Dave Dearborn and Dan Brocious, to search out evidence of Incan astronomical observations among the many strangely carved boulders at and near Ñusta Ispanan. Sara had a copy of <u>Sixpac Manco</u> along for use as a guidebook and I was curious as to how well the maps had worked out. Once they'd figured out that the lateral distances were distorted a bit to fit everything onto a single page, she said, they'd found the map of Rosaspata pretty handy **(1)**. Her only complaint was that wandering around the site they found that I'd "missed a lot." Missed a lot! At Vitcos? That was the one site I thought I'd pinned down pretty well in 1984. Hadn't José told me he'd shown us all there was to see? That I might have overlooked something there was believable enough - it was a big place, after all - but how could I have missed "a lot?" Well, we'd be there soon enough, I thought. Maybe Juvenal would know what she was talking about.

Before the evening ended, we agreed to take the next day off to visit Tipón, a beautiful and seldom visited Inca country estate Susan had been mapping about an hour outside Cuzco. I'd seen it from the air and jumped at the chance to go there with someone who knew the place well. Also, John Rowe offered us an opportunity we couldn't refuse. He explained there might be evidence in the chronicles that Machu Picchu was not entirely unknown to the Spaniards, as had long been assumed. Rodriguez de Figueroa, traveling to Vilcabamba on his mission to see Titu Cusi in 1565, noted, in passing, a bridge across the Río Vilcabamba near a place called Condormarca and a road beyond which, he said, continued from there to places called "*Picho*" (Machu Picchu?) and "*Tambo*" (probably Ollantaytambo) - via a town called Sapamarca **(2).** John had found other references to Sapamarca on several old maps, but to his knowledge, no one had ever actually looked for it. He felt that if it could be located in the country between the lower Río Vilcabamba and Machu Picchu - somewhere, he thought, around the modern town of Santa Teresa - it would confirm that Figueroa's "Picho" was, in fact, Bingham's famous lost city and that the Spaniards knew of its existence after all. Besides, John said, the search for a new site might be interesting in its own right and would, at the very least, be good training for our continued work in the Vilcabamba.

Given the visit to Tipón and what I'd just learned about the need for more work at Rosaspata, my first thought was that another site to look for was the very last thing we needed. But John pressed the attack and, after talking it over, we all agreed that finding Sapamarca might be worth postponing our arrival at Cobos's place a few days. Bruce, whom we'd all taken to calling "Vito" due to his swarthy resemblance to what we all imagined a mafia hit-man might look like, was especially glad about the change of plans. He was scheduled to return to the States before we would have otherwise gotten into any real jungle exploration, and Sapamarca promised him a taste of that rather unique experience.

After a fascinating morning at Tipón with Susan, Sixpac Manco III headed downriver. So that Ben, Susan and Vito could get a quick look at Machu Picchu, we got off the afternoon train at Aguas Calientes for a quick visit before pressing on to Santa Teresa, starting point for the Sapamarca search. Waiting as though he'd been expecting us was William Kaiser, our host from 1984. "Gringo Bill" as he now called himself, was full of news from the intervening two years and eager to learn of our adventures and current plans. Reading the copy of Sixpac Manco I'd brought along as a gift, he laughed at the part about being an "unreliable guide" and said the two guys we'd heard that from in Cuzco hadn't been among his favorite clients, either. After a good dinner and more than a few *cervezas*, we turned in glad to be back.

I was awakened early the next morning by the musical "plink...plink...plink" of a gang of masons shaping granite ashlars for the *façade* of a nearly completed village church we'd seen under construction in 1984. As I lay in bed, listening to the sound of chisels pecking away, a key missing step in the Sacsawaman stone-fitting process Vito and I were considering fell suddenly into place. I rushed next door, woke him up and we began an orgy of rock talk that went on non-stop for several days as we worked out the fine points of our theory. In a nutshell, we'd devised a practical way to achieve the fit with a single movement of each stone, finally, into place. The result was a paper delivered to Rowe's Institute the following winter and subsequently published in both English and Spanish (**3** & **4**). To this day, it remains the only serious attempt in print yet offered to solve the problem.

Since my graduate school days, I've always remembered the quip attributed to the famous Finnish architect, Alvar Aalto: "any idea that can't be pissed in the snow is too complicated." Our newly hatched theory met that test, at least. Imagine two large boulders set side by side, say four or five feet apart so that several people can work between them. Now imagine that the sides of the boulders facing one another are smoothed off with stone hammers so that a simple measuring stick exactly fits between the worked surfaces, no matter where it is inserted. Clearly, if the stones are then slid together, they should fit perfectly, whether or not the surfaces are flat.

There is a catch, of course. The measuring stick must always be inserted along exactly parallel lines, so that the points at each end will be those in contact once the stones are touching. The idea may seem moronically simple, but the devil is definitely in the details. Maintaining the stick, called a "scribe," with a constant orientation in space regardless of its position between the rocks is a bit of a trick, especially since the only device known to the Incas with which to do it is a weighted string line or plumb bob. Other serious problems arise from the fact that the shaping, or "coping" of the surfaces with hammer-stones - again, the only tools available to the Incas - is necessarily done working downward, with the help of gravity. The whole system, then, hinges on positioning the stones so that the working surfaces are convenient for the stonecutters and devising ways to keep the scribe's orientation in space constant.

Vito and I thought we'd come up with solutions to both problems, but it remained to be seen if our method could actually be made to work with large stones. Given the massive amounts of labor needed to find out, neither of us had any expectation it would ever be tried. We were wrong. As the manuscript for this book was in its final editing, the producers of NOVA, the well known TV series, called to say that ours was an idea whose time had come. Someone on their staff had gotten hold of a copy of our, by then, eight year old paper and thought wrestling with big rocks on camera would make good footage whether they ended up fitting together or not. In other words, the entire world was soon to find out if Davis and Lee were geniuses or crackpots. Much of life seems driven by the avoidance of boredom and/or embarrassment, so I quickly agreed to give it a try, but at the same time resolved not to come off looking like a jerk in the process.

I needn't have worried. Two months and nearly 1500 man-hours later, I watched as, using stone age technology, my nine Indian masons lowered the last of several multi-ton boulders neatly into place. Their craftsmanship wasn't quite up to Inca standards, but the scribing technique worked perfectly and the proverbial knife blade could not be inserted into the resulting joints. The cameras caught it all. Vito and I were, if not geniuses, at least not crackpots. As I said into the microphone, we still don't know how the Incas did it - but we know now how they could have done it, which is more than we knew before. The big surprise was how incredibly tedious and time consuming it was to shape hard rocks by any hand method. After doing it ourselves, we were all the more astounded by the Incas' numerous, mind-boggling feats of megalithic construction. All are currently attributed to the period of only about eighty years between Pachacuit's rise to power and the civil war following the death by smallpox of his grandson, Huayna Capac.

Author's sketch of "scribing and coping" method proposed for fitting the giant stones at Sacsawaman.

The walk up to Machu Picchu in the morning was spectacular, though our performance in the wake of the previous night's partying was not. By the time we got to the restaurant outside the entrance gate everyone just wanted to sit in the shade and drink Coca Cola. Eventually, we managed a tour of the ruins but, despite the sag in tourism, the place was mobbed with Peruvian visitors. As always, the city was magnificent but, compared with our private tour of Tipón the day before, the scene was a bit of a let-down and we all headed home early. That night was Gringo Bill's birthday, and since it was also our last day in town, his wife took advantage of the occasion to throw a party. It was another enjoyable evening, but for the third night in as many days, we stumbled off to bed in the wee hours. Enough was enough. We had to get to work.

Still groggy, we caught the early local downstream to Santa Teresa the next morning to start looking for Sapamarca. Like Aguas Calientes, Santa Teresa is a railroad town with the tracks doubling as the main drag. Unlike Aguas Calientes, it is beyond Machu Picchu and sees few *gringos*. The result is there's not much reason to tarry, and we quickly headed into the hills. Five days later, we were back down at the railroad, exhausted and empty handed. The search had been anything but a party. Vito had gotten his baptism in the bush and was more than ready to get back to high, dry Colorado. With considerable effort, we'd found ruins on a high ridge above a village called Yanatili, a few miles up the seldom traveled Río Sacsara, but they seemed pre-Inca and I doubted they were the remains of Rowe's Sapamarca. Ironically, I later learned that while we were looking, my newfound pen-pal, Bob von Kaupp, accidentally stumbled onto the site a few miles further down the canyon of the Urubamba. I passed his brief report of the find along to Professor Rowe, who thus got the confirmation he'd hoped for after all.

13

Into The Emergency Zone

Our fruitless search for Sapamarca done, Vito hopped a train back to Cuzco and returned to the States. His absence was quickly felt. We were finding out that ours was not a wonderfully cohesive group, but in some way Vito had managed to hold us together. Without him, I suspected it would be a different story. Nevertheless, Ben, "Susa," as the Indians called Susan for some reason, Nancy and I continued on down to Quillabamba for the night. As in 1984, the locals at first refused to drive us up the road to Vilcabamba, for any price. The situation with the terrorists had worsened and the *policía* were dangerously inclined to shoot first and ask questions later. Finally, we found someone who'd never before made the trip and boasted that he wasn't afraid. The other guys were probably right, I thought, but we needed the ride and I ignored his bragging and made a deal.

Except that our macho driver's truck was woefully inadequate to the task, we bumped and bounced up the canyon the next day without incident. By mid-afternoon, we pulled up at the police station in Pucyura with the worst of the road behind us. Though it bristled with sand-bagged machine gun emplacements manned by surly young troopers, the *jefe*, or head man, was quite friendly and offered lots of advice. The terrorists, he said, had just recently made a sweep through the lower Río Pampaconas and he advised against travel beyond Vilcabamba the New. My heart sank. It was advice which, if followed, ruled out two thirds of our reason for being there. He insisted on tediously hand-copying for us his pitifully sketchy and inaccurate map of the area before allowing us to leave. It was a nice gesture, but looking at the map, I thought it was no wonder the terrorists were winning.

On we went to the end of the road near Cobos's place. Looking around, it was clear that things had changed. The road up from Yupanka had been improved and the Saturday market was now being held in Huancacalle. The result was dramatic. What we remembered as a sleepy little farming village had since gone commercial. The main street was crowded with people and lined with hastily thrown up stalls of cardboard and tin. Town was choked with refugee families who'd been driven in from the more isolated settlements by the terrorists and we later saw that several new shacks had been thrown up right in the middle of Cobos's fields. As we unloaded our gear in the street, a circle of curious onlookers quickly formed through which José and Juvenal soon emerged to give us a hand.

The Senderistas, they said, had crossed the Apurimac from nearby Ayacucho in force, and been on the move for several months. It was a major campaign, and everyone was afraid. A large band of *guerrillas* had begun been raiding settlements the jungle below Tambo and there was fear that they'd eventually press the attack up into the high country and over the pass at Kolpacasa. Supposedly, security was provided by the *soldados* down in Pucyura, but they were loath, with good reason, to venture too far from their fortified headquarters. Instead, they'd grown surly and arrogant, molesting the local girls and generally intimidating the people they were there to protect. José had been badly beaten a month earlier, he said, because he'd not had enough money to buy drinks for a passing patrol. The result was that everyone was nervous, caught as they were between two equally nasty would-be masters. The *campesinos* over the mountains at Pampaconas were especially exposed and had formed a "*ronda* " for self-protection. Theoretically a kind of civilian militia, it was actually more of a vigilante group operating without much government control. According to Juvenal, the *ronda* took a dim view of any strangers passing through its zone of responsibility. No one had been to Espíritu Pampa for weeks and Juvenal thought even our planned explorations in the remote Río Urumbay unwise under the circumstances. It began to look like the *jefe* had been right and the sites around Vitcos would be all we'd get to see. It was a massive disappointment, but we decided to concentrate on giving the area around Rosaspata a really thorough going over.

The rain continued through the night and all the next day. We were camped in the same place we'd used in '82 and '84, but this time the mud was awful due to the incessant rooting of Flavio's pigs. Making matters worse was the stench of the droppings they left everywhere they went. Juvenal's daughter, Águeda, and her husband, Leóncio, were living in grandfather Julio's large house while their own was under construction just across the road. Sitting high and dry on their porch, they took pity on us and invited us to move into one of their several spare rooms, vacant since the old man's death five years before. We accepted without a moment's hesitation. No sooner had we gotten settled inside than a waterlogged trio of newly arrived visitors plodded into our mud-hole and began pitching up their woefully inadequate tent next to ours. They weren't very sociable, though, and our hosts made no effort to invite them in out of the weather.

During a break in the rain, they began asking around about horses and guides. It turned out they were Israeli tourists intent on seeing the ruins at Espíritu Pampa. Under the circumstances, of course, no one wanted to take them there and, like us, they were instead warned about the dangers involved. "Nonsense!" they said. "We know all about terrorists and can take care of ourselves." When it became obvious that nothing the locals could say was going to change their minds, everyone abruptly switched gears and began encouraging them, with a certain bravado, to go on alone - which they did, the following morning. Leóncio later confided that their stubborn attitude had earned them the status of human trial balloons whose fate would provide the locals with useful intelligence as to traveling conditions beyond Pampaconas.

The rain kept up and José reminded me that I shouldn't be surprised. The moon was full and he'd always said that meant wet weather. Given the horrors of camping in such conditions, we were content to stay in old man Julio's vacant rooms. Still, we could only read paperbacks so long without lapsing into terminal boredom - life's ultimate enemy - so we all fought back in one way or another. Ben took to working around the farm and was soon just another field hand. Nancy and Susa, meanwhile, checked out the handsome weavings then in progress by several of the village ladies. Susa even ended up buying one, but apparently paid too much, since we were ever after beset with vendors of all descriptions. As the self-appointed rock person, I slogged up to Rosaspata looking for whatever Sara Steck thought I'd missed last time around. She'd offered no hint as to where the additional sites might be, so I went first to the familiar palace group to get my bearings. (**Figure 19**)

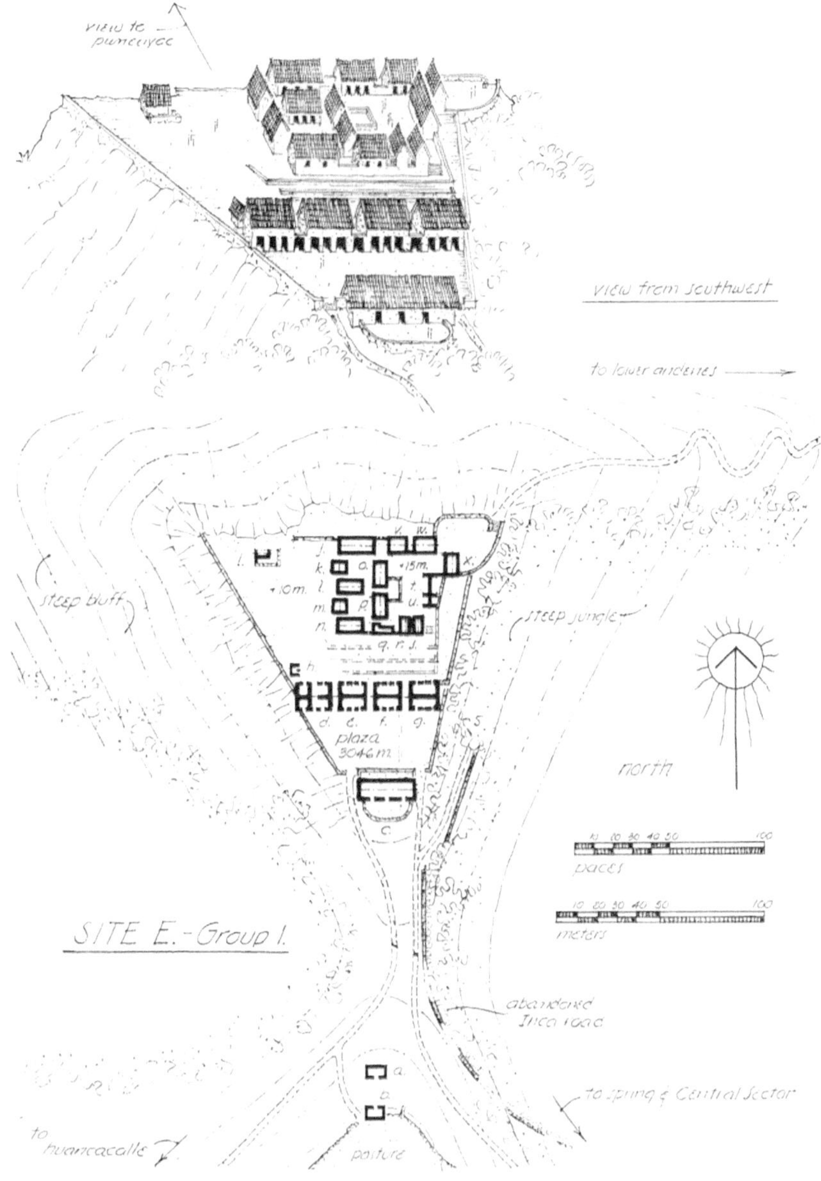

Figure 19 - Site plan of "palace" at Vitcos

Once there, I recalled that there were a few areas I'd not had time to investigate in '84. Even though José hadn't thought them places worth taking us to then, I figured it was time to find out for myself. The first was down the steep *arête* below the northeast corner of the palace. A faint trail switch-backed down the slope, but dropped off so sharply that, at first, the bottom of the valley was hidden from view beneath a band of jungle covered cliffs. About a third the way down, it came suddenly into view and I knew immediately that Sara'd been right. Spreading for nearly a kilometer along the near bank of a beautiful mountain stream, the Río de Los Andenes, was a previously unreported series of artfully planned stone terraces in nearly perfect condition. (**Figure 18**, Group 3)

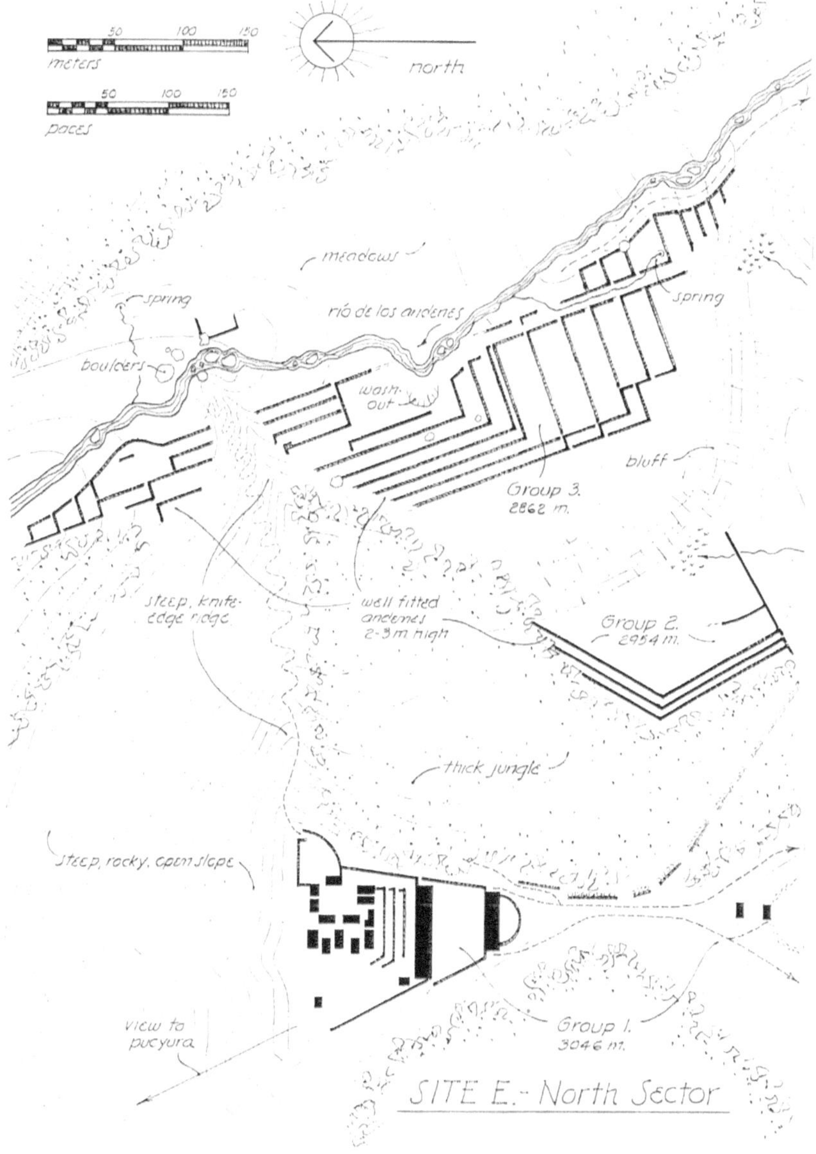

Figure 18 - "Palace" sector at Vitcos

I scrambled excitedly to the bottom only to find that the rocky crest down which the trail picked its way plunged several hundred feet straight into the river at the bottom, forcing a detour off to the left, or north side. There, another 150 meters or so of *andenes* not visible from above continued downstream as though the bedrock had somehow risen up after the fact, cutting off the lower end of what had originally been a single complex of continuous terraces. The matching alignments were especially interesting because the relationship of the two patterns was unnecessary - there being no vantage point from which both could be seen at the same time. Whoever had designed the place, I thought, certainly had a keen sense of abstract geometry and an uncanny talent for merging the natural with the man-made.

It took the rest of the morning to measure and map the complex. Although there were a few boulders strewn about, none had been carved nor did I find any shrines, fountains or other special architectural features. In contrast to the well known and highly ceremonial tier of andenes a kilometer further upstream, **(Figure 24)** the lower group was more secluded and secular in character. It seemed more like a private garden of some sort. I'd certainly spent a relaxing morning wandering around there. Maybe the Incas had done the same, five centuries earlier.

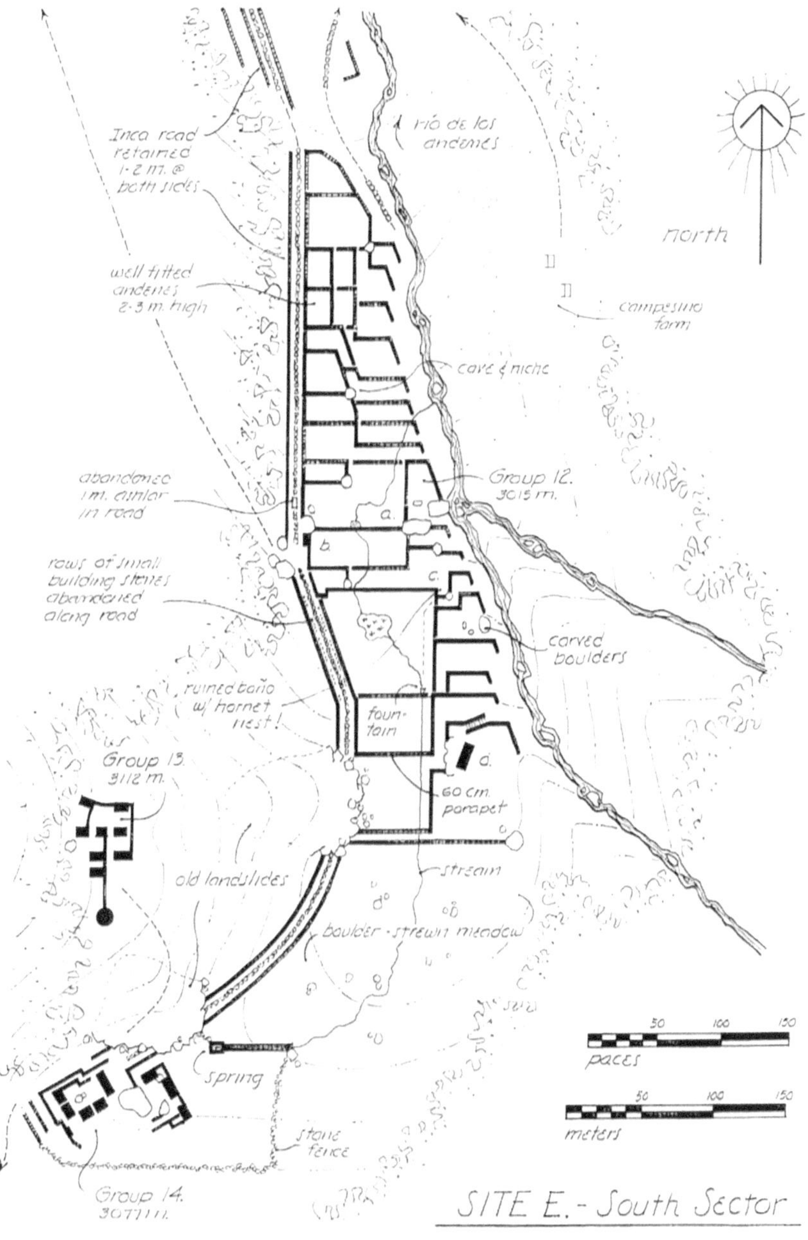

Figure 24 - "Temple" sector at Vitcos

Climbing back up towards the palace by a different route after lunch, I found more surprises waiting. In a sheltered pocket about half way up was a lovely meadow overlooking the lower *andenes* and, like them, all but invisible from above due to the steep forest by which it was hemmed in on the west. I was so taken by the serene beauty of the place it took me awhile to realize that slope just inside the tree line was retained by three beautifully built stone walls similar to those in the larger terraces down below. (**Figure 18**, Group 2) While making a hasty sketch of the layout, I noticed a boggy area near the lower edge of the meadow that seemed to be collecting runoff from someplace above. I followed the seeping water to its source and was amazed to find a running spring, oozing from thick brush just below the top of the slope. There was no sign of constructed work, but the spring turned out to be less than 100 yards across the slope from the ruined hall, or *kallanka*, José had shown us in '84. I'd been baffled then by what seemed a total lack of nearby drinking water for the people who'd lived there and elsewhere along the crest, but this new-found spring neatly solved the problem.

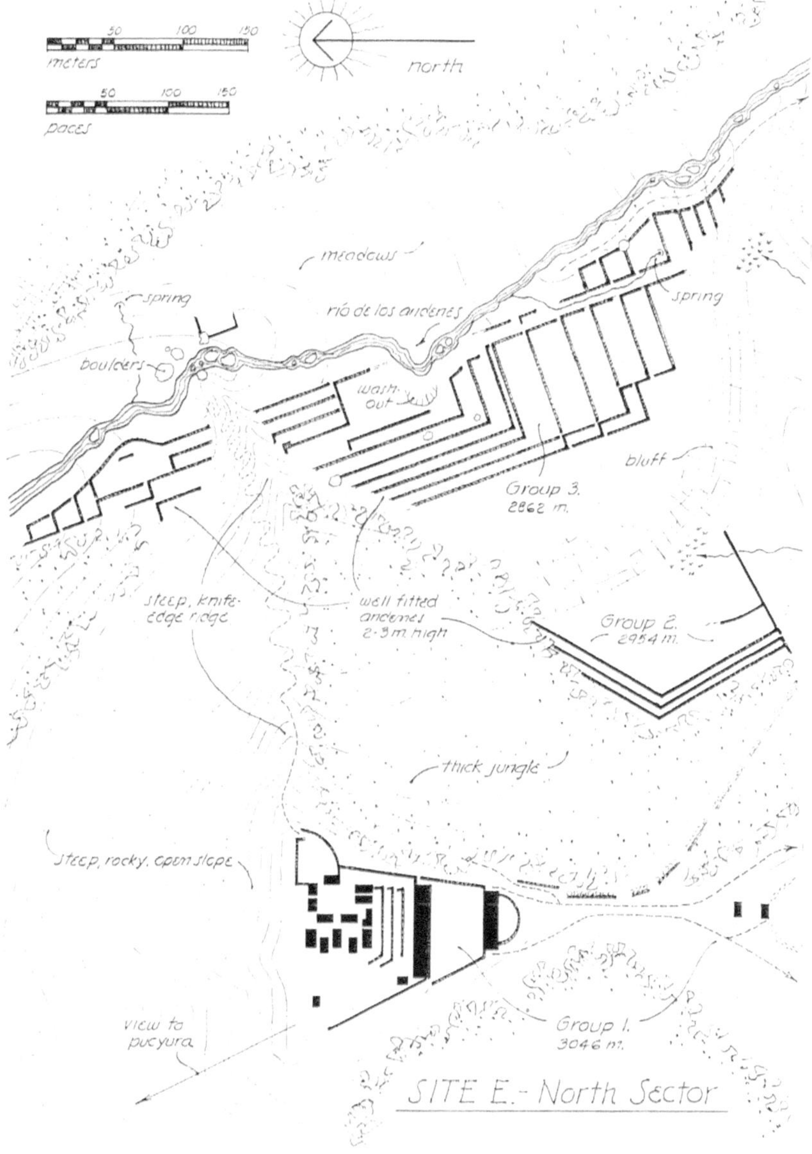

Figure 18 - "Palace" sector at Vitcos

From the great hall, I headed straight up through the woods, taking a short-cut to the trail back to camp. Heavy, dark clouds were fast swallowing what little remained of the daylight and I didn't want to get caught out at night in the rain. Even in the gloom of the forest, I could make out several overgrown rockpiles we'd unwittingly walked right past on our tour with José two years earlier. I was beginning to get the hang of exploration and knew that almost any surface rocks were worth looking into. How much more, I wondered, had we missed? Hurrying on down to camp in the dark, I was imagining all the great new finds that surely awaited me the next day when it dawned on me that everyone had warned us against travel at night. My imagination quickly shifted to the police ambush into which I was no doubt about to blunder. I began identifying myself, over and over again and in my best and loudest Spanish, to anyone who might be listening. "*Soy un gringo arquitecto, no mas, amigos - no soy terror-isto!* " Thinking back, it seems a little ridiculous, but for a few minutes, walking down that trail in the dark, I was back in the Marines on the other side of the world.

Nancy joined me in the morning as I raced back up to the wooded hillside above the *kallanka* to pick up where I'd left off. I wasn't disappointed. Not only did the overgrown mounds I'd spotted the night before turn out to be ruined buildings, there were lots more scattered along the hillside in both directions. Some were in the open and easy to spot, **(Figure 23)** but others were buried in dense brush and I had to cut through thicket after thicket to be sure I wasn't missing anything. By lunchtime, we'd come up with six entirely new neighborhoods. Together with the two José had shown us in '84, they were clustered around the great hall and spring and seemed to make up the previously unsuspected, residential quarter of Inca Vitcos. **(Figure 20)**

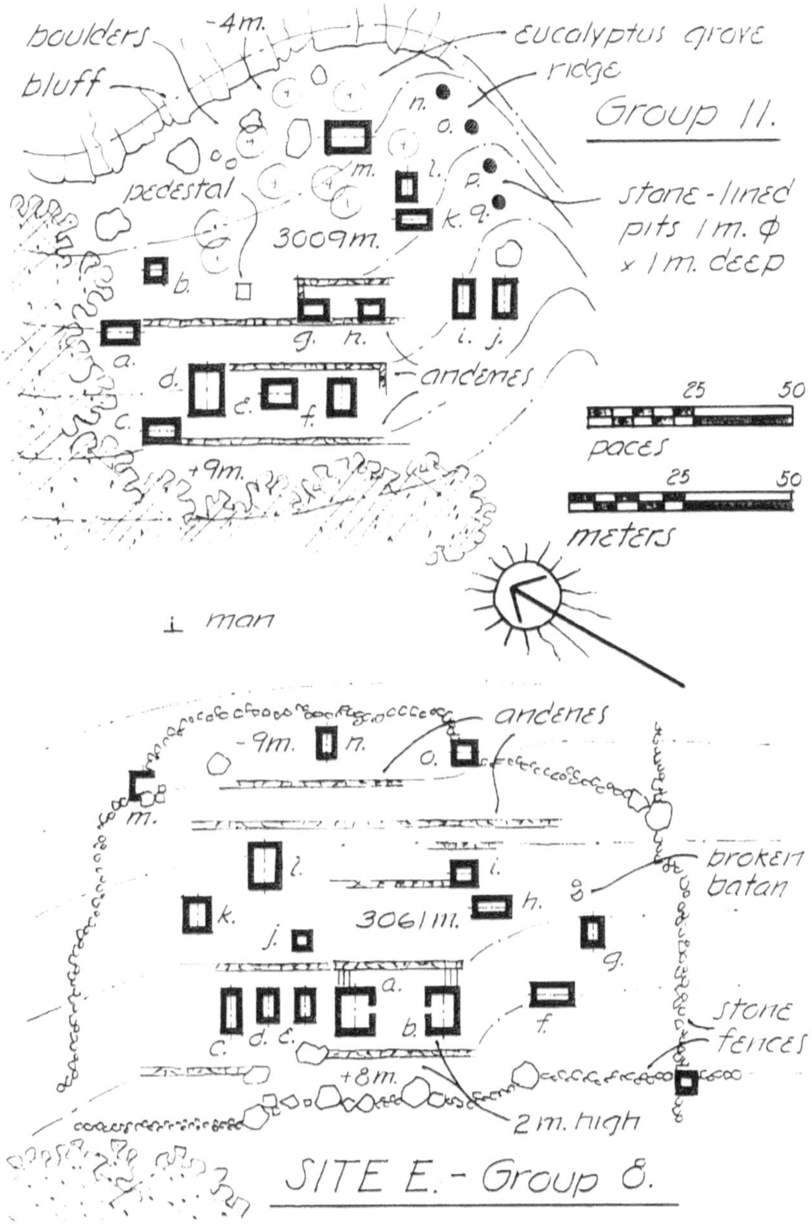

Figure 23 - Site plans of house groups

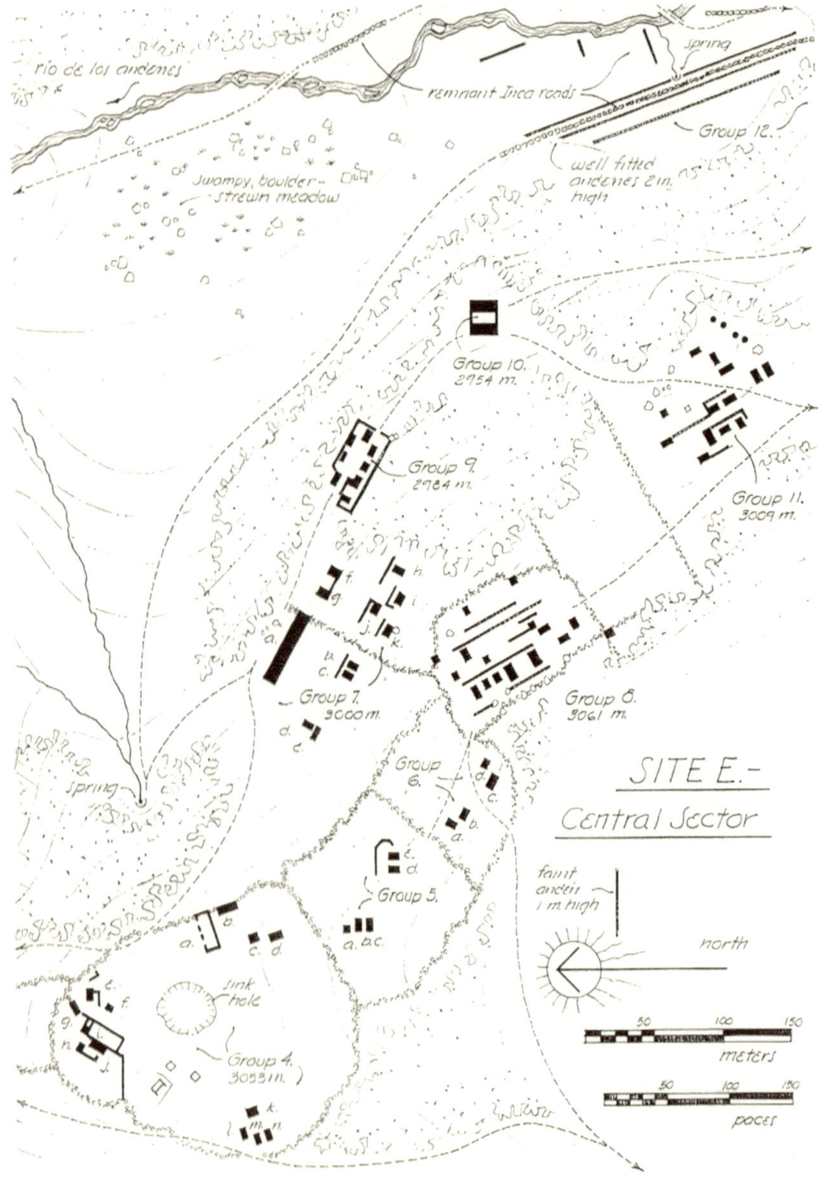

Figure 20 - "Village" sector at Vitcos

The rest of the day found us going back over Bingham's sun temple at Ñusta Ispanan and the upper tier of *andenes*. My map in Sixpac Manco (**1**) had been pretty good, but a few details of both needed refining. Careful examination of the temple group showed it to be much more complicated than I'd originally thought. **(Figures 25 and 26)** My revised plan revealed two *kanchas*, or enclosed courtyards, each entered by a monumental doorway with double jambs. The lower enclosure was built around the boulder and its associated spring and pond, which together fed the irrigation system for the elaborate tier of *andenes* below. Everything about it spoke of reverence for the Earth and the fertility of growing things. The devil worship attributed to the place by *padres* García and Ortiz may have stemmed from the medieval idea that Nature and Satan were, essentially, one in the same. In contrast, the upper enclosure was more typical of Inca *kanchas* elsewhere. It was self-contained and seemed oriented inward - or perhaps upward - not unlike the famous Corikancha, or "enclosure of the sun" in Cuzco. Probably the upper *kancha* here was the true sun temple. In any case, there wasn't much doubt Bingham had been right in assuming the whole complex was Calancha's Chuquipalta.

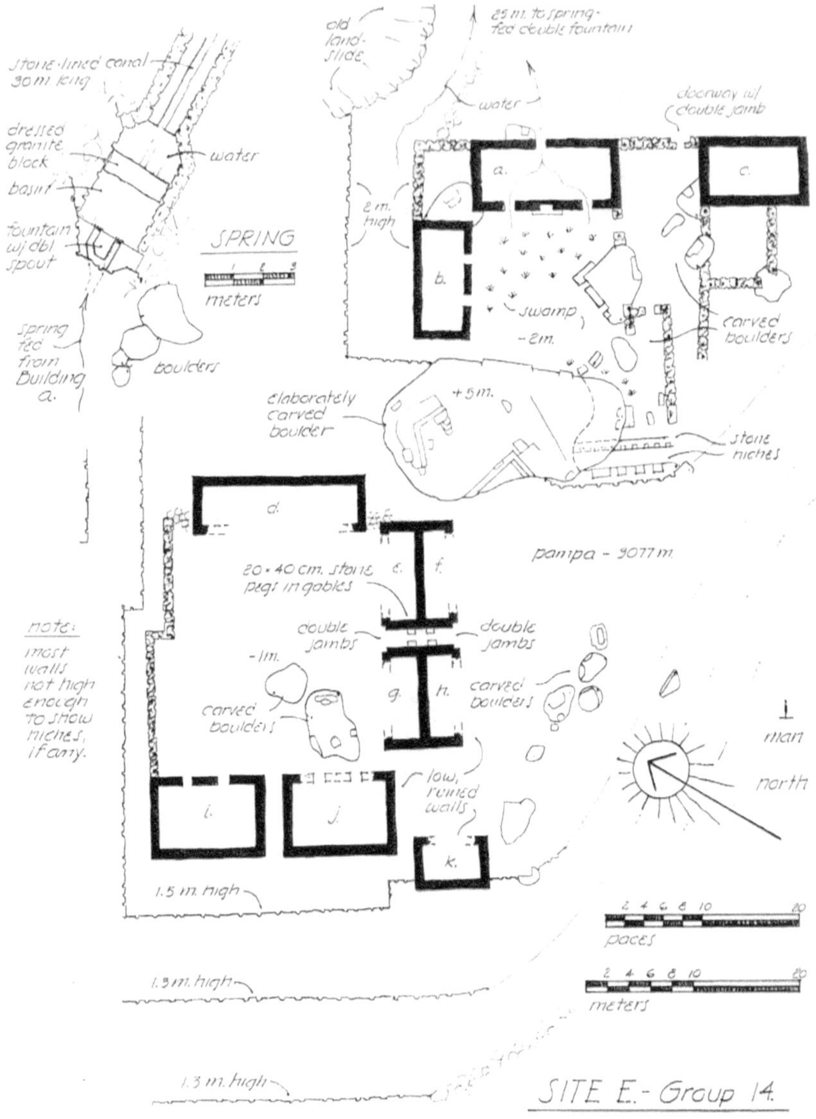

Figure 25 - Plans of sun temple and spring (Bingham's Chuquipalta)

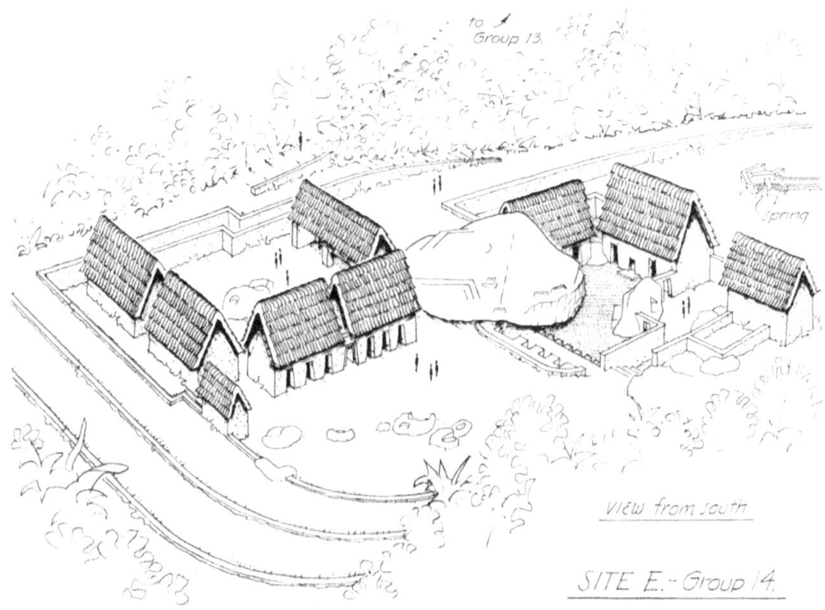

Figure 26 - View of sun temple complex

Dropping into the *andenes* below the spring, we refined my earlier mapping of a cave and boulder shrine built into the walls about midway down **(Figure 27)** and looked for other details that might have escaped me in '84. The search was quickly rewarded. Almost immediately, two new buildings turned up, one of them atop a large boulder along the road flanking the terraces on the west. Neatly laid out nearby were several rows of building stones apparently stock-piled there for some yet unfinished construction project. A few meters away, a desk-sized block of square-cut granite lay in the middle of the road, no doubt abandoned there on its way to the same destination. Elsewhere, another large and prominently placed structure stood on a small bluff overlooking the highest terraces from the east. It was reached by a flight of stone stairs built into the rock and leading up from the river. **(Figure 24**, Buildings 12b and d)

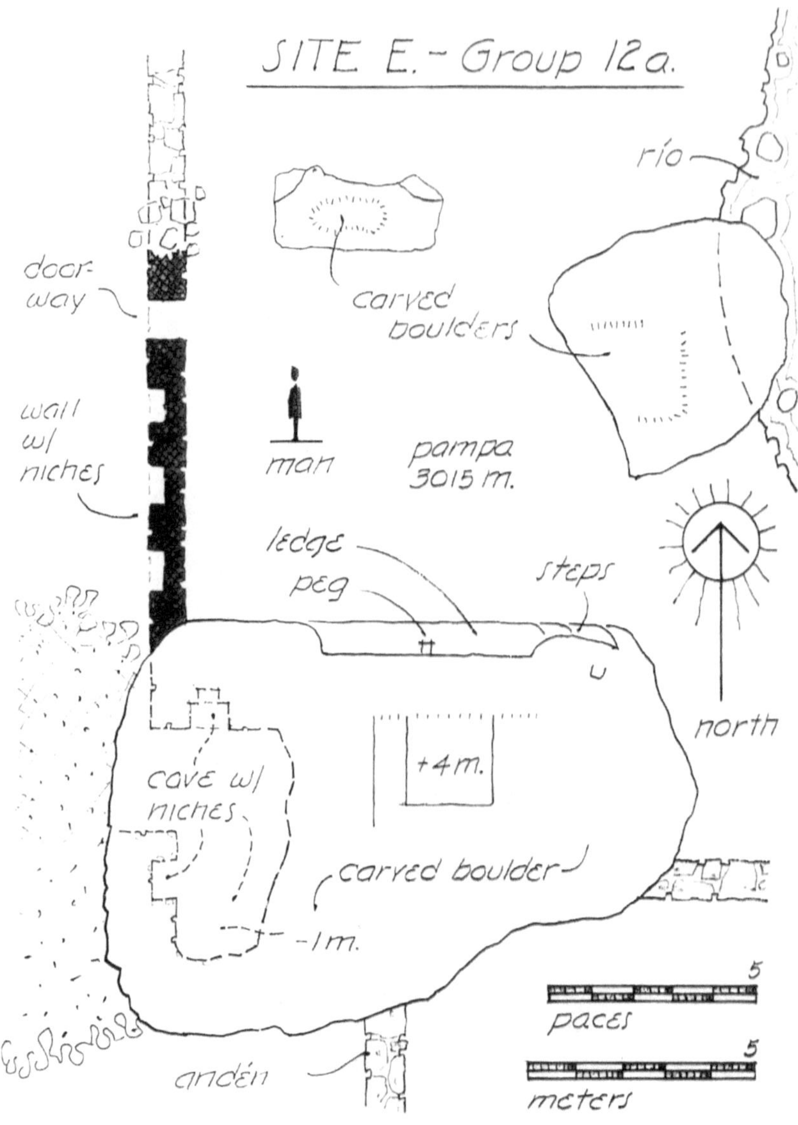

Figure 27 - Plan of cave boulder shrine

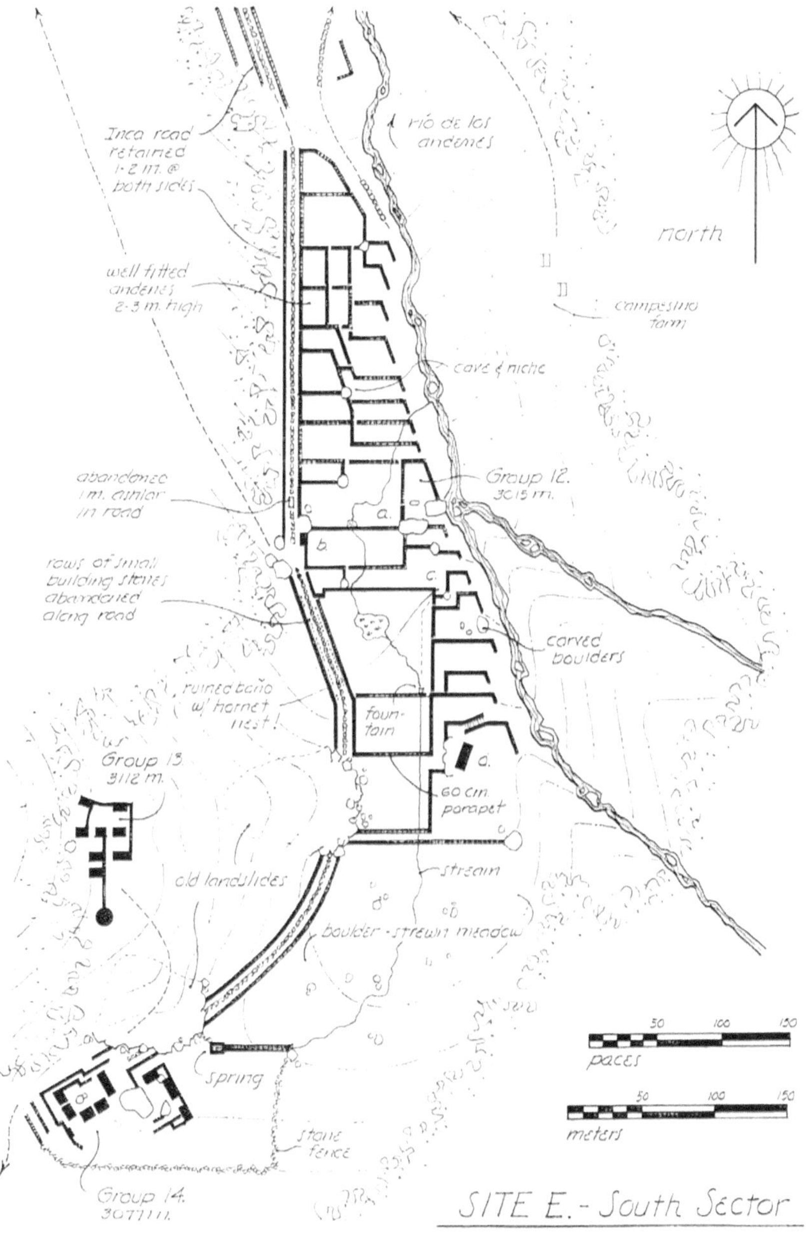

Figure 24 - "Temple" sector at Vitcos

Without warning, the sun disappeared behind a huge cloud bank that had slid unnoticed in over the mountains and a trace of rain began to falling from a rising breeze. Suddenly, it was cold and gray. I was so engrossed with all that we'd found, I hardly noticed until Nancy reminded me it was almost dark and time to head back.

Walking home together, we reflected on what we'd learned about the site. First, Sara was right. I'd missed a whole lot in '84 - probably much more than she knew - and I had her to thank for all that I'd found in the past two days. Second, the site was much larger and more complicated than most people, including me, had thought. There seemed to be four distinct sectors: the palace and its secluded terrace-gardens; **(Figure 18)** the great hall and surrounding residential village; **(Figure 20)** the sun temple, its huge carved boulder and the fancy andenes watered by its spring; **(Figure 24)** and the big fortress atop Rosaspata. **(Figures 29 and 30)** Even taken together, though, these four elements hardly amounted to a "city" anything like Cuzco. Despite its sprawling layout, we'd only found 122 buildings at Vitcos - hardly enough to house a large population. Rather, the site had about it the feel of a large country estate like Tipón and, I thought, probably that's all it really was. Founded by Pachacuti, it had been occupied from time to time by each of his successors. Finally, Manco had briefly pressed it into service as his capital-in-exile, but nothing about it had been built with that in mind. Already, I was anxious to get back to my drafting board and see what it looked like on paper. **(Figure 17)**

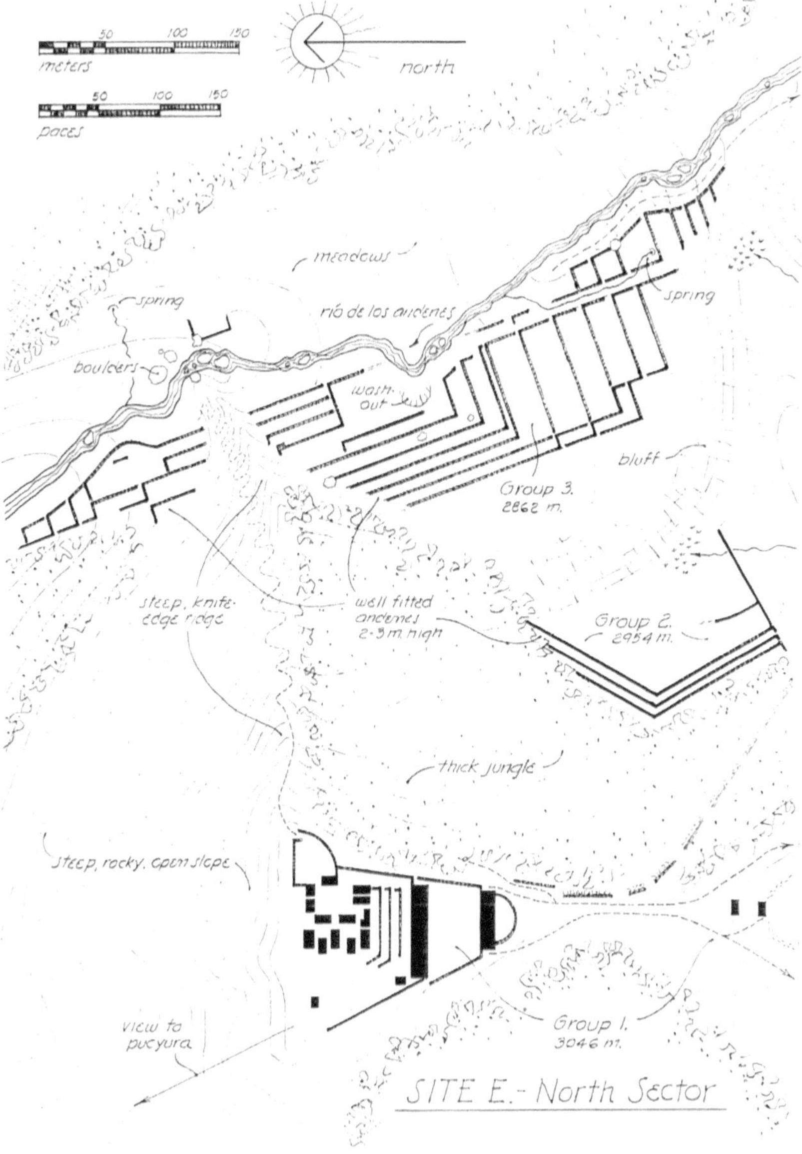

Figure 18 - "Palace" sector at Vitcos

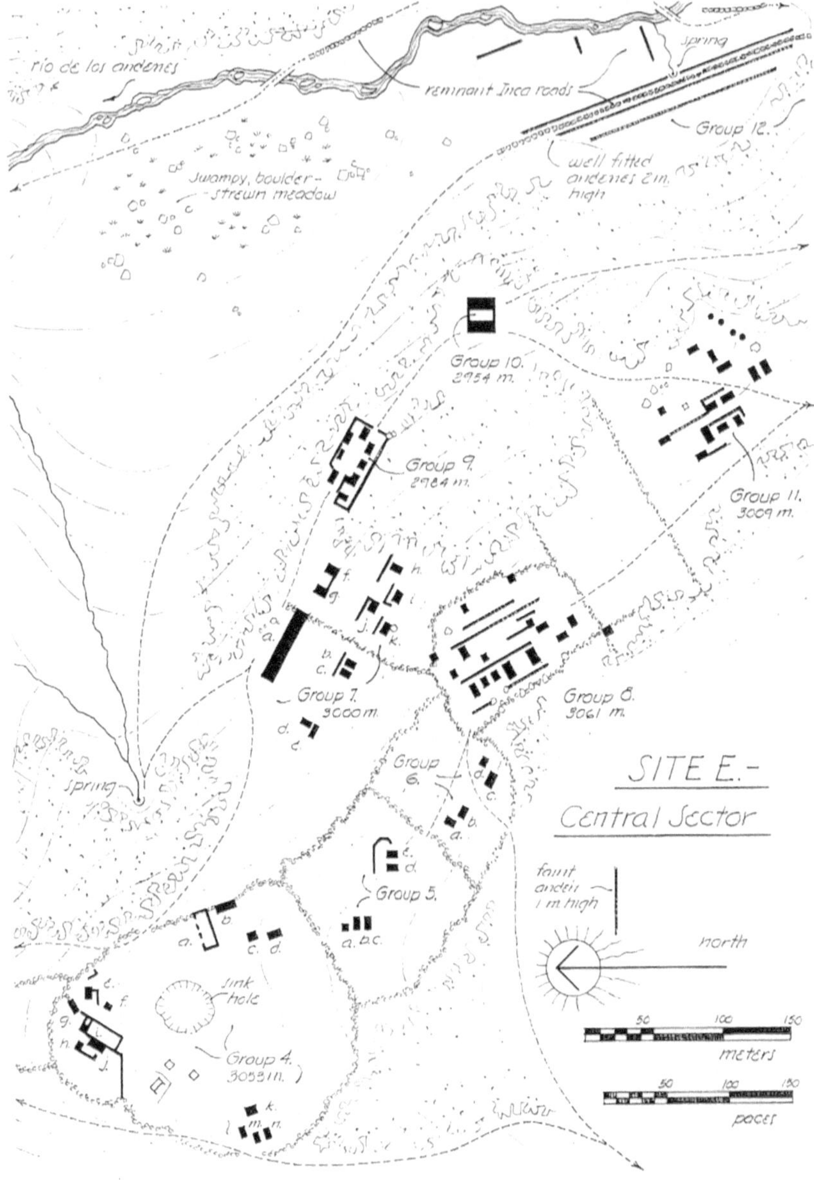

Figure 20 - "Village" sector at Vitcos

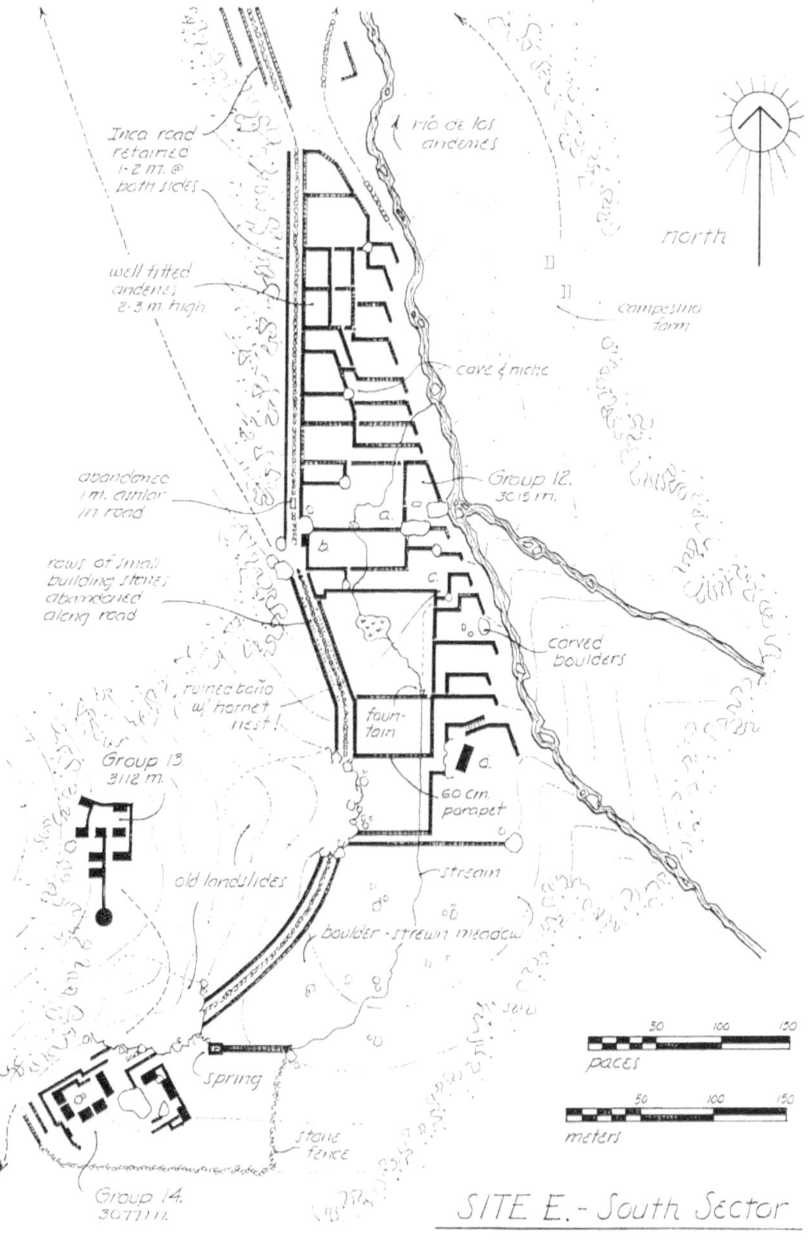

Figure 24 - "Temple" sector at Vitcos

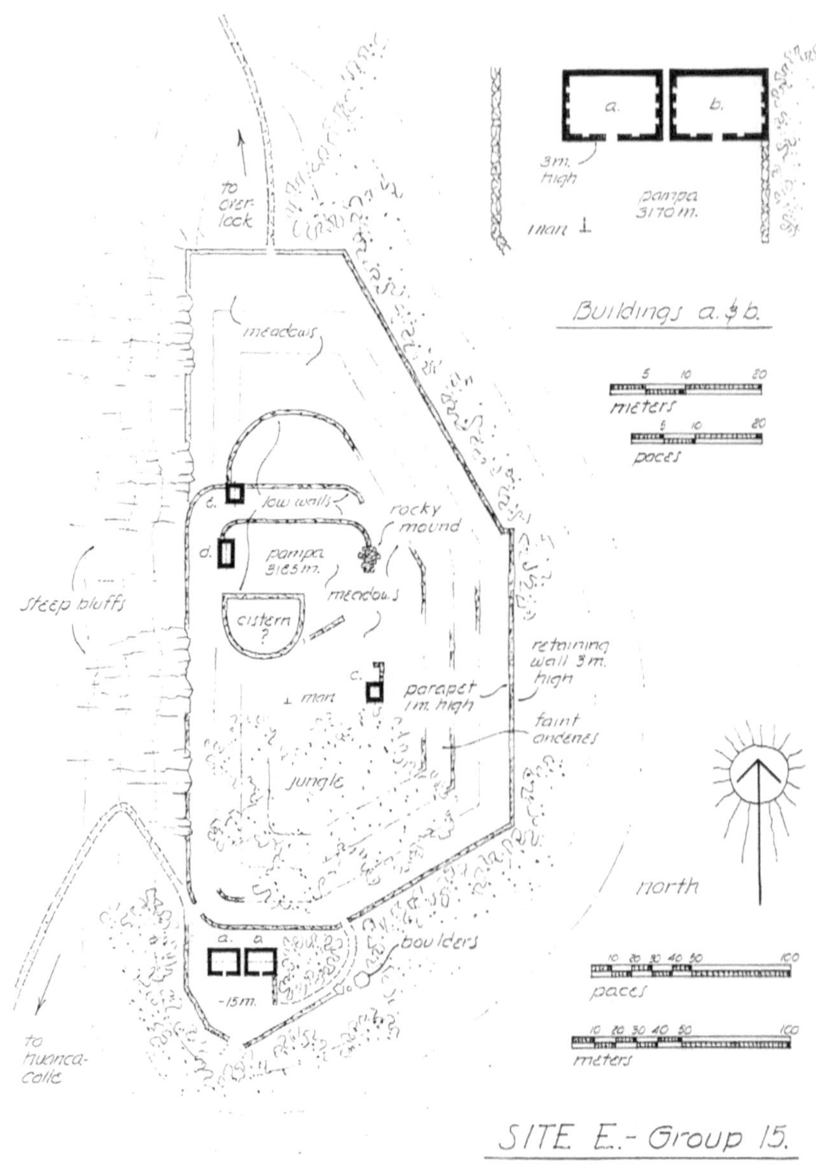

Figure 29 - Plan of "fortress" at Vitcos

Figure 30 - View of “fortress”

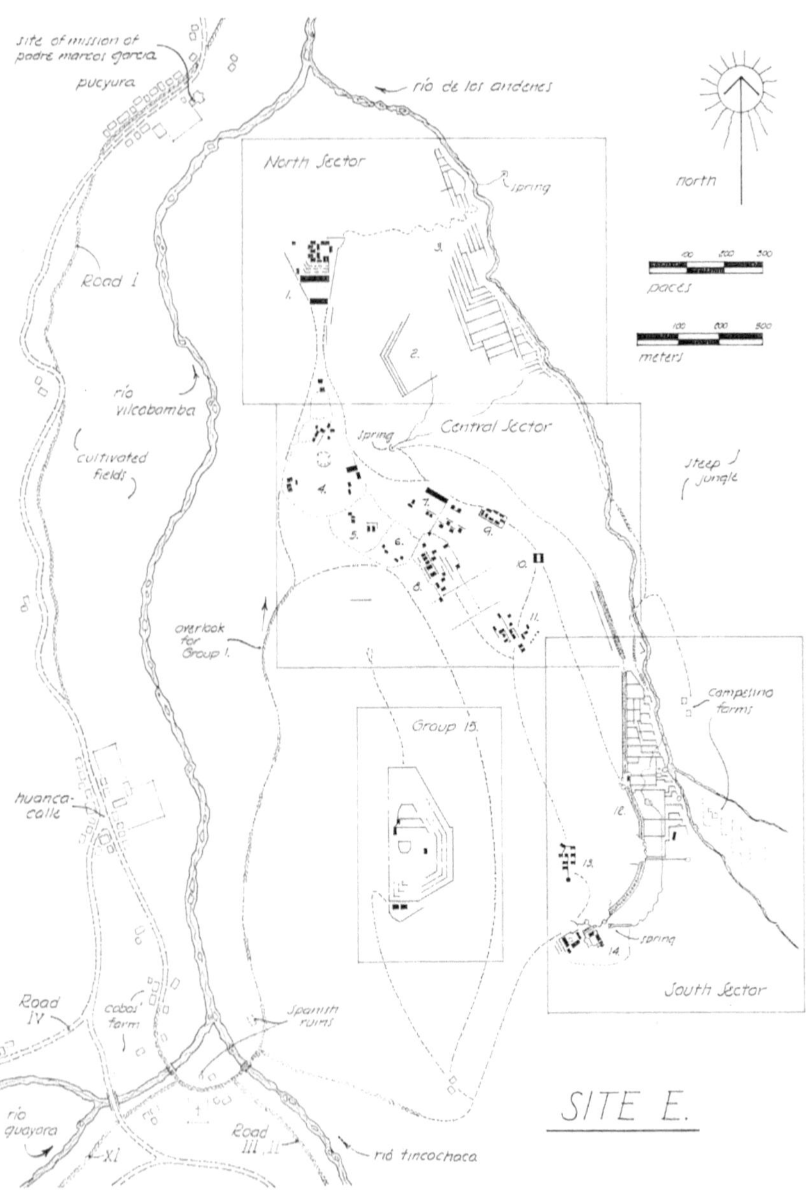

Figure 17 - Map of Rosas Pata and vicinity

Before we reached camp, Nancy told me we had a much more pressing problem than drawing pictures of rocks. She and Susa, she said, were not happy campers. They'd had it with Ben. Helpful and hard-working as he was around camp, his attitude toward them was condescending and insensitive. I'd tried hard not to notice, but I'd seen it too. He was a different guy than I'd known in Wyoming - and who could blame, him after all he'd been through. Somehow, his bitterness seemed to surface most often in his dealings with women. I assumed that was a hangover from his divorce and stayed away from it. At first, Nancy and Susa had done the same, but every so often something he did or said would really hurt, and then all hell would break loose. For my part, I was stuck in the middle, being the only "neutral" member of the team. The role of mediator was one I resented, avoided as much as possible and wasn't good when forced to perform.

Arriving back at the house just at dark, we found that things had come to a head. There'd been a blow-up of some sort between Ben and Susa. Unless I could come up with something to turn things around, she wanted out. For one thing, everyone but me was getting bored. I had my rock piles to keep me busy, but the others were just killing time. The lack of privacy and the squalor of village life is tedious under the best of circumstances, but the rain, mud and pig slop had made it unbearable. We needed to get out of town, and fast. Without a major change of plans, it looked like Sixpac Manco III was over, almost before it had begun.

14

Plan B

If we could just get up into the hills and do some real exploring, I knew we'd break out of the slump and pull back together, but where could we go? Everything south and west of Rosaspata was owned by the Shining Path. Then it hit me: Puncuyoc would be perfect! None of the others had ever seen it and being, as it was, a sort of mini-Machu Picchu, they'd love it. The full moon was past and, with luck, so was the worst of the weather. Best of all, Puncuyoc was about as far from the terrorists as it was possible to go and still be in the Vilcabamba. In selling the idea to the rest of the group, I soft-peddled my own agenda. Since 1984, I'd thought of several questions about the place that needed answering. To name two: what might we have missed during our rainy, two day visit and what about the new *baño* complex Savoy had turned up in 1985? To my surprise, everyone wanted to go. It was quickly agreed. Since we couldn't go to any of our original objectives, we'd opt for Plan B. The next day, we'd pack up and head for Puncuyoc.

A brief clearing in the morning showed a mantle of new snow over the entire Puncuyoc crest - not a good sign. Nevertheless, we were off right after breakfast. The walk down to Yupanka went well enough, but it was raining hard by lunchtime there. Just across the

Río Salinas from town, we started up the steep, muddy switchbacks into thickening cloud forest. (**Figure 4**, Road vi) The weight of our packs quickly began to tell. I tried, unsuccessfully, to beat back visions of our cold, wet tour with José two years earlier. We weren't having fun. Hours went by. Finally, late in the day, we broke out above both the forest and the clouds and camped on a scenic little meadow at about 10,500 feet. The minute we stopped, we were cold and miserable. As if to distract us, the view across to the high cordillera was superb. The huge ice peaks were plastered with fresh snow almost all the way down to our elevation. Not far above our meadow, in fact, high pockets of tropical jungle were incongruously frosted over with ice. While looking around for the best campsite, I found a circular ruin, (**Figure 4**, Building B5) the first of what I hoped would be many more. It began to look like things were going our way after all when we realized that, despite all the rain, there was no water. We looked and looked, but, like the ancient mariner, found that there was "water, water everywhere, but not a drop to drink." Desperate, I finally found some water-filled cow tracks in a swampy, jungle-choked ravine below camp. By then it was dark and, thankfully, we didn't have to look at what we were drinking. The smell might have been a problem, but we nuked the putrid liquid with so much iodine it was as though we were eating dinner in a hospital emergency room. So ended day one of our morale-building adventure.

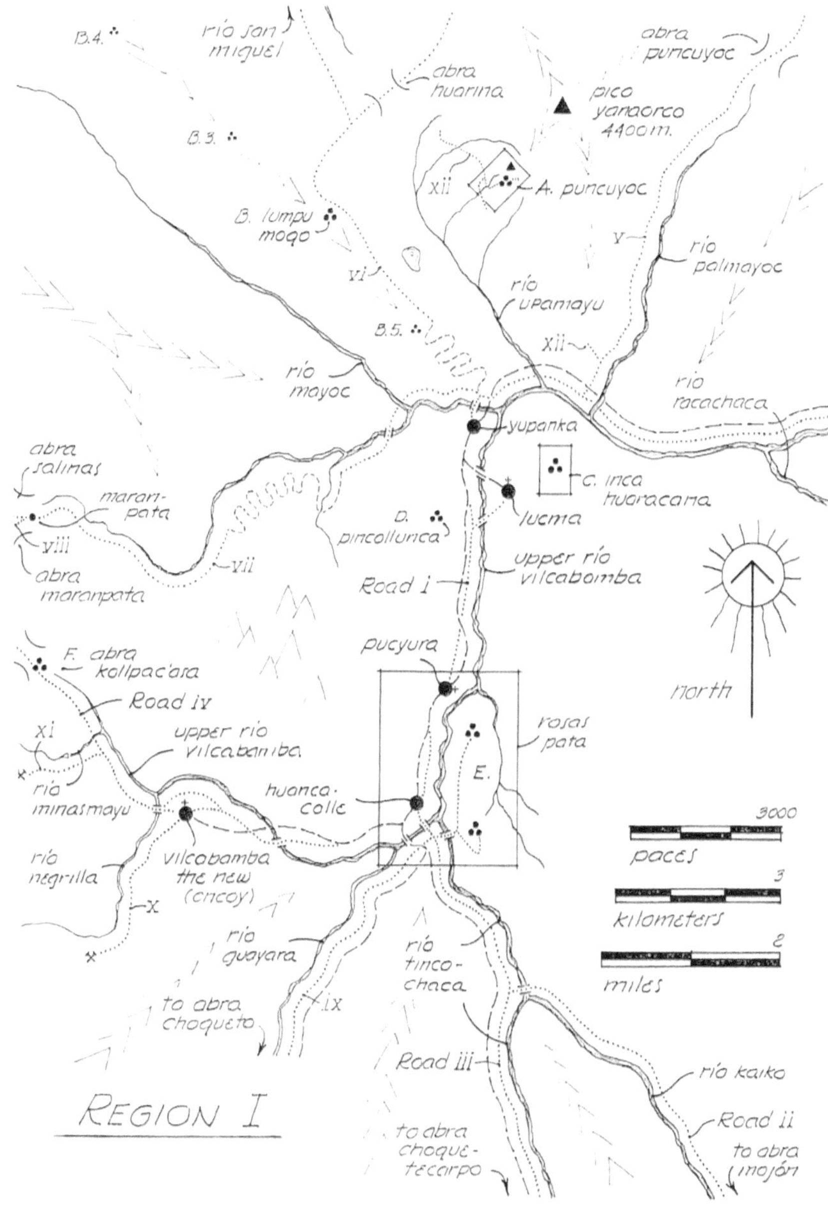

Figure 4 - Map of upper Rio Vilcabamba

Day two wasn't much better. Miraculously, no one was sick from the night before - and since the pans we'd set out to catch rainwater in the night had frozen solid, we were still dehydrated and had to go back down to the swamp for enough to cook breakfast coffee. The clouds had engulfed our route again and we unknowingly walked within a few feet of the overgrown ruins of Lump'u Moqo, **(Figure 12)** a non-Inca site Stuart White would note in his then yet-to-be-published Puncuyoc report. **(1)** Probably, it was once home to some of Beauclerk's tribesmen. Not far beyond, we topped the Huarina Pass, about 2000 feet above our soggy bivouac. From there, we should have had a spectacular view across to Puncuyoc, silhouetted on the jagged skyline several kilometers to the southeast - but there was no such luck. A few scattered snatches of paved Inca roadway in the pass were the only hints that our destination was near. Traversing eastward around the head of the Río Upamayo, we soon found the end of the Inca road which led to the site. Savoy's people had completely cleared away the tangled growth that had blocked it in '84 and, from there, we made good time up into the final cirque. **(Figure 5)**

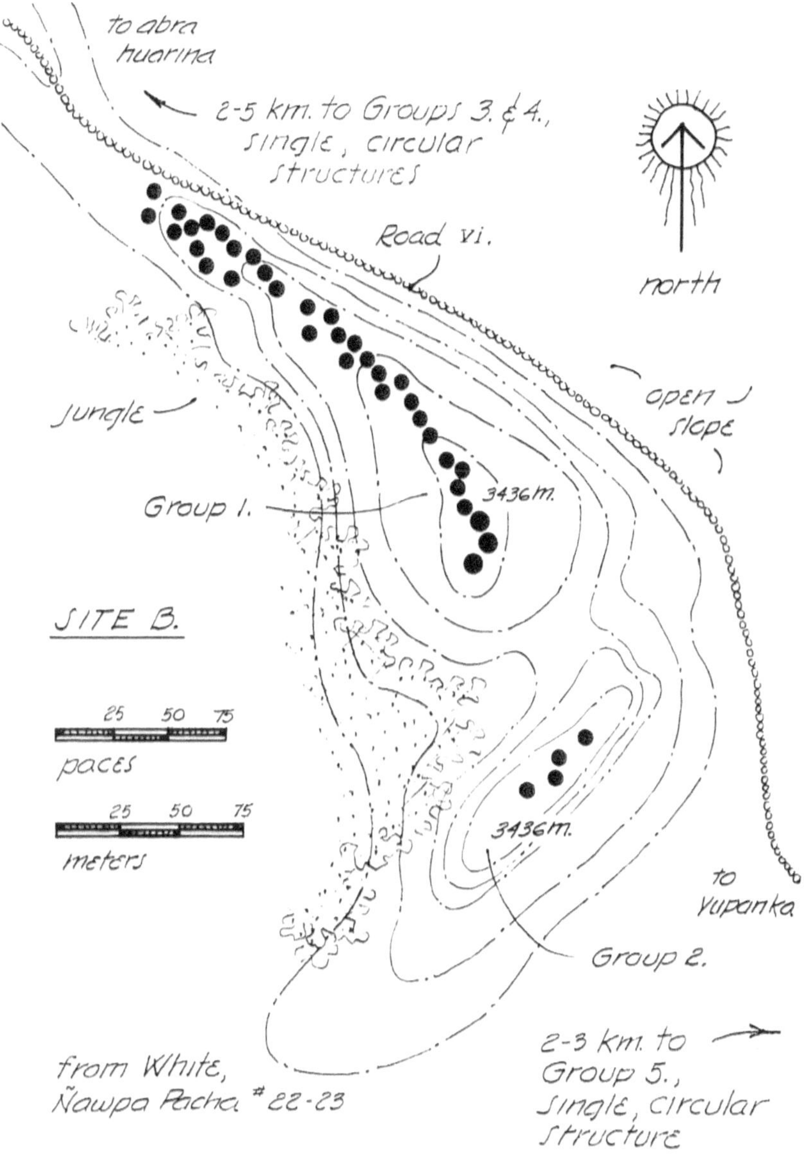

Figure 12 - Site plan of Lump'u Moqo

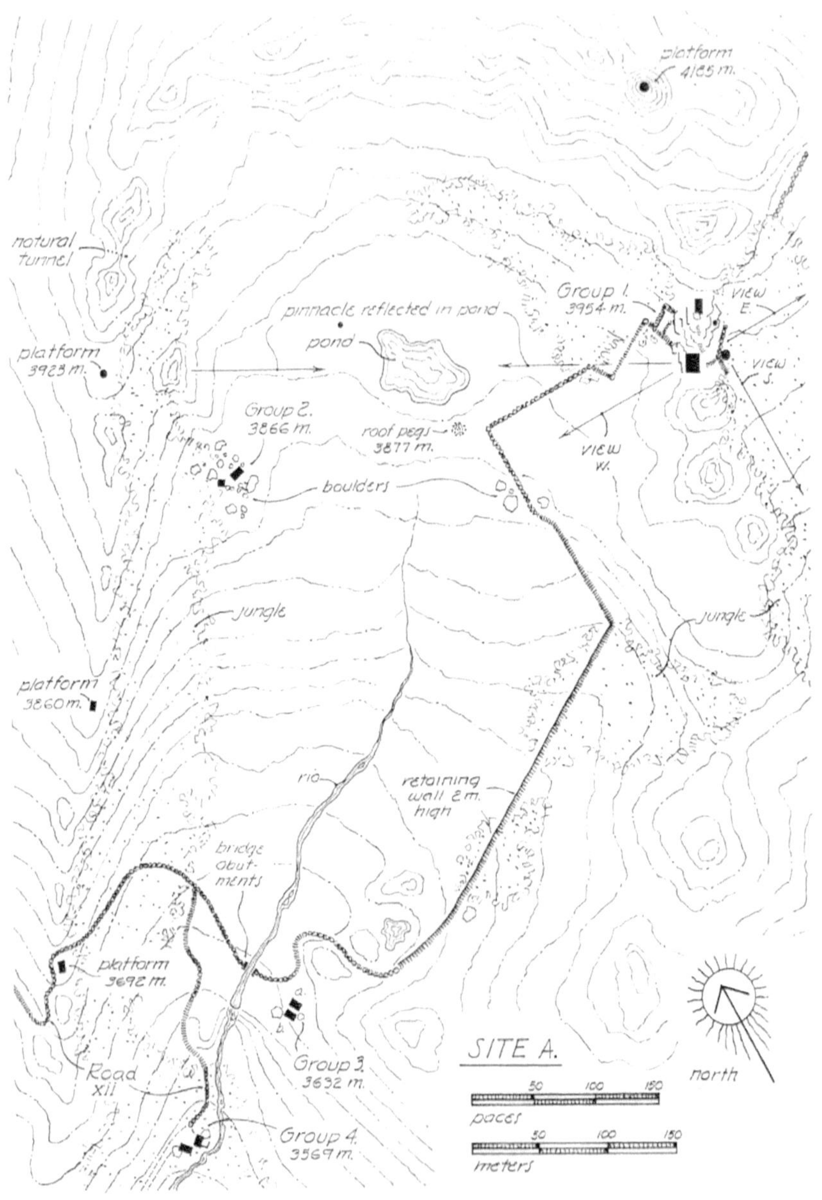

Figure 5 - Map of Puncuyoc

Even in the clouds - in fact, especially so - it was a more fantastic sight than I'd remembered. Above our heads towered rocky peaks in all directions except downstream. There, the drainage from the hanging valley plunged over a high cliff and dissipated into a gigantic plume of mist before reaching the bottom. Not far beyond the base of the cliff and close against the stream were two rectangular structures I'd not seen before, gleaming white against the surrounding jungle. Like the road, they'd probably been cleared by Savoy's crew. A steep, stone stairway, also newly opened, led down over the cliffs. Following it, I found that the buildings were part of the Inca bath group Savoy had told me about. Water had been diverted into the *baño* itself by a fountain of classic design **(Figure 11)** and the road showed some signs of having once continued on down towards the valley via the canyon of the Río Upamayo. There'd been rumors in Yupanka that a stone gateway, or *punku* in Quechua, supposedly stood lost somewhere in the forests of the lower Upamayo and I wondered if an old road hadn't once linked it with the bath. If so, it probably accounted for the name "Punku-yoc". Likely, too, it was the main access to the place in Inca times, since baths and fountains were most often found at the entrances to Inca sites. I silently vowed to explore the lower Upamayo, one day, and perhaps find there some of the features reported by von Hagen's people in the 50s, but lost ever since. "*You can never get it all*," Savoy whispered in my memory.

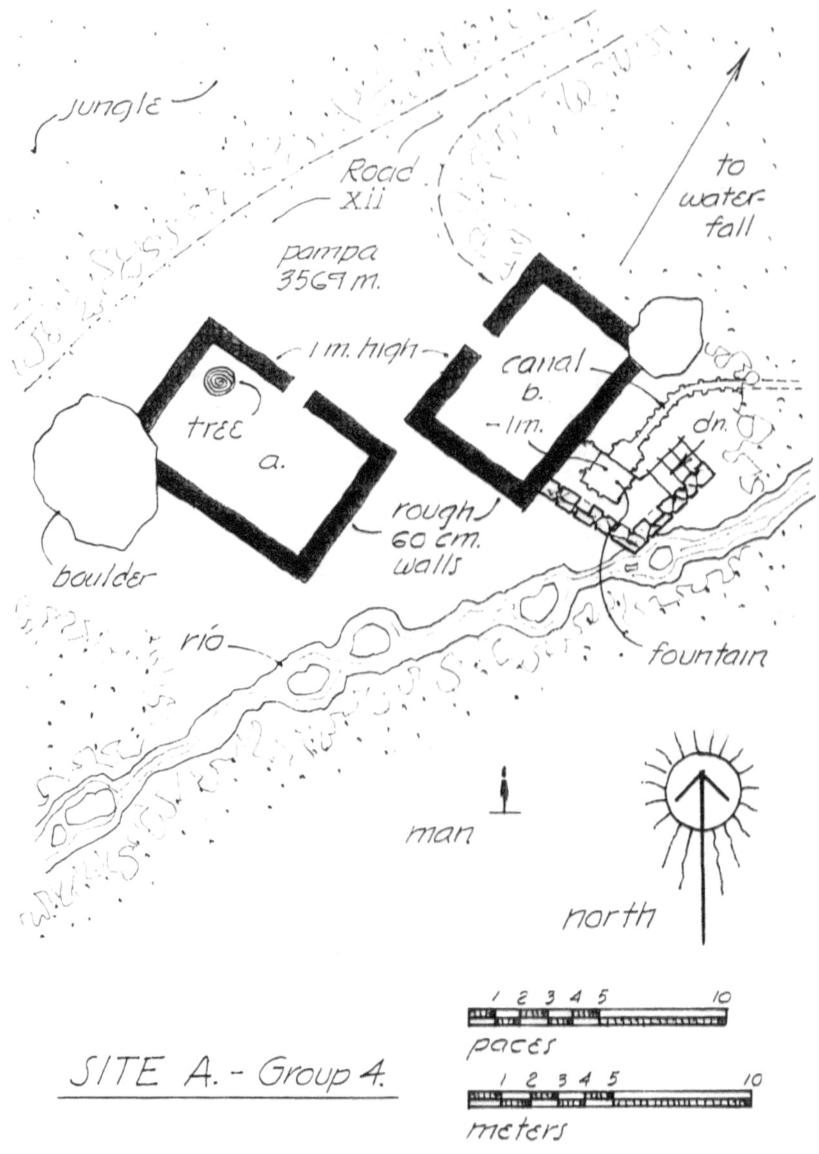

Figure 11 - Site plan of baño group

We set up a base camp in the bottom of the valley on a rise of dry ground in the midst of several ponds and small creeks. There was no point carrying our gear up the 1000 feet or so of carefully laid stone steps that led to the main building - something akin to hauling a big pack to the top of the Empire State Building without using the elevators. Just as we got the tents up, the drizzle that had persisted all day changed to a downpour. Crawling inside to shed soggy clothes, I wondered if there was anyplace wetter than the Andes in rainy weather. If so, I'd never been there. The locals believed the Puncuyoc crest was an *apu*, or sacred peak, which brought rain and thus life to their crops. I was convinced. I'd never seen the place when it wasn't raining. Even viewed from the valley, when clouds gathered, they gathered first over the Puncuyoc. Not farmers, we were becoming a bunch of borderline hypothermics, and we *gringos* were in need of a fair weather *apu*, if such there was.

We managed two more cold, wet days at the site. The perfectly preserved main building, called the Incahuasi or "house of the Inca" by the Indians, was completely cleared of vegetation and all sorts of details not visible two years earlier caught my eye. **(Figures 6-9)** I began to see exactly how the thatch roof that once covered the structure had been framed and fastened to the masonry. Clearly, it had not been done according to any of the prevailing theories I'd seen in the literature, and I made a note to write a paper on the subject when we got back to the states. **(2)** Despite the weather, I was in architect heaven and, as usual, failed to notice that my companions were descending fast into trekker's hell.

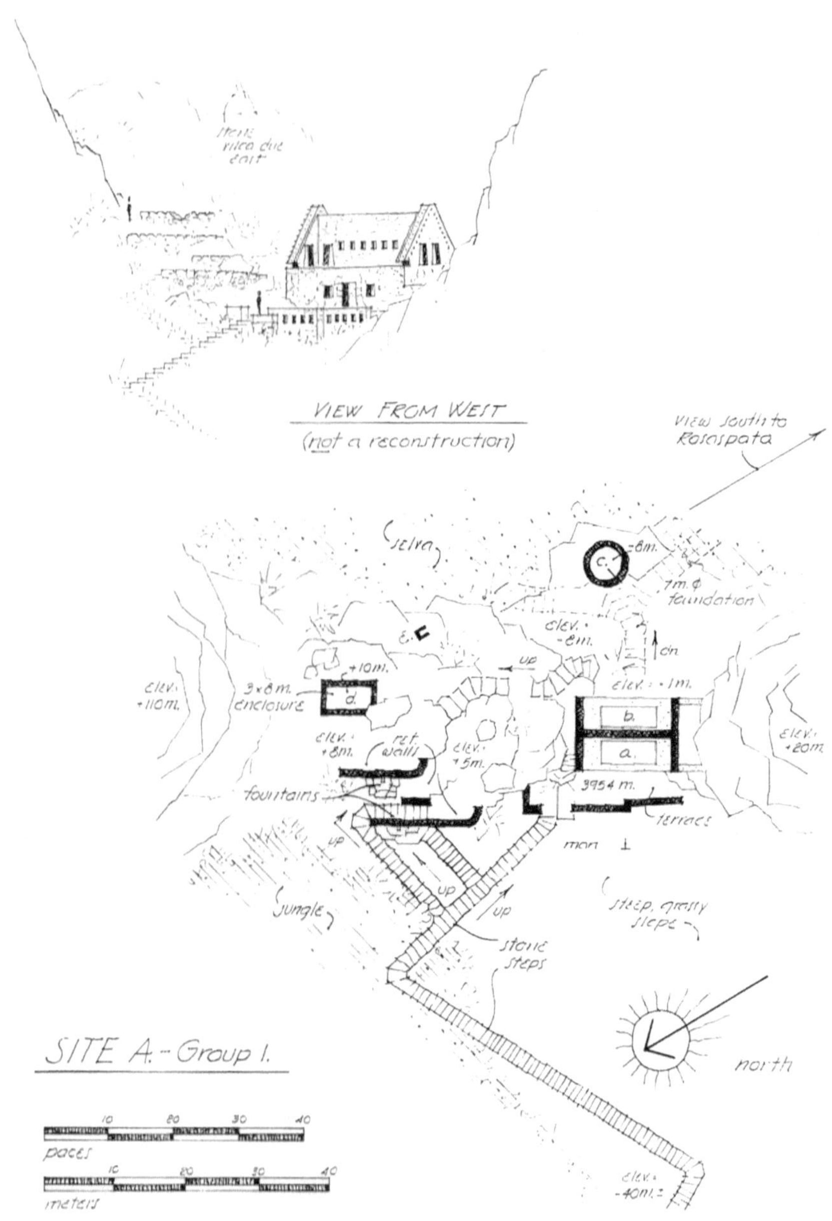

Figure 6 - Site plan and view of Incahuasi

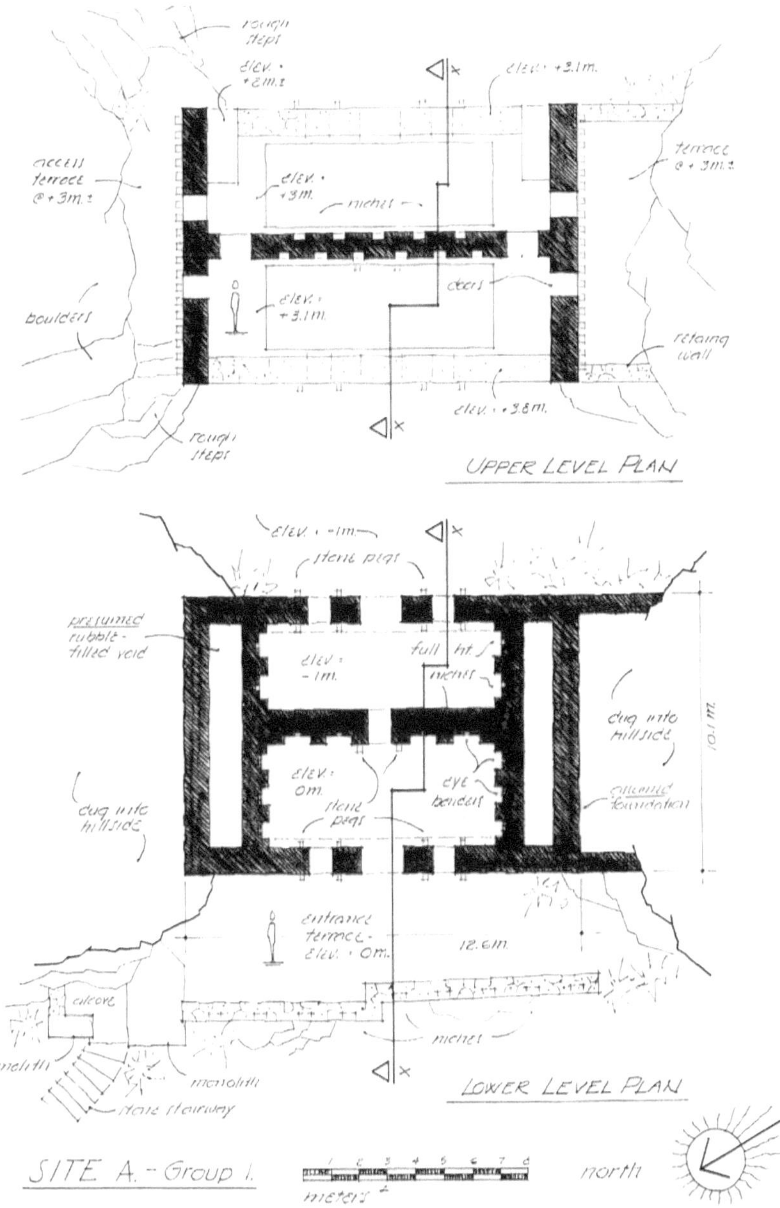

Figure 7 - Floor plans of Incahuasi

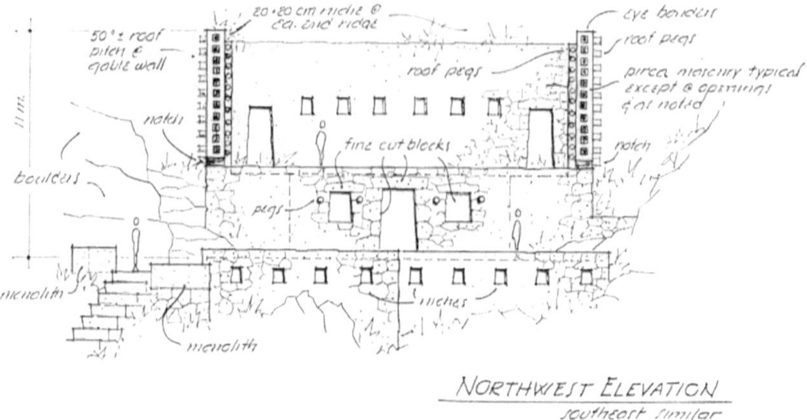

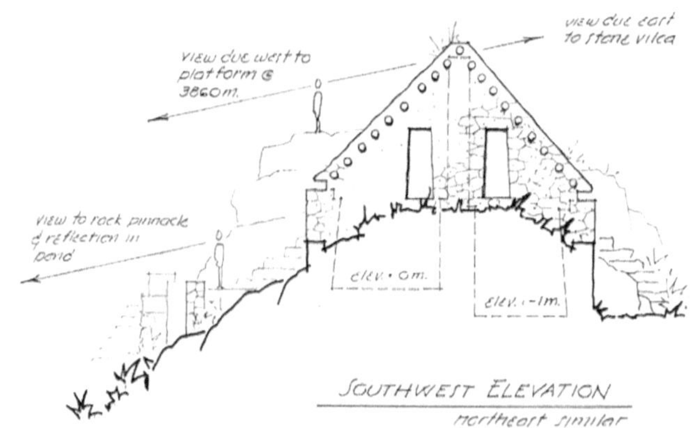

Figure 8 - Exterior elevations of Incahuasi

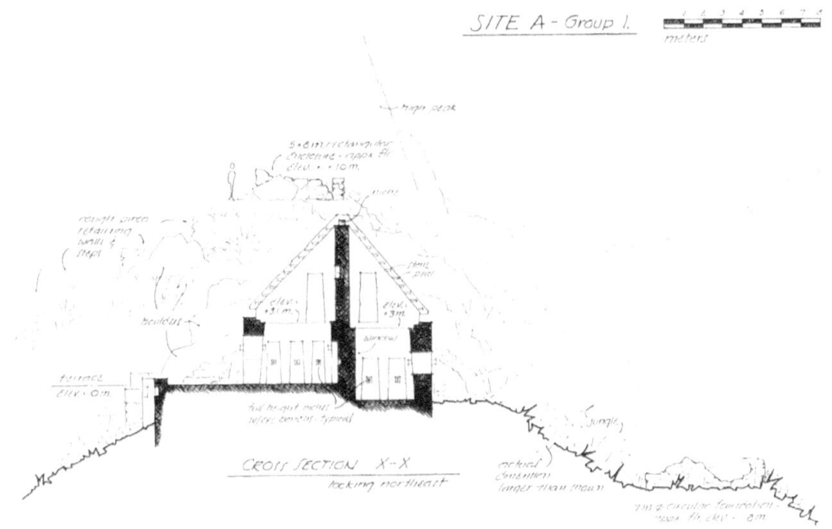

Figure 9 - Cross section of Incahuasi

Author's sketch of thatch roofing scheme proposed for the Incahuasi at Puncuyoc.

Stoic Ben was having less trouble than Nancy and Susa, though, and it was he who suggested we do some exploring elsewhere in the cirque and up on the surrounding ridgelines. Getting there was made easier than expected by a huge burn that had recently swept up from the valley and cleared most of the brush from the ledges. While the women stayed in camp and read, he and I climbed to the rock pinnacle opposite the reflecting pond below the Incahuasi to check out the great white spot at close range. It turned out to be nothing more than a slab of granite protected from the rain by a deep overhang and thus free of lichens and moss. Because it was very big and very white, we named it "Moby Dick." More interesting was the previously undiscovered stone platform we found on the ridge-top, just behind the spire. Encouraged by this new find, we scrambled up the increasingly sharp knife-edge ridge to the craggy summit that stood at the head of the valley, directly above and north of the main building. Looking like Commandos blackened with soot from the fire, we found there, too, a large circular platform. Even in the mist, we could see that it commanded awesome views all around. **(Figure 5)** I thought of my friend, Joe Reinhard, a specialist in high altitude archaeology and Andean mountain worship. He'd discovered and excavated similar platforms on scores of peaks from Ecuador to Chile, often finding there buried offerings to the mountain gods. In time, he would recover perfectly preserved mummies of Incan sacrificial victims from a tumbled platform atop a frozen peak in southern Peru. Puncuyoc looked like his kind of site and I jotted a note to tell him about it when I got back to the States.

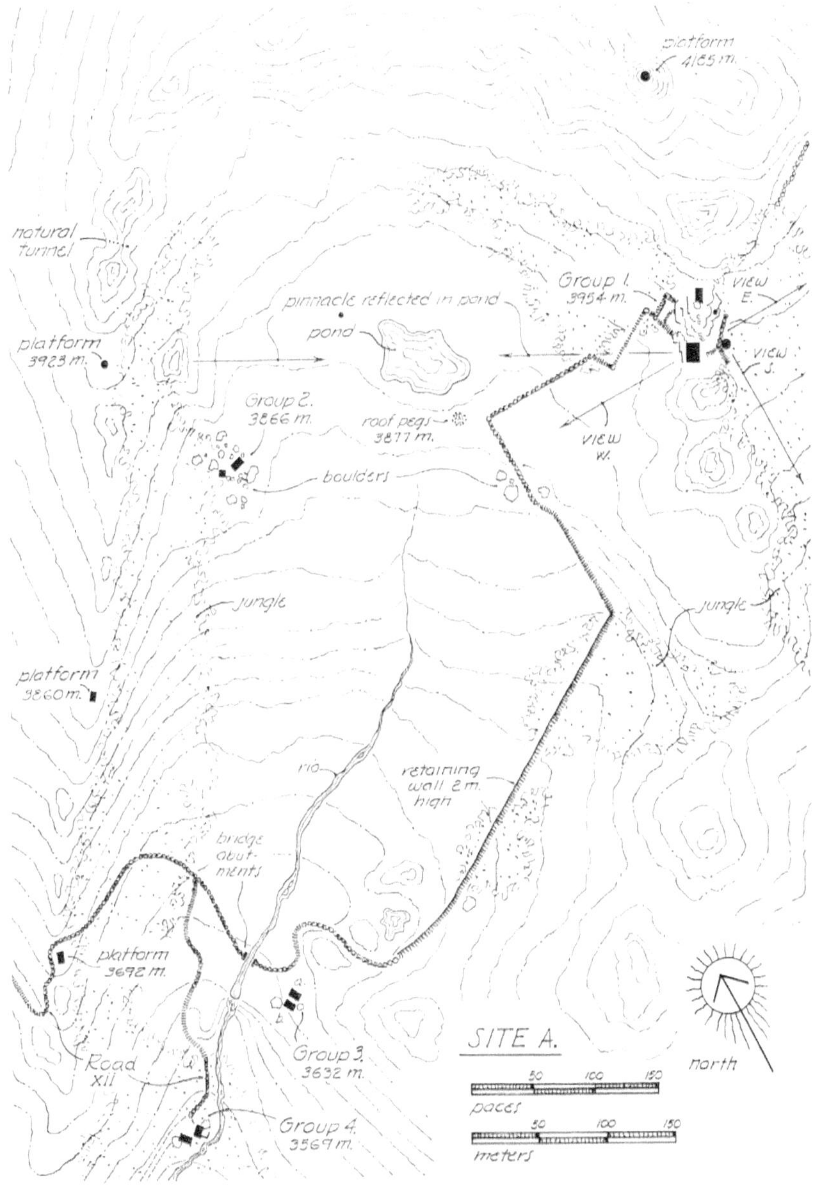

Figure 5 - Map of Puncuyoc

Dropping off the lower ridge on our way back to camp, we happened onto a fascinating group hidden in the jumble of boulders below Moby Dick. It was completely overgrown with jungle and had eluded even Savoy's energetic crews. Stuart White's Ñawpa Pacha report would describe what he termed a "cave complex" in about the same location, **(3)** and that's exactly what Ben and I found. Several caves and retaining walls had been developed beneath a house-sized boulder standing near the foundations of two rectangular buildings. **(Figure 10)** A flat bench led from there around the head of the cirque to a small, overgrown fountain near the reflecting pond. It seems likely that a road once connected the caves, via the fountain, to the main stairway up to the Incahuasi **(Figure 5)** - but, if so, no trace seemed to remain.

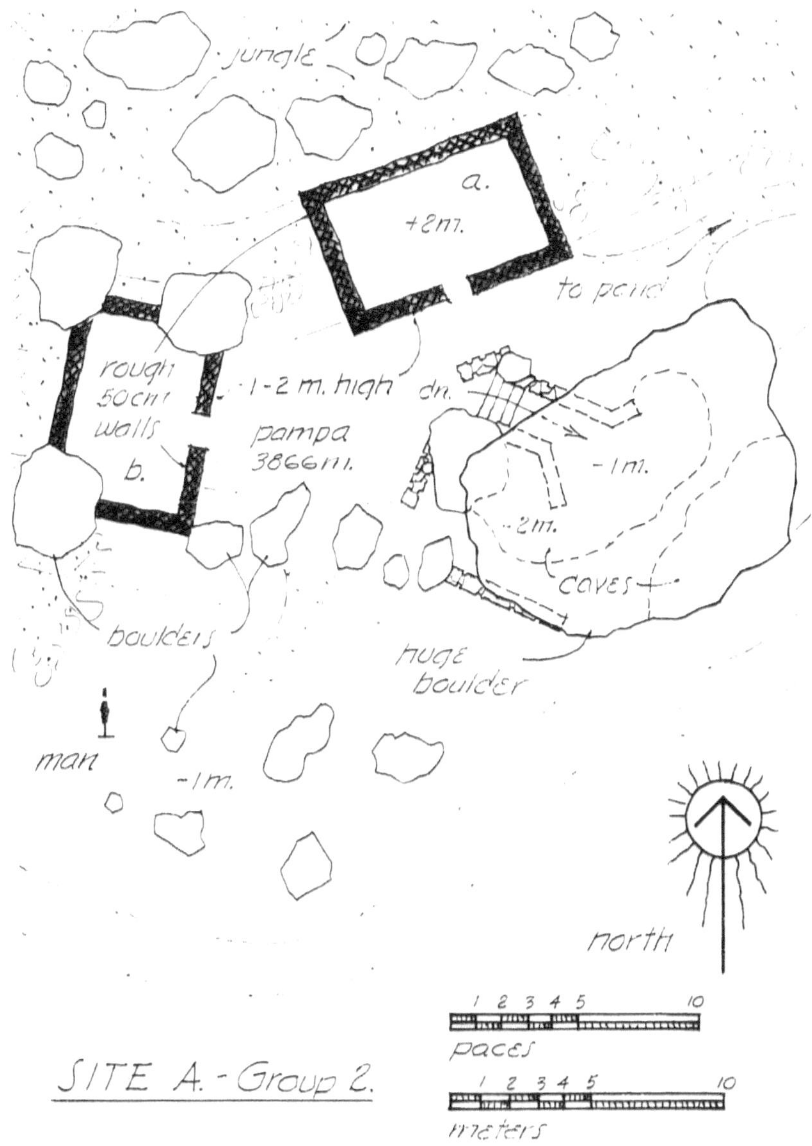

Figure 10 - Site plan of cave group

The next morning, the 25th of July, we headed back to our base camp at Huancacalle, dropping out from under the cold, damp clouds just above Yupanka. As a morale builder, the trip had failed miserably - double entendre intended. We were colder, wetter, unhappier and more tired than ever. Nancy and Susa, especially, were "ruined", a term we coined to describe anyone who broke out in hives at the mere mention of visiting another archaeological site. Aside from that, though, we'd accomplished a lot. Ben and I'd been able to thoroughly explore the entire area and had added ten new structures to my 1984 count. Far from being a single, isolated building, it was now clear that the Incahuasi had formed the focal point of a cluster of building groups, each intended for a different and specific purpose - though what, exactly, remained to be seen. White eventually concluded his analysis of the site with the suggestion that it had been an oracle to the sun, earth and various nearby huacas, such as Moby Dick, the reflecting pond and the boulder in the cave group. He speculated it might have been the place where Sayri Tupac Inca had made his fateful decision to abandon the rustic security of Vilcabamba for the seductive intrigues of Cuzco **(4)**. My own thoughts were summarized the following year in a paper which pointed out some correlations between the site and its architecture and the important Inca feast of Huarachicoy, celebrated annually in December amidst wild, high-mountain surroundings. **(5)** Maybe we're both right. The fact is, no one knows what Puncuyoc was used for and, unless solid evidence turns up in some future excavation, probably no one ever will.

Back at Cobos' place, it was good to sleep under a dry roof for a change. In the morning, we declared a rest day which was made even better by the first real sunshine we'd seen since arriving in Huancacalle. After a leisurely breakfast, we took a hard look at the rest of the trip. Nancy and Susa had had their fill. The threat of terrorism was getting on everyone's nerves, but theirs especially. As if to rub it in, a patrol passed by on one the Army's rare forays from Pucyura. The dozen or so troopers swaggered through camp brandishing their weapons like the armed adolescents they were, checking papers and lording over all they met. We had their permission, the sergeant barked, to go only as far as Pampaconas. Beyond there would be suicide, he concluded. We all knew he couldn't do squat about it if we went further, but there was an off chance he was right.

So, it looked for the moment like the only additional exploring we were going to get done was in familiar country Nancy had already visited. Susa, meanwhile, wanted to see some traditional Andean weaving and the raw, frontier settlements of Vilcabamba were anything but traditional. The best centers for old time textiles were down around Lake Titicaca, a place Nancy had been years before, but looked forward to seeing again. So she and Susa decided to pull out and spend a week or so traveling there while Ben and I did whatever we could to finish up our explorations around Pampaconas. Everybody was more or less happy with the new plan, with one condition. Nancy made me promise we wouldn't sneak off to Espíritu Pampa the minute she was out of sight, and I agreed. Finally, any lingering doubts about the women's departure were erased when Susa got a nasty dog bite on her hand. Even though others in the village had been bitten by the same dog in the past without ill effects, Vilcabamba didn't seem the best place to be in case of a medical emergency, however unlikely.

With a mixture of relief and sadness, I helped Nancy pack up and watched as she and Susa trudged off up the road to Huancacalle, where they planned to catch the next truck out to Quillabamba. Memories of her close call with the drunken *soldados* in Pucyura two years earlier probably haunted us both, but neither of us mentioned it. As things turned out, it was just as well, since the ordeal they were headed into was fated to be even worse. Their trip down to the railroad and out to Cuzco ended up being a sleepless, 48 hour marathon of bruising, mind-numbing third world travel. Even the escape they so looked forward to at Lake Titicaca didn't turn out quite as planned. After a long, icy train ride over the mountains to the Peruvian port of Puno on the lake's north shore, they found Senderista bomb squads even more active and intimidating in the city's streets than the *guerrillas* had been in the mountains. The travel agents had it right after all. 1986, we were finding, was not a great year to be journeying about in Peru.

15

Standing On The Answer

The very same day the ladies left camp, word filtered back to Huancacalle that the Israelis had gotten through okay and everyone began to breathe easier. At long last, it looked like the coast was clear. It was as if the terrorists had all gone to Puno with Nancy and Susa, although we wouldn't know anything about that for several more weeks. Ben and I immediately contracted with Juvenal for a horse and, once again, lined up José to be our packer and guide. Because he couldn't leave on such short notice, we arranged to meet him in Pampaconas three days later and left four big bags of food and gear for the horse. Glad to be getting out of town again, we headed over the pass with backpacks so small they were almost agreeable. The sun was shining and the trip was pleasant and uneventful. The beautiful section of Inca road up to Vilcabamba the New was a joy, as in the past. The only ominous note was the trail of surveyor's stakes on the hillside above the road. As an architect, I knew only too well what that meant. It was no surprise when a passing *campesino* said that a contract had been let to extend the *carretera* on up to Vilcabamba the New, the only authentic, unreconstructed sixteenth century village remaining in the province. It would be more of the same auto road that had so recently transformed the quaint farming community of Huancacalle into a cardboard, mud and tin shopping bazaar. Worse, next time it would be a one-two punch. Both the integrity of the village and the lovely stone road up to it would be swept away in an afternoon's bulldozer work. There was even talk of eventually continuing the road on over the pass to Pampaconas but, thankfully, there were no more survey stakes to be seen beyond Vilcabamba the New and the intricate Inca stairways of Mollepunku (**Figure 33**) seemed safe, at least for the moment.

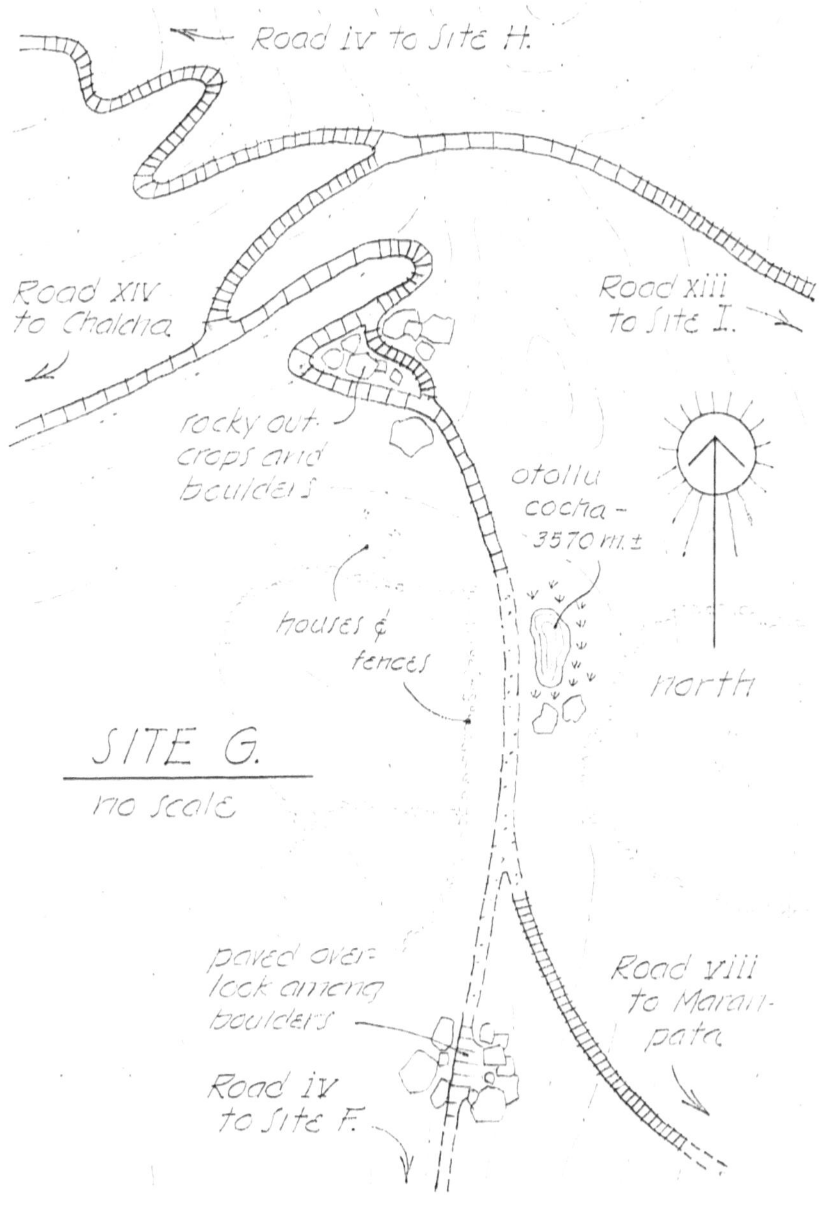

Figure 33 - Map of Mollipunku

Our first objective was to try to verify von Kaupp's claim that an Inca road crossed the ridgeline west of Pampaconas and descended into the canyon of the Río Zapateroyoc. There, he said we'd find

Inca ruins at a place called Cochayoc, appropriately near a lake - *cocha* in Quechua. The ruins were important to my plan of finding everything in the province and the road was important to his counter-theory. The Spanish invasion force of 1572 had taken eight days to march from Pampaconas to Vilcabamba the Old and had passed through the place called Anonay along the way. If, as von Kaupp thought, the Inca capital was somewhere near his sites in the Río Urumbay, he had a serious problem. Needed was an eight-day route between two places no more than a half day apart. Worse, it had to pass through the place nowadays called Ayunay which, like Edmundo Guillén, he assumed was the old Anonay. Ayunay, unfortunately, is at least half a day beyond the Urumbay from the direction of Pampaconas. von Kaupp's solution was the road Ben and I had come to find, if we could. According to Bob, it continued on beyond the Zapateroyoc for several days downstream, then doubled back upstream through Ayunay en route to the Urumbay. Far fetched as the whole thing sounded, there seemed only one way to check it out. I was 99 percent sure from my own research that it was nonsense. Sarmiento de Gamboa, the same chronicler who'd written about Anonay had also mentioned the hanging of the prisoner at Ututo, the place where Nancy, Jill and Martha had left us back in 1984. Ututo, of course, was just down the canyon a bit below Pampaconas, right smack along the Inca road to Espíritu Pampa - and nowhere near von Kaupp's round-about alternative route to the Urumbay. Still, I had to find and map the ruins at Cochayoc anyway, so looking for Bob's road while we were at it was no big deal.

The *ronderos* at Pampaconas greeted our arrival there with suspicion until we explained that we were just crazy *gringos*, looking for ruins. Incredibly, they were armed with wooden spears just as, they said, many of the terrorists were. When we inquired about the situation, they echoed the warnings of the *jefe* and his blustering *sargento*. Apparently, they agreed that the country below Pampaconas was unsafe and we were advised not to go "*adentro la selva* " - inside the forest, a phrase we heard again and again, as if the nearby jungle were an alien world of some sort. The locals seemed unaware of the litmus test performed by the Israelis and were unimpressed when we told them about it. Nonetheless, we did manage to find a couple of Juvenal's relatives willing to show us the trail over into the Zapateroyoc and arranged to go there early the next morning.

As we were soon to learn, the only Inca ruin for miles around was actually a couple of hundred yards from our camp. One of our guides casually pointed it out from the rise of ground where we'd set up the tent. I wandered over after dinner and made a hasty plan of the place in the fading light. It was a large, classically Inca platform of some sort, reached via a partially silted-in stone stairway leading up past a small, secondary terrace from a ravine to the east **(Figure 34)**. I remembered that Pachacuti had lorded over the natives from a base in Pampaconas and that Titu Cusi had met Rodriguez de Figueroa on a "square" at the same place 125 years later. The Inca kings apparently liked doing business from atop raised platforms they called "*ushnus*," and I wondered if perhaps we'd found one - and an historic one, at that. Juvenal later told me the place was called Incapampa.

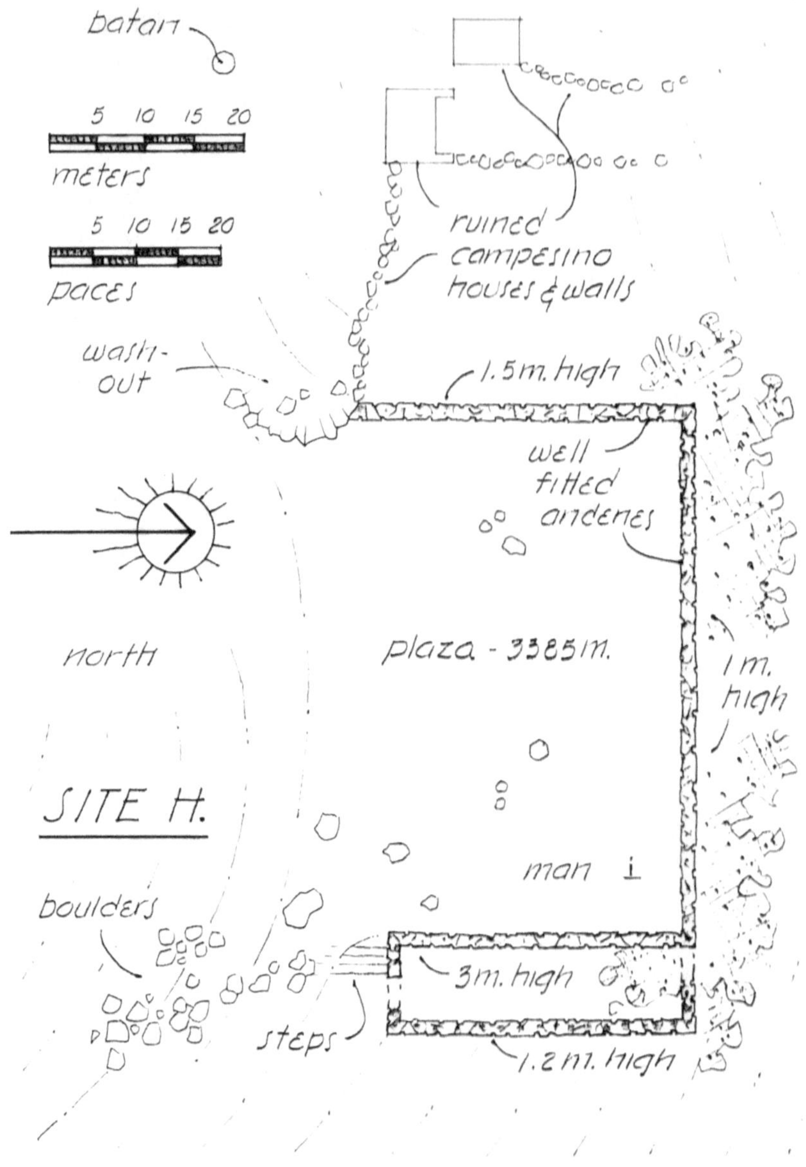

Figure 34 - Site plan of Incapampa

Although we found neither an Inca road nor any ruins whatsoever in the course of our expedition the next day, it was not a total loss. The country, including several lovely lakes, was spectacular, the weather was superb and our guides were unequivocal in their responses to my many questions. Yes, there was a small ruin called Cochayoc, but it was over in the canyon of the Río Urumbay, not there in the Zapateroyoc. No, there were no Inca roads out of Pampaconas save the commonly used one down the long, stone stairway to Ututo. Yes, there was another road, running down the spine of the ridge separating the Zapateroyoc from the Pampaconas but no, it was not Inca and no one used it anymore. The paved Inca road that crossed the river below Ututo was shorter and better in wet conditions. And, finally, yes, they'd heard there was also an old road below Ututo that didn't cross the river, but it was lost in the jungle and they'd never seen it. I thought about my own discovery of what seemed to be an abandoned and overgrown road there two years earlier.

Late in the day, as we neared Pampaconas on our way home, they stopped a few hundred feet above camp and showed us the road along the spine of the ridge. Sure enough, it was nothing more than a plain old mule track, and not a very good one. Several days later, José showed me the place where it rejoined the Inca road just above Tambo. It must have been the route followed by Bingham, I thought, as he proceeded beyond Pampaconas on his way to Espíritu Pampa in 1911. His description exactly matched the terrain: "*Leaving the village* (of Pampaconas) *we climbed up the mountain and followed a faint trail by a dangerous route along the crest of the ridge. The rains had not improved the path.*" (emphasis added)**(1)** The path to Ututo goes downhill from Pampaconas and Bingham's map of the expedition's route, published in 1914, indicates that they stayed west of the river all the way downstream **(2)**. (**Figure 32**)

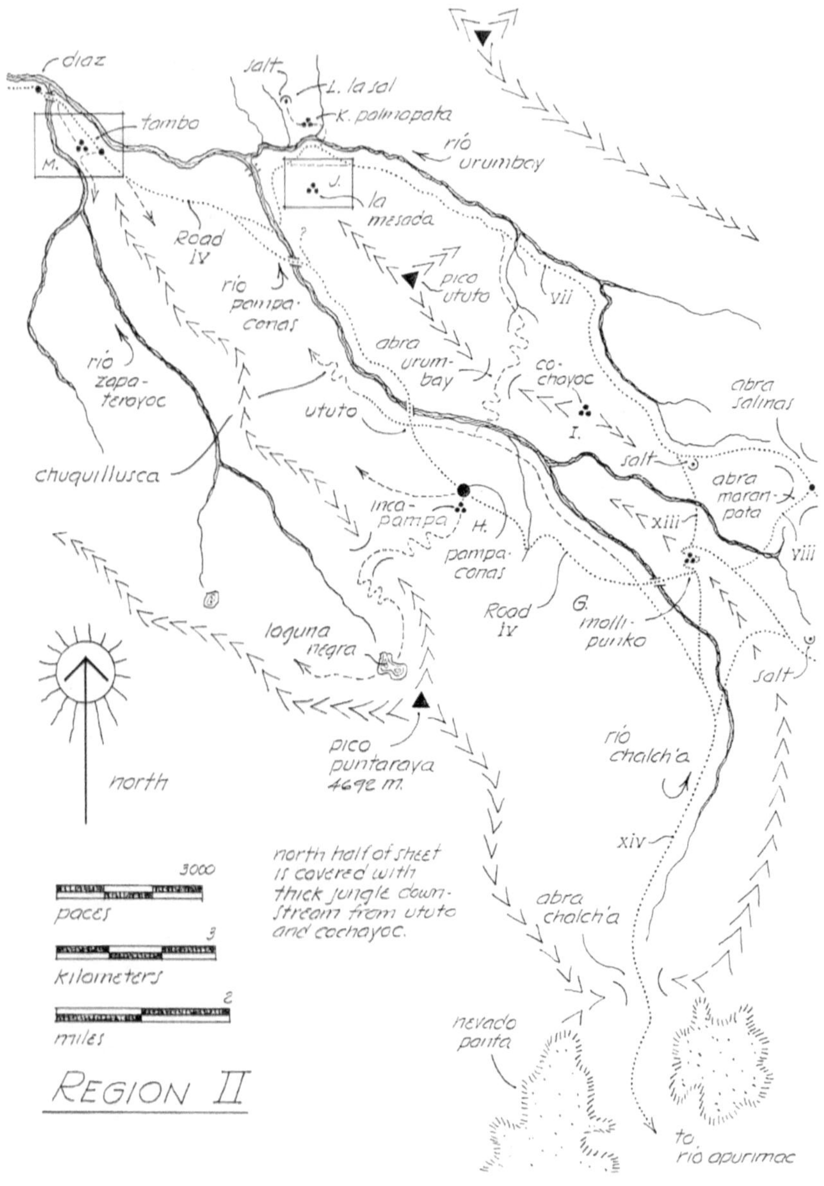

Figure 32 - Map of upper Rio Pampaconas

The report of a "lost" road west of the river, below Ututo, likewise fit nicely with the written record. After the execution of the Indian, Canchari, at Ututo, an argument had ensued among the Spanish captains regarding which road to follow, "*the road of the forts or that of the Incas*." **(3)** Since the Inca road below Ututo was definitely the one across the river, it followed that the unused path lost in the jungle on the near side must have been the "road of the forts." Ben and I got up early the next morning and slipped down there to have a look. After searching all through the wall of forest that rimmed the meadows, we found only the same overgrown trail I'd spotted on our way up from Tambo in 1984. Optimistically, we decided to spend the rest of the day cutting downstream to see where it went. By noon we'd gone less than half a mile. It was totally overgrown, and good sized trees growing right out of the pathway suggested it hadn't been used for years. It must have been the old road our Pampaconas guides had heard about, but never seen. Despite cutting nearly until dark, we never found out where it went. All we learned for sure was that it crossed lots of cliffs and ravines choked with dense jungle, just exactly as the Spaniards described the "road of the forts." When I asked Juvenal about it several weeks later, he said the old westside trail hadn't been used in his lifetime, but local tradition held that it once went all the way through to Tambo.

Walking back up the long Inca stairway to Pampaconas that night, I reflected on what we'd learned in the past two days. First, von Kaupp's theory wasn't supported by anything we'd been able to find on the ground, nor did it check out with what we'd been told by the locals. Second, the ruin called Cochayoc was somewhere in the Urumbay, not the Zapateroyoc as he'd claimed. Third, we'd verified that at least one Inca ruin did still exist at Pampaconas, a site long thought to have been barren of pre-Hispanic remains. And finally, there'd formerly been three roads downstream from Pampaconas, each of which corresponded closely with one historic account or another. **(Figure 32)** Those were the answers we'd come for and there was nothing left to do. It was time to move on, but where to? Neither of us wanted to turn back, but if the *ronda* thought the jungle downstream unsafe, who were we to disagree? Still, José was due with the horses any time, so we had to come up with something, and soon.

Sooner than we thought. José was already waiting when we dragged back into camp after dark, dead tired from our day in the bush.

He'd been talking with the locals and thought he saw a way around our dilemma. If it was the lower Urumbay we wanted to see, he knew a way in there that avoided the main road, where trouble was most likely to be waiting. Relieved, we gulped down some of the new food he'd brought up and turned in, exhausted. Still, the idea we were headed into hostile territory began working on us both during the night and neither of us ended up getting much sleep. The morning dawned cold and clear, and we were up at first light and on the trail well before sun up.

José had brought along his oldest son, Ronaldo, and all our food and gear had come up on the back of an old buckskin gelding. A seasoned packer, he was soon due to be put out to pasture and we took to calling him El Viejo, the aged one, in honor of his twenty-plus years. He was easy on the trail and Ronaldo handled him most of the time while his father walked along listening to Cuzco radio on his battery operated portable. How I came to hate that little plastic box! The idea that we'd finally gotten out into the wilds only to be assaulted by city noise all day long was more than I could handle. I prayed the batteries would die, but they never did. What were they made of, enriched kryptonite? Either that, or José had hidden a two week supply somewhere in El Viejo's pack and switched them at three in the morning, when no one was looking. It was so maddening I considered electronic sabotage - but José never let it out of his sight. I gave up instead and, after that first day, just started out early or dropped way behind, out of earshot.

Instead of leaving camp by way of Ututo, we backtracked the way we'd come a kilometer or so and dropped down a steep *quebrada*, or gulch, to the Río Pampaconas. It was running low due to the clear weather and we forded without difficulty. Across the river a steep, muddy path switchbacked up the forested slope opposite Pampaconas and by midday we'd crossed over the top, into the drainage of the Río Urumbay. Beyond, rolling meadows dotted with a few *campesino* farms angled gently down into the upper reaches of the canyon. As we descended to the river, our route joined a good trail coming down from upstream and we followed it into the thickening jungle of the lower canyon.

There was nothing down there, José said, except the salt mines at La Sal - one of von Kaupp's three archaeological sites and, thus, one of our reasons for going there. The gathering of the salt was done communally, once a year, but because of the terrorists, the mines hadn't been worked since 1984. The condition of the trail deteriorated the deeper we got into the woods. Clearly, no one had been using it. Proof turned up soon enough when we came onto a large tree fallen across the path, effectively blocking horse travel. An hour later, we'd cut through with our *machetes* only to find another tree in the way a short distance beyond. What should have been a pleasant half-day's hike was turning into a long, tedious grunt. In 1572, the Incas had reportedly felled numerous trees in the path of the invading Spaniards and we now understood just how effective that tactic could be.

I was cutting through a tangle of brush late in the day when a sharp branch snapped back and hit me in the eye. *Machetes* are dangerous tools in inexperienced hands and I'd been so worried about slicing my foot off I wasn't paying much attention to anything else. Usually, I wore sunglasses, but not in the perpetual twilight of the jungle. My right cornea was badly scratched and at first I could hardly stand to open the lid - and couldn't see anything when I did. I popped some pain killers, got some ointment into the eye and put on a patch. The pills helped, but I was immediately frustrated by how hard it was to see with one eye closed, especially in the *bosque*, where visibility was so-so to begin with. Fortunately, José said we were nearing camp and the country was beginning to open up a bit. We took the right fork at the only trail junction we'd come to, and quickly found ourselves faced with crossing the Urumbay on a very nasty looking bridge of slippery poles, high above the water. El Viejo was just barely able to struggle across the rushing stream below, so it didn't look like we had any alternative. Without thinking, I volunteered to go first, but soon realized my mistake. With only one eye, I had no depth perception and less balance. I ended up crawling across on my hands and knees and, even at that, I was spooked. To my immense relief, Ben, Ronaldo and José did only slightly better and the crossing took forever.

Finally on the other side, we followed a path up the steep bank onto an open bench bounded on the north and east by swampy jungle and elsewhere by steep drop-offs into brushy ravines. The clearing was called Palmapata after a giant palm tree that had once stood nearby. José said the old timers claimed it was Mananhuañunca, the place where a Spanish priest called "Padre Huarcuna" had been killed by the Indians many years before. The word *huarcuna* means "hanger" in Quechua, so von Kaupp had made the connection with Father Diego Ortiz. According to Martín de Murúa, the priest had been hung on a cross, among other things, during his final ordeal **(4)**. So, we'd arrived at the first of Bob's sites and looking around, I wasn't impressed. It was nothing more than a boggy meadow, strewn with loose rocks. According to José, it was the only *pampa* in the area, and was used as a campsite by the pack outfits each year when they came for salt. According to José, the mines - von Kaupp's second site - were not far up the ravine to the west.

The light was fading fast and while Ben, José and Ronaldo set up camp, I set about finding the remains described by von Kaupp in his 1983 report. **(5)** He'd written that the *padre's* "*tomb*" was located on the south edge of the clearing and that its "*entrance apparently faced south*" and had "*recently been opened.*" Expecting to find a ruin of some sort, I was disappointed when the only man made feature to be seen was a formless pile of small fieldstones no different than those found everywhere in the Andes where fields have been cleared for cultivation. Neither the "tomb" nor its "entrance" were apparent to me. von Kaupp had also noted "a series of stone lines" radiating out from the tomb. Of the larger rocks scattered about the meadow, only a few seemed to be aligned, and by natural erosion - not human intent - or so it appeared to me. Below the rockpile was the fallen palm tree that had given the place its name in recent times. Its trunk was broken into three segments which totaled more than twice the "*19.2 meters*" noted by von Kaupp. So much for accuracy, I thought. Disgusted, I made a quick map of the place **(Figure 38**, Site K) and joined the others at the fire, wondering if Bob's two remaining "archaeological" sites would be any more convincing than Mananhuañunca.

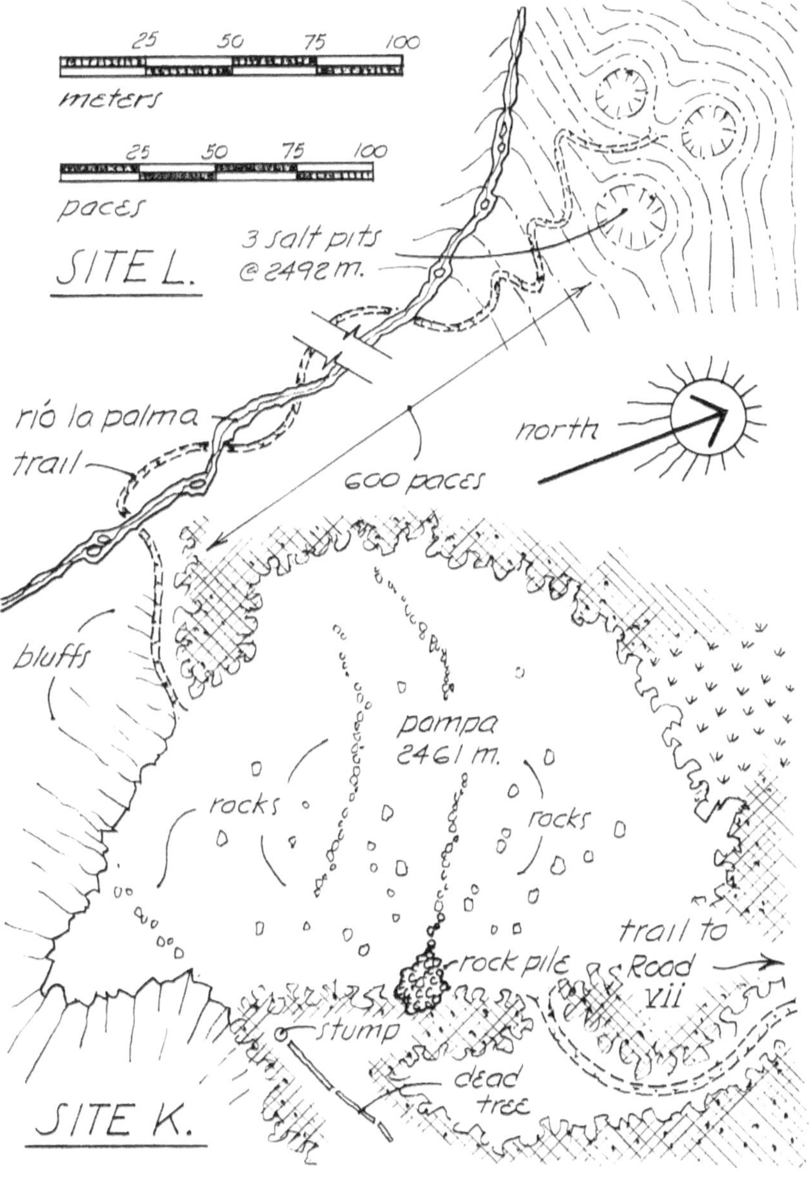

Figure 38 - Site plans of La Sal (top) and Palmapata (Mananhuañunca)

The answer wasn't long in coming. The next morning, walking up to the salt mines at La Sal, simply "the salt", my eye was better and I had high hopes. After dropping down to the creek, the Río La

Palma according to José, the path turned up the steep, narrow ravine down which it tumbled. Thick forest overhung the high embankments on both sides and water seeped from fissures in the walls everywhere. Half a kilometer upstream and after crossing and re-crossing the creek three times, José cut up the muddy slope above the north bank. At the top, he pointed to a collection of three small, shallow pits dug into the hillside and informed us that these were the objects of our search. (**Figure 38**, Site L) If von Kaupp's Mananhuañunca was a disappointment, his historic salt mines seemed, at first glance, a joke. The pits had been nearly filled by mudslides from above - the consequence of nearly two years of disuse, José said - but some evidence of crude shoring with log poles could still be seen. One of the pits, a bit below the other two, was overgrown and apparently abandoned. All that we saw corresponded pretty well with von Kaupp's description, including his report that the rocks and mud all about had a distinctly dark color. It was from the latter that he'd concluded the place was the "Yanacachi," or "black salt," mentioned in the chronicle of Antonio de la Calancha. **(6)** Maybe, I thought, but there was no evidence at all of sixteenth century occupation and José claimed to the contrary that the deposits had been discovered only about seventy years earlier by the Álvarez family, still the only *campesinos* in the lower Urumbay. For the moment it looked to me like von Kaupp was batting 0 and 2. Was the last strike waiting, I wondered, hidden somewhere in the jungle across the canyon of the Urumbay - or was his third site, Ruinas La Mesada, really the "large Inca ruin" he claimed? Finding out was our next project.

José had been to Palmapata and La Sal lots of times, but of La Mesada he'd only heard rumors. von Kaupp's report said the ruins were up "a short slope" to the "north" of the Urumbay, across from Palmapata. A sketch he'd sent me prior to the trip, however, showed them south of the river and, since our camp at Palmapata was above the north bank, the sketch had to be correct. To me, it was a perfect example of the fallibility of written accounts. One minor slip of the pen could completely distort an otherwise simple description. I'd been able to resolve Bob's goof with his sketch, but what if he'd written his report four hundred years ago, in old Spanish and left no sketch? What then? He wasn't the only one who made mistakes. I'd made plenty myself. The message was clear: it was important to be extra-careful writing directions that someone else might someday try to follow - that is, if you cared whether or not they succeeded.

After a quick lunch, we set out to try to do just that. Not knowing how high a "short" slope was, we started at the bottom and began working our way uphill. After several hours, we'd found nothing but steep, thick jungle. Finally, about 500 feet above the river, we came to a trail connecting several of the Álvarez huts. Near one was a circular mound of rocks, the first ruin we'd been able to come up with. Encouraged, we continued up into the thickening forest. Where there was one, we figured, there had to be more. An hour later, and having turned up nothing new, we weren't so sure. Then, with darkness fast approaching, we'd all but given up when several large, circular structures loomed out of a swampy bench a couple of hundred feet above the trail. They were rough and probably not Inca, but now we knew for sure there was more up there. Excited, we beat it back to camp in the dark, eager to resume the search the following day.

Discussing the prospects over breakfast coffee, we noticed something we hadn't seen before. Enhanced by the oblique angle of the early morning sun, the view across the canyon from Palmapata revealed a large bench, or *meseta*, about 300 feet above our highpoint of the previous day. It was marked by the crowns of several enormous trees that seemed to dominate the surrounding forest and José was sure we'd find our ruined city there. For one thing, the name "Mesada" probably referred to the bench. For another, the big trees meant water, he said, and lots of it - just what a populous village would have needed. Having searched lower down with only meager success, we decided to go straight for the *meseta* even though it was a thousand feet above the river - quite a bit more, it seemed to us, than von Kaupp's "short slope." By using the trail up to Álvarez place, we quickly gained most of the elevation and were cutting up into the steep forest above by mid-morning. A surprisingly short climb brought us up to the abruptly level, shelf-like expanse of José's *meseta.* A dismal place, it was choked with thick vegetation growing from a nightmare of rotting, fallen trees. Huge vines streamed down from the canopy high above and swampy bogs lay trapped behind every rise of ground. Hollywood could hardly have devised a better setting for a "lost city," but we didn't see one. It looked as if von Kaupp had struck out when I suddenly realized I was standing atop a large, overgrown mound of rocks. Looking around more carefully, we saw that there were piles of rocks everywhere, all but invisible under tons of tangled growth. Stripping it away as best we could, we found ourselves surrounded by tumbled ruins on all sides. The largest structures seemed clustered beneath the giant *matapalo* trees we'd seen from camp. Bits of wall could even be glimpsed in the gaps between their spreading roots - great buttressing teepees of growth big enough to swallow entire buildings.

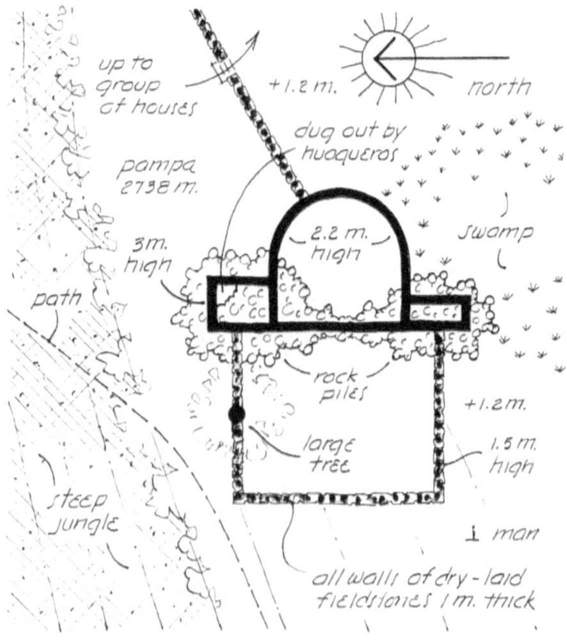

Plan of the central nucleus of Ruinas La Mesada.

It looked like we'd happened upon what Bob's report had called the "central nucleus" of the town. **(7)** We spread out and began scouring the rest of the large bench for the "eighty four Inca houses" he'd counted. An hour or so later, we re-grouped back at the nucleus and compared notes. The jungle in all directions was incredibly thick, wet and unpleasant. Still, we'd managed to find lots of circular foundations, all about a meter high and roughly built of field stones set in mud. Contrary to von Kaupp's claim that they were organized along "platforms, like *andenes,*" they were scattered all over the place, wherever the ground was flat enough to build on. Ben uncovered a small flight of stone steps just east of the largest ruin and José turned up a couple of grinding stones in houses nearby. Bob, too, had noticed some grinding stones said there was a stairway to the "left of the nucleus." Not knowing which direction "left" was, we could only assume it was the same one Ben had found.

Especially in view of such details, we were confident the ruins all around us were those of La Mesada, the same place Pancho Quispicusi had taken von Kaupp eight years earlier. This, despite the fact that neither my map of the place **(Figure 35)**, nor close inspection of the buildings themselves disclosed anything remotely "Inca" about the place. As for his claim that the ruins were those of Marcanay, we found no evidence either way. The bottom line seemed to be that von Kaupp had neither struck out nor scored. From what we'd seen, however strongly his ideas might be supported by his reading of the chronicles, they were neither confirmed nor contradicted by anything on the ground.

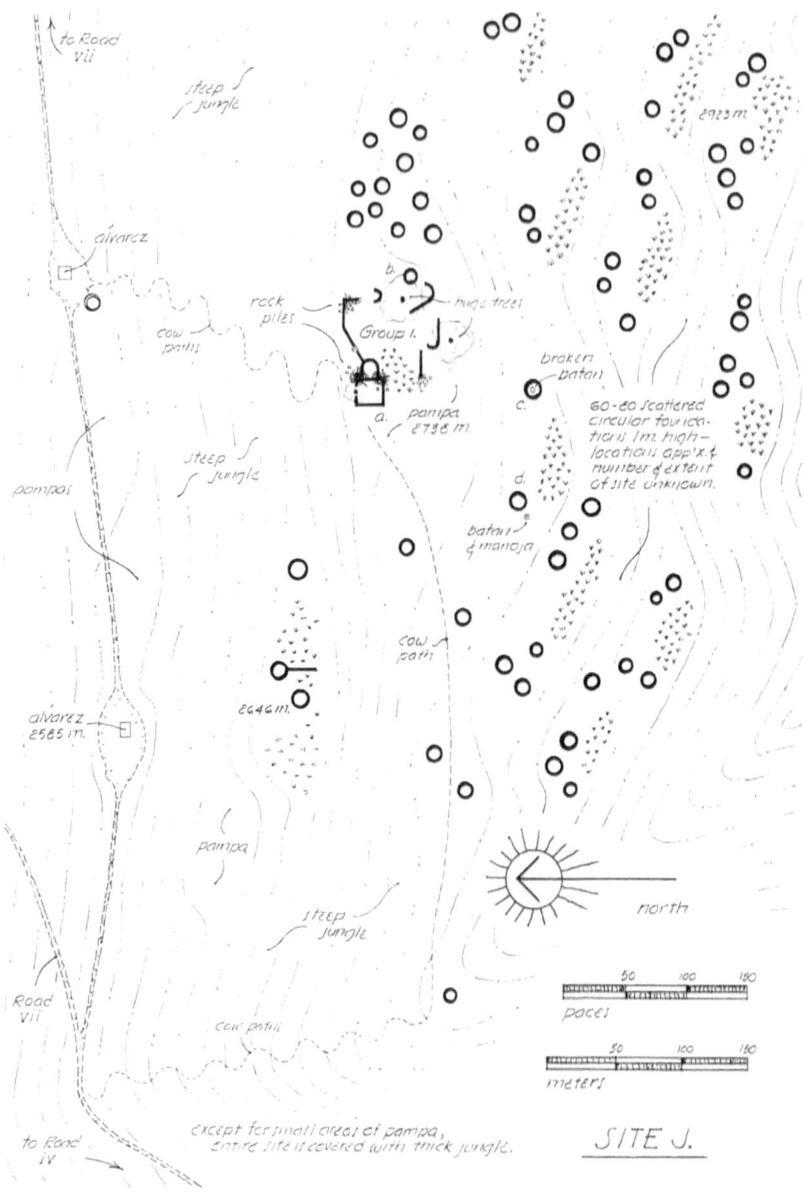

Figure 35 - Site plan of La Mesada

There was nothing more to do in the ruins, so we went back to camp for a late lunch and decided to move on that same afternoon. I was torn between feelings of relief that the evidence in favor of von Kaupp's counter-theory had turned out to be so weak and disappointment that his sites hadn't been more interesting. Theories aside, I'd been excited by the prospect of exploring and mapping the interesting places his descriptions had led me to expect, and viewed that way, the past week had been pretty much of a bust. Besides, we'd been in the field for 33 days straight and were starting to drag. My eye was better, but still useless. Ronaldo, who'd been keeping an eye on El Viejo, had gotten stepped on, somehow, while messing with the horse and could hardly walk. In true *macho* fashion, José offered little sympathy and saw his son's painful injury as no more than a learning experience. Ben was beginning to wonder if the boring ruins we'd seen so far were worth all the trouble. It seemed to me that what we all needed was some excitement to get us going. Ben felt the same way and, terrorists be damned, we figured the best place to find it was at Espíritu Pampa. Forgotten was my solemn promise to Nancy. There, we knew for sure there'd be scores of new and possibly important ruins to be found. The idea had a rejuvenating effect on everyone, even José. He nodded quick approval, turned up the volume on the damned radio and went right to getting El Viejo packed and ready for the trail.

Continuing a kilometer or so down to the mouth of the Urumbay that afternoon, I was struck by how close La Mesada was to the main Inca road between Ututo and Tambo. **(Figure 32)** Once we were across the Pampaconas, it was just a short, steep scramble up to the heavily traveled trail. In fact, the ruins of the New Fort were actually visible from von Kaupp's site if you knew where to look. Based on their many circular houses, both settlements must once have been the homes of Beauclerk's indigenous, non-Inca natives. But, aside from that, I couldn't help wondering how La Mesada fit into the larger history of the region. The only reason to think it was the site of Marcanay was the Huarcuna legend and the local tradition about Mananhuañunca - and we'd found no hard evidence to support either one. Maybe the locals were just plain wrong, or maybe Huarcuna wasn't Ortiz after all. Maybe, but I didn't really think so. von Kaupp was onto something. I was sure of it, even though exactly what, remained to be seen.

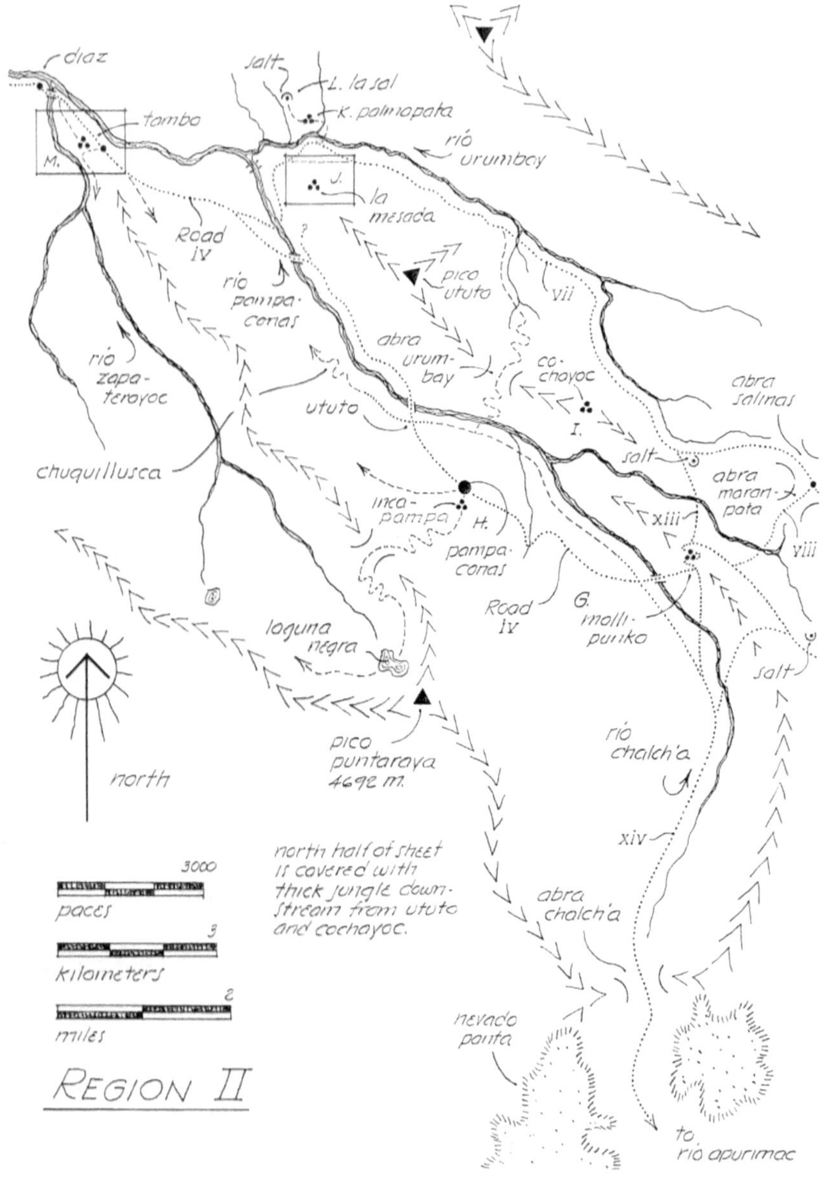

Figure 32 - Map of upper Rio Pampaconas

16

Un Poco Loco

Back up on the main road, we turned downstream to the vantage point from which we'd first spotted the New Fort two years before. The farms at Tambo were all deserted - a reminder that we were getting deeper into hostile country with every step. How serious that was, we had no way of knowing. Assuming José would let us know if or when we started pushing our luck, we pressed on. San Fernando was abandoned, its fields overgrown. At dusk, we arrived at the big gravel bar just above Vista Alegre and made camp. There were no kids or barking dogs, no fire smoke, nothing but the river and the sounds of the *selva*. We were utterly alone and even José seemed nervous despite the fact it was his 36th birthday. No celebration was planned. To avoid drawing attention to ourselves, we made no fire and cooked a silent dinner on the kerosene stove. Afterwards, there wasn't much to do but stare off into the darkness, listening for any sign of activity. I couldn't help imagining that every firefly was a terrorist's cigarette. For the second time on the trip, I was back in the Marines until, finally, I dropped off to sleep.

The next morning, we passed through what had once been Vista Alegre. The Luques and all their neighbors were gone. José said the Senderistas had crossed the Markacocha Range from Osambre on the Río Apurimac and entered the Vilcabamba via the same trail Curtis, Brooke and I had used to reach the high country during our Icma Coya climb. Their first act had been to destroy Vista Alegre. Now, all was in ruins. The houses and school had been burned along with the unharvested *maíz* crop. The soccer field was covered with brush and the jungle was fast reclaiming the whole settlement. José had heard that most of the people had gotten wind of the attack and fled to the San Miguel valley, across the Santuario mountains to the east. But several of the more isolated *campesinos* had apparently been caught unawares and killed.

Walking through the ashes of the burnt corn, I was haunted by the memory of Luque's youngest son, a boy of five or six, leading us to the bottom of the Markacocha trail in 1982. We'd come to the Río Vista Alegre and had to cross on a series of long, slippery logs. It was early morning and matters were made worse by the frost. I couldn't imagine how we'd keep from slipping off. Without hesitation, the boy reached down and filled his hat with sand, which he sprinkled in front of him as he went. Across the creek, he laughed and laughed when I told him that, simple as his trick was, in all my years in the mountains I'd never before seen it done nor thought to do it myself. I hoped he'd been among those who escaped with his father.

Continuing down the ominously deserted canyon, we stopped at Urpipata and I showed José the ruins of the Old Fort. I'd told him about the place in '84, but he'd never been there and was openly skeptical. The very idea that a *gringo* knew something about his mountains that he didn't, was unthinkable. Not until we actually got to it did he believe it existed. Once there, though, he excitedly helped clear the largest and best preserved structure (**Figure 45**, Building b) and began rooting around in the dirt for artifacts. There's a bit of *huaquero*, or treasure hunter, in the heart of every *campesino* and any new ruin offers the chance, at least, to find something valuable. The odds of getting rich are tiny, but every now and then someone hits a jackpot - just like Las Vegas, but much more destructive. And so the looting continues, as it has for centuries. There's no use trying to prevent the locals from digging, since they'll just come back, long after you're gone. Unfortunately for him, but lucky for the rest of us, José turned up nothing at Urpipata but a few common potsherds.

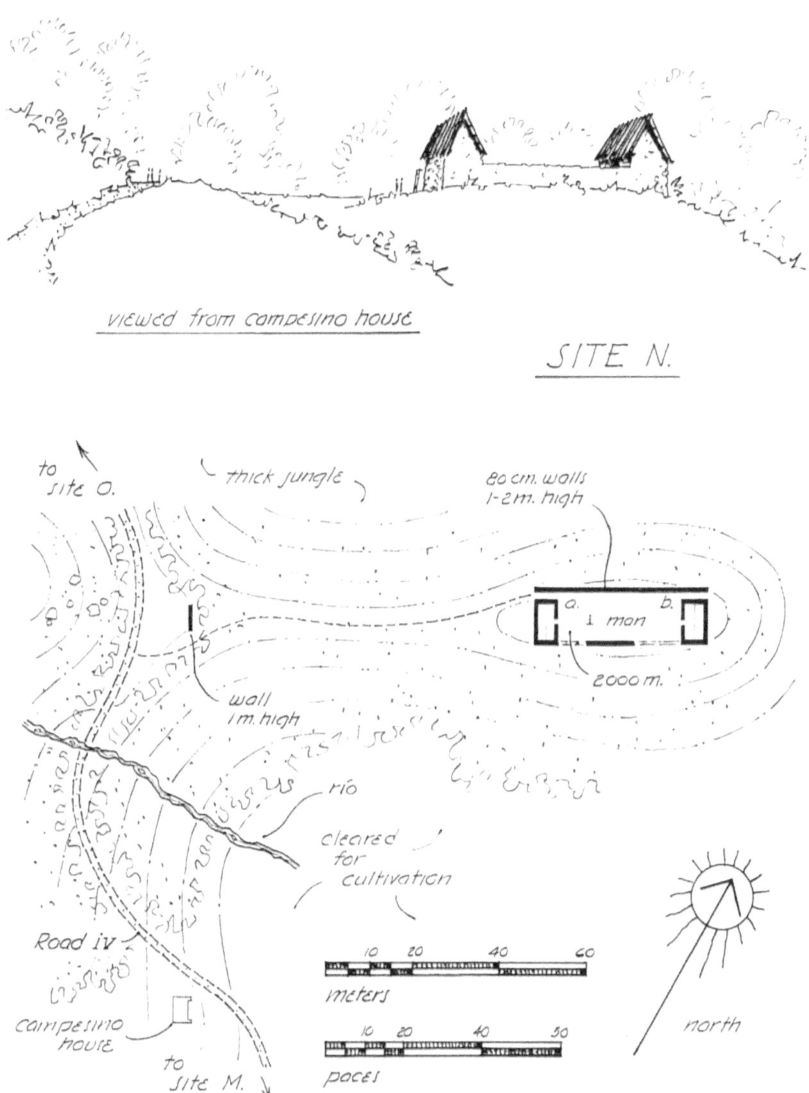

Figure 45 - Site plan and view of Urpipata (probable site of Machu Pucara)

I showed him around the site and he agreed that it looked Inca. He added that it's location meant that the modern trail must once have been the old Inca road. It was an important point, since not everyone agreed. Savoy, von Kaupp and even some of the locals thought that the modern trail was of recent origin and that the Inca road still lay lost in the forest somewhere else. If they were right, then the forts and Marcanay were still lost in there too - and I was all wet. The ruins at Urpipata told me that the old road must have passed somewhere nearby. I knew there was no abandoned road anywhere below the site. Two years before, during our unsuccessful first try at finding the fort, Chris and I had covered the entire slope down to the river and found nothing at all. With José's comment in mind, I decided to check the mountainside above the ruins, just to be sure. Back on the trail, Ben, Ronaldo and José stayed with El Viejo while I climbed several hundred meters up a steepening ridge looking for any sign the old road might have been higher up. Aside from a few isolated boulders, there was nothing. It looked like José was right and another piece of the puzzle had fallen into place.

Hurrying on down the canyon to reach Espíritu Pampa before nightfall, we were encouraged to find a few people still living at Consevidayoc. I tried to show José the ruins we'd found there, but the whole area was so overgrown we decided to save them for another day. The village had been spared by the terrorists, but the fields hadn't been worked and were in awful shape. Most of the crops at Consevidayoc were grown by highland farmers who'd long since fled the area. The few residents who'd hung on looked frightened and thin. I thought of the Spanish descriptions of the countryside during their march into the Inca Empire in 1532. The civil war that had raged for several years had depopulated whole villages and broken the back of the vast agricultural base on which everything else rested. More than 450 years later, nothing much had changed, it seemed.

We reached Espíritu Pampa late, ate quickly and went right to bed, anxious to get to work early in the morning. It came soon enough. The revolution had seemingly bypassed Cobos's farm and nothing much seemed to have changed since our last visit. After a quick breakfast under oppressive, cloudy skies - the remains of rain in the night - off we went into the city. It was hot, muggy and wet. Huge black flies swarmed all around us, perhaps attracted by our increasingly ripe body odors. Their only virtue was that they were slow and easy to swat and their immense size made each kill quite satisfying. I began work by verifying a few points still unclear from my mapping in 1984, and found that my notes then had by and large been correct. I'd brought along Harth Terré's maps to be sure we didn't overlook anything Savoy had found, two decades before us. His plan of the plaza, as published in the Explorer's Journal, **(1)** showed its northeast end to be square, not angled as my notes indicated. Rechecking the compass azimuths confirmed that my version was right. The same article included drawings of the Mexican-looking group Savoy called "Palace of the Platforms" and his site map showed where it was supposed to be. After two hours of searching, we'd found lots of new ruins, but nothing at all that matched his descriptions. The missing "palace" finally turned up several days later, almost a mile from where he'd reported it. **(Figure 60,** Group 26)

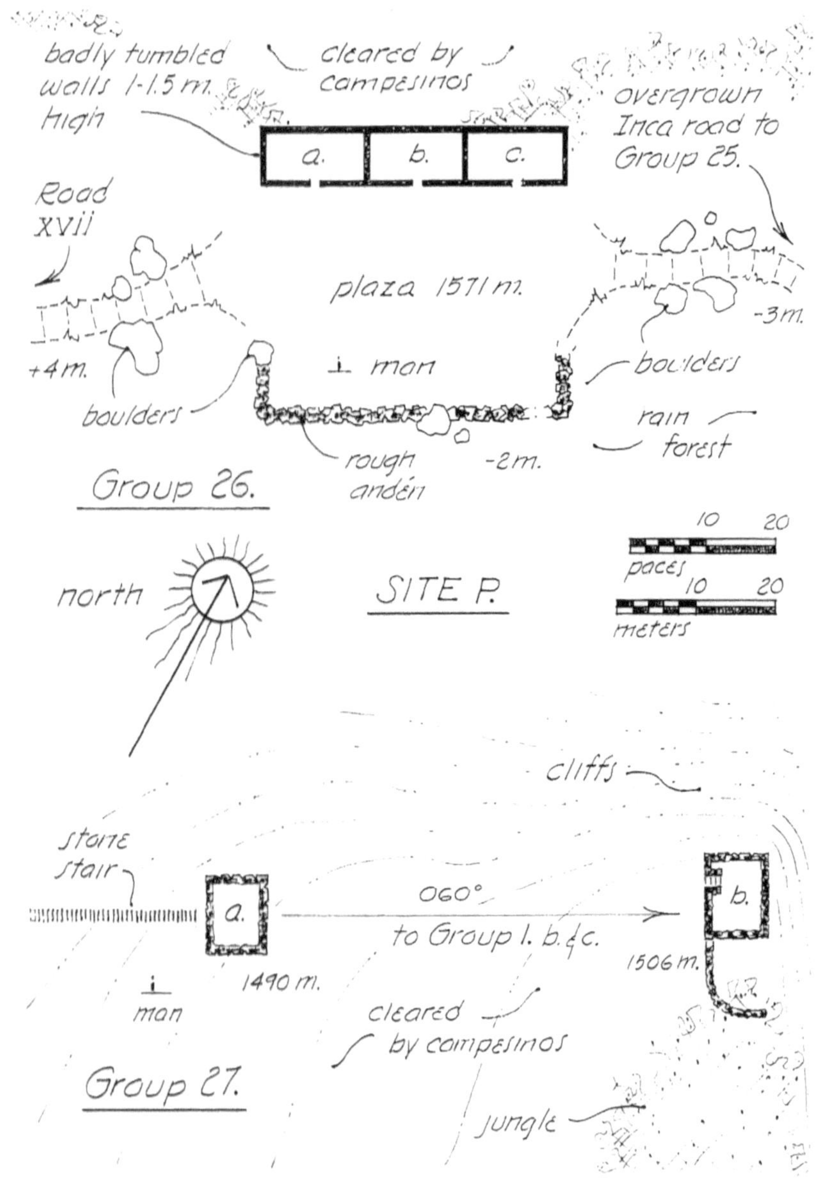

Figure 60 - Plan of southernmost group (Savoy's Palace of Platforms) Plan of platforms above city

Next, we plunged into the dense jungle above and below the plaza where Savoy's plans showed scores of buildings I'd not seen. He was right. There were ruins everywhere - though what we found again bore little resemblance to what was shown on his maps. Not twenty paces above the trail leading to the stone bridge, we uncovered a well built terrace 130 paces long and nearly 50 wide, with five buildings still standing chest high. A sixth, 43 paces long and 14 wide, was set off to one side and included six rooms and ten doorways. (**Figure 51**, Group 5) It was an impressive complex, still standing and larger than a football field. Bingham had missed it entirely and Savoy hadn't bothered to record it with much care, since his maps had it all wrong. Below the plaza he'd plotted a group he called the "Palace of the Large Stones" on a huge platform ten feet high and built of Volkswagen-sized boulders. But, instead of the four buildings shown on his plan, we found seven. One of the missing structures was almost 100 feet long with two large rooms and walls still head high. (**Figure 53**, Group 19) How could he have possibly missed it?

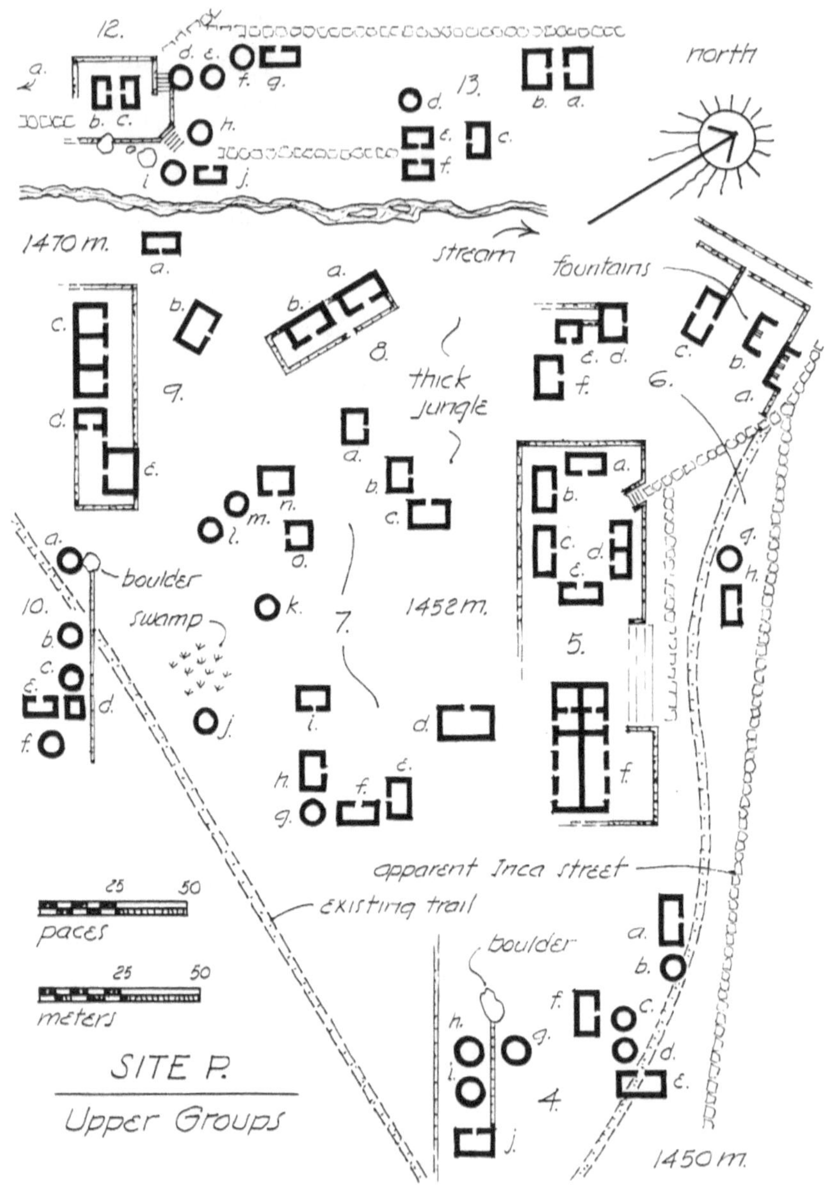

Figure 51 - Plan of Hanan Vilcabamba

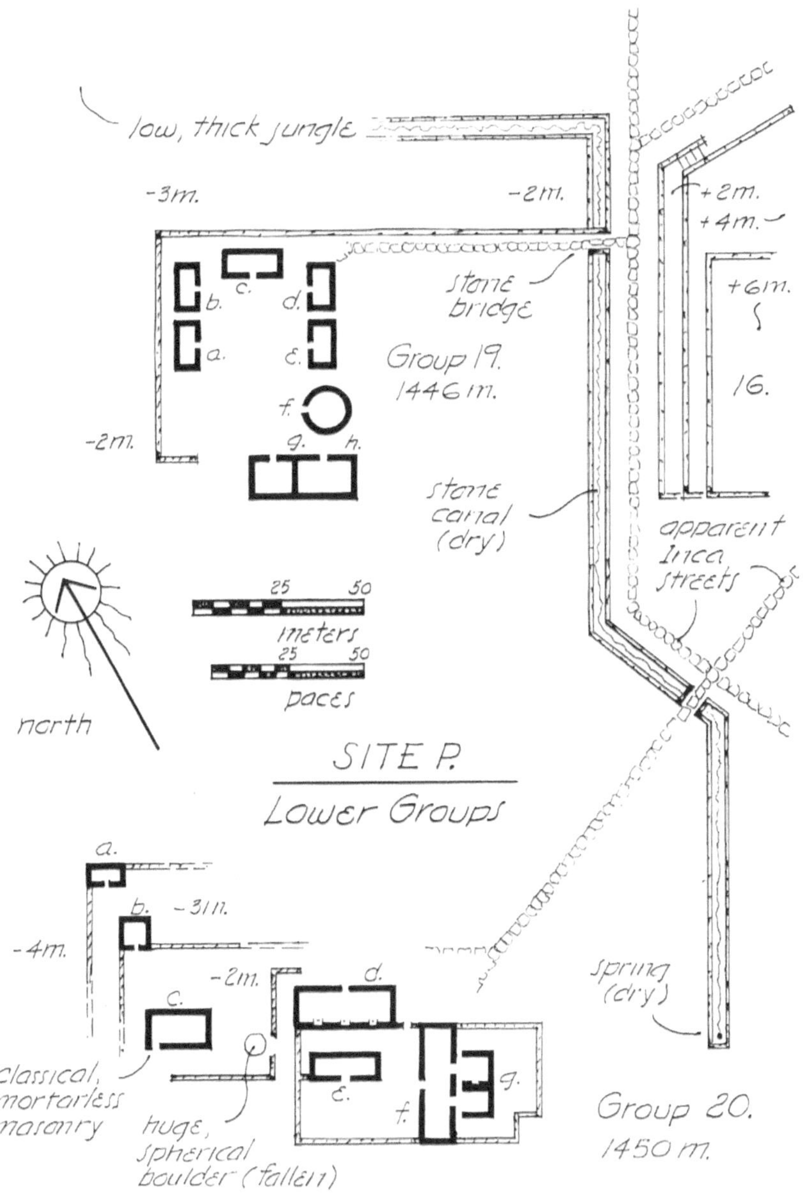

Figure 53 - Plan of Hurin Vilcabamba (Savoy's palaces of large Stones and Fine Ashlars)

Equally mysterious was Savoy's siting of another group he called the "Palace of the Fine Ashlars," which he showed about 500 yards west of the plaza. **(2)** Angling southwest from the Palace of Large

Stones, we were hunkered down for a long cut when no more than a hundred paces out we came to a large building with three niches still evident inside its rear wall. As we excitedly began clearing and exploring the surroundings, more buildings, walls and terraces appeared. Thinking we'd found something new, I was disappointed when my sketch of the layout instead began to look a lot like Savoy's group, still supposedly a quarter of a mile away. (**Figure 53**, Group 20) Then we found it. In a thick patch of jungle on a terrace below the main group was a waist-high, rectangular foundation of beautifully fitted stones - not technically "fine ashlars," but close enough. Almost three feet thick, it was the only Cuzco-style, mortarless masonry we'd seen anywhere in the city. The plan of the large, one-room structure was also unusual. It's only door was in a corner, an atypical design suggesting some special purpose. Finally, there were dressed blocks scattered in the brush all around the perimeter, as though the walls had been intentionally thrown down. Taken together, the high quality masonry and unique floor plan indicated an especially important building, one which someone - either offended by, or greedy for, its contents - had gone to a lot of trouble to destroy.

And so it went for several more days. Eventually, we added 95 new buildings to our 1984 count, (**Figures 51**, **54**, **57** & **58**) increasing the total to more than half of the 400 reported by Arbieto. (**3**) The weather had gradually cleared, but the work was still hot and buggy. The insects seemed thickest in the most claustrophobic tangles of vines and brush. Swarms of the huge black flies buzzed around our heads while tiny no-seeums of some sort worked their way beneath our clothes. Each afternoon, we emerged from the forest filthy dirty and covered with a garish assortment of bites and welts plus untold scratches from the diabolical combination of thorns, spines and nettles that pressed in from all sides. The constant machete work was tedious and exhausting, but offered at least a modicum of satisfaction in the uneven contest with the jungle. One large, leafy stalk, in particular, repaid a single easy slash with a van-sized opening in the curtain of growth. Watching them fall felt so good that we often went out of our way just to cut them down. Most satisfying of all, though, was the work itself - as in a boyhood dream, we were searching for hidden treasure and finding it at every turn.

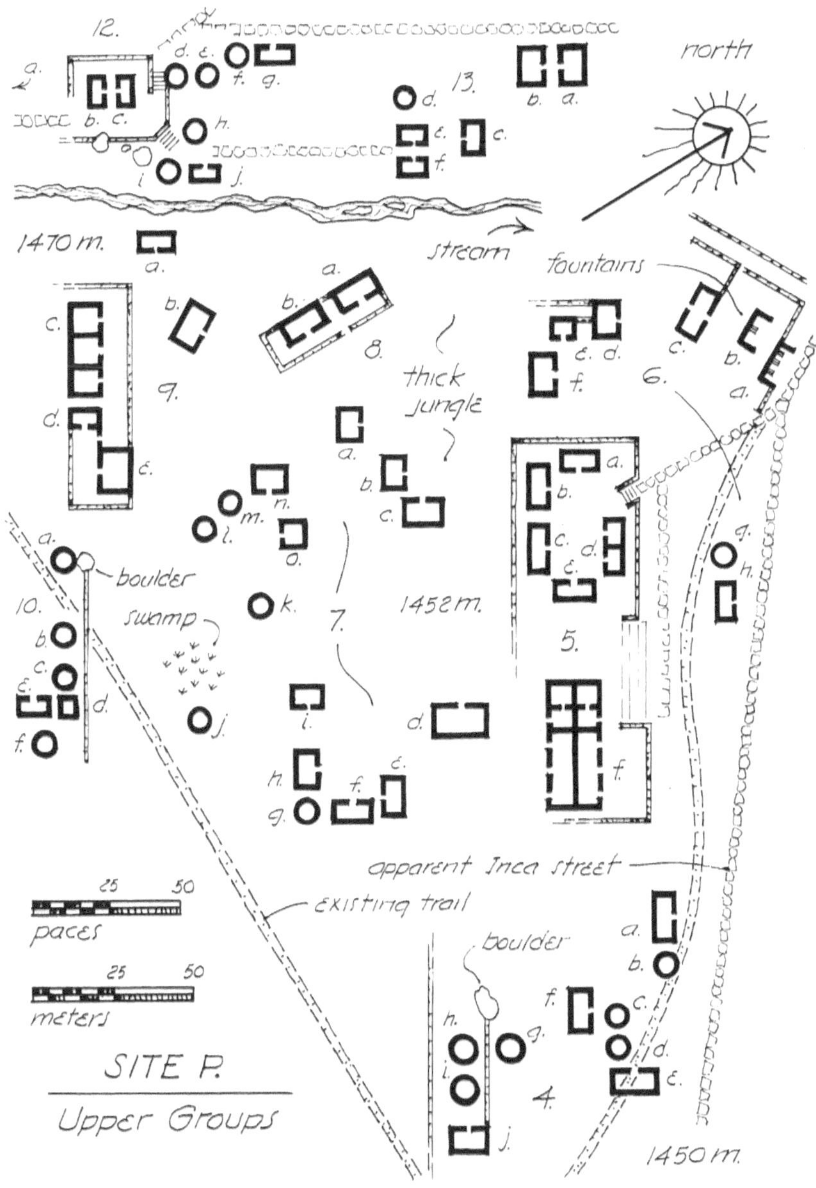

Figure 51 - Plan of Hanan Vilcabamba

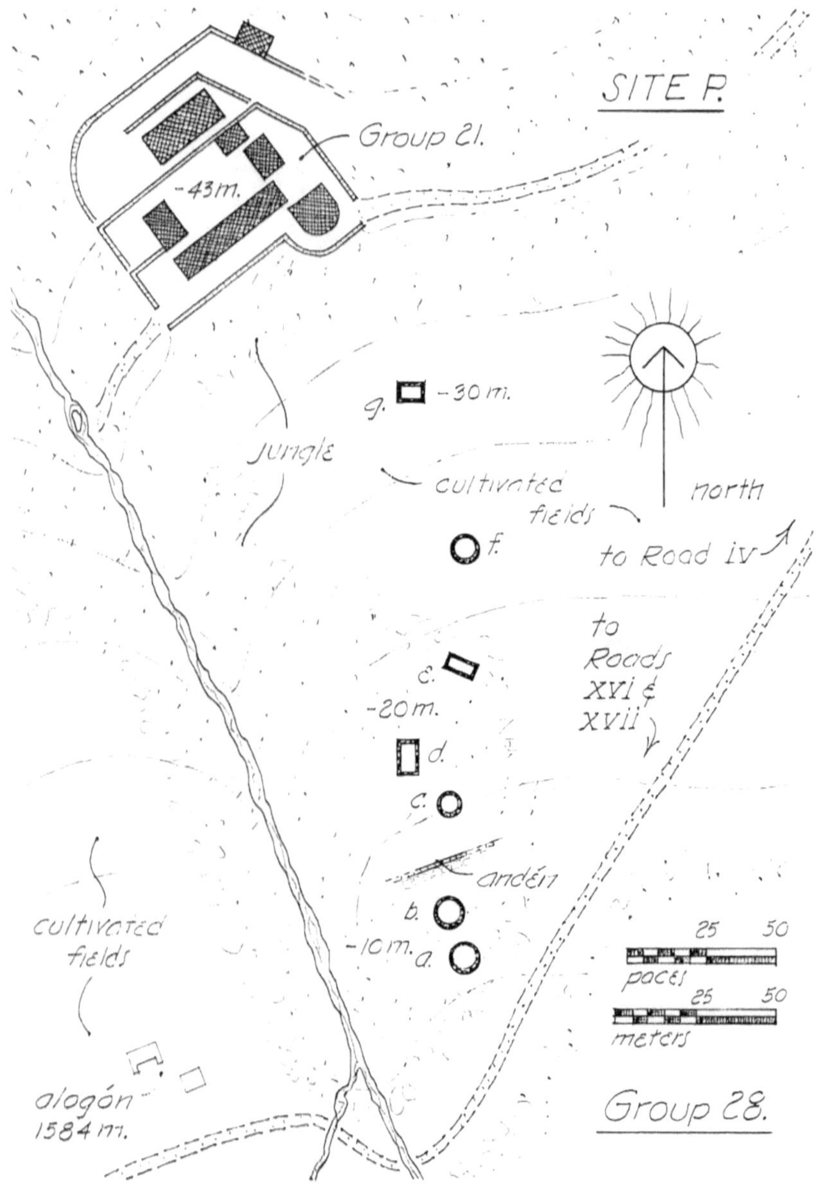

Figure 54 - Group above Tendi Pampa

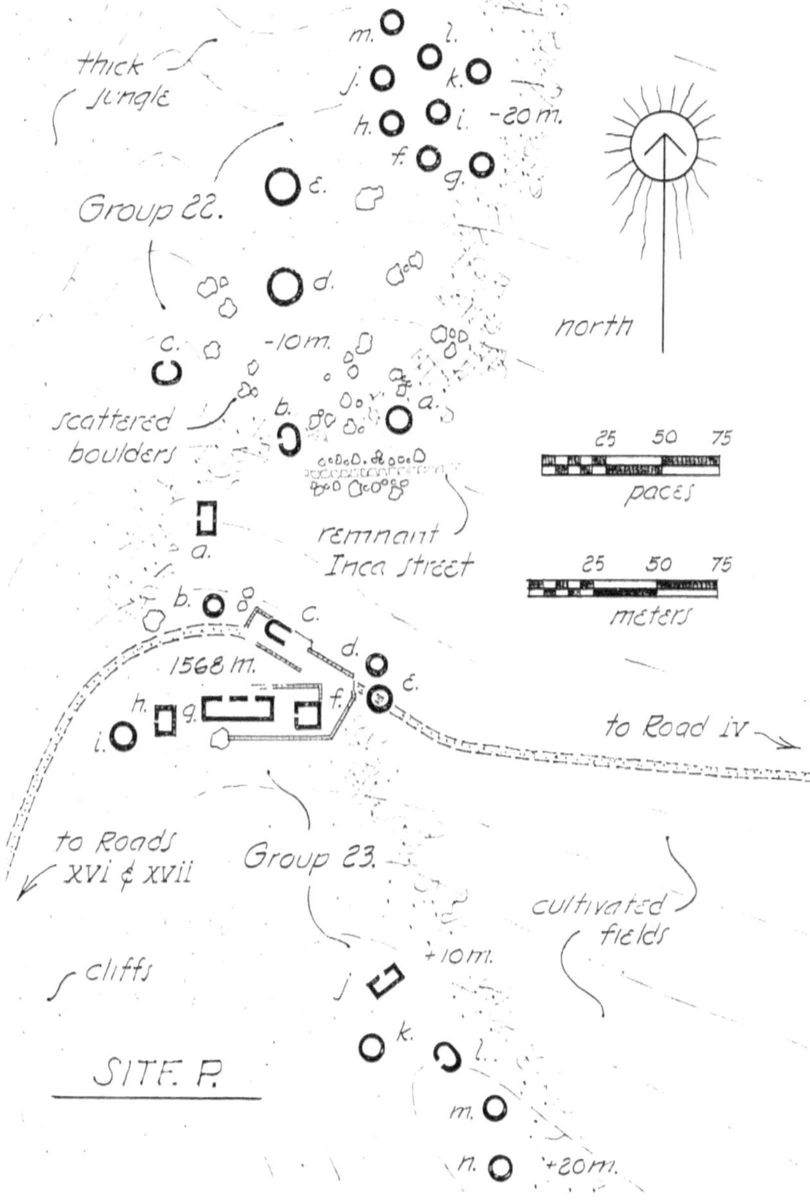

Figure 57 - Site plan of outlying groups

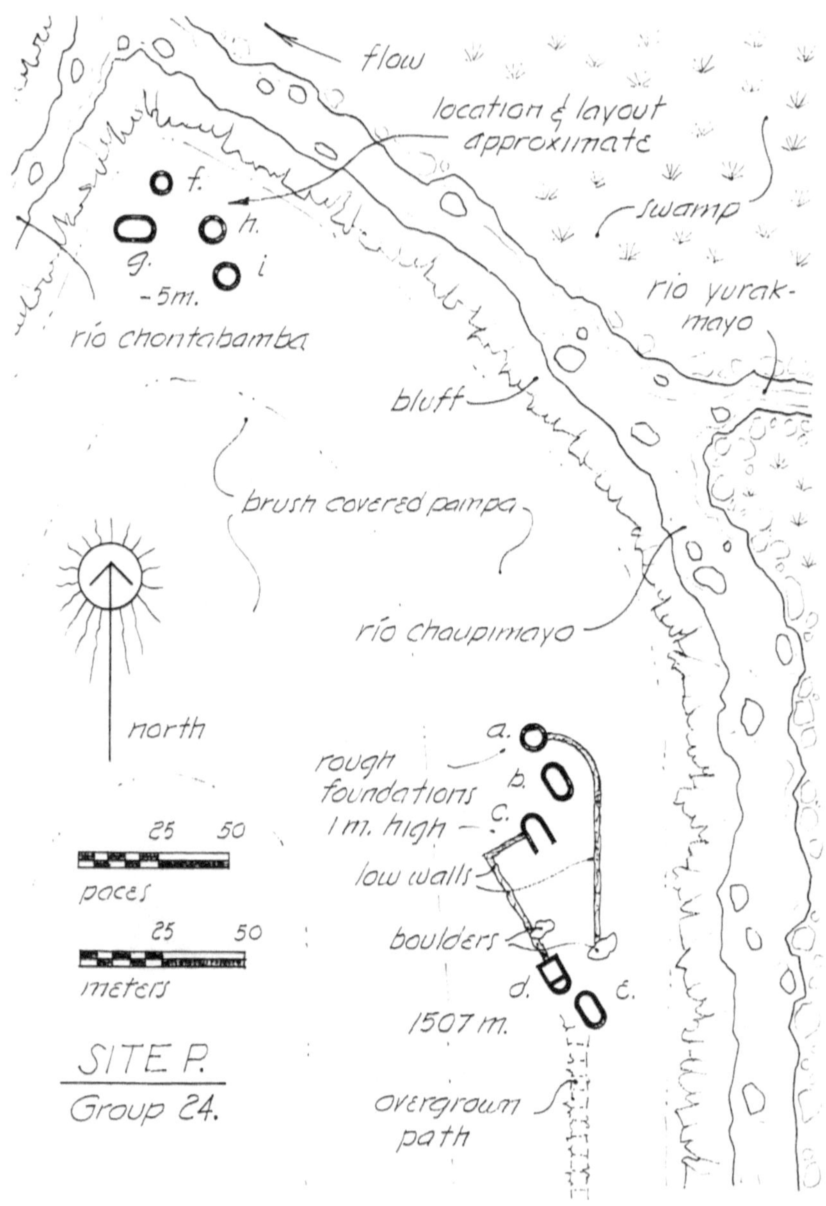

Figure 58 - Non-Inca groups across river

We weren't really "discovering" most of the buildings, of course. Bingham and Savoy had done that years earlier. Our contribution wouldn't become clear until what we were mapping was plotted weeks later. Savoy had characterized the city as strongly non-Inca due to what he saw as the predominance of circular structures scattered among the more typically Incan rectangles. **(4)** von Kaupp, who'd never even been there, took this as further evidence that Espíritu Pampa wasn't the site of Vilcabamba the Old after all. Francescutti, who had seen at least some of the the ruins, agreed and, like Bingham, thought the site too small and roughly constructed to be Manco's lost capital. As my maps and plans later proved, all of those judgements were wrong. The site was large, reasonably well built and classically Incan in every detail of its architecture and planning. **(Figures 47-51)** As a result, Espíritu Pampa's future detractors would not only have to find a credible alternative for the Incas' final redoubt, they'd also have to convincingly explain away the sprawling Inca metropolis shown on my maps. To date, neither von Kaupp, nor Francescutti nor anyone else has been able to do so.

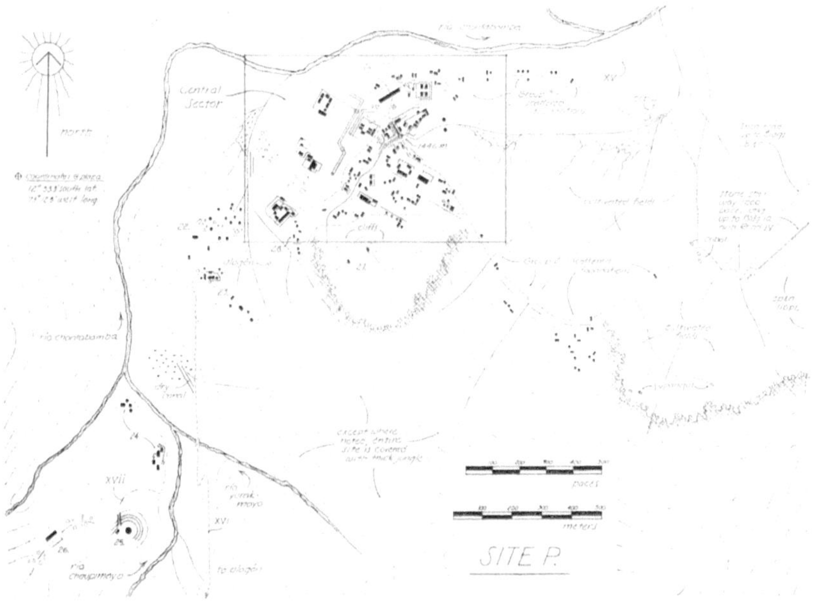

Figure 47 - Map of Espiritu Pampa (Vilcabamba the Old)

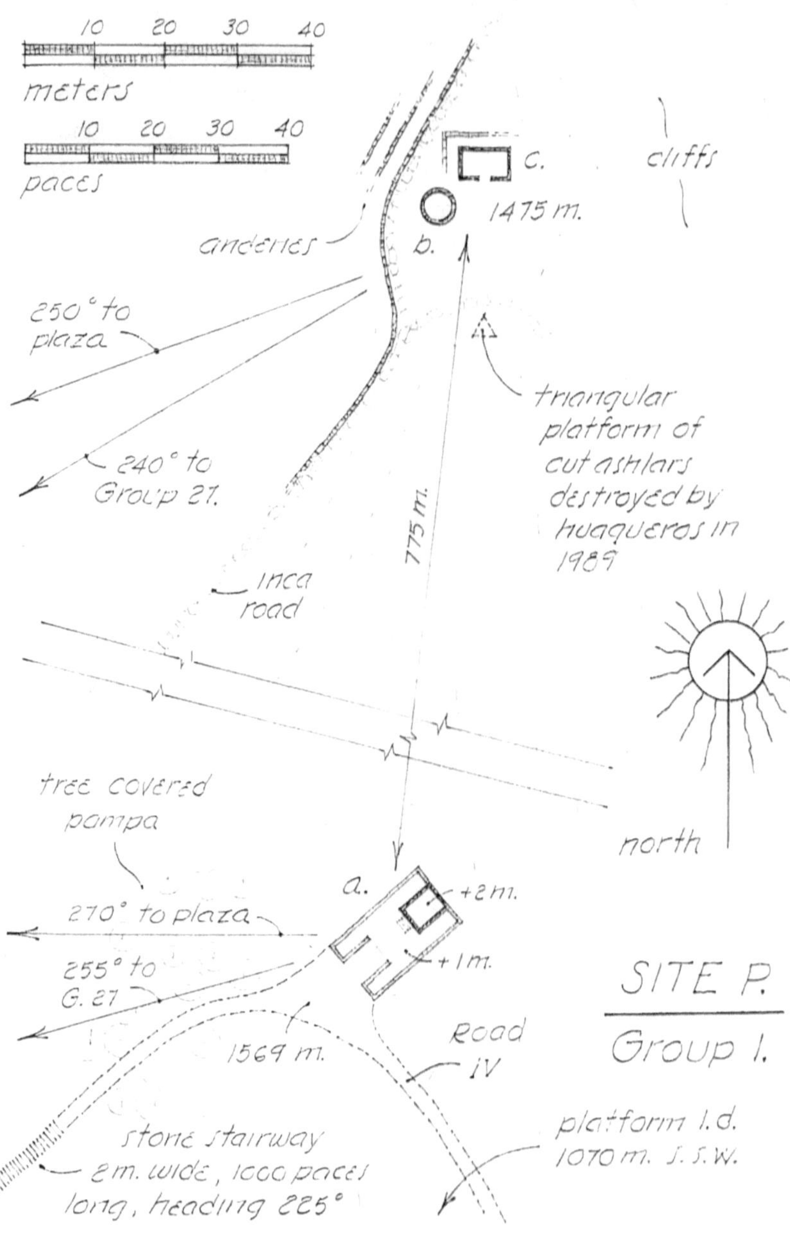

Figure 48 - Group at top of stone stairway

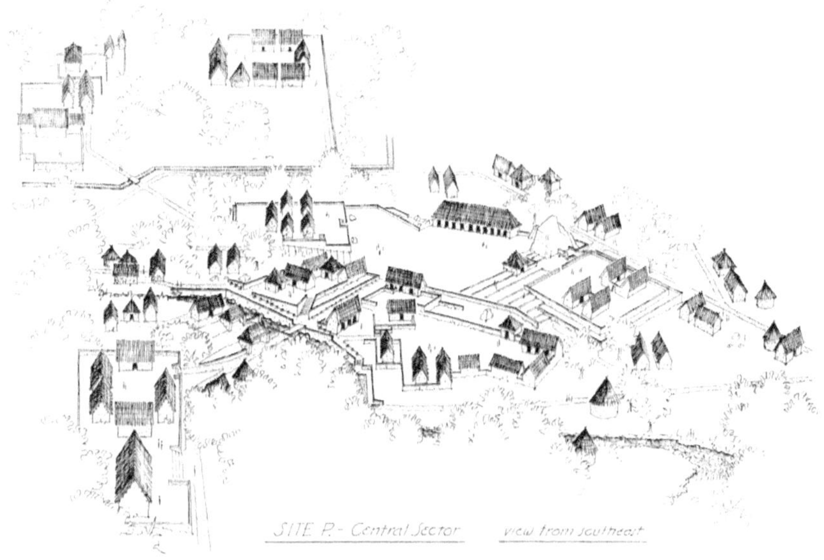

Figure 49 - View of city center

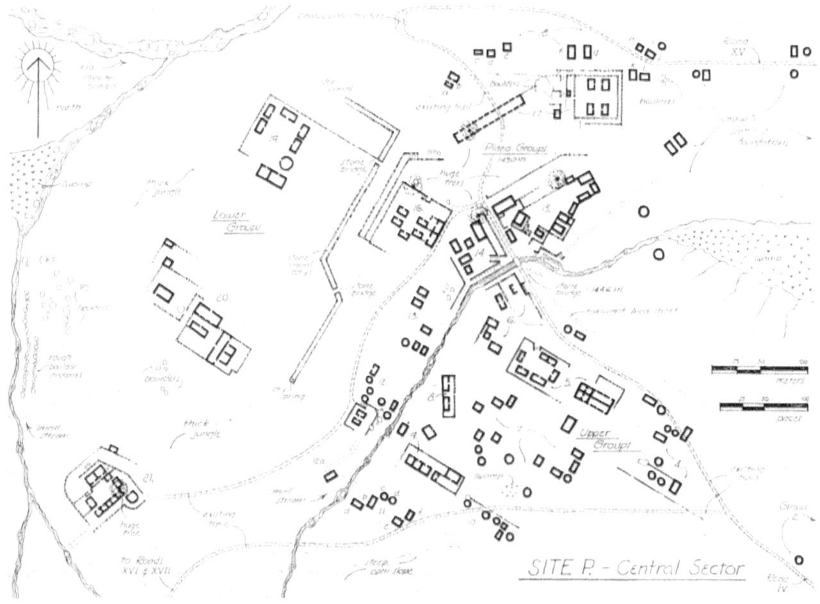

Figure 50 - Site plan of city center

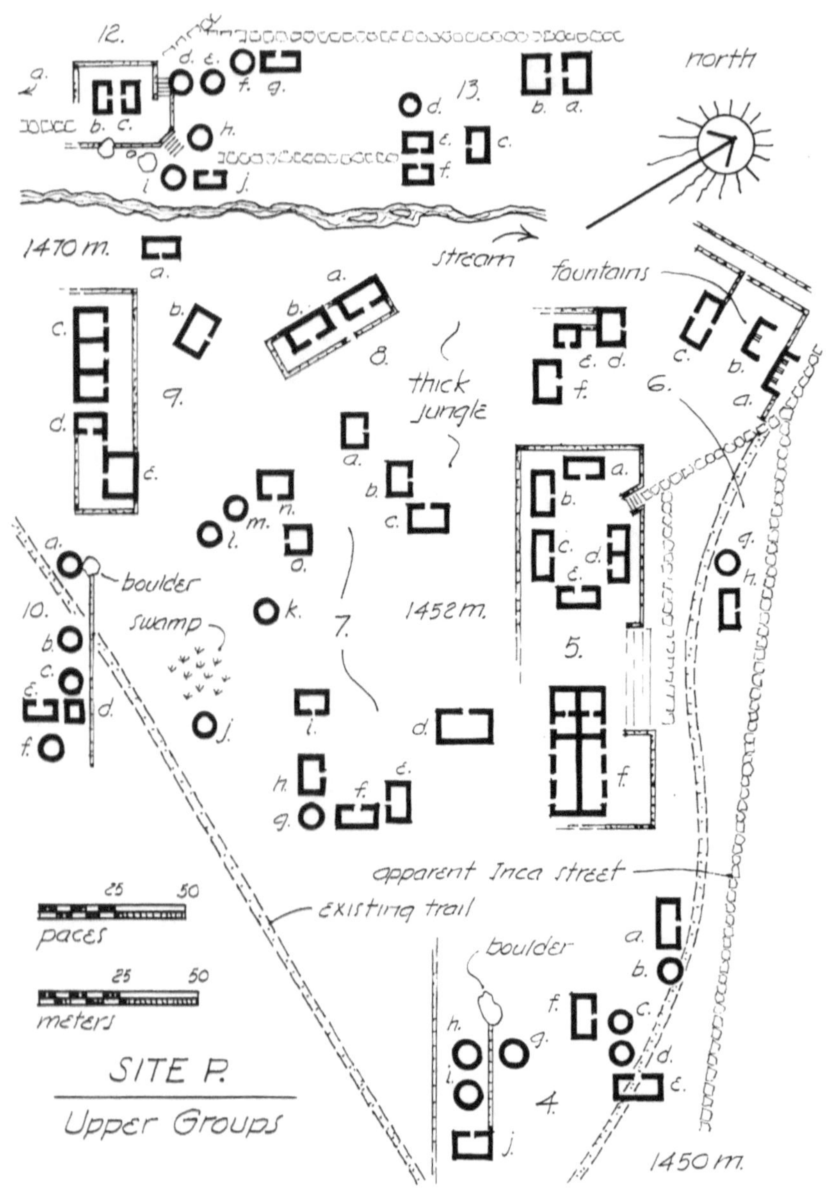

Figure 51 - Plan of Hanan Vilcabamba

The day before we were to leave, I decided to thoroughly explore the country upstream from the city, between the Ríos Chaupimayo and Chontabamba, where Savoy claimed to have found the ruins of

Marcanay and Mananhuañunca. Barefoot and I had ventured there briefly two years earlier, but hadn't had time to reach either of Savoy's reported sites. After fording the Chaupimayo, cold and swollen by rain in the cloud-capped Markacocha peaks, we fanned out. Ben and José began cutting into the brush covered *pampa* in the confluence of the two rivers, while I turned southwest up the ridge that separated them. (**Figure 47**) Shortly, I came onto the overgrown remains of a stone road (Road xvii) which led up to a large circular building atop a terraced hill. (**Figure 59**) It was almost certainly the same place Savoy had called Mananhuañunca and sure enough, the road continued on to his candidate for Marcanay, several hundred yards beyond. (**Figure 60**, Group 26) The layout of the latter matched Savoy's mis-mapped Palace of the Platforms, but nothing about either of the ruins supported his identifications.

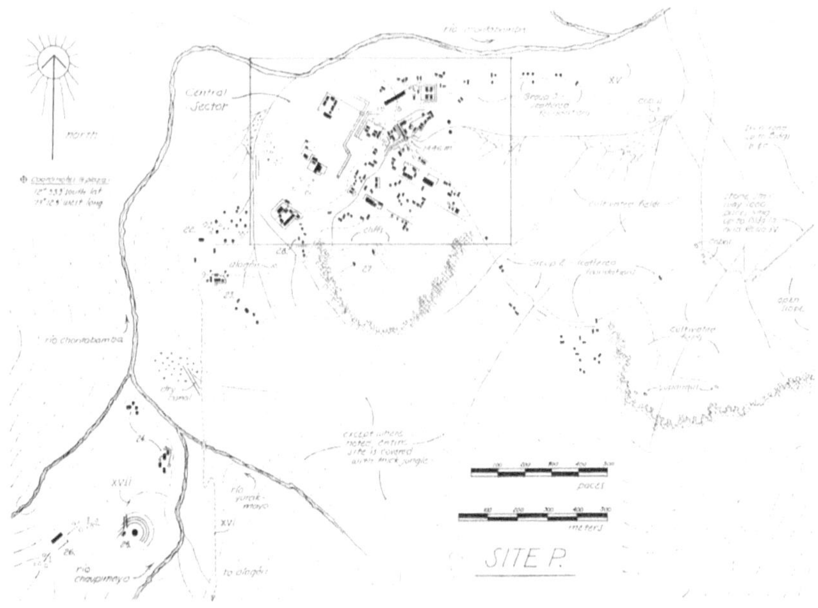

Figure 47 - Map of Espiritu Pampa (Vilcabamba the Old)

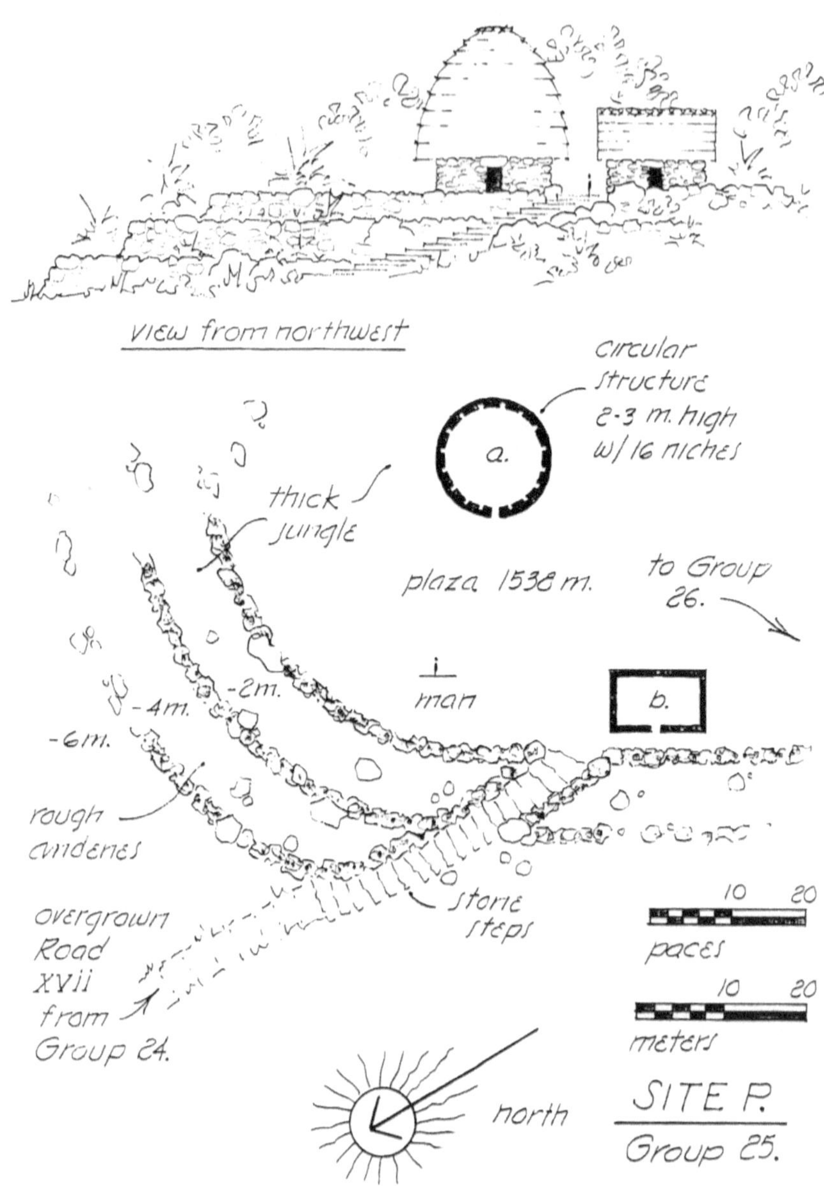

Figure 59 - Plan and view of circular group (Savoy's Marcanay)

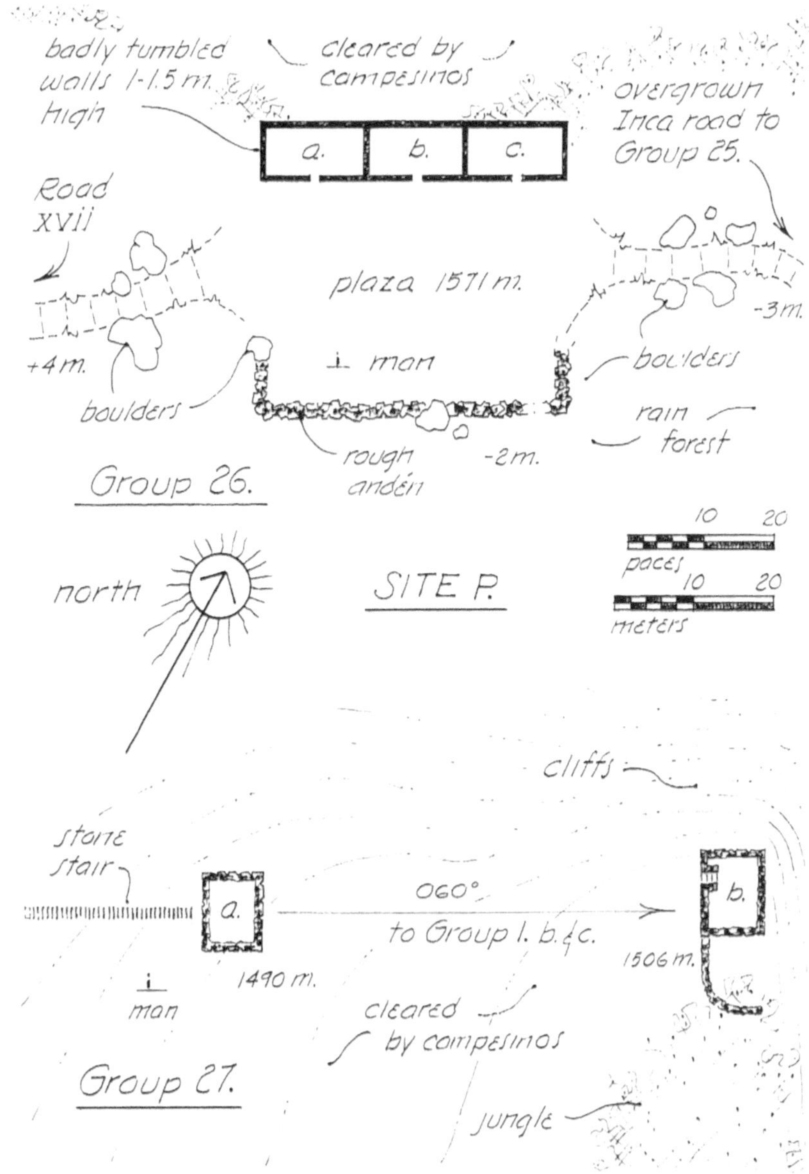

Figure 60 - Plan of southernmost group (Savoy's Palace of Platforms) Plan of platforms above city

After mapping both, I methodically explored a mile or so further up the gentle ridge to the south. There were no more ruins, but my progress was aided by a faint trail through the jungle. Occasional machete cuts showed it had recently been used, but by whom? The thought that it might be the terrorists was beginning to work on my nerves when the scream of a large cat shattered the silence from not far off and sent two pairs of dark, boy-sized spider monkeys - *maquisapas*, José called them - chattering into the canopy high overhead. I never saw the cat, or *tigre*, as the Indians say, but José later thought it probably a puma, down from the nearby peaks - Espíritu Pampa being too high for the jaguars of the lower Amazon. None of that mattered as I watched the terrified monkeys. Momentarily frozen with fear, myself, I suddenly realized how foolish I'd been to wander alone so far from the others. I turned and, with frequent glances over my shoulder, beat a hasty retreat back to Savoy's palace group.

Ben and José were there waiting. Aside from another isolated cluster of the same kind of rough, non-Inca structures Barefoot and I had seen in 1984, (**Figure 58**, Buildings f-i) they'd found nothing interesting. Instead, they said, they'd run onto a band of Machiguenga Indians passing through. That explained the freshly cut trail, I thought. There'd been four of them - two men with bows and arrows, a boy with a *machete* and an enormously pregnant woman carrying, all the gear. Ben said they looked like refugees from the Stone Age, but according to José, the "Machis" still hunted the country beyond Espíritu Pampa and were a fairly common sight in the ruins.

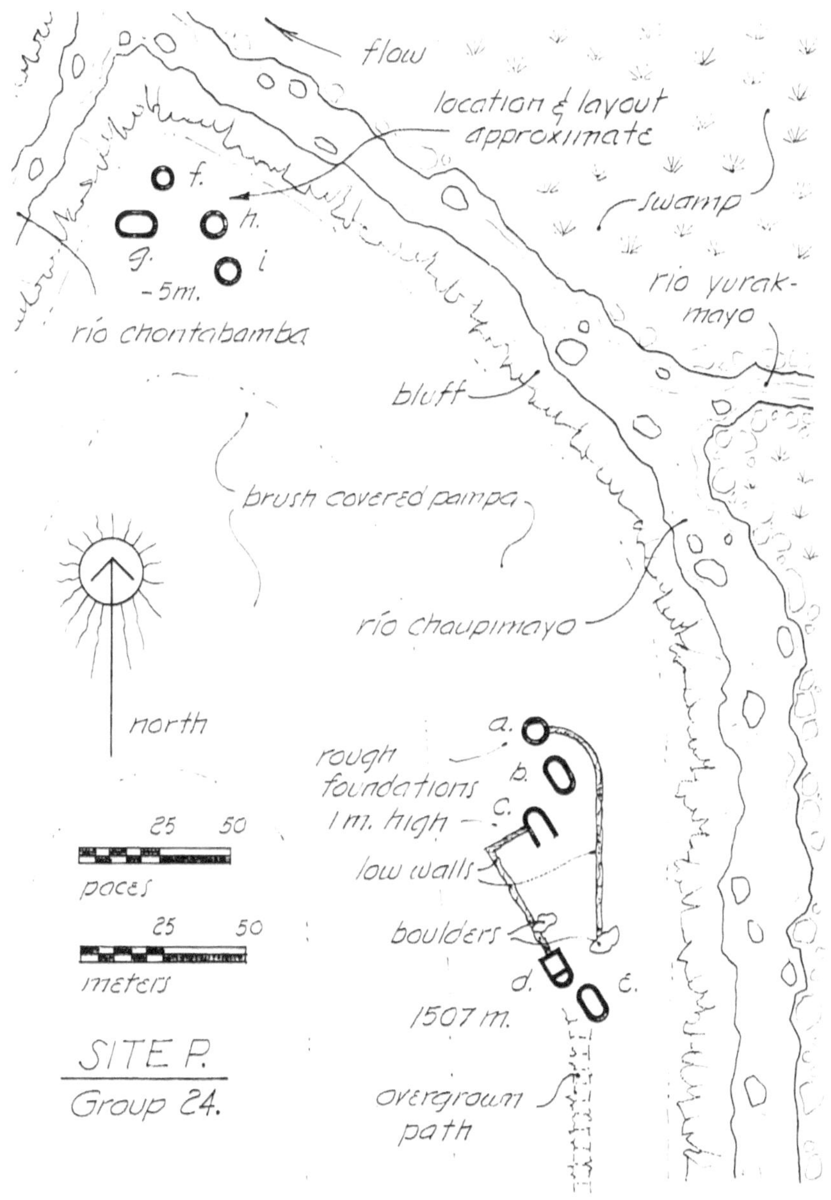

Figure 58 - Non-Inca groups across river

"They claim to be the true descendants of the Incas," he said, "and think of themselves as the guardians of these places. Sometimes they talk about 'great stone ruins' in the forest several days northwest of here, but nobody's ever seen them. It's terrible country and no one ever goes there except the Machis."

I wondered if the trail I'd followed might eventually have led to the great stone ruins no one had ever seen. A glance at the satellite photo showed that the ridgeline it ascended curved off to the northwest not far from where I'd turned back. With Machi guides, how big a deal could "several days" in the bush be, no matter how awful the terrain? Now that, I thought, would make for one hell of a future expedition! It wasn't until some months later that I learned several others before me had heard similar rumors and gone in there to have a look. In the mid-1950s, an Englishman named Julien Tennant had written a book about a strange expedition down the Urubamba. **(5)** He'd heard tales of lost ruins in the forest at the head of the Río Montaro, a tributary flowing into the Urubamba many miles downstream, below the Pongo de Mainique. With a companion named Sebastian Snow, he'd hired Machiguenga guides to take him up the Montaro in search of the rumored site.

After two harrowing weeks of desperate bushwhacking, they arrived, he said, among huge stone walls constructed of oddly shaped, interlocking blocks. Sick and almost out of food, they barely got out alive, but he brought back photos and sketches of the place, none of which were, however, very convincing. The walls looked like natural cliffs and none of his drawings were backed up by clear pictures. The only real "evidence" of his lost city was a single Inca pot that he claimed he'd found in the ruins, but could as easily have been bought in Cuzco. Despite Tennant's persistent claims to the contrary, his story was largely dismissed as a hoax. Several years later, the well-known adventure writer, Peter Mathiesen, made a stab at going back in for another look, but never quite made it. **(6)**

Both expeditions were before Sputnik, and there were no real maps of that part of the world. No one knew just where the head of the Montaro was, relative to anyplace else. There still aren't any good maps, but with satellite photos, the terrain is a lot less mysterious. After reading Tennant's account, I studied the maze of drainages north of the Pongo. For the first time, really, I had some idea what I was looking for - and there it was! The Río Montaro, sure enough, ran into the Urubamba a few miles downstream from the famous rapids, but its main headwaters flowed from the back side of the remote, mist shrouded peaks that loomed on the skyline, not far northwest of Espíritu Pampa.

Furious that I'd missed out on what might have been my only opportunity, ever, to experience contact with actual Stone Age people, I grudgingly agreed to head back to camp. It was getting late and we had a long way to go. We re-forded the frigid Chaupimayo further upstream than where we'd crossed in the morning. Once back on the trail, our route home soon arrived at the Río Yurakmayo, the large tributary of the Chaupimayo Barefoot and I had forded near its mouth two years before. **(Figure 47)** A high bridge of poles had been thrown across by the *campesinos*, but it looked as though no one had used or repaired the crossing in weeks - likely another side effect of the season of terrorism. Still, none of us wanted to wade another icy creek, and over we went, one at a time with José in the lead and me in the rear. Just as Ben was about to disappear into the forest on the far side, I stepped out onto the logs and heard a resounding "crack!" In an instant, I found myself hanging from a slippery pole by one hand and clutching my journal in the other. "Ben!" I screamed, "the journal!" and flung it as hard as I could towards the other side just as my hand lost its grip and I dropped into the rapids below.

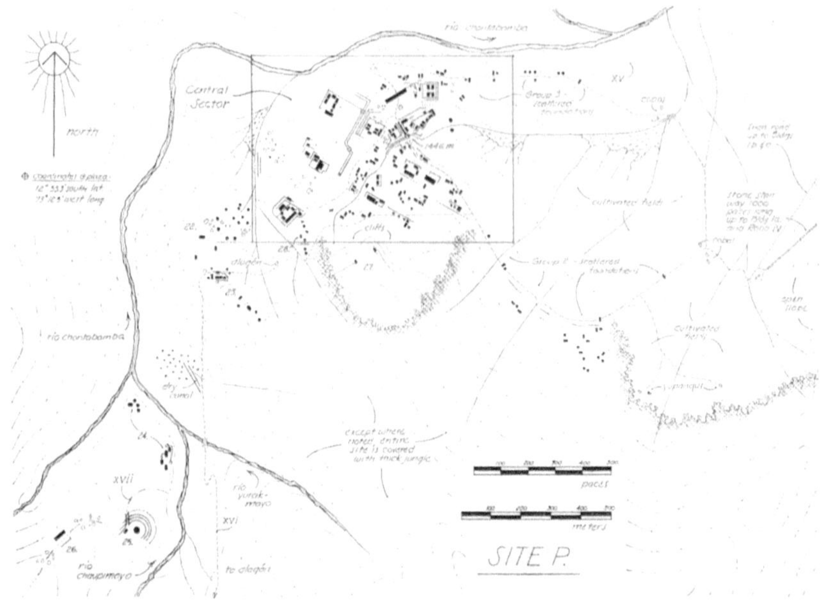

Figure 47 - Map of Espiritu Pampa (Vilcabamba the Old)

In a flash, on the way down, I remembered a curious comment Savoy had made months before. Describing how he'd lost everything - wife, family, land - when he'd been run out of Peru years ago, he said, "at least I got out with my journals." At the time, Nancy and I had thought it a strange comment, but now I understood with crystal clarity. The little book I'd just thrown away was all I had to show for five long weeks of backbreaking work. Replacing it would be out of the question, at least for another year, and who knew what might happen in a year's time. Fortunately, I landed in a deep pool and although swept immediately into some boulders, I scrambled out scratched, shivering and shaken, but unhurt. Ben had the book, wet because my throw had fallen short, but he'd grabbed it before it was caught by the current. I flopped down on the bank, panting with relief. Later that night, I dried the soaked journal, page by page, over an open fire. To this day it smells of fire smoke and brings back powerful memories of the Plain of Ghosts. At the time, though, and for the second time that afternoon, my heart was racing out of control - and it wasn't over yet.

The gloomiest part of the trail back to camp was just beyond the stone bridge that had once been the entrance to the center of the city. By the time we got there it was nearly dark and visibility was nil. We'd been talking about how most snakes were nocturnal and it was best to stay out of the woods at night. José said that was true, especially over in the San Miguel valley where there were lots of *shushupes*, as he called the huge bushmasters that stalked the lower elevations to the north. He'd always insisted that *serpientes* - snakes - were not a problem at Espíritu Pampa and he routinely crashed about in the bush bare-legged in sandals as if to prove it. We'd always followed suit, but nervously, since to us ignorant *gringos*, the country thereabouts looked for all the world like snake heaven.

Being in the lead, I turned to warn the others about a rock in the trail just as I moved uneasily to step over it myself. Uneasily, because I didn't remember anything being there earlier in the day. Out of the corner of my eye and in mid-stride I thought I saw the rock move. As my vision slowly focused in the fading light I recognized the long tail and hind legs of a rat-like animal about 18 inches long disappearing into a grotesquely distended mouth in the midst of a huge mass of writhing, slate gray coils. "Yeeoow!" I yelled and jumped back, my heart once again pounding, seemingly in my own mouth. "What the hell is that?" I barked rhetorically, knowing only too well what it was. We'd interrupted a very large snake in the midst of it's dinner. José insisted on killing the poor thing even though I was against it once I calmed down. It was, he said, an *asp'a* - but thankfully, no relation to Cleopatra's. Rather, it was a fairly beneficial and harmless constrictor - except to 18 inch rats, it seemed. This one was about eight feet long and as big around as a man's upper arm. Harmless or not, I'd have gone into cardiac arrest, I know, if I'd ever tangled with one face to face during our countless episodes thrashing about in the bush.

The next day we had to begin the long return trip upriver. We'd done all we'd planned, but there was half a roll of extra-fast film left and I decided to go back into the city alone for a few more shots before breakfast. The low-lying area west of the plaza **(Figure 53)** was thickest of all and it received so little daylight that even using special film, I had to cut away lots of vines and foliage to get decent pictures. It was a tedious routine because I'd have to cut and then check the light, cut and check, over and over again. A *machete* in the jungle, I'd learned, is much like an ice axe in the mountains. When needed, it's needed badly, but at all other times it's just in the way. To free both hands for the light meter, I'd gotten into the careless habit of sticking mine in the ground, blade first, but it wasn't smart. Anything left loose in the jungle blends quickly into the foliage and I'd nearly lost the it that way several times already. Still, I figured a few final shots wouldn't make any difference. Not so. I'd just snapped my very last picture when I got the feeling something was wrong. It took a minute to realize the *machete* was missing. Not only did I need it to get out of there, but - I belatedly recalled - it was special. I'd traded it from a Negrito pygmy in the Philippines when I was there with the Marines back in the 1960s. Unlike the Collins & CO. *el cheapos*, available for a buck or two in every *mercado* in Latin America, it had been forged from an old jeep spring and had a hand-carved handle made from a water buffalo horn. Over the years, I'd come to think of it as an old and valued friend. I looked everywhere, but couldn't find it. Frantic, I went back over every step I'd taken since I last remembered having it in my hand - but it was gone. I began to imagine it was Tupac Amaru's way of telling me, "Go home, gringo! There's nothing more for you to do here."

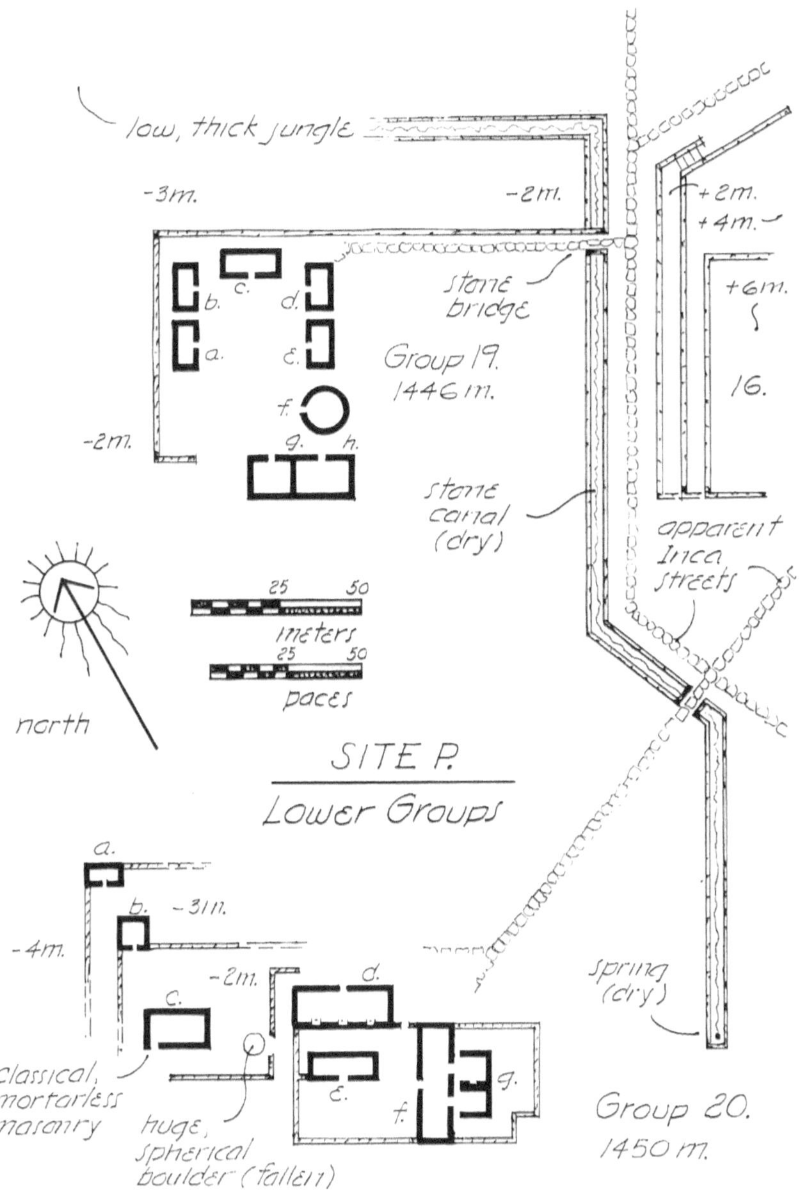

Figure 53 - Plan of Hurin Vilcabamba (Savoy's palaces of large Stones and Fine Ashlars)

Empty-handed, I turned back towards camp, discouraged and thoroughly depressed. Standing there motionless in the forest watching me were the Machiguengas. From Ben's description, it was the same outfit they'd seen the day before - except now there were five. Sometime in the night, the woman had given birth and the tiny baby was now at her enormous breast. She held it with one arm while still carrying all the group's possessions with the other. The men both had *chonta* palm bows half again taller than they were and an assortment of meter-long arrows, some barbed for fishing and others blunt-tipped, I guessed for stunning birds. Wrapped twice around the older man's waist and tied at one side was the slate gray skin of our *asp'a*, apparently eaten for dinner. José had flung it off into the forest. How had they found it? And what about the rat? Had they had him for breakfast, I wondered? The thought of it gave new meaning to the phrase "hunter-gatherer." All five were nearly naked, none wearing more than a few filthy rags. The only exception was the grimy red, white and blue wool "US SKI TEAM" hat worn incongruously by the younger man. We grinned at each other and shook hands all around in limp, Andean fashion, but they seemed to understand little Spanish. Besides Machi, they spoke Quechua like their highland cousins - but either way, I was pretty much out of the loop. Still, by eye contact, gestures, and an occasional word or phrase, we chatted as best we could and they nodded tentative agreement with José's story about ruins beyond the mountains. Nevertheless, there wasn't much doubt we were separated by a lot more than a language barrier. In fact, we might as well have lived on different planets, for what little we had in common. As if to underscore the point, the early Aero Peru flight from Lima passed high overhead on final approach into Cuzco, only a few minutes away by jet. We all looked up and watched it, silently lost in our own thoughts. What on earth did they make of that, I wondered? I tried asking, but they just shrugged and pointed to the sky, grinning at one another.

On that note, the trip effectively ended. The plane reminded me how much I wanted to get the hell out of there and back to the world of cold beers, clean sheets and sweet, *café cortado* in the morning. After a brief goodby to the locals, what was left of Sixpac Manco III trudged up the long Inca stairway under heavy loads. An unburdened El Viejo limped along behind, having at the last minute gone lame. Forty eight hours and a snowy pass later, we staggered into Huancacalle, confirming Calancha's seventeenth century report that it was "*dos jornadas largas* " - two long days - from Vilcabamba the Old to Vitcos. For Ben and me, a cold, rainy day of re-packing gear and bidding elaborate farewells was followed by a demonic 24 hour truck ride down to the railroad at Chaullay. A shrill diesel horn rudely awakened us from a few fitful hours of sleep on the concrete station platform there. All our visions of sipping *cervezas grandes* in the comfort of our first class seats were dashed as the train rumbled in looking like something from the evacuation of Saigon. We'd haplessly chosen the day after a two week holiday for our emergence from the jungle. Though we had no way of knowing it, Nancy and Susa had endured the opening hours of the very same *fiesta* sixteen days earlier. It was instantly clear that we, like they, had seriously screwed up. Hundreds of Cuzqueños, returning from the tropical diversions of Quillabamba had mobbed the train while we slept and lay sprawled over the roofs of the cars or hung clinging to every available finger and toe-hold below. We thought about climbing onto the engine, but instead fought our way aboard one car back just as it clanked and clattered off into the darkness.

Perched on the front of the tauntingly named *primera clase* coach with my feet balanced precariously on the lurching iron couple of the baggage car ahead, there wasn't much to look at. Behind me, 16 stoic Peruvians stood crammed into the vestibule without any hope of seats for the twelve long hours to Cuzco. The interior of the car behind held a formless mass of humanity and luggage, impenetrable even to the conductor. There I was again, I thought. Hadn't I known only too well what to expect? The past six weeks had gotten me back into shape and re-sharpened my skills in the bush, but nothing ever prepared one for the tedium of third world travel. My patience was all but exhausted and my sense of humor was little more than a vague memory. However successful, the expedition had been long and hard and now - as if to validate Zeno's paradox - no amount of effort seemed sufficient to bring it to an end.

All the way up the grand canyon of the Urubamba we stood sweating in the front of the jammed vestibule, unable to move. Only the pitiful misery of those between us and the door had saved us from the agony of our entrapment all the way to Cuzco. As the train pulled into Ollantaytambo, the first stop accessible by automobile, those nearest the doors rushed off in a mad scramble for seats in the two dilapidated taxis that theoretically offered alternative transport back to the city. Ruthlessly we lunged back into the car, captured and held a momentarily vacated seat. Maniacally, we braced ourselves against the wave of frantic returnees, clambering back onto the rapidly accelerating train, their only ticket home after all. Smug grins flickered across our faces as we realized our incredible good fortune - the result of their folly. Cuzco, the Oz of our dreams now seemed within reach. Alicia's doorway on Calle Huayna Capac loomed as the entrance to the Garden of Eden. We had both gone *un poco loco*.

Briefly on level ground, the train picked up speed. The seemingly endless Inca terraces of the Sacred Valley rushed past like some sort of archaeological speed reading course. A platoon of soldiers flashed past as we swung across the strategic bridge over the Urubamba at Pachar. They were mostly teen age kids, smoking cigarettes and fondling their automatic weapons. On such as these, it seemed, the future of democracy in Peru had for the moment come to rest. Uncomfortable with the thought, my mind returned to the question of why we were there and what, if anything, the last few weeks had meant. As the horrendously overloaded train emerged from its laborious ascent of the canyon of the Río Huarocondo and crept slowly out onto the broad, flat Plains of Anta, I thought of Pachacuti Inca's great victory over the marauding Chancas there in 1438. It had been an engagement of pivotal importance for much of South America and thus the world, for without it there would have been no Inca Empire. Yet it was a little known event, even among Peruvians. Like the battle of Hastings or Waterloo, it had reshaped the flow of history, but unlike those it had occurred among the aboriginal peoples of the New World and was thus thought to be of little account. Miserable as I was, I realized that I was glad we'd come back to finish the job begun two years earlier. With all the new information our explorations had uncovered, perhaps the true story of Vilcabamba, the final chapter in the saga of the Incas, could finally be written and thus not forgotten.

Now less than an hour from Cuzco, such positive thoughts were coming more easily to mind when, for no apparent reason, the train screeched to a stop. For a moment, everyone hesitated, expecting it to move on again. Instead, a rumor swept through the crowd that a strike among the trainmen in Cuzco would delay our arrival there indefinitely. Quite accustomed to that sort of thing, our fellow passengers began streaming resignedly across the quarter mile or so of open pasture that separated us from the highway, and began hitching on in to town. Ben and I stretched out, exhausted, each on our own seat in the abandoned coach. The last thing I remember before dropping off to sleep was a bicycle going by with either six or seven people aboard - it wasn't easy to tell.

17

Death Of A Martyr

Back in Jackson Hole, it was weeks before I could even look at my journals, let alone begin following up on the enormous amount of work we'd done. I was suffering from Vilcabamba overload and instead busied myself with the stone-fitting theory Vito and I had come up with early in the trip. I received a "call for papers" from John Rowe and decided to try our idea out on his Institute membership at their upcoming annual meeting in Berkeley. The paper was accepted and my presentation went pretty well. Not everyone agreed that we'd solved the mystery, but our theory stirred up enough interest to warrant publication in the Institute journal, Ñawpa Pacha (**1**), and in the Spanish language Boletín de Lima (**2**). It was shortly after that meeting that I received a letter from John informing me that I'd been elected a member of the Institute and was appointed a Research Associate as well. Totally unexpected, it was more than a little gratifying and was exactly the boost I needed to get off my duff and back to work on Inca Vilcabamba.

Right off, I wrote to von Kaupp and outlined our attempts to check out his theory. I told him that what we'd found in the field hadn't, by and large, matched what I'd read in his report. Specifically, I said, there was no "large Inca town" at La Mesada and that it had clearly been a settlement of forest Indians, either pre-Inca or subject to their rule. The normally courteous and even ingratiating von Kaupp took no time nor minced his words in responding. I had "obviously gone to the wrong place," he said, and should have "hired his guide" to take me there. In the face of our thorough and, to my mind, conclusive field work, I'd naively expected some softening of his position. No way! He was more adamant than ever. Soon there followed a thick packet of material re-stating again, and in minute detail, all the reasons why La Mesada was unquestionably the site of Marcanay and Vilcabamba the Old thus could not be located at Espíritu Pampa. Once again, I sat down and went through the whole thing from start to finish.

There was nothing new or startling about his arguments, but I had to admit that it was theoretically possible we'd somehow missed his site. But more than that, I found myself interested in the tragic story of Padre Diego Ortiz, really for the first time. My focus from the beginning had been the Incas, and just as Beauclerk had sparked my interest in their indigenous neighbors, von Kaupp now made me realize I'd paid too little attention to the Spanish players in the drama of Vilcabamba. From their point of view, the Indians had all the bit parts and the stars were their fellow Europeans. And of these, Ortiz had been among the most important - at least according to the chronicles of Murúa and, especially, the verbose Antonio de la Calancha. The ramblings of the latter were formidable - hundreds of pages of old Castilian, still available only in the original small-print edition intended for readers blessed with God-like eyesight. Up to that time, I'd had neither the interest nor the patience to wade through it all, but I now suspected that had been a mistake. With the help of Paula Dimler, a home town friend, former Peace Corps volunteer and Spanish teacher, I began going through page after page of Calancha's ornate and tedious text to be absolutely sure I wasn't missing something important.

The destruction of Vilcabamba had begun innocently enough, with the arrival there of the Augustinian missionary, Marcos García, in

1568. Diego Ortiz joined him a year later. At first, Titu Cusi cautiously restricted their potentially subversive activities to the easily watched village of Pucyura. A rebuilt version of García's mission church is still there, though used infrequently, there being no resident priest. Towering above town, atop the hill of Rosaspata across the river to the south, Vitcos still keeps silent tabs on the comings and goings below, as it did in Inca times.

CORONICA
MORALIZADA
DEL ORDEN DE
SAN AVGVSTIN EN EL
PERV, CON SVCESOS
EGENPLARES EN ESTA
MONARQVIA.
DEDICADA A NVESTRA SEÑORA
de Gracia, singular Patrona i Abogada de la
dicha Orden.

COMPVESTA POR EL MVY REVERENDO
Padre Maestro Fray Antonio de la Calancha de la misma
Orden, i Difinidor actual.

DIVIDESE ESTE PRIMER TOMO EN QVATRO
libros; lleva tablas de Capitulos, i lugares de la sagrada
Escritura.

Año 1638.

CON LICENCIA

En Barcelona: Por Pedro Lacavalleria, en la
calle de la Libreria.

Title page from the chronical of Padre Antonio de la Calancha, 1638.

After a brief stint as García's side-kick, Ortiz began lobbying the Inca for permission to build a church of his own, elsewhere in the province. In time, Titu Cusi consented, choosing for Ortiz' mission a town called Guarancalla, somewhere between Vitcos and his sprawling jungle capital at Vilcabamba. Though the place-name has since disappeared from the map and the country between Rosaspata and Espíritu Pampa now stands silent and empty, Calancha reported that Guarancalla was in those days a populous district, teeming with pagan souls in need of Ortiz' ministry.

He noted that the *padre's* new mission was two or three day's journey from Garcia's church in Pucyura, in the midst of and well located to convert the Indians of several nearby villages. Among these, was the place called Yanacachi, ancient home of the people conquered by Pachacuti 137 years earlier and named for a nearby deposit of black salt. In a short time, Calancha says, Ortiz built a church, house and hospital, all "*poor buildings*." Thus established, he began preaching the gospel throughout the surrounding mountains, planting thereon tall crosses and sacred trees where once the native idols had stood. **(3)**

Father García was a dour and judgmental pastor from the start. He was no favorite of the apparently fun-loving Titu Cusi, by whom no excuse for a party was ever overlooked. Ortiz, on the other hand, was by all accounts a good man, preoccupied with the welfare of his flock and tolerant of the drinking, debauchery and other excesses of Inca. Before long, he even became a trusted advisor at court, especially in matters involving the Spaniards, in whose ways he was presumed an expert. Still, Ortiz' growing popularity and influence among the natives was potentially troublesome and many of the Inca's captains spoke against the priest behind his back. It was finally agreed that both of the arrogant Christians needed a lesson in humility and Titu Cusi devised a plan. In early January of 1570, he extended them a fateful invitation. "*I wish to take you to Vilcabamba,*" he told them. "*Neither of you has seen that town and I want to feast there with you.*" **(4)**

They accepted eagerly. Calancha describes Vilcabamba as the largest town in the province and the epicenter of its pagan idolatry. He claims that the priests secretly planned to throw out the "*masters of the abominations*" practiced there and preach instead Christianity to the city's many residents. Why they thought the Inca would ever allow that to happen is unclear, but if that were indeed their intention, it was hopelessly naive. The folly of any such hopes were dashed when, at the outset, the Inca insisted that they make the entire three day journey from Pucyura to Vilcabamba barefoot! Along the way, he ordered them to walk waist deep down a frigid river with the idea that the route would thus appear so bad to them and the terrain so harsh that they'd give up and leave the province. Not content with that, according to Murúa's account of the trip, Titu Cusi arranged that they be tempted and scorned day and night by various pairs of particularly comely Campa tribal women dressed in long and sensuously revealing gowns, reminiscent of their own monk's habits. The stalwart *padres* resisted these native sirens of the rainforest and persevered toward their goal. Despite their best efforts, they never reached the sacred center of Vilcabamba. Upon arrival, the Inca allowed them to go no further than the outskirts of the city so that they would not see any of its *huacas*, or shrines, nor witness the many rites and ceremonies the Indians performed there. After eight frustrating days bickering fruitlessly with the Inca, the priests gave up and trudged back over the passes to Pucyura, humiliated and disgusted with the whole affair. **(5)**

A month after their return, Murúa claims that García and Ortiz were still stinging from their ill treatment by the Inca. As if cued by fate, some of the *padres'* parishioners came to them saying that near Vitcos was a place called Chuquipalta, where there was a temple dedicated to the sun and a great white rock standing above a spring of water. The locals believed that a devil lived in the rock, actually appearing there from time to time, according to Calancha. This apparition threatened and frightened all those who refused to worship him with offerings of gold and silver and the Indians begged the priests to free them from this evil. **(6** & **7)** Seizing immediately on what seemed an opportunity to recoup their failure to do God's work at Vilcabamba and at the same time repay Titu Cusi's many abuses of them there, the holy men unwisely consented. Accompanied by the many neighboring Indians they'd converted to Christianity, they marched to Chuquipalta, burned the temple and set a huge blaze all around the rock. It was a momentous mistake. The devil may or may not have thus been purged from the rock, but he certainly remained alive and well in the province, as the events of the coming months would tragically demonstrate.

Titu Cusi was enraged, the destruction of a sun temple being an unthinkable offense. Padre Marcos García was summarily stoned and banished from the province. He drowned crossing a river while attempting sometime later to return in defiance of the Inca's sentence. Ortiz was spared for the moment, but not forgiven. He and the Inca soon quarreled over the unjust but politically expedient execution of a roving gold prospector named Romero. The Spaniard had wandered out of the mountains and witlessly announced his intention to inform the new Viceroy of the the region's rich mineral deposits. Titu Cusi knew that couldn't be allowed and had the man killed over Ortiz' strenuous objections.

The *padre* insisted that the unfortunate fool's body be given at least a Christian burial. The Inca refused, having it thrown, instead, into a ravine. Ortiz recovered the remains and buried them anyway. It was the final straw. Titu Cusi's patience with his one-time friend and advisor was exhausted and his captains began openly to plot the priest's downfall. Yet, in the event, Ortiz' demise stemmed from a totally unexpected cause and, though ironically unjustified, was inflicted with unspeakable cruelty.

A few days after the murder of Romero, Murúa says Titu Cusi went to a shrine at Vitcos, near the place where the seven Spaniards had assassinated his illustrious father. There, the Inca soon became embroiled in what amounted to an orgy of feasting, singing and drinking *chicha*, the native booze. At some point, he apparently became violently ill and passed the remainder of the night "*vomiting and bleeding through the mouth and ears*." **(8)** Calancha adds that the Inca awoke the following morning "*complaining of chest pains*." Several trusted attendants, including his long-time, half-breed secretary - a man named Martin Pando - offered up various supposed remedies. At first Titu Cusi refused, fearing the cure more than the sickness. But seeing that Pando was among those giving it to him, he drank the medicine down and almost immediately lost his power of speech. Within twenty four hours, Calancha says, the Inca expired. **(9)**

Though not among those who had prepared the faulty remedy, Ortiz was present at Titu Cusi's death-bed, presumably to administer the Last Rites to his old friend and nominally Christian host. The distraught Indians had begged him to use his priestly powers to restore the Inca's life, but he replied that "*only God could do such a thing*." With his one time benefactor now dead, the natives' growing disaffection with Ortiz flared into vengeance. An Indian woman, the Inca's mistress, wanting to put an end to Ortiz' preaching and meddling once and for all, lied and told the captains that it was Ortiz who had poisoned the Inca, together with Pando. From that moment, the *padre's* fate was sealed, even though Murúa claims that many of those present knew that he was innocent of any complicity in the affair. For his part, Martin Pando was immediately seized by the Indians and killed. Ortiz was not so fortunate. **(10)**

Calancha's description of what followed may be suspect. He was writing 68 years after the fact and clearly thought his fellow Augustinian a worthy candidate for canonization. Whether he embellished his account of the doomed holyman's final ordeal to shorten his road to sainthood, we'll likely never know. To date, the Church has not seen fit to so honor Ortiz' martyrdom, but this brief excerpt from Calancha's account gives an idea of its severity. More to the point, it tells us most of what little we know about the sites of Guarancalla, Marcanay and Mananhuañunca.

"*Ortiz was first hung on a cross in the cemetery,* (of García's church in Pucyura) *and tied by the throat, legs and arms so tightly that the ropes cut his flesh. He was then beaten so badly that he bled streams of blood. Afterwards, they loosened him from the cross and continued to torment his body as they walked him through the country with his hands tied in back. He was led by a rope tied through a hole in his jaw toward Marcanay, a town two leagues from Vilcabamba the Old, where the new Inca, Tupac Amaru, was waiting. From Pucyura until Marcanay is a distance of nine Inca or twelve Spanish leagues* (either way, about 36 miles) *which includes highlands, woodlands and a few icy plateaus and rocky plains. The martyr was flogged, stoned, persecuted, starved, left naked in the cold and put in a cave over night, drenched by an incessant flood of icy water. Expecting to find him dead in the morning, his tormentors instead found him more valiant and took him from the cave, dragging him like a dead beast to the town of Guarancalla, where he had built his church and used to teach. They continued beating him as they dragged him though the town and on to Marcanay, having traveled three days.*"

"*Upon arrival,* (at Marcanay) *he was taken to the Inca, Tupac Amaru, who sentenced him to death in whatever way his tormentors elected. As soon as they heard this they dragged him down a steep slope to a river between some hills, the place they used to call the 'gallows of the Inca', where the the wicked were executed. The Indians now call this place Mananhuañunca, which means 'he will not die', since despite all their tortures, the priest continued to live. This name is conserved today at a place between two rivers. They whipped him there for the fifteenth time and thrust the slender thorns of the chonta palm under the nails of his hands and feet, spitting their foul saliva on him all the while. They shot their arrows at him, making his body look like a cactus. They blew smoke in his nostrils, taking away his breath to smother him, but still he would not die. Finally, one of the executioners who had an axe delivered a mortal blow to Ortiz head, but before the holyman expired, they inserted a stick underneath his groin and pulled it out through the nape of his neck, driving it into the ground with the priest's head pointing downward. Finally, they covered his body with dirt and rocks.*" **(11)**

It is a powerful story and a reminder that the sword of tragedy cut both ways in the deadly, final days of Inca Vilcabamba. Within a year of his death, Ortiz' executioners would be cut down by unwitting avengers. There would be no heroes or villains, no victors or vanquished - just survivors and corpses. In the end, Vilcabamba would turn out to be no great prize for the Europeans, nor much of a loss to the Indians, whose fate had been sealed decades earlier by the inexorable march of history.

Engraving of the martyrdom of Padre Diego Ortiz from the very rare, First Edition of Calancha's Coronica Moralizada, published in 1638 (courtesy of John Howland Rowe).

Much as I'd hoped to find the key to some sort of breakthrough hidden among Calancha's ramblings, it didn't happen. Rather, I came away with the same nagging feeling I'd had leaving La Mesada. Von Kaupp was onto something - but what? Paula and I gradually expanded our readings to include other sources, old and new, and eventually put together translations of almost everything that had ever been written about Vilcabamba. We found there a whole layer of interesting new details, but no real shockers. A lot of the material was repetitive, but much was confused and a few points were downright contradictory. By selectively choosing certain passages, I could make a strong case for almost anything, von Kaupp's counter-theory included. My suspicions about the reliability of the written record returned and the "truth" remained far from clear.

If anything, I was more sure than ever that Marcanay was at Consevidayoc, not La Mesada, as Bob insisted. Murúa was clear that the village the Spaniards passed through two leagues before entering Vilcabamba the Old was a lush, tropical farming community - to this day a perfect description of Consevidayoc, but one that could hardly apply to anything at or near La Mesada. Now, Calancha had added that Marcanay was about 36 miles from Pucyura, exactly the trail distance to Consevidayoc, but nearly twice the distance to La Mesada by any of the several possible routes.

But if von Kaupp was wrong, what then was La Mesada? Except for the Mananhuañunca legend, all there was to go on was its proximity to La Sal, the place Bob thought was Calancha's Yanacachi. The latter was named for a source of black salt, all right, but the *padre* went on to say Yanacachi had been "*a great town in ancient times*." **(12)** Where was the great town at or near La Sal? Maybe *that's* what we'd found at La Mesada, I thought, and von Kaupp's "large Inca town" was somewhere else, just as he claimed. And, if so, was it Guarancalla, the "*populated place*" not far from Yanacachi where Calancha said Ortiz had built his church? **(13)** There was a problem with that, too. In 1978, Quispicusi had shown von Kaupp what he claimed were the ruins of that very same church, but at a place called Maranpata, almost twenty kilometers from the lower Urumbay and thus nowhere near La Mesada.

Hoping to make sense of it all, I tried various alternative explanations out on von Kaupp, but he wasn't interested. Savoy didn't much care. He'd made up his mind years ago. John Hemming was in Brazil and all of our Berkeley friends figured I was their expert on Vilcabamba, not the other way around. I turned to Nancy, but she threw up her hands. "How can you even remember all those crazy names, let alone keep track of what they were and where they are?" I was still sure von Kaupp was wrong, but was getting nowhere in my attempts to prove it on paper. Finally, a long letter from

Edmundo Guillén in Lima further complicated matters by restating his reservations about my forts. It was an unwanted reminder that we'd never really gotten around to dealing with that one on the last trip. Reading books and exchanging letters had raised all sorts of new problems, but I knew it would never solve them. There was only one way to do that. And so, less than six months after getting home from what we'd thought was the expedition to end all expeditions, Nancy and I decided to go back.

18

The Final Piece

It was mid-November before we could get away - a wet time in the *montaña* - but we planned a quick three week visit and figured a brief exposure to the dreaded rainy season might even be interesting. Strange as it may seem to readers familiar with Andean weather, we were right. Sixpac Manco IV was to be a good trip. Not that there weren't the usual tip-offs that we were headed into harm's way - a terrorist bomb took out all the lights of Lima just as our flight was on final approach into the city - but it somehow didn't matter. Our arrival at Alicia's in Cuzco was nothing short of a family homecoming. There was even a list of phone messages waiting from various friends and acquaintances. Peter Frost, expatriate British author of the most popular English language guidebook to the city, invited us out to dinner before we left for the mountains. No one knows the city better and we had a wonderful evening with him, especially in the the uncrowded conditions of Cuzco's off season. Peter was fascinated by my stone-fitting theory and asked if he could include it in the up-coming reprint of Exploring Cuzco **(1)**. The big news, he said, was that my old friend Renzo was back and claimed he had *millions* of US dollars to spend on tourist development in the Vilcabamba! No one had actually seen any of the money yet, but the Italian had supposedly raised it in Europe from corporate donors. Why anyone would contribute that kind of cash to a project with such marginal prospects for return, remained a mystery. Still, on the off chance there was something to it, Nancy and figured we'd better get back in there ASAP, while we still had the chance.

By late 1987, terrorist activity in the countryside had begun to taper off. Like all revolutionaries on a roll, the Senderistas had shifted their focus to the capital in Lima, and we received our Vilcabamba permit without much fuss. We headed downriver to Quillabamba the next afternoon. The following day found us once again at our friend Juvenal's doorstep in Huancacalle, where he, too, welcomed us back warmly and offered to accompany us on our expedition. He'd farmed the country all the way down to Espíritu Pampa for decades and was more knowledgeable about the region than anyone else we knew. I was delighted that at long last we'd have his company in the field. Once we got settled for the night, we went up to his house for dinner and a few beers. He said the political situation had improved since we'd last been there and things were momentarily *tranquilo* - peaceful. As if to prove his point, he showed us a pet red fox he'd captured and kept tied on a leash. He joked that keeping the fox out of trouble was his biggest problem

I often think back to that idyllic evening. Since our departure the previous September, the ominous line of surveyor's stakes up to Vilcabamba the New had been transformed into the *carretera* promised by the government contract. The lovely old Inca road had been effectively obliterated in the process, but, ironically, not replaced. No funds were available for a needed concrete bridge across the Río Vilcabamba, and the new road remained unusable and abandoned. Horse and foot traffic continued to pick its way through the barren, boulder-strewn moon-scape left behind by the bulldozers. Early in 1988, the denuded mountainside washed out, saturated by heavy rains. Thousands of cubic yards of boulders and mud swept down the canyon, killing nine *campesinos*, including three small children, and burying Cobos' entire farm under tons of rock. His house and family were spared, but his livelihood was ruined. For decades among the most prosperous men in the valley, he and Flavio were wiped out in a matter of minutes. Juvenal had to sell his surviving livestock - the only real capital left to him - just to feed his household, but they all got sick anyway and he, himself, nearly died of dysentery in the aftermath of the disaster. Archaeology teaches that nothing is forever - a truth our old friend Juvenal was soon to learn the hard way.

But all that was months in the future. Anxious to get back up to speed on happenings in the Vilcabamba, I asked him about Renzo and the rumors we'd heard in Cuzco. They were true, he said. The Italian had indeed been back, but the locals hoped it was for the last time. In classic Francescutti fashion, he'd apparently talked big but accomplished little. Like von Kaupp, he was after the "real" Vilcabamba the Old, but his slant on the story was very different from Bob's. Since Bingham's time, an alternative name for Manco's lost capital had been Vilcabamba "Grande" or, in Quechua, "Hatun Vilcapampa". Both names had been used for years, along with Vilcabamba "the Old," to differentiate the ruins at Espíritu Pampa from the old Spanish village at Vilcabamba the New. But by 1986, Hatun Vilcapampa had somehow become a mysterious new and undiscovered city, distinct from Savoy's by then well known site and far more important, if the rumors were to be believed. Whether Francescutti instigated these stories or they were invented for his benefit is unclear. He nevertheless proclaimed that they described yet another "lost city" and hinted that he had a satellite photo showing just where it was, off in the jungle northwest of Rosaspata. According to Juvenal, who provided horses for the expedition, the search for these ruins several months earlier had been a total fiasco.

A young Machiguenga boy, pressed by Renzo into service as an unwilling guide, finally tried to escape. Tragically, he fell off a cliff and was killed in the attempt. Towards the end of the trip, rations became so short the Italian ended up commandeering food at gunpoint from poor, pioneering farmers back in the bush. One defiant *campesino* had refused, and watched as his prize pig was shot dead by one of the hungry soldiers. Despite all, the expedition found nothing. In the end, Renzo paid Juvenal only half his contract for the horses because the expedition had failed to turn up the fabled city, even though the Italian had been assured beforehand there was none to be found. Despite such penny pinching, Francescutti circulated color brochures advertising his grandiose development project for Vilcabamba. Included features were to be improvement of the road up from Chaullay, better medical facilities for the residents and various programs to study and reconstruct some of the ruins. Hopes in the region were running high, of course, because those are precisely the kinds of things both the government and the locals wanted very badly to see. But so far, Juvenal said, nothing much had come of it all.

Dinner done and gossip over with, talk turned to the project at hand. I told Juvenal why we'd come back and how much time we had. The rain was increasing daily, he said, and swollen rivers might soon block our way down in the jungle. It would be best to get going without delay. We agreed, and set out the very next morning with two pack horses loaded with food and excess gear. Four short days after leaving home, there we were, heading out the trail back into the sixteenth century. Bringing up the rear was an 11 year old orphan named Policarpo. Juvenal had recently taken him in after the boy's father was murdered by the Senderistas, his throat cut while his family was made to watch. Policarpo's mother had been spared, but was left so poor she could no longer support the family. She'd soon been forced farm her three kids out to whomever would take them. Tragic as the situation was, Policarpo, at least, had ended up in good hands. He and Juvenal got on well and the boy played the roll of sidekick to the hilt. Despite occasional bouts of loneliness for his family, he was a joy to have around and his good cheer constantly rubbed off on us three adults throughout the incessant rains and mud of the next two weeks.

Our plan was simple. We were going to hire von Kaupp's guide, Pancho Quispicusi, to show us every single rock he'd shown his former client in the course of their 1978 Urumbay explorations. There were to be no slip-ups this time; no lingering questions as to where we'd gone or what we'd seen. I wanted to settle the issue once and for all. Afterwards, if time and conditions permitted, I also hoped to check out Guillén's imagined fort locations below Urpipata, even though we'd given the area a pretty good going over with

José in 1984 and found absolutely nothing. Quispicusi's house was right on the rocky road intersection that doubles as Yupanka's plaza. He was well known around town as a "guide" and we quickly saw why. Unlike Juvenal and José - farmers, basically, and men of few words - Pancho had made a career, of sorts, out of dealing with visiting *gringos*. He talked constantly and, like guides everywhere, figured his job was to keep us entertained and tell us whatever it was he thought we wanted to hear. Although the chatter was tiresome and there was more than a little pathos in his name dropping and past tales of derring-do, he was helpful and we liked him. His fees, not surprisingly for one whose profession was milking *touristas*, were a bit pricey.

Since we already had Juvenal and only needed Pancho's help in the Urumbay, we decided to go on up to Maranpata, von Kaupp's site for Ortiz' church, on our own. Pancho said he'd join us there in a couple of days. Before we'd even left Yupanka, though, he more than earned his pay by telling me the location of Bingham's buildings at the nearby site of Inca Huaracana. Unable to find them during our visit with José, I'd long wondered where they were. I'd deduced only two possible locations from the famous explorer's 1912 description and site plan **(2)** and had gone to one in 1984, but found nothing. Pancho confirmed that, sure enough, it was the other. That news, in turn, solved the mystery of why Bingham hadn't found the plaza and buildings I'd uncovered in the nearby undergrowth. Upon reaching the pass above Lucma, he'd turned right, up the ridgeline to the south, and thus missed our half of the site altogether. **(Figure 13)**

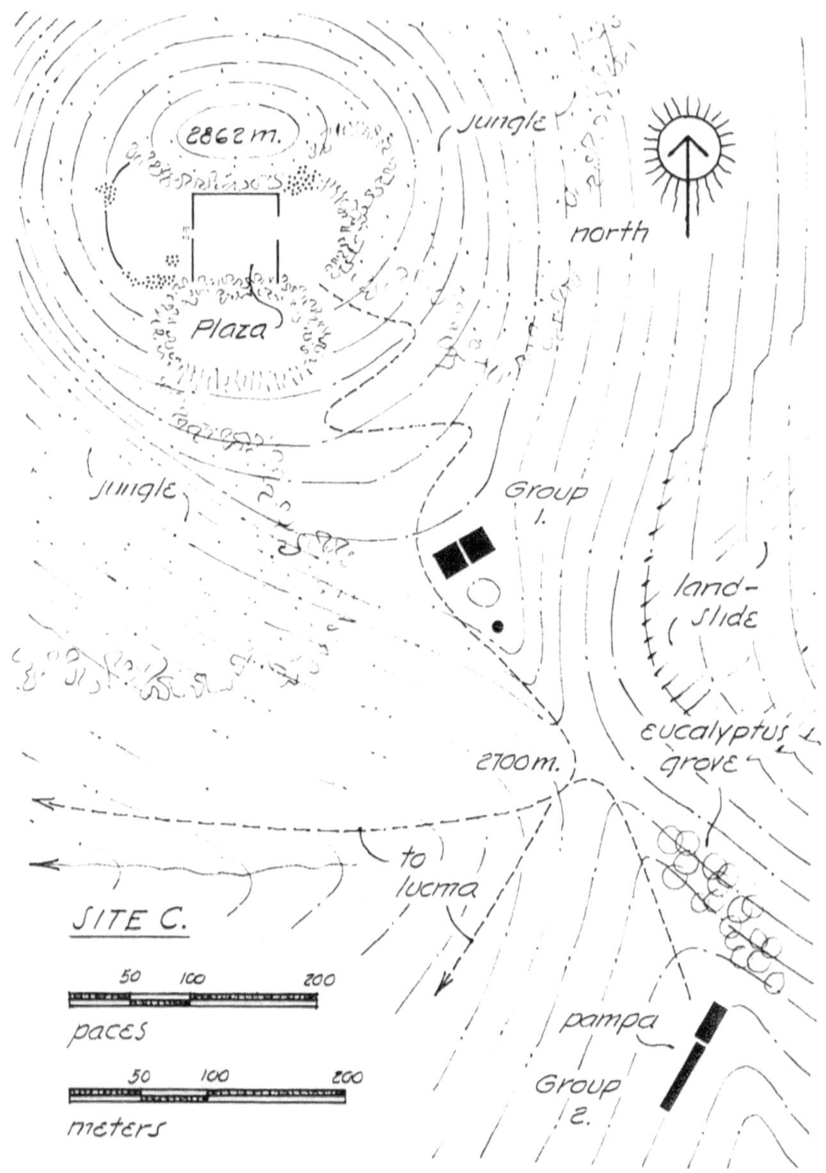

Figure 13 - Map of Inca Huaracana

Leaving Yupanka, we ascended the steep drainage of the Río Salinas all the way to its headwaters, below a pass of the same name that leads over into the head of the Urumbay. Although there were patches of old paving stones in the bottom and near the top of the canyon, most of the route was up narrow, muddy switchbacks. (**Figure 4**, Road vii) Just short of the pass, at about 12,300 feet, the terrain opened into a broad, marshy valley called Maranpata. There were several farms scattered around, but the climate at that altitude didn't encourage much in the way of agriculture and there was no evidence that the place had ever supported more than a few families. We camped under a threatening sky near the highest house, owned by an old friend of Juvenal's. Once we were set up and the stove was hissing away for a badly needed pot of afternoon coffee, I took a quick look around.

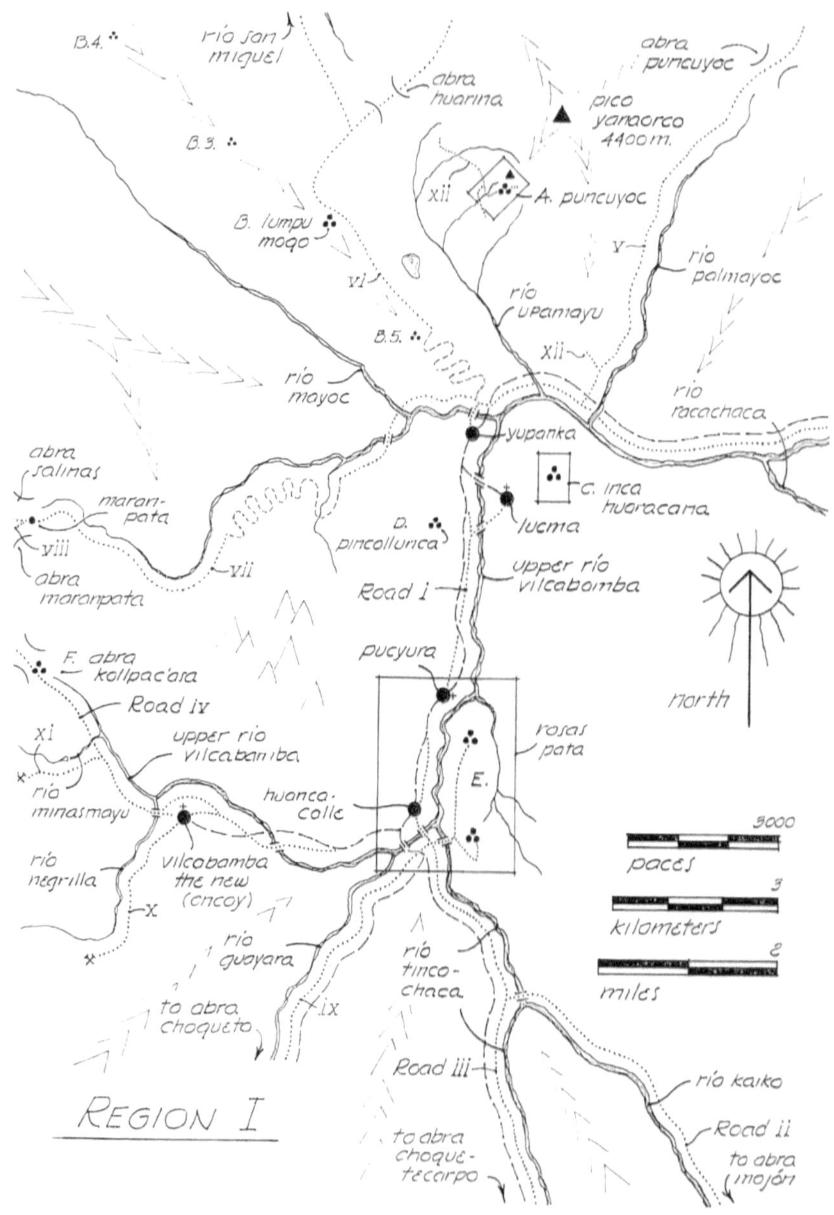

Figure 4 - Map of upper Rio Vilcabamba

Wandering up to a low gap in the ridgeline just above our tent, I found I could look down the other side to Mollepunku (**Figure 33**) on the Pampaconas road, no more than a mile or so away. Juvenal said the gap was called Abra Maranpata and the remains of a paved Inca road could still be seen winding down to and across the intervening valley. (**Figure 32**, Road viii) Bleak and unimpressive as it was, Maranpata was thus at the junction of no less than three old roads in Inca times. I'd always thought that there was just one way from the upper Río Vilcabamba into the upper Río Pampaconas - the road we'd always used, over the pass of Kolpacasa. I now saw I'd been wrong. The route we'd just followed up the canyon of the Río Salinas had once provided an alternative - a major short cut, actually - from the area around Lucma over to Pampaconas or on downriver to Tambo and Vilcabamba the Old.

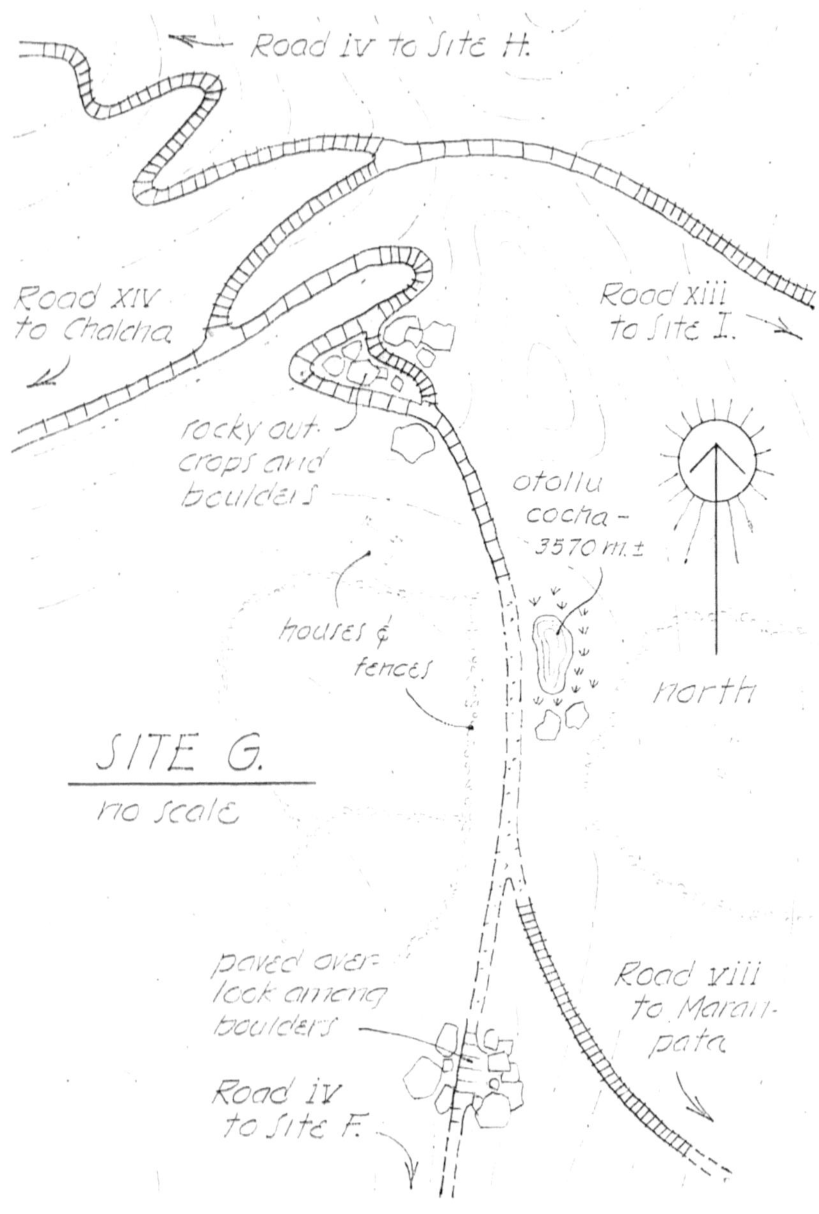

Figure 33 - Map of Mollipunku

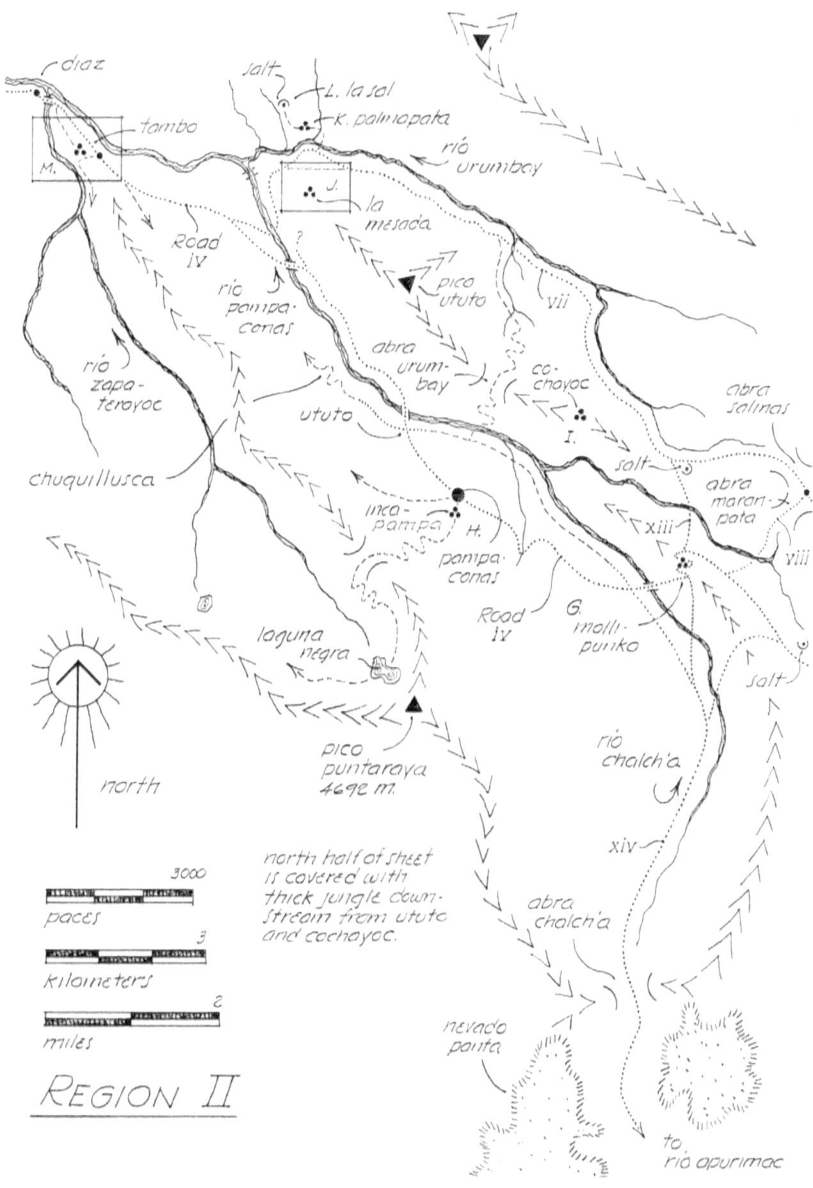

Figure 32 - Map of upper Rio Pampaconas

That, in turn, answered a question that had bothered me for some time. During the invasion of 1572, the Incas had broken off contact with Arbieto's army somewhere below Vitcos and reappeared in full force at Tambo, several weeks later. Apparently, they had bypassed both Vitcos and Pampaconas in the process, since the Spaniards encountered no resistance at either place. Now, it was obvious where they'd gone. By retreating up the Salinas and over into the Urumbay, (**Figures 4** & **32**, Road iiv) the Indians had easily beaten the Europeans down to Tambo, meanwhile keeping tabs on them by posting lookouts along the high points separating the two routes. Unappreciated at the moment, my newfound alternate route also answered another important question, but it was one I wouldn't know to ask for several more days.

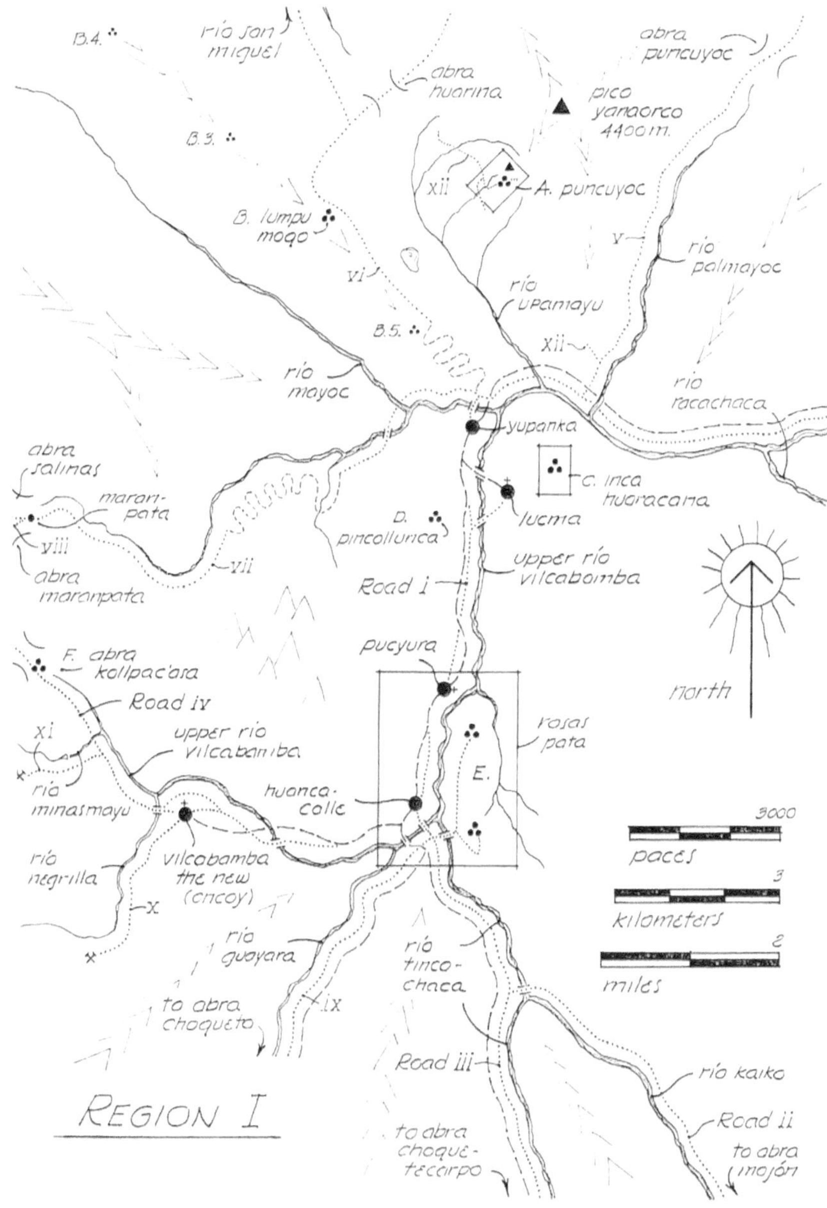

Figure 4 - Map of upper Rio Vilcabamba

Towards dark, the weather turned nasty and horrendous winds and rain swept our ridiculously exposed campsite all through the night and half the next day. Juvenal and Policarpo slept inside the farm house, but Nancy and I stayed out on the theory that only the dead weight of our bodies would keep the tent from blowing away. It was a long, sleepless night. We should have struck the thing and gone inside, but by the time we realized that, it was too late. Effectively, we were camped on a flatbed truck, barreling down the interstate at 50 miles an hour. Doing anything other than just hanging on was out of the question. I thought of the ruins at Puncuyoc and shuddered to think what conditions must be like up there. As the wind blows, they're not very far from Maranpata, and are more than 500 feet higher. The gale that was battering us must have funneled around the super-exposed Incahuasi with hurricane force. **(Figure 6)** It was obvious from the masonry details I'd seen there the previous year that the roof had been tied down with elaborate care, and now I knew why.

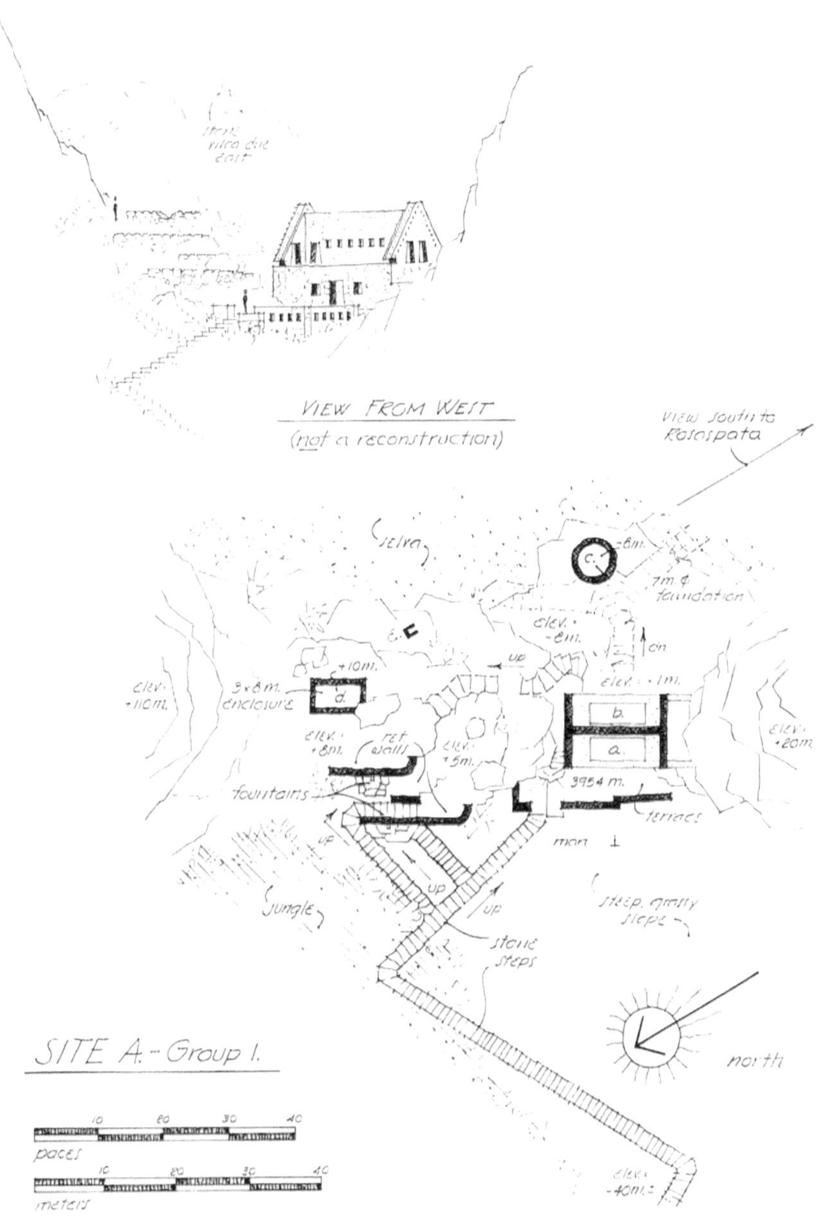

Figure 6 - Site plan and view of Incahuasi

By early afternoon, the storm began to slack off and Pancho showed up. Relieved to escape at last from our little nylon prison, we decided to take advantage of the improving weather and check out the ruins von Kaupp thought were those of Ortiz' mission. Pancho led off up a nearby hill and stopped, finally, at the very top. Four tumbled stone fences met at a lumpy cairn on the highest point. A couple of holes had been dug close by and there were a few loose rocks lying about. What we were looking at, according to Pancho, were the remains of the church where a folk hero named Padre Huarcuna had once preached.

There was nothing to be gained by arguing the point, but it was ridiculous. There wasn't enough flat ground on the steep-sided summit to lie down, let alone build a church. Nor were there enough stones to build even a tiny shepherds hut. Calancha had reported not only a church, but a house and hospital. I began to get the sinking feeling that in '78, Pancho had quickly picked up on what it was von Kaupp wanted to find and led him down the garden path to this and all his other sites. If so, we were in for more disappointments down the Urumbay. As I made a sketch of what little there was to record, I wondered how such a place could ever have become confused with the site of Ortiz' church. Calancha said the *padre* often preached from mountaintops and occasionally left large, wooden crosses behind to commemorate the event. **(3)** Supposedly, he'd done so at Kolpacasa, the Salty Pass, only a mile away. I figured he might well have done the same here, above Maranpata. With its panoramic, 360 view of the surrounding countryside, it would certainly be an inspiring place for a sermon. In any case, the forlorn valley spread below us had never been "*very populated*," as Calancha described Guarancalla. Clearly, Ortiz' church had been somewhere else.

The next day Pancho, Juvenal and I crossed the Abra Salinas and headed down the canyon of the Urumbay under oppressive, gray skies. Nancy wasn't feeling well and Policarpo stayed behind to give her a hand around camp. The plan was for us three to get down to the "real" La Mesada and back to Maranpata as quickly as possible. Going downhill we made good time despite several interesting encounters along the way. (**Figure 32**, Road vii) Not far beyond the pass, a trail came in from the left that Juvenal said led over to

Mollepunku. (**Figure 33**, Road xiii) I realized right away it was one of the side roads that joined the main downstream thoroughfare at the picturesque pedestrian interchange there.

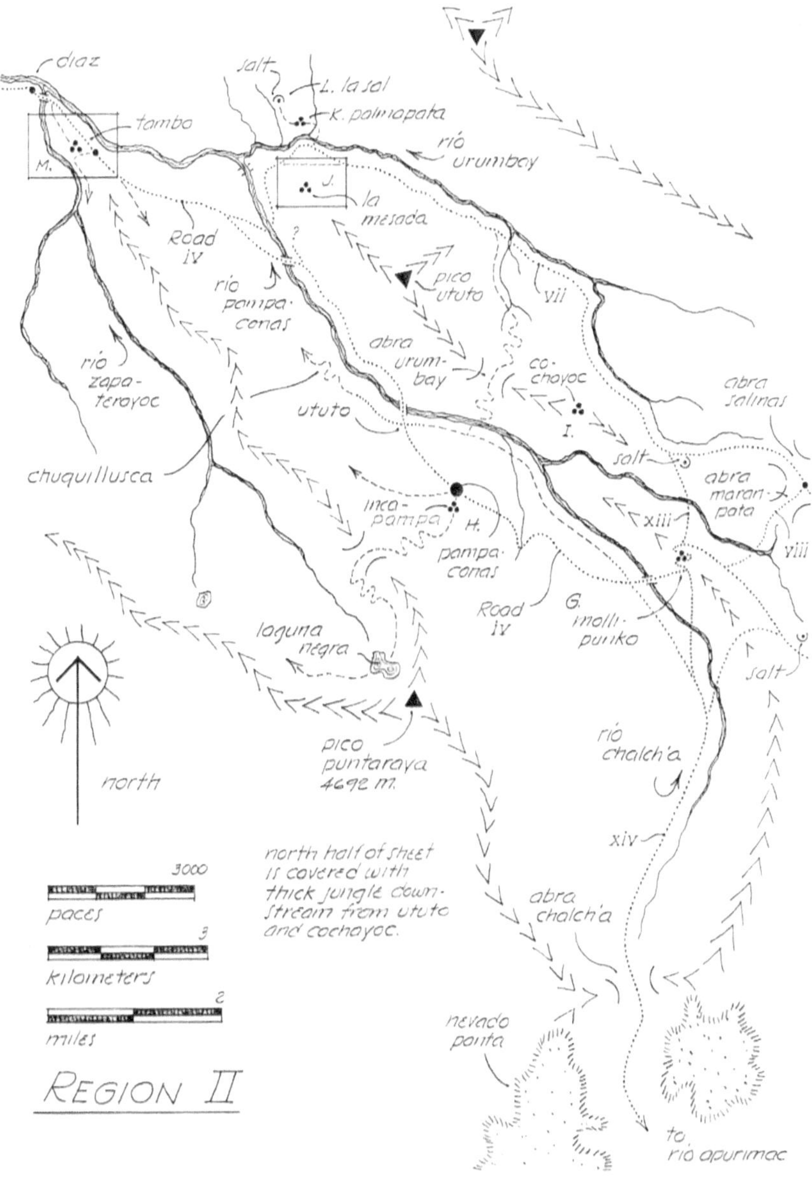

Figure 32 - Map of upper Rio Pampaconas

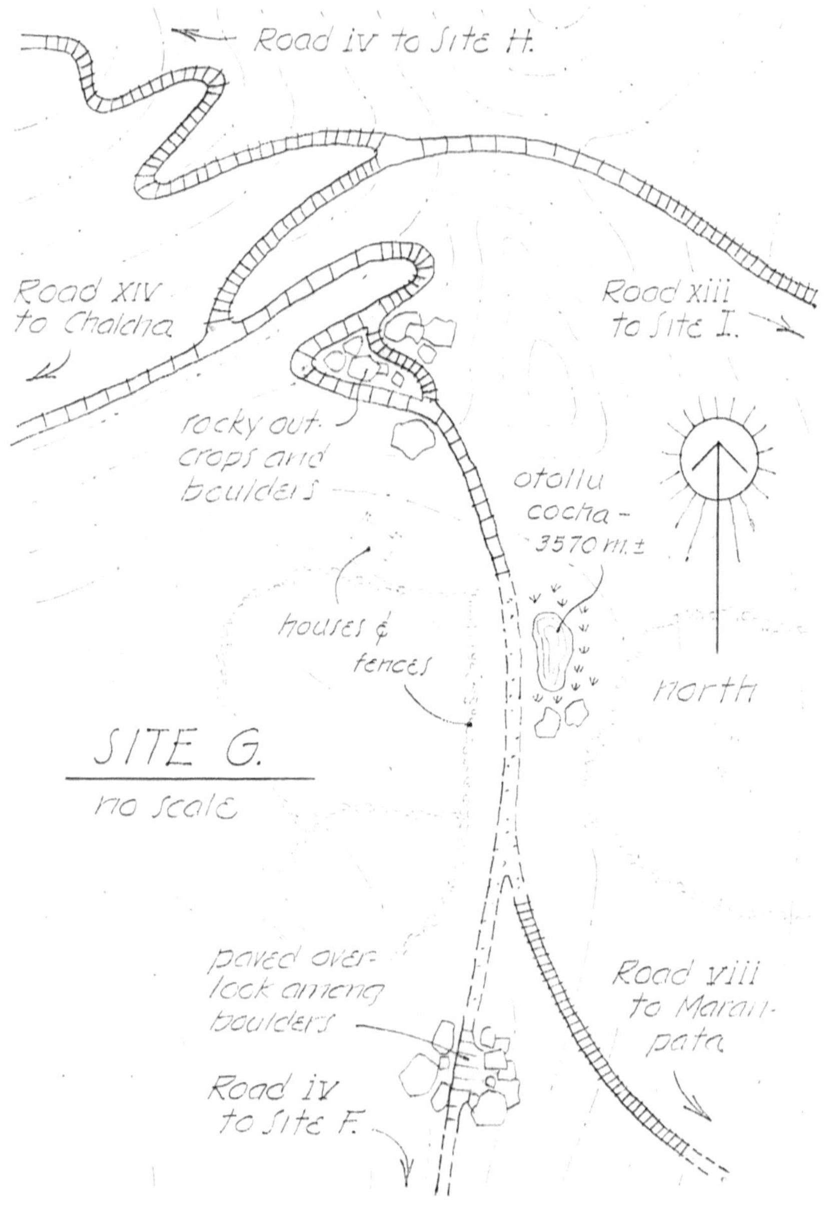

Figure 33 - Map of Mollipunku

An hour further downstream, the canyon opened a bit and a small bench appeared a few hundred feet up the left-hand slope. Both *campesinos* agreed that there were ruins there at a place called

Cochayoc - the place Ben and I had been told of in Pampaconas the previous year - but they were just a few circular houses, badly tumbled, overgrown and uninteresting. I made a mental note to go there on our way back upstream, but we never did. Below Cochayoc, we eventually rejoined the route José, Ben and I had followed on our first trip to La Mesada and the country became familiar for the first time since we'd left Yupanka. The trail was still in bad shape, but at least there weren't any trees down and we reached the first of Álvarez huts just before dark.

The others slept inside, but the place was so filthy and filled with fleas and spiders that I couldn't do it. I rolled my bag out on the narrow porch by the door. The thatch overhung a bit, lucky for me, because the rain that night came down in sheets. I'd heard that phrase all my life and never before known what it meant. Nancy later said the storm up in the pass was the most violent she'd ever experienced. By morning it had stopped, but the jungle was drenched, visibility was down to a few feet due to the fog and mist and the ground underfoot was a more or less continuous swamp. The humidity must have stood right at 100% and the whole scene was straight from a grade B jungle movie. Pancho led off with his *machete* as we left the road and started up the mountainside toward La Mesada. Never having been off the trail above the Álvarez place, Juvenal followed, curious about what we were about to find. To me, the surroundings seemed depressingly familiar. Not wanting to influence Pancho in any way, though, I said nothing. After an hour or so the angle laid back and we emerged onto José's meseta, not far from the giant matapalo trees. The bush was even thicker than I'd remembered, I guessed because of all the rain. No ruins were visible and Juvenal thought we'd just stopped for a rest. I knew better and, sure enough, Pancho pulled some vines away from one of the walls of the large, central structure and announced that we'd arrived. "*Aquí estamos!* " There was no doubt, he said. It was the same "large Inca ruin" he'd shown von Kaupp almost a decade before. In retrospect, I suppose I knew all along we weren't going to find anything new - but for the moment, visions of all the time, money and sweat I'd dumped into returning to that same, nasty, uninteresting, rat hole of a place danced in my head. I lost it.

"Pancho", I snapped, only half-heartedly trying to control myself, "this place is about as Inca as my ass! I've been here before. I know this place. I know Inca architecture when I see it and there are no 84 Inca houses anywhere near here!" Visibly hurt - so much so that I was immediately ashamed of myself - he insisted that they were "all around us." Actually, on second thought, they were "higher up" the slope, he said. Not wanting to give von Kaupp any further ammunition, up we went. For an hour or more, we searched, ever higher into the soggy cloud forest. The circular foundations we'd found with José were everywhere. A dubious benefit of that second visit with Pancho was an expanded grasp of the scale of the place. I had to agree with Bob about that , at least. There were, indeed, "84 houses, and probably many more" as he'd reported. They just didn't seem to be Inca. There was, theoretically, a possibility they were *store* houses - one of the few circumstances where the Incas favored circular floor plans. But such sites were typically organized into orderly rows and included some of the Inca's classically rectangular structures for living quarters, administration and the like. Of either of these features, we found no trace. Also, the quality of Inca construction was generally better than what we were finding. The whole idea of a storehouse was to keep out weather and vermin, and the walls of La Mesada would have provided scant protection from either. In response to Pancho's continuing promise that the Inca buildings were "higher up," I finally, in desperation, offered a nominal cash reward for the discovery of any building with square corners and told both *campesinos* that I'd be back down at the large central structures if they found anything. As I turned to backtrack down through the area we'd already searched, they eagerly disappeared up into the thick jungle above.

In 1984, I'd regarded the ruins that made up what von Kaupp called the nucleus of the site as anomalous, since they seemed neither Inca, nor at all similar to the rough, circular houses all around. Bob was right, I thought. There was something special about the place, but what? I guessed it had been the modest "downtown" district of the old settlement, probably made up of its temples, meeting halls or other public structures. Having little else to do, I decided to spend the afternoon trying to find out. After an hour or so of clearing with my *machete*, the layout of the ruins was easier to see. What I'd thought to be a group of buildings connected by high walls instead turned out to be two large rooms or enclosures separated by a pair of high mounds, filled with loose rocks. One of the latter had been dug out, probably by *huaqueros*, and appeared to be the base of a roughly square tower about 6 paces on a side. The other mound, too, showed signs it had once been rectangular, though a bit smaller than the first. Of the two enclosures, the larger - 20 by 25 paces - had never been more than five or so feet high, while its smaller neighbor was still standing well over my head and had the form of an elongated semi-circle with a diameter of about 16 paces. No doors, windows or niches were visible anywhere, though the wall separating the two enclosures was buried beneath at least ten feet of debris and the mid-point of the only side of the larger enclosure which wasn't dug into the slope was obscured by the tangled roots of one of the gigantic *matapalos*. For the first time, I began sketching what I'd found **(Figure 36)** and suddenly realized what it was. In an instant, everything fell into place. I'd found the final piece of the puzzle of Inca Vilcabamba!

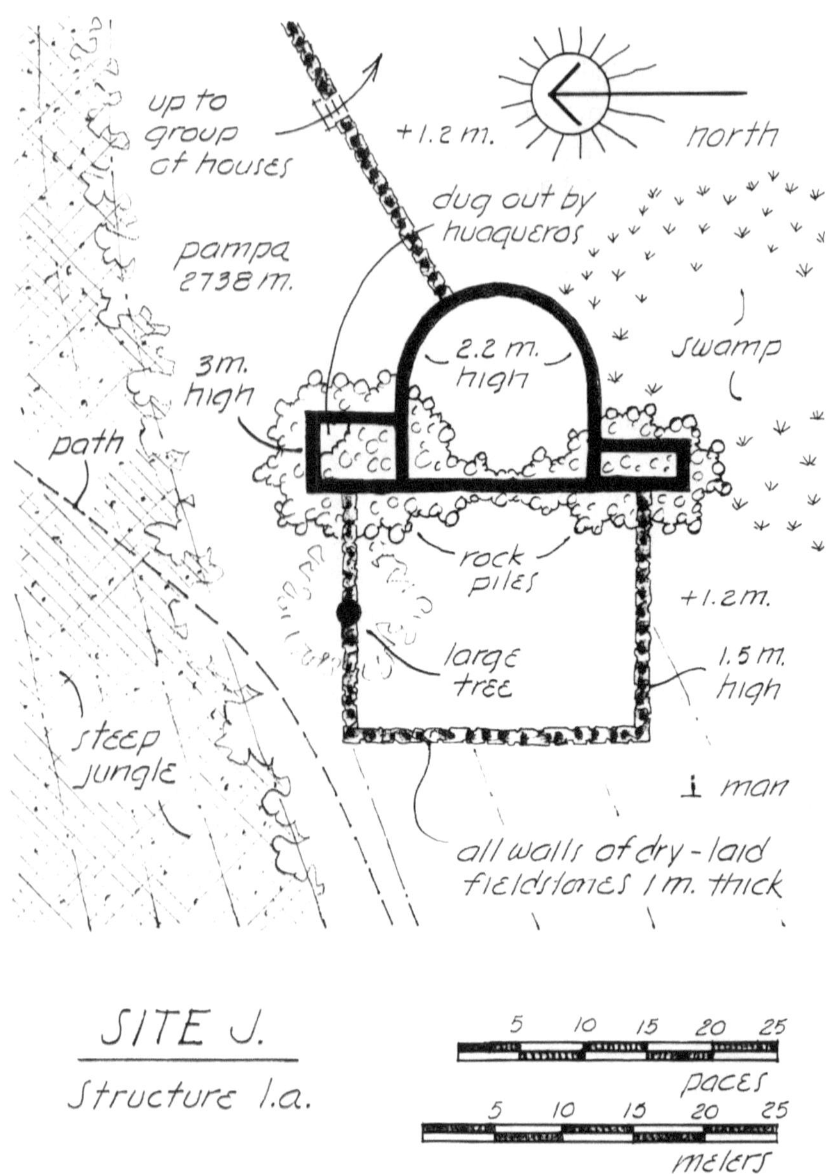

Figure 36 - Plan of anomalous structure

Just then, Juvenal and Pancho emerged from the forest, the latter looking distinctly sheepish. Despite their best efforts, they couldn't claim a single *inti* of reward money. They'd found a few more of the circular constructions above where I'd left them, "*...muchos redondos!* "

Pancho exaggerated, hopefully. But nothing with square corners, "*...pero, ningunos cuadrados*," Juvenal added, knowing they'd struck out. I wasn't surprised. Von Kaupp himself had located his "*Inca*" site up a "*short slope*" from the river **(4)**, hardly a description that would apply to ruins as much as two thousand feet up the mountainside. Besides, who cared? I now saw that it was a moot point. Even if there were Inca remains hidden somewhere in the surrounding forest, it made no difference. The ruin I'd just finished clearing told the whole story.

The nucleus of La Mesada was a small Spanish church, a classic example of the so-called *capilla abierta*, or open chapel. It was a building type especially favored by sixteenth century missionaries in largely Indian parishes. I'd learned about them in my readings with Paula, not thinking much about it at the time. Now it all came back. According to the experts, the interior of the church itself was reserved for the offices of the priest, while the often unruly congregation received the mass from a balcony between the bell towers while standing in a large, open *atrio*, or courtyard, in front of the building. **(5)** The generally semicircular sanctuary of such a chapel was invariably at the east end of the nave, opposite the bell towers, and the *atrio* was usually a walled enclosure beyond them to the west. A glance at my sketch showed exactly that layout at La Mesada. Probably, there'd once been a doorway between the towers on the west, now buried in the rockpile, and a gate into the courtyard where the big tree now enveloped the wall. I projected those features onto the ground plan and *viola!* - there was my church. **(Figure 37)**

Figure 37 - View of anomalous structure (Ortiz' mission at Guarancalla)

La Mesada, then, was Guarancalla, the lost mission of Padre Ortiz. It had to be. Titu Cusi had allowed only two Christian churches to be built in the entire province. A rebuilt version of the other, the mission of Ortiz' partner, Marcos García, still stands opposite the police station at Pucyura. According to Calancha, Guarancalla was several days' walk from García's church, at a "*populated place*" somewhere between Vitcos and Vilcabamba the Old. **(6)** In every way, it was an apt description of La Mesada. Significantly, Calancha did not identify Guarancalla as an "Inca" town - he inferred only that it was inhabited by subjects of the Inca. From the crude, round houses surrounding the church, I guessed they were Beauclerk's forest Indians, the same people who'd comprised the bulk of Titu Cusi's retinue during his meetings with Figueroa at nearby Pampaconas in 1565. **(7)**

If La Mesada was Guarancalla, then it couldn't be Marcanay, as von Kaupp believed. My placement of the latter at Consevidayoc thus stood unchallenged and Bob's revolutionary counter-theory evaporated, no matter what the locals thought about Padre Huarcuna and his supposed execution at Palmapata. That, in turn, meant that Tambo, the only other town anywhere near La Sal, had to be Calancha's Yanacachi, the ancient village named for a nearby deposit of black salt. Both identifications were further strengthened by Calancha's inferences **(8)** that Guarancalla and Yanacachi were nearby places - La Mesada and Tambo being no more than a half hour walk apart. Finally, the route of Ortiz' martyrdom made sense for the first time. Calancha reported that, from Pucyura, the Indians dragged the priest through "*Guarancalla, the town where he taught and made his church*" on their way to Tupac Amaru in Marcanay. **(9)** No such place was known on the main road over the Kolpacasa to Pampaconas and beyond, and I'd always wondered where they'd gone. The answer was now clear. They'd followed the same route we had, up to Maranpata and down to La Mesada, (Road vii) before rejoining the main, downriver road at Tambo.

Walking back up the canyon of the Urumbay later that afternoon, I was struck by the ironic turn of events. Ortiz' church was the one building in the Vilcabamba no one, including me, had ever bothered to look for. In retrospect, it would have been one of the easiest to find, or at least identify, since there was none other like it in the province. And once found, it was so unimpressive that neither von

Kaupp nor I had paid much attention to it or assigned it any significance - yet, all along, it had been the key to a riddle explorers had been trying to solve for the better part of a century.

After returning to Maranpata, we shifted our attentions to Guillén's proposed fort locations. Pancho went home to Yupanka, unconvinced about my church. Nancy was feeling better and she, Juvenal, Policarpo and I crossed the Abra Maranpata to the main road and headed downstream. After a long day on the trail, we set up camp near the Río Tunquimayo, the tributary to the Pampaconas below Urpipata where Guillén theorized the location of Huayna Pucara, the New Fort. (**Figure 44**) It was steep, thick country and Nancy and Policarpo again tended camp while Juvenal and I ventured off into the bush. José, Jim Little and I had checked the most likely terrain in 1984 and found nothing. Now, Juvenal and I systematically searched all the surrounding canyons and ridgelines for any sign of old roadways or fortifications. All the *campesinos* were good cutters, but Juvenal was a wizard with a *machete*. In two days we covered what I'd have taken a lifetime to explore. We found nothing. Our next and last objective was Guillén's version of Machu Pucara, the Old Fort. I'd hoped to look for it somewhere around La Roca, but high water in the Río Lucumayu a kilometer further down the trail prevented our going there. Juvenal said not to worry. He'd spent his entire 50 years working that country and assured me there was nothing there.

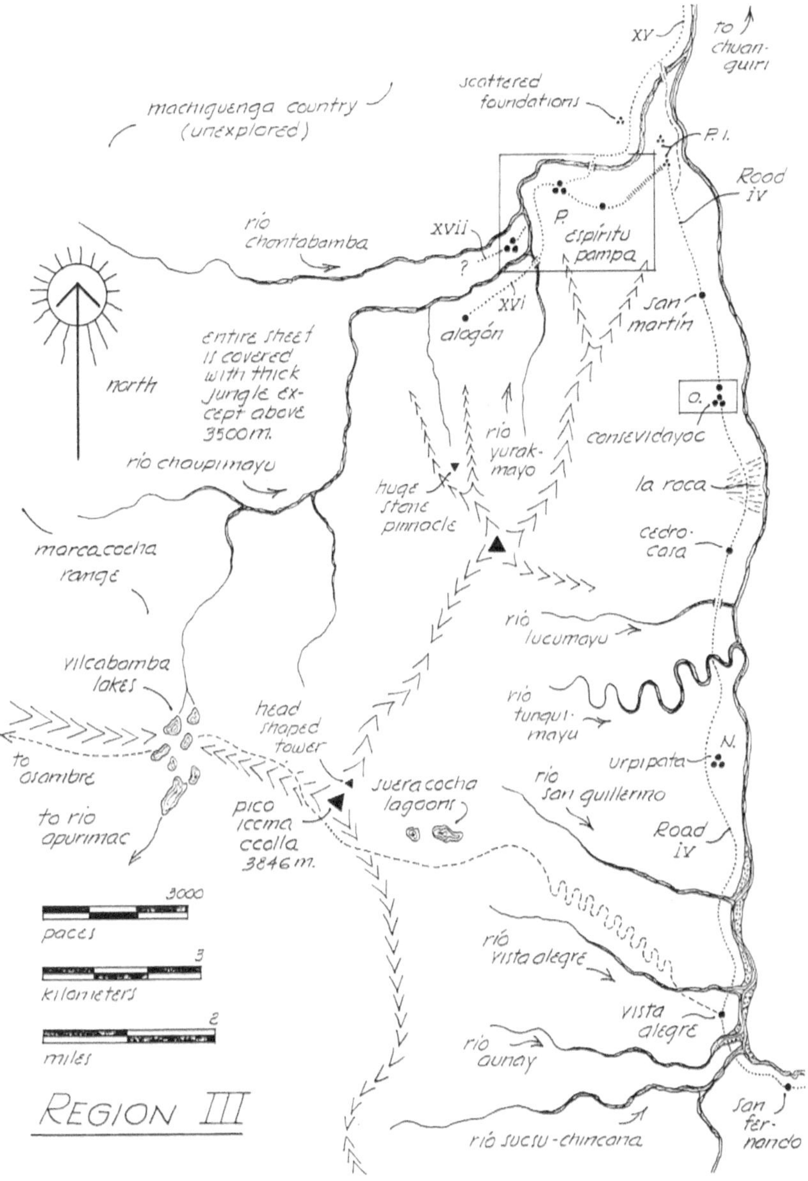

Figure 44 - Map of lower Rio Pampaconas

According to him, the only ruins further downstream, other than those at Espíritu Pampa, had been at Consevidayoc. Years ago, it was a village of circular houses, he said, much like those we'd just seen at La Mesada. As a boy, he'd helped his father, Julio, clear the area for crops and they'd found scores of badly tumbled, round foundations under the tangled growth. **(Figure 46)** The old stones had been needed, he said, for building the school, houses and fences of the modern settlement. They'd used them all. That did it, I thought. We'd been right about Consevidayoc all along. Juvenal's recycled ruins had once been Marcanay, the native village everyone agreed was the last stop on the road to Manco's lost capital.

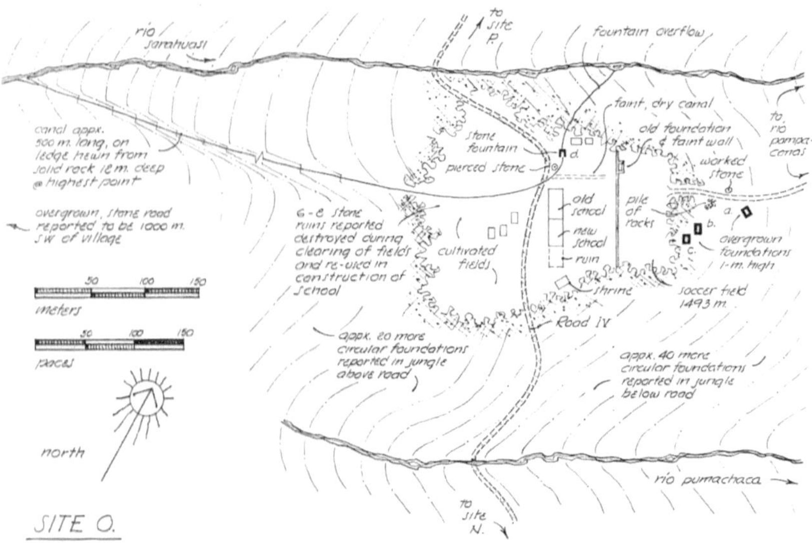

Figure 46 - Map of Consevidayoc (probable site of Marcanay)

So, it was over. Strangely, every piece of the puzzle had finally fallen into place except Mananhuañunca, the one that had drawn von Kaupp into the search in 1978 and thus led me to piece together all the rest a decade later. To this day, local tradition places Mananhuañunca at Palmapata, the clearing in the forest across the canyon from La Mesada - yet the chronicles all imply it was near the town of Marcanay, fifteen miles further downstream. The physical description of the place of Ortiz' martyrdom given by Calancha **(10)** closely matches the terrain at Palmapata and several other obscure references can be read to belie its proximity to Marcanay. Yet, there's little doubt the unfortunate *padre* was dragged before the Inca Tupac Amaru for sentencing at Marcanay prior to his execution. Could it be he was dragged all the way back up to Palmapata before the deed was done? No one knows. Probably no one ever will - that is, unless Bob von Kaupp and his friend Pancho Quispicusi one day make good on their promise to find the "real" Vilcabamba the Old somewhere in the steamy jungles of the Urumbay. I wish them luck.

Epilogue

As Aero Peru flight 66 rose out of Cuzco and began its long turn northwest toward Lima, the terraces of Tipón slipped beneath the tip of the port wing. A scattering of cheers and nervous applause testified to the relief of passengers, ourselves included, from the previous day's flight. Partway down the runway, that plane - that crashed two days later on final approach into Puerto Maldonado - had shuddered to a loud, metallic crunch, forcing the pilot to abort our take-off seconds before that option would have disappeared forever, likely taking us and all aboard with it. It had been a close call, and ironically so after years of tramping around among the peaks and jungles of that terrorism plagued land. We were glad to be airborne, at last.

Moments later, the crags of Pachatusan drifted past and the stupendous canyon of the Río Vilcanota yawned beyond. Pisac, Ollantaytambo and Machu Picchu appeared, one after the other, echoing in a matter of seconds Manco Inca's lengthy retreat after his failure to retake Cuzco from the Spaniards in 1536. Like his army, the path of flight 66 began to veer off into the jumble of peaks, glaciers and forested canyons west of the river. Almost suddenly, the impossibly steep summit ridge of Pumasillo loomed close outside the starboard windows, its icy flanks gleaming silver blue in the early morning light. Two miles below lay the Vilcabamba, just emerging from the long, August night.

Fascinated, I watched as, one by one, the obscure places that had consumed five years of my life came into view. Tiny patches of pale sunlight pinpointed Puncuyoc, Rosaspata, Pincollunca and Inca Huaracana, proof positive that Manco and his followers revered the rising sun no less than their ancestors. Further west, across the pass of Kolpacasa the darkness still held sway and seemed more opaque, magnified by the deepening forest. Streamers of mist clung to the sharp ridgelines. As if by Inca design, La Mesada, Tambo, Urpipata and Consevidayoc remained concealed, hidden yet by the natural camouflage of the jungle. Off to the north, the valley of Espíritu Pampa lay shrouded beneath heavy clouds, the real "lost city of the Incas" avoiding still the prying eyes of unwelcome outsiders. Silhouetted against the cloud-tops, the peak of Icma Coya stood like an enormous headstone, as if to mark the end of one of mankind's moments of greatness. As I turned away, it struck me that our brief over-flight had somehow symbolized, in a matter of seconds, the entire 36 year history of Inca Vilcabamba. When I returned to the window for a last look, like the Incas themselves, it was gone.

In the weeks and years past, we had traveled east into the dank rain forests of the Amazon, south beyond sky-high Lake Titicaca, west along the parched coastal deserts of the Pacific and north among the frigid glaciers of the towering Cordillera Blanca. Always, we were within Tawantinsuyo, the Four Quarters of the Inca World, the realm of those remarkable people. Often the image of their final stronghold passing silently outside my plane window returns to my thoughts. Why, I wonder, does that memory haunt me so? What relevance could all those piles of lifeless stones possibly have in our world?

It is this. In their way, the Incas were much like us. The Romans of their time, as we are of ours, they were builders, civilizers and believers in order and prosperity. They, too, bent the land to their will without hesitation or shame. Yet, unlike us, the Incas never lost touch with their origins - with Pacha Mama, Mother Earth. None among the aboriginal Caesars of the New World had greater license to take its wonders for granted than the mighty Sapa Inca, yet few embraced them with more vigor. Master, literally, of all he surveyed and possessor of absolute power to work his will, the Son of the Sun chose to celebrate, not simply manipulate, Nature. Lifeless stones his monuments may now be, but they tell more of importance about his world view than libraries filled with tales of palace intrigue.

The Incas have been popularly characterized as a clever but artless people. Others before them were better weavers, potters, metalsmiths and, perhaps, musicians. The Incas were builders, but even in this they have been praised always as engineers and craftsmen; seldom as designers and architects. Our attitude in this is an absurd condescension, an eloquent statement of our own chaotic architectural heritage more than a critique of anything Incan. In the Andes, it was once clear that, great as a man or a nation might be, the Earth was greater still - and that to open the Earth was an act of significance. Whether planting corn or building a city, the Incas knew that only their best would do.

For us, the result is the lingering footprint of an alternative world, an architecture so unlike our own that it seems to some the work of an alien race. But it is we who have alienated ourselves from much that is real and built, instead, a world in which the Earth is trivialized as real estate - and sunlight, space, pure water and growing things are seen as amenities affecting largely its price. We build as if integrity were no more than a costly, and thus dispensable, design strategy. As surely as with the Incas, time will one day reduce our works to lifeless tangles of steel and concrete - and though much of our essence may then be lost, it will be clear that few of us began our days blowing kisses to the sun.

Postscript

In the nearly two decades since the work presented here was first begun, dramatic changes have taken place throughout Peru, and nowhere more than in the Zona de Vilcabamba. The political and economic crises that held the entire country hostage throughout the late 1980s and early 1990s have, for the moment, ended. As a result, tourism in general and adventure travel in particular have exploded, with more and more people seeking alternatives to the increasingly overcrowded standbys around Cuzco, Machu Picchu and the Inca Trail.

For better or worse, Vilcabamba is absorbing some of the overflow. It has traditionally been a difficult, or at least tedious, place to get to. Once there, travelers have found no developed sites or accommodations and absent maps or guidebooks, they have been entirely reliant on their own resources to explore a region reputed to be "unknown" and perhaps, even dangerous. Precisely these rigors first drew me to Vilcabamba in 1982. You may find them attractive as well, but like all things adventurous, they are often more fun to anticipate and recall than they actually are to do. With this in mind, take heart. While the splendors of the countryside and its rich archaeological heritage remain more or less intact and untrammeled, some of the misery formerly associated with enjoying them is now gone.

As I speculated after Sixpac Manco II in 1984, the road up the Río Vilcabamba has been improved such that one or more inexpensive mini-busses now go daily to and from the roadhead at Huancacalle. For those willing to pay more, private vehicles, or *expresos*, can be hired from Quillabamba (half a day each way) or even Cuzco (a very long day each way). Satellite-based and topographic maps are now available (see Appendix B) and show the area in fairly accurate detail, although many place-names are either incorrect, improperly located, or both. Several restaurants and hotels have sprung up in Huancacalle, including one run by the Cobos family featuring clean rooms, *gringo*-length beds, bottled drinking water, flush toilets, hot showers and electric lights - all unheard-of amenities only a few years ago. A telephone is even said to be on the way. Guides, horses and mules for day hikers, multi-day trekkers or major expeditions are also available.

In cooperation with the local *campesinos* , the government is clearing parts of Vitcos and has plans to rebuild the nearby ruins of Ñusta Ispanan. An official resident guardian oversees the project. The many other archaeological sites in the region remain largely abandoned and overgrown. An exception is the valley of Espíritu Pampa, where a hundred new families no longer fearful of terrorism, have settled in and cleared portions of the ruins. A government guardian watches over their activities, but no restoration work is yet underway. Many opportunities for archaeological exploration remain, and each season produces claims of "new" finds at this place or that, but so far nothing of consequence has been added to the inventory presented here. Commercial trekking companies from Cuzco, the U.S. and Europe offer guided trips into the region, with the most popular trips going to Espíritu Pampa (4 days) and Choquequirau (5-6 days), where substantial clearing and reconstruction has been underway for several years. A day or two beyond both sites, return transportation to Cuzco is available, eliminating the need for a round trip back to Huancacalle.

During the exceptionally rainy El Niño season of 1997-8, a gigantic landslide roared down the Río Aobamba just below Machu Picchu damming the Urubamba and backing up a lake which then washed out, scouring the lower canyon of the Urubamba all the way to Quillabamba. The railroad was obliterated and five downstream bridges were carried away, including the heavily traveled Chuquichaca tressle at Chaullay together with its old Inca abutments and the enormous, three story mid-stream boulder that once divided the span. Plans are underway to restore the crossing, but absent the old railroad, only the tortuous, twelve hour drive over the 14,000 foot Abra Malaga (Panticalla Pass) will link the region to Cuzco in the future. Perhaps it is just as well. For centuries, the essence of Vilcabamba has been the lure of its remoteness. Something 0f this magic will be lost forever if it one day becomes easy to go there.

About the Author

Vincent Lee is an architect, archaeologist, explorer and author. His insatiable curiosity to solve ancient architectural mysteries has led him on numerous adventures to the mountain jungles of the Andes, the shores of Easter Island, and the arid climes of the Middle East. Vincent lives in southwestern Colorado with his wife, Nancy, and is a Member of the Institute of Andean Studies at Berkeley, a Fellow of The New York Explorers Club and a Research Associate with the San Diego Museum Of Man.

Appendix - Explanatory Notes

IMPORTANT EVENTS AND DATES

- ca. 1440 : Invasion of Vilcabamba by Pachacuti Inca
- 1532-3 : Pizarro's arrival in Peru and occupation of Cuzco
- 1533 : Manco Inca given puppet throne in Cuzco by Pizarro
- 1536 : Manco revolts and burns Cuzco but native rebellion fails
- 1536-7 : Manco retreats to Ollantaytambo and on to Vitcos
- 1537 : Diego de Almagro overthrows Pizarro in Cuzco
- 1537 : Almagrist Rodrigo Orgóñez attacks Vitcos, Manco escapes
- 1538 : Pizarro regains control in Cuzco
- 1539 : Gonzalo Pizarro invades Vilcabamba, Manco again escapes
- 1544 : Manco assassinated at Vitcos by seven Almagrist refugees
- 1544 : Sayri Tupac Inca succeeds Manco Inca in Vilcabamba
- 1557 : Sayri Tupac leaves Vilcabamba for new estates in Yucay

- 1560 : Sayri Tupac dies in Yucay under suspicious circumstances
- 1560 : Titu Cusi Yupanqui Inca takes control in Vilcabamba
- 1565 : Rodriguez de Figueroa meets Titu Cusi at Pampaconas
- 1566 : Titu Cusi signs (peace) Treaty of Acobamba
- 1568 : Titu Cusi baptized, Marcos García builds church in Pucyura
- 1569 : Diego Ortiz arrives and builds church in Guarancalla
- 1569 : Viceroy Francisco de Toledo takes control in Cuzco
- 1570 : García and Ortiz humiliated at Vilcabamba the Old
- 1570 : García and Ortiz burn Sun Temple at Chuquipalta, Garcia banished 1571 : Titu Cusi dies, Ortiz martyred at Mananhuañunca
- 1571 : Tupac Amaru Inca assumes throne in Vilcabamba
- 1572 : Atilano de Anaya killed by Indians at Chuquichaca
- 1572 : Toledo's final invasion of Vilcabamba, Incas defeated 1572 : Tupac Amaru captured and executed in Cuzco ca. 1865 : Antonio Ramondi visits Vilcabamba but finds no ruins
- 1911 : Hiram Bingam finds Machu Picchu, Vitcos and Espíritu Pampa
- 1921 : Christian Bües makes the first map of Vilcabamba
- 1948 : Bingham's *Lost City of the Incas* published
- 1953 : Victor Wolfgang von Hagen's crew finds Puncuyoc
- 1964 : Gene Savoy claims Espíritu Pampa is Vilcabamba the Old
- 1965 - present : Various modern explorations
- 1970 : Savoy's *Antisuyo* and Hemming's *The Conquest of the Incas* published
- 1982 - present : Sixpac Manco expeditions

UNFAMILIAR WORDS, SPELLINGS AND TRANSLATIONS

The story told here necessarily involves the occasional use of Spanish terms and a few words in Quechua, the unwritten language of the Incas. An attempt has been made to define all of these within the text so that no glossary is needed. Much Spanish is rapidly finding its way into the vernacular anyway, but the same cannot be said of Quechua, an idiom spoken by millions in the Andes, but hardly anyone else. Its unusual sounds and unavoidably phonetic spelling have led to a wide variety of written forms, depending on the usage of the writer. In recent years, Andean scholars have attempted to rectify this by acceptance of discipline-wide conventions independent of the authors' own languages. The familiar "Inca," for example, is increasingly seen as "Inka." Nevertheless, since virtually everything else ever written about Vilcabamba has used the traditional spelling, I have used it here as well for continuity's sake. Also, I have simplified the spellings of several Quechua place-names in hopes their pronunciations will come easier to the general reader. Some minor inconsistencies between the text and the figure captions have resulted, but only purists will notice the difference.

The text contains a number of excerpts, quoted from the Spanish chronicles of the sixteenth and seventeenth centuries. In their original forms, some were written in the ornate Castillian of the period and others in the old Spanish of common soldiers or lowly friars. All include long, complicated sentences, erratic or non-existent punctuation and the imaginative spelling variations noted above. In order to make these ramblings more comprehensible to twentieth century English language readers, I have translated, punctuated and simplified the contents of all quoted passages to convey their apparent essences as clearly as possible. As all scholars know, however, this is risky business. Some nuance of the chronicler's intended meaning can easily be misinterpreted or missed altogether on the turn of an obscure phrase or even a single word. For this reason, my sources for all such quotations are given in the Chapter Notes for those interested in reading them in their original forms.

Chapter Notes

PART I

Chapter 1 - The World Turned Upside Down

1 Bauer, 1992, Ch. 9

2 Cobo, 1979, pp 135-6

3 Calancha, 1639, pp 787

4 Cobo, 1979, pp 137

Chapter 2 - Trust No One

1 see Appendix B, Satellite Photos

2 Savoy, 1970, pp 82-3

3 Savoy, personal correspondence

Chapter 3 - Back To Vitcos

1 Pedo Pizarro, 1978, pp 195-6

2 Titu Cusi Yupanqui, 1916, pp 88-9

3 Ibid., pp 92-3

4 Raimondi, 1876, pp 161

5 Bingham, 1910, pp 525

6 Ibid., 1912, pp 182

7 Ocampo, 1907, pp 216

8 Bingham, 1912, pp 186-7

Chapter 4 - Explorer Beware

1 Rodriguez de Figueroa, 1913, pp 178-80

2 Ibid., pp 189-90

Chapter 5 - Beginner's Luck

1 Guillén Guillén, 1980, pp 36

2 Murúa, 1962, pp 251

3 Calancha, 1639, pp 787

4 Murúa, 1962, pp 146

5 Ibid., pp 148

6 Ibid., pp 254-5

7 Ibid., pp 255-6

8 Arbieto, 1935, pp 146-8

Chapter 6 - The Plain Of Ghosts

1 Murúa, 1962, pp 257

2 Titu Cusi Yupanqui, 1916, pp 88-9

3 Murúa, 1962, pp 257

4 Arbieto, 1935, pp 148

5 Murúa, 1962, pp 258

6 Bingham, 1979, pp 136

7 Murúa, 1962, pp 258-60

8 Ibid., pp 259-64

9 Oviedo, 1908, pp 406

10 Ibid., pp 407

11 Ibid., pp 408

12 Bingham, 1914, pp 185-8

13 Ibid., pp 196-7

14 Ibid., 1911 Journal, pp 100

15 Ibid., 1979

16 von Hagen, 1975, pp 101-2

17 Savoy, 1970, pp 105

18 Ibid., 1978b, pp 161

19 Ibid., 1970, pp 122

20 Howel, 1967, pp 45

21 Murúa, 1962, pp 259

Chapter 7 - A Promise To The Inca

1 Savoy, 1970, pp 127

2 Spiess, 1966, pp 119-37

3 Pardo, 1972, pp 107

4 Calamcha. 1639, pp 796

Chapter 8 - A Star In The Forest

1 Hyslop, 1984, Ch. 19

2 Ibid., Ch. 20

Chapter 9 - Icing On The Cake

1 Clark, 1959

2 Bingham, 1979, pp 116

PART II

Chapter 10 - Second Thoughts

1 Hemming, 1982

2 Rowe, 1944

3 Ibid., 1946

4 White, 1985

5 Savoy, personal correspondence

6 Lee, 1985

7 Savoy, 1985

Chapter 11 - Back To Square One

1 von Hagen, 1975, pp 103-4

2 Buck, 1993

3 Bingham, 1911 journal, pp 83

4 von Hagen, 1953

5 von Kaupp, 1983

6 Guillén Guillén, 1977, pp 127

7 Murúa, 1962, pp 253

8 Calancha, 1639, pp 787

9 Guillén Guillén, 1994, pp 187

10 Ocampo, 1907, pp 216

11 Rodriguez de Figueroa, 1913, pp 177

12 Guillén Guillén, 1980, pp 26

13 Ibid., 1994

14 Beauclerk, 1979

15 Ibid.

16 Kendall, 1984

Chapter 12 - Fitting The Stones

1 Lee, 1985, pp 77

2 Rodriguez de Figueroa, 1913, pp 175

3 Lee, 1986b

4 Ibid., 1990

Chapter 13 - Into The Emergency Zone

1 Lee, 1985, pp 77

Chapter 14 - Plan B

1 White, 1985, pp 136

2 Lee, 1988, pp 10-18

3 White, 1985, pp 133

4 Ibid., pp 134-5

5 Lee, 1988b, pp 14

Chapter 15 - Standing On The Answer

1 Bingham, 1979, pp 132

2 Ibid., 1914b, pp 211

3 Guillén Guillén, 1980, pp 36

4 Murüa, 1962, pp 267

5 von Kaupp, 1983

6 Calancha, 1639, pp 787

7 von Kaupp, 1983

Chapter 16 - Un Poco Loco

1 Savoy, 1978b, pp 161

2 Ibid., pp 160

3 Arbieto, 1935, pp 148-50

4 Savoy, 1989

5 Tennant, 1958

6 Matthiessen, 1961

Chapter 17 - Death Of A Martyr

1 Lee, 1986b

2 Ibid., 1990

3 Calancha, 1639, pp 787

4 Ibid., pp 803-4

5 Murúa, 1962, pp 232

6 Ibid.

7 Calancha, 1639, pp 807

8 Murúa, 1962, pp 234

9 Calancha, 1639, pp 812

10 Murúa, 1962, pp 235

11 Calancha, 1639, pp 824-5

12 Ibid., pp 787

13 Ibid., pp 801

Chapter 18 - The Final Piece

1 Frost, 1989

2 Bingham, 1912, pp 177-9

3 Calancha, 1639, pp 801

4 von Kaupp, 1983

5 Gisbert, 1985, pp 145-9

6 Calancha, 1639, pp 794-801

7 Rodriguez de Figueroa, 1913, pp 178-90

8 Calancha, 1639, pp 787 & 822

9 Ibid., pp 823

10 Ibid., pp 824

About the Graphic Logos

The geometric patterns that accompany the chapter titles are authentic Inca "tucapus" copied from a checkerboard tunic in the Dumbarton Oaks Pre-Columbian textile collection. Geometric forms arranged in checkerboard grids are common in Inca decorative art. The significance, if any, of the various patterns is not known.

Attempts to assign meanings to recurring logos and organize them into a graphic

"alphabet" have not produced decipherable results. The temptation to see something more than abstract ornamentation remains strong, but absent some yet unfound key,

like the Rosetta Stone, the patterns remain enigmatic.

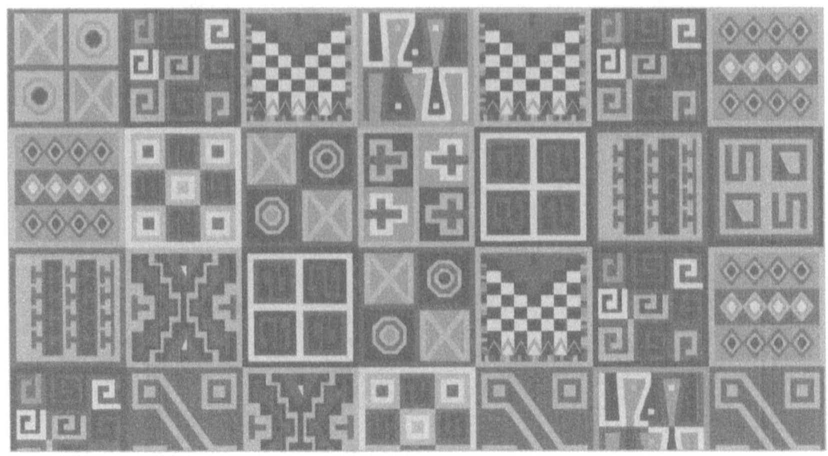

Image: https://www.isned.org/inca-tocapu-for-fun

Bibliography

Publications and other sources referenced in the text and appendices are listed below.

For a complete bibliography of Inca Vilcabamba, see Hemming, 1970.

Angles Vargas, Victor - *Historia del Cuzco Incaico*, 1988; published by the author, Cuzco.

Arbieto, Hurtado de - *Report to Viceroy Francisco de Toledo...*, (1572); from R.Levillier- Don Francisco de Toledo..., 1935; Madrid.

Bauer, Brian - *The Development of the Inca State*; 1992; University of Texas Press; Austin.

Beauclerk, John - *La Cordillera Vilcabamba, Ultimo Refugio de los Incas*, 1979; *Boletín de Lima*, Nos. 4 & 5, Lima.

Bingham, Alfred M. - *Portrait of an Explorer*; 1989; Iowa State University Press; Ames, Iowa.

Bingham, Hiram - *The Ruins of Choquequirau*; 1910; *American Anthropologist*; N. S.,

12.

Unpublished journal of 1911 Yale Peruvian Expedition; in archives of Yale

University Library; New Haven.

Temple of the Sun at Ñusta Ispana; 1911+; undated and unpublished map in archives of Peabody Museum, Yale University, New Haven.

*Vitcos, the Last Inca Capita*l; 1912; *American Antiquarian Society*; April.

The Ruins of Espíritu Pampa; 1914; *American Anthropologist*; N.S., 16.

The Pampaconas River; 1914b; map in *Geographical Journal*, 44, No. 2; August.

Lost City of the Incas, (1948); paperback cited; 1979; Atheneum, New York.

Bowman, Isaiah - *The Andes of Southern Peru*; 1916; American Geographical Society; Henry Holt and Company; New York.

Buck, Daniel - *Fights of Machu Picchu*; 1993; *South American Explorer*, No. 32; Ithaca, NY.

Bües, Christian - *El Señorio de Vilcabamba*, map by (1921); revised and reprinted 1989, Instituto Nacional de Cultura, Cuzco.

Calancha, Antonio de la - *Crónica Moralizada del Orden de San Agustín en el Perú*, 1639; Barcelona.

Cieza de Leon, Pedro de - *The Incas*, (1553); translated by Harriet de Onis: edited by Victor W. von Hagen, 1959; U. of Oklahoma, Norman.

Clark, Simon - *The Puma's Claw*; 1959; Little, Brown and Co.; Boston and Toronto.

Cobo, Bernabe - *History of the Inca Empire*, (1653); translated by Rowland Hamilton, 1979; University of Texas Press, Austin.

Deyermenjian, Gregory - *Vilcabamba Revisited*; 1985; *South American Explorer*, No.

12; Ithaca, NY.

Drew, David - *The Cusichaca Project: the Lucumayo and Santa Teresa Valleys*, 1984; BAR Series 210, No. 44, Oxford.

Fejos, Paul - *Archaeological Explorations in the Cordillera Vilcabamba of Southeastern Peru*; 1944; Viking Fund Publications in Anthropology; No. 3; NewYork.

Francescutti, Renzo - *Vilcabamba and Urubamba*; 1982; draft map of region; 1:

120,000; from the author; Trieste, Italy.

Frost, Peter - *Exploring Cuzco*; 1989; Nuevos Imagenes; Lima.

Garcilaso de la Vega, El Inca - *Royal Commentaries of the Incas and General History of Peru*, (1609); 1966; University of Texas; Austin.

Gasparini, Graziano and Luise Margolies - *Inca Architecture*, 1980; translated by Patricia J. Lyon; Indiana University Press, Bloomington.

Gisbert, Teresa and José de Mesa - *Arquitectura Andina 1530 - 1830*, 1985; Coleccíon Arsanz y Vela, Embajada de España en Bolivia, La Paz.

Guillén Guillén, Edmundo - *Vilcabamba, La Ultima Capital del Estado Imperial Inca*,

1977; *Scientia et Praxis*, No. 12, Lima.

Restauracíon Geografica del Itinerario Belico Sequido por los Españoles....; 1978; *Primera Journada del Museo Nacional de Historia*; Noviembre 1976; Lima.

El Testimonio del Capitán Pedro Sarmiento de Gamboa, (1572); 1980; *Boletín de Lima*, No. 9; Lima.

Vilcabamba: El Último Fortín Inca; 1994; *Peru Tour*, Año 1, Vol.3; Lima.

La Guerra de Reconquista Inka; 1994b; published by the author; Lima.

Hemming, John - *The Conquest of the Incas*; 1970; Harcourt Brace Jovanovich, San Diego - New York - London.

Author's Addendum to *The Conquest of the Incas*; 1970b; available only with

second and subsequent paperback editions.

Hemming, John and Edward Ranney - *Monuments of the Incas*; 1982; New York Graphic Society; Little, Brown and Company, Boston.

Hornberger, Esteban and Nancy - *Diccionario Tri-lingue: Quechua de Cuzco*; 1983; Qoya Raymi; La Paz, Bolivia.

Howell, Mark and Tony Morrison - *Steps to a Fortune*; 1967; Geoffrey Bles, Ltd.; London.

Hyslop, John - *The Inca Road System*; 1984; Academic Press, New York.

Kendall, Ann - *Archaeological Investigations...at Cusichaca Peru*; 1984; *B.A.R. Series* 210, No. 44, Oxford.

Lee, Vincent R. - *Sixpac Manco: Travels Among the Incas*; 1985; published by the

author, P. O. Box 107, Wilson, Wyoming 83014.

Preliminary Field Report: Sixpac Manco Expedition III; 1986; published by the author, P. O. Box 107, Wilson, Wyoming 83014.

The Building of Sacsayhuaman; 1986b; *Ñawpa Pacha*, No. 24; Berkeley.

The Lost Half of Inca Architecture; 1988; published by the author; Box 107, Wilson, WY 83014.

Function, Form and Method in Inca Architecture; 1988b; published by the author, P. O. Box 107, Wilson, Wyoming 83014.

Chanasuyu - The Ruins of Inca Vilcabamba; 1989; published by the author; Box 107, Wilson, Wyoming 83014.

Guarancalla: the Lost Mission of Padre Ortiz; 1989b; published by the author, P. O.

Box 107, Wilson, Wyoming 83014.

La Construccíon de Sacsayhuaman, Cuzco; 1990; *Boletín de Lima*, No. 69; Lima.

Inca Choqek'iraw; 1997; published by the author, P. O. Box 107, Wilson, Wyoming 83014.

Matthiessen, Peter - *The Cloud Forest*; 1961; Viking, New York.

Murúa, Martín de - *Historia General del Perú*, (1590); edited by Manuel BallesterosGailbrois; 1962; Madrid.

Ocampo, Baltasar de - *Descripción de la Provincia de San Francisco de la Vitoria de Vilcapampa*, (1610); translated by Clements R. Markham; 1907; Hakluyt Society, Series II, No. 22, Cambridge.

Oviedo, Gabriel de - *Relacíon of...*, (1573); translated by C. R. Markham; 1908; supplement to Hakluyt Society, Series II, No. 22; Cambridge.

Pardo, Luis A. - *El Imperio de Vilcabamba; 1972; Revista del Patronato Departamental de Arqueología del Cuzco*; Cuzco.

Pizarro, Pedro - *Relacíon* of..., (1571); Fondo Editorial; 1978; Pontifica Universidad Catolica del Peru, Lima.

Prescott, William H. - *History of the Conquest of Peru*; 1847; E.P. Dutton & Company, New York.

Raimondi, Antonio - *El Peru*; 1876; Tomo II; Lima.

Reader's Digest - *The World's Last Mysteries*; 1978; Pleasantville, NY.

Robinson, Richard - *Vilcabamba Peru*; 1988; unpublished paper available from author; 67 Christchurch Rd., Tring, Herts., HP23 4EL, U.K.

Rodriguez de Figueroa, Diego - *Relación of...*, (1565); translated by C. R. Markham; 1913; Hakluyt Society, Series II, No. 31, Cambridge.

Rowe, John Howland - *An Introduction to the Archaeology of Cuzco*; 1944; Papers of

the Peabody Museum, Vol. XXVII, No. 2; Harvard University; Cambridge.

Inca Culture at the Time of the Spanish Conquest; 1946; *Handbook of South American Indians*, Vol. 2; Smithsonian Institution; Washington D.C.

Samanez Argumedo, Roberto - *Choquequirau*; 1986; architectural plans and elevations available through COPESCO, Cuzco.

Savoy, Gene - *Antisuyo*; 1970; Simon and Schuster, New York.

The Discovery of Vilcabamba; 1978; *The Explorers Journal*, March; New York.

Return to Vilcabamba; 1978b; *The Explorers Journal*, December; New York.

Gran Vilaya; 1985; *South American Explorer*, No. 12; Ithaca, NY.

La Ultima Aventura, 1989; revista *Somos*, No.146, Lima.

Spiess,Ernst - *A Topographer in the Cordillera Vilcabamba*; *The Mountain World*

1964/65; Zurich; 1966; pp 119-135.

Squier, George Ephraim - Peru: *Incidents of Travel and Exploration in the Land of the Incas*, (1877); 1973; AMS Press, Inc.: New York.

Tennant, Julian - *Quest for Paititi*, 1958; Max Parrish, London.

Titu Cusi Yupanqui - *Relación of...*, (1570); edited by C. A. Romero and H. H. Urteaga,

1916; Colección de libros y documentos referentes a la historia del Perú, Series I, Vol.

2; Lima.

von Hagen, Victor W. - unpublished journals of...; 1953; from Adriana von Hagen; Lima.

Highway of the Sun; 1975; Plata, Ltd., Switzerland.

von Kaupp, Robert - *Preliminary Report: Urumbay Finds*; 1983; available from the

author, 152 N. Carolina Ave. S.E., Washington, D.C. 20003.

Sapamarca: Preliminary Report; 1988; available from the author, 152 N. Carolina Ave. S.E., Washington, D.C. 20003.

White, Stuart - *Preliminary Survey of the Punkuyoq Range, Southern Peru*; 1985;

Ñawpa Pacha, No.22-23, Berkeley.

www.ingramcontent.com/pod-product-compliance
Lightning Source LLC
Chambersburg PA
CBHW030326130626
46554CB00011B/14

* 9 7 8 1 9 6 9 0 3 0 0 0 0 *